G.I. JOE

G.I. JOE vs. COBRA

The Essential Guide 1982–2008

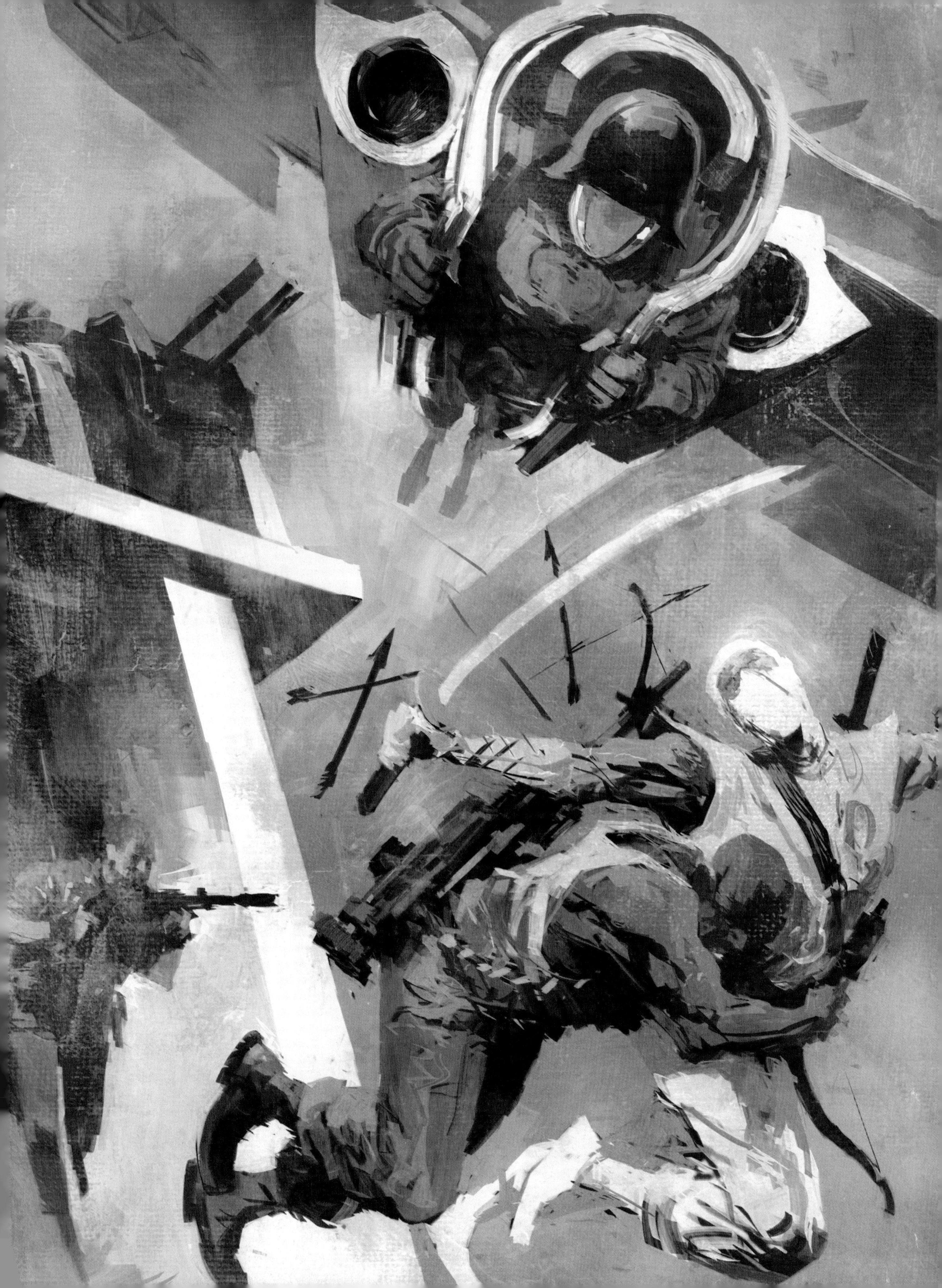

G.I. JOE vs. COBRA

The Essential Guide 1982–2008

Pablo Hidalgo

Licensed by:

BALLANTINE BOOKS · NEW YORK

To Larry Hama, for breathing adventure and drama into plastic and young imaginations.

A Del Rey Trade Paperback Original

Published in the United States by Del Rey, an imprint of The Random House Publishing Group, a division of Random House, Inc., New York.

DEL REY is a registered trademark and the Del Rey colophon is a trademark of Random House, Inc.

ISBN 978-0-345-51642-8

Printed in the United States of America

www.gijoe.com
www.delreybooks.com

2 4 6 8 9 7 5 3 1

Book design by Foltz Design

ACKNOWLEDGMENTS

This book is a result of an unrelated business dinner that turned into an unexpected round table of geek love stories for G.I. JOE and the storytelling power of Larry Hama. The enthusiasm showed by Del Rey editors Erich Schoeneweiss and Keith Clayton made this guide possible, and for that I thank them. A special "Yo, JOE!" to the rest of the team at Del Rey: Shona McCarthy, David Stevenson, and Phil Balsman, as well as Foltz Design for the passion and skills they brought to the book. Also, thanks to Laura Jorstad, a consummate copy editor.

The dedication and passions of G.I. JOE fans worldwide served as both inspiration and valuable resources, particularly the minds behind YoJoe.com, HissTank.com, and JoeBattleLines.com. A special thank-you goes out to fellow G.I. JOE fan James McFadden, who is a veritable encyclopedia of classic G.I. JOE lore.

This book is of course indebted to all the sculptors, illustrators, toy designers, and brand managers who have shepherded the G.I. JOE line since the 1980s, and the people at Hasbro, Marvel Comics, Blackthorne, Devil's Due Publishing, IDW Publishing, Sunbow Entertainment, DIC, and Reel FX, who brought the legend of G.I. JOE to life. Thank you to Andy Schmidt at IDW Publishing for supplying the excerpts and covers from the great new line of G.I. JOE comics. Special thanks to Michael Kelly at Hasbro for helping to direct this project during a very busy and exciting time in G.I. JOE history.

My sanity owes a huge debt of thanks to my beloved Kristen for helping me see through two monstrous projects with tight deadlines back-to-back.

And finally, a shout out to Gene Bartlett, the kid who, in fourth grade, brought a G.I. JOE action figure to the playground of Margaret Park Elementary School, introducing the future author to an incredible adventure that has lasted decades.

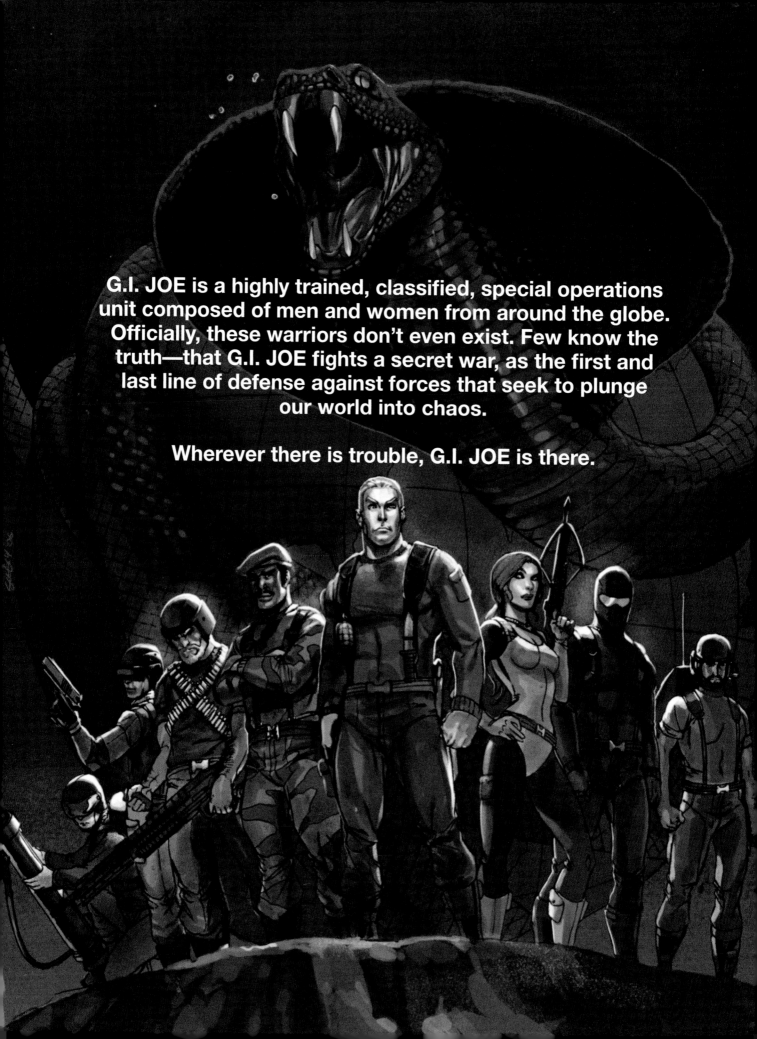

G.I. JOE is a highly trained, classified, special operations unit composed of men and women from around the globe. Officially, these warriors don't even exist. Few know the truth—that G.I. JOE fights a secret war, as the first and last line of defense against forces that seek to plunge our world into chaos.

Wherever there is trouble, G.I. JOE is there.

CONTENTS

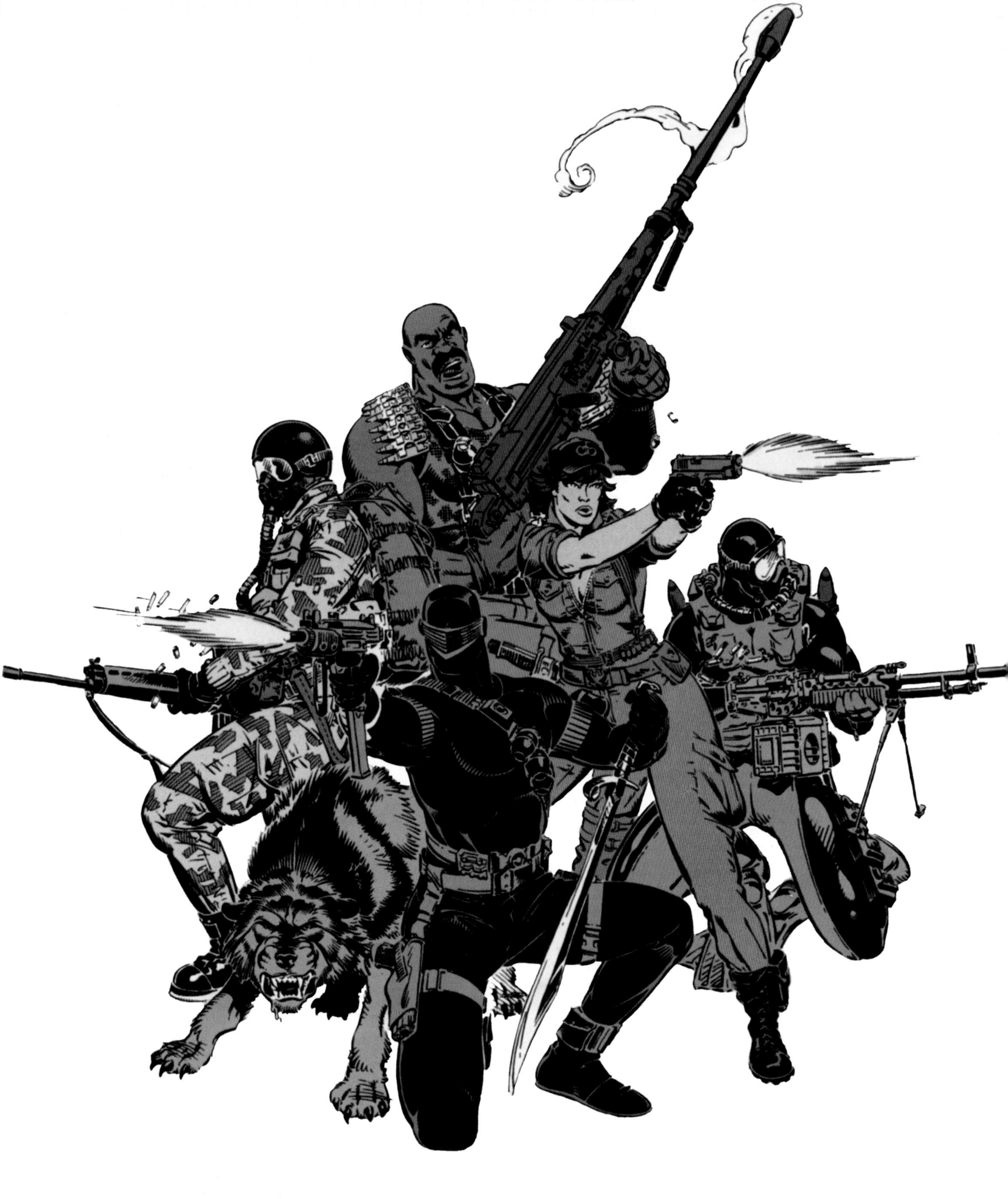

INTRODUCTION

CLASSIFIED ORIGINS

> *The world is changing. The task of protecting the country isn't as simple as it used to be. The enemy has changed its shape, altered its plan of attack, and we are changing to meet the challenge. This unit reflects that change: you are the best of the best—the finest soldiers we have to offer. The team roster is intended to stay minimal for the immediate future. Our plan is to develop a tight-knit team of specialists that can act with one mind; an entity with one common goal...*

Modern G.I. JOE operations exist in no searchable database. Their documentation graces no paper, no recordings, no memoranda. They can barely be said to exist at all—but if not for the vigilance, skill, and courage of the men and women who make up the ranks of this elite organization, the world would be a far more dangerous place. There are no medals to bestow upon modern G.I. JOE soldiers. No parades welcome them home after grueling, extended service in the most hostile of foreign nations. Though their tools are on the bleeding edge of technological innovation, and their talents are beyond extraordinary, their task is the same as that of soldiers throughout history—to do the impossible and then be forgotten.

Though the current incarnation of G.I. JOE exists in the shadows, with inscrutable chains of command, this was not always the case. What history has not been redacted and concealed behind the darkest of marker strokes points to G.I. JOE evolving over time. Its origins reach back to a primordial incarnation hatched by President John F. Kennedy in 1963. He saw the need for a new army unit that bypassed the regular chain of command and was answerable directly to his office. It was not an elitist praetorian guard, but rather "a cadre of knights errant fit for a modern Camelot." He never saw his framework for an elite subset of Special Forces realized, for he was killed by an assassin's bullet in November of that same year.

The innocuous code name of G.I.JOE finds its cultural roots in World War II, as it combines two slang terms of the era. *Joe* was an everyday stand-in appellation for just about any man: Don't know the name of the newspaper vendor or shoe shine kid on the corner? You could do worse than to refer to him as "Joe." *G.I.* is commonly mistaken to stand for "general issue," but is in fact an unrelated

military acronym for "galvanized iron." It came to refer to anything military. Merged together, *G.I. JOE* came to describe the everyman American soldier of World War II. It was pure coincidence that the man Kennedy handpicked to build up this earliest incarnation of the G.I. JOE team was also named Joe—Lieutenant Joseph Colton, a highly trained and effective Green Beret.

Colton's exploits as the first G.I. JOE remain classified, and he eventually retired from active military service. The name *G.I. JOE* was shelved for a time before resurfacing as the code name for Special Counter-Terrorist Group Delta, an elite unit that would draw from all branches of the US military to counter the emergence of a worldwide terrorist threat. Generals Lawrence J. Flagg and Aaron "Iron-Butt" Austin began formulating the framework for what would eventually become the "first class" of the modern G.I. JOE team. *"Duty. Honor. Courage."* would be their motto. The team's battle cry is the unmistakable rally, "Yo, JOE!"

From a small team of soldiers handpicked by Flagg, Austin, and General Clayton Abernathy, G.I. JOE evolved and grew to adequately counter the threat posed by COBRA and other subversive agencies around the world. Subgroups and specialty teams formed and disbanded, and G.I. JOE headquarters moved from secret locale to secret locale.

In the current G.I. JOE incarnation, the chain of command remains classified. While Abernathy serves as executive officer in command of the team, where he gets his orders from is unknown. Prospective G.I. JOE candidates are effectively wiped from all records, "killed in action," and reinstated under a code name as part of the G.I. JOE team. The current location of the Pit—G.I. JOE's subterranean headquarters—is a top military secret. G.I. JOE ranks are now made up of more than just the best of the US military branches; they also include military specialists from around the world.

The face of G.I. JOE continues to change, a fluid evolution made necessary by the turbulent and uncertain times the planet finds itself in. But wherever there's trouble, G.I. JOE will be there.

MILITARY GRADES

Ranks within G.I. JOE largely conform to the standards of the United States military—a coded system of grades that translate across the branches of service. During specific missions, individual experience and military specialties may trump listed grades, putting what would be an otherwise lower-ranking G.I. JOE in command if the demands of the assignment dictates it.

Grade	Army	Navy / Coast Guard	Marine Corps	Air Force
E-1	Private (PVT)	Seaman Recruit (SM)	Private (PVT)	Airman Basic (AB)
E-2	Private (PVT)	Seaman Apprentice (SA)	Private First Class (PFC)	Airman (AMN)
E-3	Private First Class (PFC)	Seaman (SN)	Lance Corporal (LCPL)	Airman First Class (A1C)
E-4	Corporal (CPL)	Petty Officer 3rd Class (PO3)	Corporal (CPL)	Senior Airman or Sergeant (SRA)
E-5	Sergeant (SGT)	Petty Officer 2nd Class (PO2)	Sergeant (SGT)	Staff Sergeant (SSGT)
E-6	Staff Sergeant (SSG)	Petty Officer 1st Class (PO1)	Staff Sergeant (SSGT)	Technical Sergeant (TSGT)
E-7	Seargant First Class (SFC)	Chief Petty Officer (CPO)	Gunnery Sergeant (GYSGT)	Master Sergeant (MSGT)
E-8	Master Sergeant (MSG); First Sergeant (1SG)	Senior Chief Petty Officer (SCPO)	Master Sergeant (MSGT) First Sergeant (1stSGT)	Senior Master Sergeant (MSGT)
E-9	Sergeant Major (SGM) Command Sergeant Major (CSM)	Master Chief Petty Officer (MCPO) Command Master Chief Petty Officer (CMDCM) Fleet Master Chief Petty Officer (FLTCM)	Mastery Gunnery Sergeant (MGYSGT) Sergeant Major (SGTMAJ)	Chief Master Sergeant (CMSGT) Command Chief Master Sergeant (CCM)
W-1	Warrant Officer (WO1)	Warrant Officer (WO1)	Warrant Officer (WO1)	
W-2	Chief Warrant Officer 2 (CW2)	Chief Warrant Officer 2 (CW2)	Chief Warrant Officer 2 (CW2)	
W-3	Chief Warrant Officer 3 (CW3)	Chief Warrant Officer 3 (CW3)	Chief Warrant Officer 3 (CW3)	
W-4	Chief Warrant Officer 4 (CW4)	Chief Warrant Officer 4 (CW4)	Chief Warrant Officer 4 (CW4)	
W-5	Chief Warrant Officer 5 (CW5)	Chief Warrant Officer 5 (CW5)	Chief Warrant Officer 5 (CW5)	
O-1	Second Lieutenant (2LT)	Ensign (ENS)	Second Lieutenant (2ndLT)	Second Lieutenant (2ndLT)
O-2	First Lieutenant (1LT)	Lieutenant, Junior Grade (LTJG)	First Lieutenant (1stLT)	First Lieutenant (1stLT)
O-3	Captain (CPT)	Lieutenant (LT)	Captain (CAPT)	Captain (CAPT)
O-4	Major (MAJ)	Lieutenant Commander (LCDR)	Major (MAJ)	Major (MAJ)
O-5	Lieutenant Colonel (LTC)	Commander (CDR)	Lieutenant Colonel (LTCOL)	Lieutenant Colonel (LT COL)
O-6	Colonel (COL)	Captain (CAPT)	Colonel (COL)	Colonel (COL)
O-7	Brigadier General (BG)	Rear Admiral (lower half) (RDML)	Brigadier General (BGEN)	Brigadier General (BRIGGEN)
O-8	Major General (MG)	Rear Admiral (upper half) (RADM)	Major General (MAJGEN)	Major General (MAJGEN)
O-9	Lieutenant General (LTG)	Vice Admiral (VADM)	Lieutenant General (LTGEN)	Lieutenant General (LTGEN)
O-10	General (GEN)	Admiral / Commandant (ADM)	General (GEN)	General (GEN)

GENERAL JOSEPH COLTON
(THE ORIGINAL G.I. JOE)

File Name: Joseph B. Colton
SN: 1033-1027-HAS93
Primary Military Specialty: (Current) G.I. JOE
 X-O—executive officer
Secondary Military Specialty: (Current) Combat
 Infantry—training and intelligence
Other Military Specialty: Strategic Defense
 Initiative Systems
Birthplace: Central Falls, Rhode Island
Grade: (current) O-10 (four-star general)

Joseph Colton graduated from the United States Military Academy at West Point, receiving the institution's highest honors. An expert marksman, he quickly became proficient with a wide variety of modern weaponry. Colton was recruited by Special Forces and soon distinguished himself as an outstanding Green Beret. He participated in numerous combat operations in trouble spots around the world, but as they were "ultra" top classified, he saw minimal accolade or acknowledgment for his service. His only measure of distinction was the respect he engendered in those under his command, and his permanent badge of service was the scar on his right cheek, earned under circumstances still classified.

During service overseas First Lieutenant Colton was rushed from an ambushed landing zone by an unmarked black helicopter exempted from any known command chain.

Within 36 hours of this hairy extraction, Colton found himself standing in the burnished Oval Office, awaiting a private meeting with the president of the United States, who offered the lieutenant command of the initial G.I. JOE team.

Over the course of five years, Colton built his team with the toughest soldiers the armed services could muster. G.I. JOE operations took Colton and company around the world. With his innate combat skills and indefatigable spirit, Colton would change the course of military history and redefine the word hero ... at least for those with the clearance necessary to read up on the deeply classified exploits.

Colton ultimately retired from active military service, but continued to serve as a valued adviser to the Pentagon. He joined a team of globe-trotting civilians dubbed the Adventure Team, offering security and services to scientific and cultural missions around the world. With his teammates, Joe helped save world leaders stranded in hostile territories and confounded would-be grave robbers planning to raid history's most treasured tombs.

Joe continued to liaise with the Pentagon on-and-off over the intervening years, and was aware of the reinstatement of a modern G.I. JOE team to counter the emergence of a new worldwide military threat, COBRA. Generals Lawrence J. Flagg and Aaron "Iron-Butt" Austin began formulating the framework for what would eventually become the modern G.I. JOE team.

Though in many ways this new team mirrored the ideals and objectives of Colton's original team, he remained far from the formation of this modern incarnation. Colton was long retired from service at that point, and he gladly stayed out of the picture to let young blood lead the way.

Colton and his longtime associate, Jane Ann Martelle, were transferred to command a top secret Strategic Defense Initiative installation hidden within the upper floors of the Chrysler Building in Manhattan. The orbital pulsed laser system contained within the famed skyscraper would figure into G.I. JOE escapades in later years, bringing Colton face-to-face with the modern soldiers who now continue his legacy. Later, when the team's traditional leader, General Clayton "Hawk" Abernathy, became indisposed, General Colton returned to active duty to lead the G.I. JOE team, and later shared the role with Hawk upon his return.

To this day, he continues to advise the G.I. JOE team.

Joe and Jane Ann

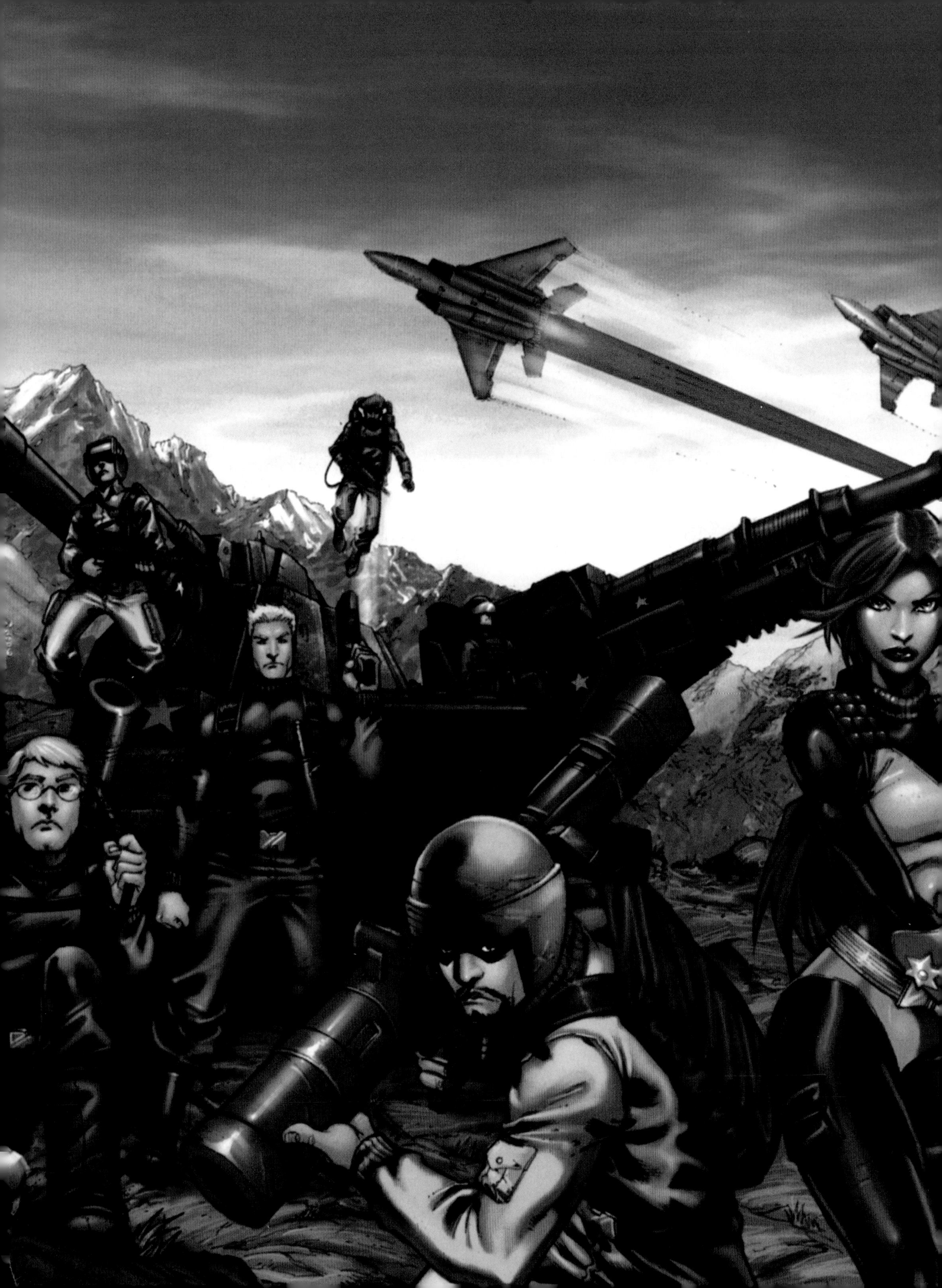

G.I. JOE vs. COBRA

The Essential Guide 1982–2008

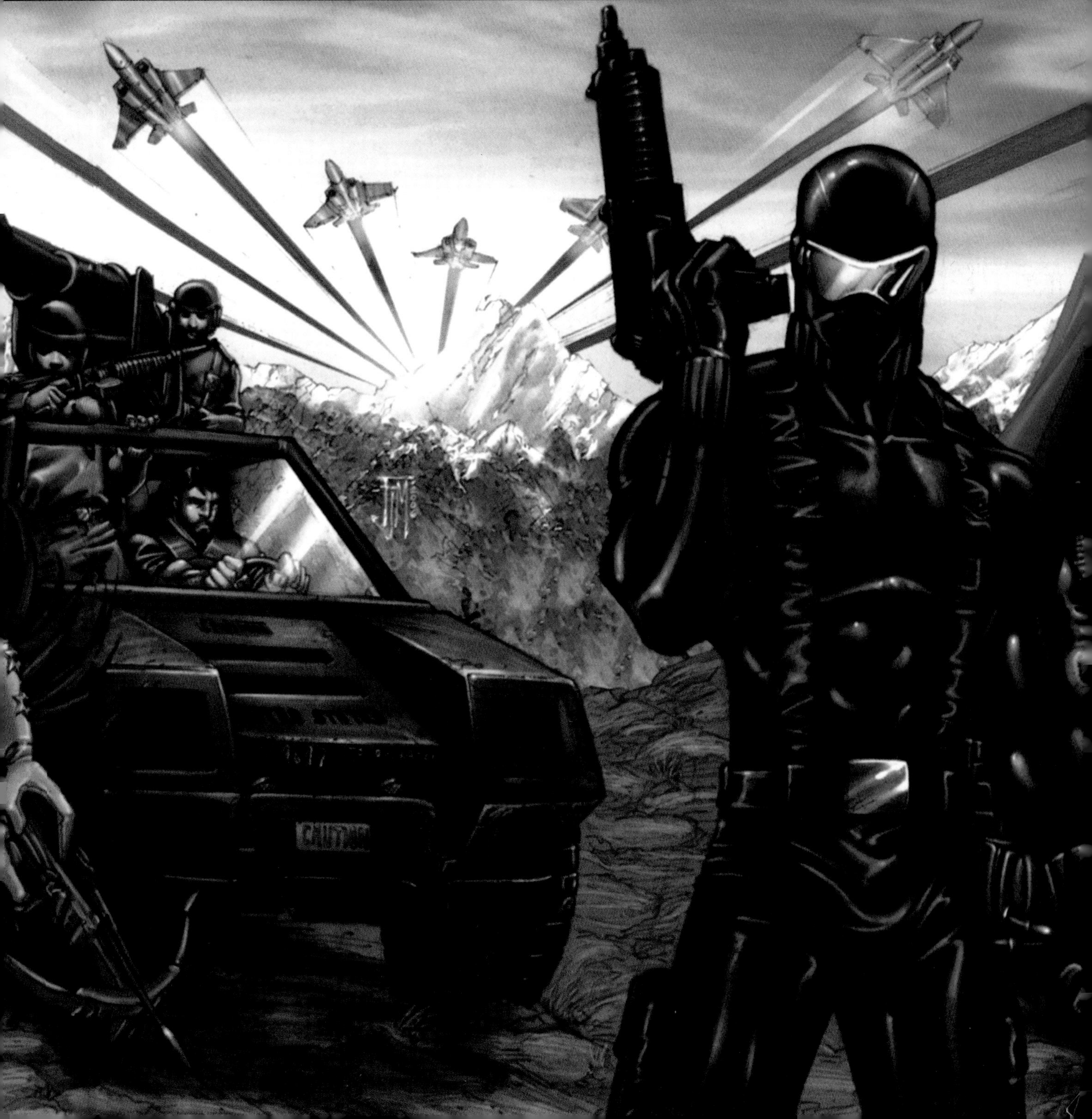

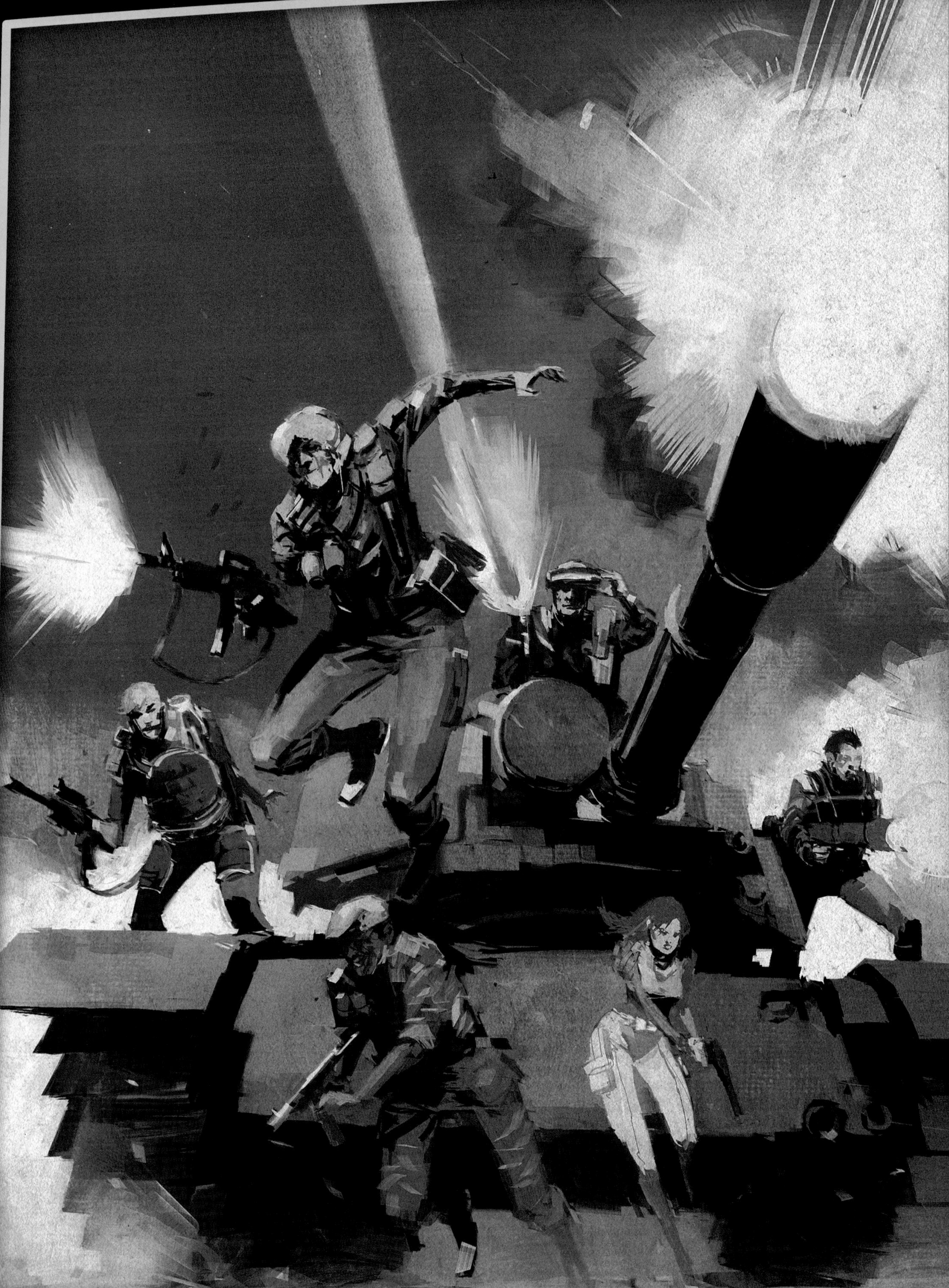

G.I. JOE

CHAPTER 1

G.I. JOE CHARACTERS

ACE
(Pilot)

DATA FILE

ACCESS GRANTED

File Name: *Brad J. Armbruster*
SN: *233-035-BJ74*
Primary Military Specialty: *Fixed-wing pilot (single and multiple engine)*
Secondary Military Specialty: *Intelligence operations*
Other Military Specialties: *Ordnance officer; battle copter pilot*
Qualified Expert: *F-5E; F-15; F-16; XP-14/F; Ghost Striker X-16; Conquest X-30; A-10 ground attack jet*
Birthplace: *Providence, Rhode Island*
Grade: *0-3 (captain, USAF)*

G.I. JOE's hotshot fighter pilot, Ace has been flying since his teen years, paying for lessons during high school by doing odd jobs. After graduation, he flew Alaskan pipelines and later enjoyed a two-year career as a stunt-flier for Hollywood. Seeking the opportunity to get behind the stick of the most advanced aircraft available, Armbruster enlisted in the US Air Force at age 22. He served as a member of Tactical Air Command (TAC, now Air Combat Command), and as a senior instructor for the Fighter Weapons Squadron known as the "Aggressors."

Though his code name suits his piloting ability well, it's not actually the source of his sobriquet. Armbruster was known as Ace well before enlisting because of his unmatched skills as a cardsharp. Ace is a cutthroat poker player, but in his case it can hardly be considered gambling since he never loses.

A fast thinker with great judgment skills, Ace's knowledge of air combat and dogfighting is extraordinary. Enemies are lucky to get a shot at him—and if they do, they only get one before it's his turn to make a COBRA crash and burn. He's a man the good guys can trust anytime—except at the card table.

■ Mission Report: Jousting Air Knights

What was intended to be a simple Skystriker shakedown run to test out new electronic black boxes and ECM pods turned into a much-talked-about aerial duel between Ace and Wild Weasel. Ace launched from McGuire Air Force Base in New Jersey, with Lady Jaye serving as his "backseat" navigation officer. Before long, they clashed with Wild Weasel and the Baroness aboard a Rattler tank smasher. Outmaneuvering the Rattler, Ace was able to tag it with 20mm Vulcan nose-cannon fire, but could not bring his missiles to bear on the enemy because of their close proximity to civilian neighborhoods.

Wild Weasel, of course, had no such reservations. He launched a bracket of heat-seeking missiles, but Ace evaded with a screen of rapid-blooming chaff (RBC) and infrared flares that befuddled the enemy ordnance. The near-miss missiles detonated and took out the Skystriker's transmission antenna, leaving Ace without means to contact the base. The Rattler raked the Skystriker with machine-gun fire from its tailgunner turret, shattering the canopy and turning Ace's helmet visor into a sheet of spidered glass.

Ace doffed his helmet and continued the cat-and-mouse game with Wild Weasel over suburban housing developments, highways, and junkyards. Each pilot acquitted himself formidably, outmaneuvering the other until both aircraft were scarred and out of ammunition. Both Skystriker and Rattler completed another pass at each other, but this time, rather than target a weapon at his opponent, Ace saluted to Wild Weasel, a gesture of honor and respect the COBRA pilot returned in kind.

BEACHHEAD
(Ranger)

DATA FILE
ACCESS GRANTED

File Name: *Wayne R. Sneeden*
SN: *902-46-SW14*
Primary Military Specialty: *Infantry*
Secondary Military Specialty: *Small-arms armorer*
Other Military Specialties: *Special operations weapons sergeant; armored vehicle driver*
Qualified Expert: *All NATO and Warsaw Pact small arms*
Birthplace: *Auburn, Alabama*
Grade: *E-7*

We sure found out pretty quick why this guy's a legend in the military: It's 'cause he likes to try an' kill his green shirt recruits. Before you know it, you're running wind sprints with a 90-pound pack an' Beachhead's yelling at you like you ain't never been in the real military before.... It's a tradition that green shirts get joke nicknames until they earn a G.I. JOE code name. Come time to assign our nicknames, he tells us that from now on we're gonna be known as One, Two, Three, Four, an' Five. You know what that does to a man? It makes him hate his sergeant major like he's never hated anyone in his life....

Hard as nails, Beachhead has become the first obstacle that G.I. JOE recruits face. He excels at kicking green shirts and rawhides into shape. Beachhead brooks no insubordination. The only thing that rattles him are those who aren't willing to try their best. It's a tall order for rookies—anything less than grueling labor is a luxury in Beachhead's book. He *likes* getting up at 0600 hours to take on a 10-mile run and PT session before breakfast. He *delights* in squatting in festering jungles for three days at a stretch to ambush the enemy. As far as Beachhead is concerned, being pushed to the limits is the only way to emerge with a solid understanding of what those limits are.

Prior to service with G.I. JOE, he served as lane instructor at Ranger School in Fort Benning. He was also an observer/adviser at Covert Ops School. Beachhead is authorized to wear the Master Explosive Ordnance Disposal Badge, the Combat Infantryman's Badge, and the Good Conduct Medal with Oak Leaf Cluster. He is a perfectionist with a high pain threshold: resilient, tenacious, efficient, and downright scary.

Mission Report: Aeroflot Flight 213

An example of Beachhead's calm under extremely volatile circumstances was the defusing of a hostage situation aboard Aeroflot Flight 213 out of San Francisco. The Fourth International, a radical activist group based in the Bay Area city, hijacked the Russian passenger liner with a trio of terrorists, intent on crashing the plane into a top-secret chemical warfare depot in Beringovskiy, Russia. Before the plane took off on its transpacific journey, it stopped for refueling in Anchorage, at which point Beachhead, Flint, and Lady Jaye infiltrated via the landing gear wheel wells. Beachhead used a compact cutting torch to slice his way into the passenger compartment, emerging beneath the seat of American chess team prodigy, 17-year-old Carlisle Anderson. Anderson did not blow Beachhead's cover, allowing him to emerge and hide in his row until it was time to neutralize the hijackers. While Lady Jaye Tasered the explosives-laden terrorist with a dead man's switch, Beachhead overpowered another of the hijackers, holding her at knifepoint and subduing her with the no-nonsense words, "I'm no gentleman and I have no compunctions." The terrorists thwarted, the plane was routed back to San Francisco.

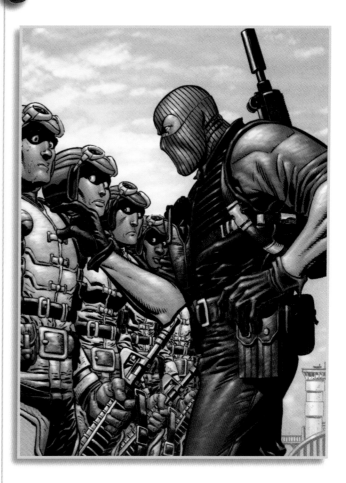

BREAKER
(Communications)

File Name: Alvin R. Kibbey
SN: 757-79-AR35
Primary Military Specialty: Infantry
Secondary Military Specialty: Radio telecommunications
Other Military Specialty: Computer technology
Qualified Expert: M-16; M-1911A1 auto pistol; Ingram MAC-10
Birthplace: Gatlinburg, Tennessee
Grade: E-4

Breaker was the youngest of the original G.I. JOE team. Brilliant with technology, he is efficient and self-assured. Alvin Kibbey's interest in communications stemmed from a ham radio set he'd owned as a 10-year-old boy, which allowed him contact with similar amateur enthusiasts from around the globe. In time, he became fluent in seven languages (though which ones remain classified).

Efficient and self-assured, he has the uncanny ability to turn adverse situations to his favor. His one annoying trait is that damn bubble popping. The team often wonders what's stickier: his gum or the situations that he seems to always get out of.

Upon enlistment, Kibbey's skills proved valuable when he served in a highly secret Special Forces unit conducting intelligence operations in Southeast Asia. His other specialized training included covert electronics and Signal School in Fort Gordon, Georgia. As a hobby, Specialist Kibbey ran advanced crystalline fracture point programs at MIT. He was busted by the Criminal Investigations Division for decrypting top-secret military transmissions. CID agent Philip Provost led an interrogation that uncovered Kibbey's language proficiencies and electronics skills, as well as confirmed that there was no malicious intent behind his activities. Rather, this was a bored genius eager for a challenge.

Colonel Clayton Abernathy interrupted the interrogation with two full packs and told Kibbey to put one on. They went for a run up a mountain as part of a test to see if Kibbey had physical skills in addition to his technical aptitude. Kibbey never tired, and overtook Hawk in one stretch. He was then recruited to G.I. JOE, his hacking transgression wiped from his record. He served for years as a valu-

able link between field missions and command. It was Breaker who would call for medevac, radio in artillery coordinates, or call for an air strike. Breaker's talents for cracking COBRA ciphers and jamming their transmissions saved the team time and again.

■ The Pop Heard 'Round the Block

Early in the struggle between COBRA and G.I. JOE, prior to the evil organization's bolstering of its arsenal with the latest armaments from M.A.R.S. Industries, Cobra Commander relied on stolen technology to advance COBRA weaponry. The enemy leader had his sights set on the MOBAT, G.I. JOE's advanced main battle tank, and hatched a complex scheme to capture it. The tank would feature as a bold centerpiece in an Armed Force Day Parade marching through Manhattan. COBRA infiltrated the procession with troops dressed up as a marching band and a capture vehicle disguised as an enormous float behind the tank.

The MOBAT's crew—Steeler, Clutch, and Breaker—clued into COBRA's intentions before it was too late, and escaped the clever snare. They fled down the avenues of midtown Manhattan in the most impossible-to-conceal escape vehicle, the polished and unarmed MOBAT tank. The COBRA soldiers revealed antitank weapons hidden among their musical instruments, and gave pursuit, ultimately cornering the tank in Central Park. But the clever G.I. JOEs turned the tables on COBRA by firing a booming warning shot over their heads and demanding their surrender. The COBRAs laid down their arms, even though they were capitulating to an illusion.

The MOBAT's main cannon had no shells. The thunderous report was actually the tank's external speakers, amplifying the sound of Breaker's popping bubblegum. The power of suggestion did the rest. For all the grief that Breaker gets for his rather immature habit of constantly chewing pink gum, it has actually saved lives on other documented occasions as well.

CHUCKLES
(Undercover)

DATA FILE

ACCESS GRANTED

File Name: Philip M. Provost
SN: 299-58-5214
Primary Military Specialty: Criminal
   Investigations Division (CID)
Secondary Military Specialty:
   Intelligence
Birthplace: Little Rock, Arkansas
Grade: E-5

If he didn't have such a refined sense of right and wrong, Chuckles could have retired a wealthy grifter. He is eminently likable, able to talk his way out of any situation. This made him well suited for undercover operations. Chuckles is unusual in that he strives to become memorable while on duty, as opposed to disappearing into the shadows. In essence, his gregarious nature earns the trust of his marks, so that they simply cannot believe he's actually spying on them.

Chuckles has worked in undercover for so long that no one is truly certain which agency he works for. He has undertaken many covert ops for G.I. JOE, including a lengthy stint spent infiltrating Extensive Enterprises, the corporation headed by Tomax and Xamot.

Chuckles's natural likability is his greatest asset. He can sit around all day with a bunch of COBRAs, grinning, cracking jokes, and punching shoulders, all the while wearing a miniature transmitter that's being homed in on by the G.I. JOE team. He's aware of the consequences of being found out. He's also confident in his ability to fight his way out of any situation.

■ The Invisible Agent

It would take someone with Chuckles's unparalleled detective skills to find evidence of his shadowed path, which has woven through the foundations of the modern G.I. JOE and COBRA teams both. When the top brass were putting together G.I. JOE, they turned to Philip Provost's investigative work to identify worthy candidates for the team and bring to light examples of character that did not get reported in dossiers or after-action reports. Provost looked through the ugliest, most classified operations undertaken by the likes of Clayton Abernathy and Lonzo Wilkinson, and sifted through to the heart of the matters that exemplified the unerring strength of personality these soldiers exhibited under the most arduous of circumstances. Based on Provost's findings, these men would become some of the first modern G.I. JOE operatives—Hawk and Stalker—and yet they would have no knowledge of Provost's involvement.

Thus is the mercurial nature of his specialty. What Chuckles does, he does not for any accolade or recognition—for few ever know what he has accomplished. It is believed that Chuckles was the one who first found evidence of the formation of COBRA, though there is no record on file crediting him with this intelligence. Even if there was, it would have been gathered by one of a string of aliases that has long since been deleted with a few keystrokes.

COVER GIRL
(Intelligence/Armor)

DATA FILE
ACCESS GRANTED

G.I JOE

File Name: Courtney A. Krieger
SN: RA973-24-4860
Primary Military Specialty: Counterintelligence
Secondary Military Specialty: Armor
Other Military Specialties: AFV mechanics; recruitment
Birthplace: Peoria, Illinois
Grade: E-5

Courtney Krieger's natural beauty and poise had her winning pageants in Peoria at a young age. She soon broke into the big time, gracing the runways in New York and Chicago and magazine covers nationwide. The flashbulbs and glamour, however, weren't fulfilling, and as she approached adulthood she grew tired of showbiz superficiality and began seeking out ways to make a difference. Rather than heed the advice of a dozen wannabe agents suggesting she use her looks to support charities and causes, she spun her life around entirely and enlisted in the army, specializing in a field where cheekbones, facial symmetry, and good skin offered no advantage whatsoever. Trading glitz for grease, she found she had a talent for heavy vehicle repair, making things that run on diesel purr at her command. She learned the ins and outs of armored fighting vehicles (AFVs) at Fort Knox before joining the G.I. JOE team.

Cover Girl constantly has to work against her beauty to prove herself. Her chosen specialty often leaves her vulnerable to preconceptions and misjudgments, but she couldn't have picked a field more different from her civilian life. When she chooses to use them, though, her self-assurance and beauty reduce most men to stuttering fools. Of course, Clutch does tend to ask for it.

■ Unleash the Wolverine

Proficient in diesel mechanics and gas turbine technologies, Cover Girl can perform diagnostics, maintenance, and repair on any AFV. She is also a qualified expert with anti-armor weapons such as LAW rockets and M-47 Dragon anti-tank missiles. Her true love is the Wolverine armored missile carrier. This 20-ton armored tank is her signature vehicle, and is armed with a dozen anti-tank or anti-personnel medium-range optically sighted laser-designated missiles.

■ Intelligence and Covert Ops

Though her specialty was primarily armor-based, there were several early calls for Cover Girl to use her expertise in makeup and stagecraft to go undercover on covert and intelligence-gathering ops. She resented assignments that took advantage of her natural beauty, such as when she posed as a cheerleader to provide security to the president while he attended a baseball game, or when she modeled the Watchstar diamond to lure COBRA agents into capturing her so she could uncover details about their weapons development program. She nonetheless heeded the call of duty and put aside her discomfort. Rather than feel compromised or unsettled in such tasks, Cover Girl expanded her knowledge of undercover work at Fort Huachuca Military Intelligence School (MIS). She emerged a capable field agent, increasing the scope of her skill set to the G.I. JOE team.

■ The Greaser and the Pirate

Whoever coined the maxim *Opposites attract* would find no better example than the relationship that blossomed between Shipwreck and Cover Girl. Krieger became the object of uninvited attention many times over the years, deflecting the advances of oafs such as Snow Job and Clutch with either a witty rejoinder or a well-placed elbow. With Shipwreck, though, it was different. Somehow the salty sailor got past her guard, and she saw what lay beneath his gruff exterior.

Although some commands would have frowned on such relationships within the ranks, General Hawk encouraged them. He knew from tragic personal experience that the dangers of being a G.I. JOE often meant putting aside certain fundamental comforts of life, like love and companionship.

DUKE
(First Sergeant)

File Name: Conrad S. Hauser
SN: 234-55-GI89
Primary Military Specialty: Airborne infantry
Secondary Military Specialty: Military intelligence (G-2)
Other Military Specialties: Ranger; Star Brigade battle commander; artillery; small-arms armorer
Qualified Expert: CLASSIFIED
Birthplace: St. Louis, Missouri
Grade: E-9

There are three things that make Duke see red: ignorance, disorder, and deliberate evil. Even as a young boy growing up in Iowa (where the Hauser family resided for a time before returning to Missouri), he took school bullies down a peg whenever he could. Young Hauser felt it his duty to excel and make the best of himself—a trademark he saw at the heart of America. Becoming an expert in history, a champion football player, an able gymnast, and a Yale student was not enough for Duke. He strived to give his best in the service of freedom.

Duke has more combat experience than some of those generals in the Pentagon. He's the kind of grunt you want to have right by your side when the going gets rough. He can assess any hostile situation with lightning speed and act upon it instantly. The man doesn't know the meaning of the word fear.

Aside from his native English, Hauser was already fluent in French and German when he enlisted. He graduated at the top of his class from Airborne School in Fort Benning, and opted for the US Army Special Language School, gaining the linguistic and cultural chops he'd need in executing two of the eight primary missions of Special Forces: unconventional warfare and foreign internal defense. Hauser learned Han Chinese and a host of Southeast Asian dialects. He would return from overseas a decorated hero, receiving a Congressional Medal of Honor and two Bronze Stars for single-handedly rescuing 34 POWs from a heavily guarded enemy compound.

Hauser took refresher language courses in numerous Middle Eastern languages, including Farsi, as well as Spanish, and ran four Special Forces schools. He led RDF (Rapid Deployment Force) troops into various hot spots in Central America and the Middle East.

At a young age, Hauser was given a commission as an officer, but declined. "They tell me that an officer's job is to impel others to take risks … so that the officer survives to take the blame in the event of total catastrophe," Hauser said in response. "With all due respect, sir… if that's what an officer does, I don't want any part of it." Hauser opted to stay in the front lines, where the action was.

As part of the G.I. JOE team, Duke would fill the role of first sergeant, a position also referred to as the "First Shirt," "Top Kick," or "Top Hat." In this role, he served as a rough and rugged leader by example, a careful listener, a precise giver of orders, a font of lore and knowledge, and a fair settler of disputes. Duke served as field commander under Hawk, supervising the training of the noncommissioned officers in G.I. JOE. As the team fluctuated in size and structure over the years, Duke was a fixture in command, leading special units such as Tiger Force, Star Brigade, and Sigma 6. Duke spends his spare time reading history, which he views as a catalog of mistakes of the past, ones he does not intend to repeat.

A Captive of COBRA

A risk any G.I. JOE leader runs is capture by COBRA, which deemed command figures as targets to be taken alive whenever possible. Duke was netted by COBRA agents during the theft of the RelayStar satellite by the COBRA M.A.S.S. (molecular, assembly, scrambling, and sending) teleportation device. Taken to COBRA's mountain citadel, Duke was fitted with a mind control headband that allowed a COBRA agent to direct his muscles through a simple joystick. In this manner, Cobra Commander pitted Duke against a hulking slave combatant, Ramdar, in the gladiatorial arena of sport. Duke was able to hold his own against the titan, and with the help of fellow prisoner Selena, he disrupted the mental sway of COBRA technology and escaped the citadel. He left Selena his command ring, which contained a homing beacon allowing the G.I. JOE team to home in on COBRA's mountain headquarters.

Massacre at Trucial Abysmia

One of the most grueling crucibles endured by Duke occurred in the Middle Eastern nation of Trucial Abysmia. Duke and Falcon led a small G.I. JOE armor team, operating out of the neighboring Emirate of Benzheen, in a rapid assault on COBRA Terror Drome installations. They were outflanked by COBRA vehicles, and the team—10 in all—were taken captive. Duke refused to go quietly and spat on his captors, Tomax and Xamot, receiving a brutal beating in return. Though he tried to center the attention of the COBRAs on himself, a cold-blooded S.A.W. Viper soldier instead opened fire on the entire group of prisoners, who were held helplessly in a ditch. Four G.I. JOEs died before Falcon was able to momentarily stop the Viper.

Duke and his surviving teammates escaped in a commandeered COBRA Rage vehicle, taking their dead comrades with them. The S.A.W. Viper gave pursuit, leading a charge of COBRA artillery that destroyed the Rage, killing three more men. Of the original team, only Duke, Falcon, and Cross-Country remained standing. Just as the S.A.W. Viper was about to kill the trio, he received an order from COBRA Command to cease hostilities.

Duke swore vengeance, but when he finally encountered the S.A.W. Viper, the COBRA soldier was unarmed. Despite his disgust and rage, Duke could not open fire on an unarmed man. He also could not take the S.A.W. Viper prisoner, because the G.I. JOE team was operating in Trucial Abysmia illegally. He was forced to turn away from the maniacal murderer who was responsible for killing seven troops under his command.

The Black Ops Years

> Duke, I remember you as the toughest, proudest First Shirt I'd ever served under. You rode me pretty hard sometimes, but you helped me heal when I needed it. After the team disbanded and you spent those years in black ops doing who-knows-what … you're not Duke anymore. You're this man that I really don't trust and I really don't like. That bothers the hell out of a lot of people these days. It's not just me.
> —Ripcord

The G.I. JOE team was briefly disbanded following the apparent defeat of COBRA, and the team members scattered, some transferring to other assignments while others retired from military life altogether. Duke essentially vanished for a time, turning in his khaki fatigues for the black suit and tie of a secret government agency. Duke carried out numerous black ops that remain highly classified to this day before returning to the reinstated G.I. JOE. The time spent operating on the shadowy fringes nurtured a secretive, solitary side to Duke that took some of his longtime colleagues by surprise.

When Duke operated off-the-books to send an unauthorized G.I. JOE team to Sierra Gordo to flush out Destro's operations there, he went too far. Though the team successfully captured Destro, they took casualties. Tunnel Rat and Low-Light were severely injured, while new recruit Dart suffered a nervous breakdown. Disgusted by what he saw as maverick and dangerous behavior, Flint asked for Duke's resignation, a request Hawk seriously considered before letting Duke remain for another chance.

Mission Report: Trailing Bludd

Prior to the reestablishment of hostilities between G.I. JOE and COBRA, Duke (or rather, Agent Hauser) was sent on a black ops mission to locate and detain wanted mercenary fugitive Major Sebastian Bludd. Duke was air-dropped into the former Soviet Union, where he infiltrated a swanky cocktail party, complete with tuxedo and witty Russian conversation. He snuck away from the soiree to tap into an unprotected computer system, pulling up contract records of Major Bludd.

With this information, Duke trailed Bludd to Italy, where the one-eyed gunman was attempting to broker an arms deal. True to his treacherous ways, Bludd double-crossed his buyers and fled the scene in a speedboat, only to be pursued by Duke and two other agents on Jet Skis. The breakneck pursuit continued on land once Bludd commandeered a sports car and Duke a motorcycle. Though Bludd escaped, Duke located his Italian residence and there found proof that Cobra Commander had returned to American soil. This discovery precipitated the reinstatement of G.I. JOE.

Family Ties

Family has long been a sore spot for Duke. He and his half brother Falcon rarely saw eye-to-eye, and tensions between the two would erupt in heated arguments despite their difference in ranks. It was the estrangement with his father that bothered Duke the most, though.

Conrad Hauser was a gifted artist as a child, a talent nurtured by his father, Max, and his ailing mother. His mother succumbed to cancer, leaving Connie to be raised by Max alone. Max was an ardent pacifist, and would take part in protests against the US government's use of military abroad. The lesson learned by young Conrad was to stick to his convictions. It was not an act of youthful defiance when he enlisted in the army. Rather, it was following his father's example and acting upon his beliefs.

When COBRA uncovered classified information regarding G.I. JOE families, Max Hauser was targeted for capture. Duke was visiting at the time, and both father and son were taken prisoner by the COBRA agent known as the Interrogator. The COBRA attempted to coax information regarding G.I. JOE counterintelligence operations in the Middle East by playing on each Hauser's psychological weakness when it came to the other. A disguised COBRA operative playing a US military officer tried to convince Max Hauser that his son had gone rogue. Max refused to believe the claims, and the Interrogator's efforts were cut short when Roadblock stormed the COBRA safe house, rescuing the Hausers.

Max was shot and wounded during the rescue, but in his pain managed to make peace with Duke. He was treated for his injuries, and the two now remain in much more civil contact than in years previous.

DUSTY
(Desert Warfare)

DATA FILE

ACCESS GRANTED

File Name: *Ronald W. Tadur*
SN: *371-11-RT05*
Primary Military Specialty: *Infantry*
Secondary Military Specialty: *Refrigeration and air-conditioning*
Qualified Expert: *M-16; M-16A2; M-14; M-1911A1; M-60; M-203 40mm grenade launcher*
Birthplace: *Las Vegas, Nevada*
Grade: *E-4*

To young Ron Tadur, the lights and extravagance of his native Las Vegas paled in comparison with the promise and allure of the open desert. After he enlisted and underwent basic training at Fort Bliss, Texas, his expertise in desert ecology earned him the position of the first dedicated desert trooper on the G.I. JOE team. An excellent tracker, he is fluent in Arabic and Hebrew, and conversant in Kazakh and the Oirat-Khalkha languages of Central Asia.

If there was ever any shortage of evidence revealing how capable Dusty is in desert environs, just look to Sandstorm. After an extended operation in the Utah deserts, Dusty "adopted" this coyote as a "pet." The terms are applied loosely—Sandstorm doesn't regularly enter the G.I. JOE desert bases or get taken on walks. The animal only emerges from the shadows of the bluffs when Dusty is on patrol. It's as if the coyote respects and acknowledges Dusty as a fellow creature of the desert. Spirit has described Sandstorm as Dusty's animal totem. Mutt can't stand the cur, and insists that Dusty keep it far away from his beloved Junkyard.

Dusty can track like a hungry wolf, go to ground like a spooked prairie dog, and fight like a wounded bobcat. He's got the patience of a diamondback, the social graces of a gila monster, and the taste buds of a coyote. He excels at sneaking up behind bad guys in the desert and popping a can of firefight.

■ Mission Report: Dusty's Double Deception

Dusty had a starring role in a complex ploy designed to thwart COBRA's plans to concoct a mind-control gas. The subterfuge exposed Dusty as a traitor to G.I. JOE, ingratiating him to the upper echelons of COBRA. The scheme came at a time of great personal difficulty to Dusty. His mother, Gladys Tadur, was ailing, succumbing to faltering health and growing medical expenses. At the end of his wits and finances, Dusty was approached by Tomax and Xamot representing Extensive Enterprises. The twins offered to pay for Gladys's medical bills in exchange for Dusty handing over the classified formula behind an experimental G.I. JOE armor treatment that rendered vehicles and infantry impervious to laser weaponry and munitions.

Dusty at first violently rejected the COBRA offer, but in time, he contacted Extensive Enterprises. He did not have the formula in hand, but he could provide crucial intelligence to COBRA regarding G.I. JOE movements and operations. Dusty warned COBRA of a forthcoming G.I. JOE ambush, a treacherous act that began to earn the trust of Cobra Commander. These actions also raised the suspicions of his fellow G.I. JOEs, who were soon certain that they had a traitor in their ranks.

Duke and Flint engineered a plan to expose Dusty, based on Duke's initiative. They purposely leaked intelligence in Dusty's presence of an upcoming investigative mission to an abandoned COBRA base in the Gulf of Mexico. Dusty was not part of the mission; when the G.I. JOEs arrived, COBRA triggered the booby traps within their derelict outpost. Duke was caught in an explosive blast and knocked into a coma.

In the meantime, Dusty succeeded in capturing and transmitting the formula data to COBRA. He was also finally confronted by the incensed G.I. JOEs, particularly Shipwreck, who engaged the desert trooper in an unrestrained brawl. Dusty nearly escaped, but was caught by G.I. JOE security. He was promptly court-martialed, found guilty of treason, and sentenced to life of hard labor at a military prison.

En route to incarceration, Dusty was freed by COBRA agents, and soon welcomed personally by Cobra Commander into the serpentine ranks. While COBRA scientists attempted to replicate the armor treatment formula, Cobra Commander had Dusty lead the remaining raids on chemical stores needed to concoct the mind-control toxin. When Dusty had secured all the elements, Cobra Commander tasked him to gas captive G.I. JOEs as a final act of his loyalty.

Dusty's *true* loyalty shone through, as he instead freed his G.I. JOE teammates, and used the chemicals in a special mixture and concentration that unraveled the armor treatment formula. Unbeknownst to almost everyone involved, the G.I. JOE armor formula was a crock—it was too unstable to be practical. When Dusty was first approached by COBRA for its composition, Dusty loyally informed Duke, and the two of them concocted the plot to have Dusty appear as a traitor, and use the formula lure to insinuate Dusty into COBRA to thwart the mind-control program.

The mission was successful, but the unforeseen injury suffered by Duke meant that no one in G.I. JOE could be sure of Dusty's true intentions until the final moves of this complex chess game. With COBRA thwarted, Dusty was finally able to concentrate on his ailing mother, having been given the funds needed to pay for her treatment.

FLINT
(Warrant Officer)

DATA FILE

ACCESS GRANTED

307-62-4107

File Name: Dashiell R. Faireborn
SN: 307-62-4107
Primary Military Specialty: Infantry
Secondary Military Specialty: Rotary-
wing aircraft pilot
Other Military Specialties: Demolitions;
paratrooper operations; commando;
LAV operator
Birthplace: Wichita, Kansas
Grade: CW2 (chief warrant officer 2)

Outsiders may credit the rapid advancement of young Dash Faireborn to luck, but the future Flint always made his own fortune. He moved through school at a rapid pace, earning a Rhodes Scholarship and studying English literature at the University of Oxford. Not content with that achievement, Faireborn enlisted upon graduation and returned to the United States. He applied the same intense level of concentration to his military training as he did in academia, moving his way through Airborne School, Ranger School, Special Forces School, and Flight Warrant Officers School. Faireborn's high-reaching goals and the seeming ease with which he achieved them rubbed some of his fellow students the wrong way; they took his rakish grin and the gleam in his eye to be signs of insufferable arrogance. In truth, Faireborn secretly worked extra hard to make it look so easy.

Don't mistake that assured grin and cocksure swagger for empty grandstanding. He's got the brawn and the brains ... the whole package. It's not bragging if you've got the goods to back it up.

Prior to their enlistment in G.I. JOE, Dashiell Faireborn and Conrad Hauser served together as a special ops team in the strife-torn Middle Eastern nation of Trucial Abysmia. The neighboring Emirate of Benzheen had hired mercenaries to exacerbate a long-running series of border disputes with the Abysmians. Throughout the operation, Faireborn had proven himself to have a keen tactical mind, able to apply his broad intellectual background and sharp insight into implementable solutions. Though the details remain classified, it is known that Flint planned and led six missions into hostile territories that saw the rescue of American hostages prior to his experience with G.I. JOE.

As the G.I. JOE team expanded, Hauser became the team's first sergeant, code-named Duke. In looking to fill out the brain power of

the team's tacticians, he turned to Faireborn. Dash, always on the lookout for a new challenge to conquer, saw the G.I. JOE team as the ultimate achievement in military service. He readily accepted the job, becoming Warrant Officer Flint.

Skills and Abilities

A qualified expert with all NATO modern small arms, Flint displays a strong preference for a 12-gauge pump-action shotgun. A skilled rotary-wing pilot, he can capably man the stick of all current US military helicopters as well as those in the services of most Western and former Soviet Bloc powers. He is an expert in desert battle tactics and training, quipping that he can lower his body temperature at will to better withstand the punishing desert heat. Flint also has received special recognition as a top-notch paratrooper. He has executed HALO (high-altitude/low-opening) jumps from altitudes of 40,000 feet. Flint's strong tactical mind and leadership abilities have landed him in command of several special mission groups, such as Tiger Force and the Eco Warriors.

A Lady's Man

Flint met Lady Jaye during his first assignment for the G.I. JOE team, combat-testing the new Armadillo mini-tank. He proved to be a crack shot and a skilled driver, but his self-congratulatory airs did little to impress Jaye. She expressed her skepticism about Flint's abilities, though Roadblock (who had served with Flint in Trucial Abysmia) vouched for him. Despite a frosty start, Flint and Lady Jaye grew closer as they were paired on assignments and got to know and trust each other's remarkable abilities. The tenuous romance that blossomed was, at first, kept a secret in an effort to remain professional, but in a small, tight-knit group like G.I. JOE, word spread quickly enough.

After the team was briefly decommissioned and many G.I. JOEs retired from military service, Flint and Lady Jaye stayed close to each other. Jaye went into semi-retirement, while Flint continued in the army. The two married and settled in Fort Meade, Maryland, allowing them to remain close to the Pentagon in times of need. Faireborn became a bestselling author, effectively outing his formerly classified status as a G.I. JOE. Despite public knowledge of his role in the team, when G.I. JOE was reinstated, Flint and Lady Jaye were among the first members brought back to active service.

The Ritual

We're prepared for one another to jet off to some far away, top-secret mission at a moment's notice, and we've learned to live with that. Which is why we ... have this little ritual. When one of us has a mission like this, we leave a little sign to let the other know. Flint leaves this little army man from his childhood on my pillow. I have my own little trinket....
—Lady Jaye

Mission Report: The Pleasant Cove Incident

While on a two-week leave, Flint ventured to Pleasant Cove, a new residential community along the shores of California, to visit his cousin Ted Harris. Flint's unannounced visit to Harris's family revealed a multifaceted plot by COBRA. Using subliminal control signals broadcast through local television, Cobra Commander had turned the denizens of Pleasant Cove into subservient drones who carried out drudge labor in building a new underwater headquarters. When the G.I. JOEs uncovered this plot, they closed in on Pleasant Cove to thwart the COBRA operation. Cobra Commander tried to compel Flint to harm Lady Jaye, but Flint's feelings for her were powerful enough for him to resist the overwhelming mind control.

Strange Bedfellows

Upon release of his novel *The Fight for Freedom,* Flint was kidnapped by an international coalition of criminal and rogue military leaders seeking vengeance on Cobra Commander. He was taken to the Czech Republic and imprisoned alongside the Baroness. A Yakuza interrogator attempted to painfully carve from the captives any information leading to the Commander's whereabouts. Despite the torture, Flint stayed resolute, singing at the top of his lungs "The Army Goes Rolling Along." Flint and the Baroness worked together to overpower and escape their captors. During Flint's time tied to the Baroness, there was an unmistakable chemistry between the two, but each remained faithful to their respective long-term companions.

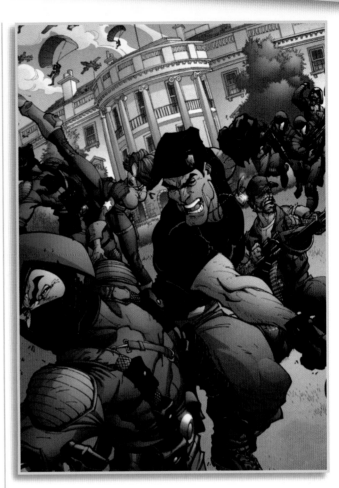

Dark Days

During the rise of the Red Shadows—an international terrorist organization with the technological clout and ruthless ambition to momentarily eclipse COBRA—Flint was targeted for capture. Red Shadow agent Dela Eden ran Flint off the road not far from his home in Maryland. His car flipped over in a ditch, and Flint was injured and trapped. Lady Jaye intuited that something was amiss and followed, tackling Eden before she could close in on her husband. Lady Jaye pulled Flint from the burning car before Eden stabbed her with a sharp metal piece of wreckage.

Flint's world fractured, and the ordinarily clean-cut, rational, and professional man became haggard, impulsive, and vengeful. Gone were the charm and bravado, replaced by a cold intensity and dangerous fatalism. The high command of the G.I. JOE team had deep doubts over Flint's effectiveness and considered retiring him. Flint took a self-imposed sabbatical from the team, composing himself and quelling his hunger for revenge. When Flint returned to active duty, his nature may have seemed muted, but he had realigned his priorities, putting country and service before his inner demons.

GUNG-HO
(Marine)

File Name: Ettienne R. LaFitte
SN: MC564-88-3900
Primary Military Specialty: Recondo instructor
Secondary Military Specialty: Jungle warfare training instructor
Other Military Specialties: Reconnaissance; battle wagon driver; anti-armor; bio-military expert (Mega Marines)
Birthplace: Fer-de-Lance, Louisiana
Grade: E-9 (sergeant)

A LaFitte family reunion has to be seen to be believed. The large Cajun clan lives in the depths of Bayou Country and convenes at a cottage that can turn from cozy to terrifying in the span of a few steps. Unchained in what passes for a backyard is Little Chouchou, the family gator, yet she's not the most dangerous one there. The LaFitte men—and more than a few women—are always looking to spar. And if you manage to avoid an unsolicited wrestling match, you had best galvanize your tongue and insides before you get a taste of the spicy family gumbo recipe.

If our operations weren't classified, the USMC couldn't do much better than use Gung-Ho as a poster boy. That Creole will run into subzero combat zones shirtless so that no one will miss his corps tattoo on his chest. All marines are crazy, but Gung-Ho is the scariest, craziest jarhead that ever scratched, kicked, and bit his way out of that hole-in-the-swamp they call Parris Island!

G.I. JOE operations have more than once pitted Gung-Ho against COBRA enemies who were supposed masters of swamp terrain, but the combative Cajun has found them wanting. Zartan is too reliant on technology and tampered genetics ("cheating," in Gung-Ho's book). If Croc-Master were really a master, he wouldn't need the leashes. The only one of the COBRA swamp fighters Gung-Ho grudgingly admits can hold his own in the bayou is Copperhead.

Conversely, Gung-Ho holds a special connection to fellow jungle fighters such as Recondo, Pathfinder, and Muskrat. Gung-Ho's strong sense of family extends to the entire G.I. JOE operation, and he feels fiercely protective of his fellow soldiers. Any hint of disloyalty gets his formidable temper cooking. For this reason, Gung-Ho has never warmed up—and likely never will—to Storm Shadow. While the ninja was under the influence of COBRA, Storm Shadow slashed Gung-Ho across the back with his katana blade. Though the cut was deep and Gung-Ho needed to convalesce for weeks, the sting that truly lasted was that Storm Shadow threatened his fellow G.I. JOEs. Gung-Ho is not one to forgive.

Mega Marines

After COBRA scientists opened up a genetic can of worms through rampant bio-experimentation following their successes with the Serpentor project, the top US brass saw the need to counter the proliferation of weaponized biotechnology through the development of the Mega Marines. Gung-Ho served as commander for the short-lived unit, working alongside Clutch, Blast-Off, and Mirage. By no means an expert at genetic engineering, he left the details of polymerase chain reactions and restriction enzymes to others, and instead offered his expertise in "force projection" and quick-strike scenarios.

A Quick Guide to Cajun

Gung-Ho's crawdaddy gumbo accent comes and goes, much to the confusion and amusement of his friends. Here are some of the things the marine might say:

ain?—Can you repeat that?
bag daer—back there
beb—sweetheart, babe (affectionate)
coo-wee—Well, look at that!
don matta—It doesn't matter
drawz—underwear/BDUs
freesons—goose bumps
lagniappe ("lan yap")—something extra
meenoo—cat
peeshwank—runt
podnah—partner
zeerahb!—gross!

Gung-Ho grew up in tough surroundings. He claims to be swampproof: that mosquitoes, leeches, and gators can't handle blood as thick as his. At the age of 13, LaFitte entered the family poaching business. He eventually moved out of the swamps and in his late teens gained a reputation as a knife fighter and bare-knuckle brawler in New Orleans. After one close call too many, he sought structure for his impulsive streaks and to channel his energy and strength toward something bigger than him. LaFitte enlisted in the US Marine Corps at age 18, and graduated at the top of his class from boot camp in Parris Island, South Carolina. LaFitte attended Airborne School, Recondo School, and Marine Ordnance School.

Gung-Ho's jungle expertise often saw him stationed in strife-torn Sierra Gordo, or the thick primordial rain forests on Cobra Island.

HAWK
(G.I. JOE Leader)

File Name: Clayton M. Abernathy

SN: 212-75-CM36

Alternative Code Name: General Tomahawk

Primary Military Specialty: Strategic
command operations

Secondary Military Specialty: Artillery

Other Military Specialties: Radar; Star
Brigade Armor Bot command

Qualified Expert: M-16; M-1911A1 auto
pistol; JUMP jet pack

Birthplace: Denver, Colorado

Grade: O-8 (major general)

Finding the right man to lead G.I. JOE was no simple task. The modern incarnation of the special missions team needed a courageous, highly intelligent leader ready to push already seasoned soldiers to the very limits of their ability. Only in this way could the G.I. JOE team emerge as the fearless defenders of freedom, ready to protect the world against the forces of evil. The military masterminds who reinstated G.I. JOE for modern operations sought out a man of integrity, finding a capable candidate in Lieutenant Colonel Clayton Abernathy.

Abernathy's military career had taken him around the world. He graduated at the top of his class from the US Military Academy at West Point. As a young officer, he served en cadre with the North Atlantic Command and put in three years at the USA ENG COM EVR missile and radar training station. His other credentials include Advanced Infantry Training, Covert Ops School, and the Officers Space Program at NASA.

General Hawk is the type of commander who goes out and gets shot at like everyone else. Troops respect that. They know he won't ask them to do anything he isn't willing to do himself. And that's why they're willing to do anything he tells them.

The last known operation involving Abernathy prior to his involvement with G.I. JOE was a United Nations peacekeeping mission in the fragmented nation of Borovia. Whatever occurred there has been redacted from any published account, but somehow elevated Abernathy into serious consideration for the leadership of the G.I. JOE team. After several years as field commander, Hawk earned his stars and was promoted to brigadier general. Such advancement did not anchor him behind a desk, however. Hawk's stubbornness

and his indisputable ability to anticipate COBRA strategies and deliver victory after victory kept him in the thick of battle, and in the hearts of the troops he commanded.

Field Command and Promotion

Hawk proved himself to be a commanding officer who led from the front. He earned the admiration of those in his command through his willingness to face risks head-on. During a COBRA attack on the US Treasury in Washington, D.C., Hawk even suffered three gunshots in the back from Cobra Commander himself, who was unaware that the G.I. JOE leader was protected by a bulletproof vest.

After General Flagg was killed, command oversight of G.I. JOE operations fell to Austin, who promoted Hawk to full commander upon the refurbishment of the team headquarters, the Pit. As Hawk became accustomed to his new role, he stepped back from front-line duty, leaving field operation of the team to Duke. Austin suffered a heart attack shortly thereafter, and while recuperating, the general saw the need to give Hawk increased scope and authority in shaping the future of the team. He promoted Hawk to brigadier general and commander in chief of the G.I. JOE team.

Mission Report: The Defection of the Montana

Hawk was a close friend of Admiral George Latimer, longtime commanding officer of the USS *Montana,* a battleship being decommissioned after 45 years of service. When the *Montana* returned to the Philadelphia Naval Shipyards, Latimer broke ranks, refusing to relinquish command. He allied himself to COBRA to prevent the ship from ending in the scrapyard. COBRA B.A.T.s (battle android troopers) overran the *Montana,* and Destro used the warship as a test bed for his new weapon to attack the Seventh Fleet of the US Navy. The Pulse Modulator device could create an electromagnetic bubble extending two miles outward from the *Montana,* leaching all electrical power from any approaching ships, planes, or weapons.

US Navy Admiral Overton ordered the *Montana* to be sunk, but Hawk recognized the power of Destro's weapon and creatively reinterpreted Overton's orders into a very dangerous, and *very* unauthorized, strategy. With volunteers from the G.I. JOE team, Hawk commandeered the USS *Constitution,* the oldest ship still in active duty in the navy. The three-masted, wooden-hulled sailing ship had no electrical systems to disrupt, and under Hawk's command "Old Ironsides" pulled alongside the *Montana,* allowing them to board and destroy the Modulator. Before retreating, Destro locked the *Montana*'s automated weapons to fire on the fleet. Hawk and Latimer worked together to disable the firing controls, but it was too late for the *Montana.* The fleet's return fire hulled the ship. Latimer refused to leave his sinking vessel, but Hawk punched him unconscious and took him from the *Montana* to answer for his transgressions.

Decommission and Reinstatement

COBRA operations wrapped around the globe, entangling nations such as Frusenland and Benzheen, even encompassing home soil activities in Broca Beach, Millville, and New York City. What was once a silent war hidden behind a veil of government secrecy grew highly visible and impossible to conceal. As the years passed, G.I. JOE and COBRA became household names in the United States

the venomization chamber, he had mutated into a horrible, monstrous brute, a hybrid forged of reptilian cold-blooded detachment, insectile focus, and feral savagery. The good man that was Clayton Abernathy had been eclipsed by Venomous Maximus.

Maximus was genetically connected to his V-Troops, forming an unbreakable bond of command and loyalty. Not surprisingly, Cobra Commander found he could not control the strong-willed Maximus. The ambitious Venomous sought to rule COBRA, and conspired with Overkill to overthrow the Commander. COBRA forces captured a G.I. JOE launch base in South America with the intent of spreading an airborne venomization serum into the atmosphere to transform civilians worldwide into COBRA V-Troops. The G.I. JOE team thwarted this effort and, using a counteragent concocted by Hi-Tech and Dr. Link Talbot, were able to cure Hawk of Mindbender's genetic tampering. Abernathy spent weeks recuperating, undergoing extensive gene therapy. While convalescing, he continued to advise Duke, who had become commander of a pared-down G.I. JOE special missions team, Sigma 6.

Twilight

After the defeat and dismantling of a COBRA splinter group called the Coil, G.I. JOE succeeded in capturing Destro, but the clever arms dealer negotiated his freedom by promising to deliver Cobra Commander instead. Staging a prisoner transfer by rail as bait, COBRA forces attacked the train supposedly carrying Destro. The battle degraded into fisticuffs between Cobra Commander and Hawk. Tragically, Hawk was shot in the back by the Commander (in actuality, Zartan in disguise, but that's *another* story). The bullet lodged into Abernathy's spine, rendering him a paraplegic.

Confined to a wheelchair, Hawk withdrew from G.I. JOE command. Lost in despair, General Abernathy reflected on the choices in his life and the losses he had faced, such as the sudden death of his fiancée Carolee years ago in a car accident, when he was still a colonel. The selfless drive that had led Abernathy to a storied career in the military resurfaced, however, and Hawk returned from this bleak period of depression. During the rise of the Red Shadows, he was targeted for assassination but rescued by Kamakura, who became a protector of sorts to the general. After the defeat of the Red Shadows, the G.I. JOE team was scaled down once more, and placed under the command of General Joseph Colton.

Hawk was obsessed with the capture of the ever-slippery Cobra Commander. He asked G.I. JOEs Spirit and Duke to undergo separate covert missions to investigate any trace of the vanished villain. Colton would eventually invite Hawk back into the G.I. JOE ranks, and shortly afterward Cobra Commander returned, revealed to be disguised as the White House chief of staff. In this position, Cobra Commander was privy to some of the most guarded secrets of Washington and G.I. JOE. Armed with such knowledge, and with complete control of M.A.R.S. Industries, Cobra Commander started his most ambitious campaign ever, igniting and fanning flashpoints around the globe to begin World War III.

In the final battlefield of the Appalachian Mountains, Hawk took to the air once more. Procuring a jet pack, he soared in to tackle a fleeing Cobra Commander, finally capturing the head snake once and for all. With all the strength he could muster, Hawk pummeled the Commander into submission as efforts around the world turned the tide on COBRA's destructive rampage.

This defeat of COBRA did not herald the end of G.I. JOE. The president of the United States instead fully activated the G.I. JOE team to its largest roster, and placed Generals Hawk and Colton in joint command.

and abroad. General Clayton Abernathy became the best known of the G.I. JOE team, for he served as the public face of the team. Though the G.I. JOE operations remained classified, Abernathy still reached out to a frightened populace, appearing on news programs (such as *Twenty Questions* with Hector Ramirez) to discuss the ongoing efforts to defeat COBRA.

When G.I. JOE was decommissioned following the apparent disbanding of COBRA, Hawk continued to ascend in rank, becoming a lieutenant general. When COBRA then returned with cutting-edge nanotechnology fueling its terrorist campaigns, it was the start of a renewed conflict that saw the reinstatement of G.I. JOE with Hawk as commander in chief, and field command falling to Duke and Flint. It was a changed team for a different era, and it took an old dog like Hawk some time to catch up with the new tricks. He initially saw bold additions like the ninja Kamakura as a misstep, and he took exception to the number of off-the-record rogue assignments taken on by hardheaded teammates such as Duke and Snake-Eyes.

The Rise of Venomous Maximus

COBRA scientists under the command of Dr. Mindbender continued to push the envelope in genetic experimentation and weaponization, resulting in their Evilution program. Destro and the Baroness kidnapped Hawk, transporting him to COBRA's Antarctic bioresearch facility, the Viper Pit, where Cobra Commander subjected him to the venomization process.

The program combined the DNA of COBRA Viper "volunteers" with that of the deadliest animals on the planet. The resulting V-Troops had the tenacity and ferocity of wild beasts combined with the precision training and obedience of COBRA infantry. The apex of Evilution was merging the DNA of the best modified troops with Hawk's, to create the ultimate military commander with the inside knowledge required to defeat G.I. JOE. When Hawk emerged from

HEAVY DUTY
(Heavy Ordnance Trooper)

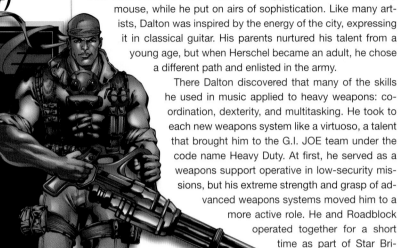

File Name: Herschel Dalton

SN: 807-46-LM65

Primary Military Specialty: Heavy anti-armor weapons

Secondary Military Specialty: Indirect-fire infantryman

Other Military Specialties: Laser weapons systems operator; tank commander

Birthplace: Chicago, Illinois

Grade: E-5

The man is an artist. As far as he's concerned, the ability to play Bach's Two-Part Invention in D Minor and hit a distant, fast-moving COBRA target are two sides of the same coin.

Roadblock's big-city cousin Herschel Dalton loved the sights, sounds, and smells of metropolitan living. Chicago was a world apart from Biloxi, and Herschel likened his bigger cousin to the country mouse, while he put on airs of sophistication. Like many artists, Dalton was inspired by the energy of the city, expressing it in classical guitar. His parents nurtured his talent from a young age, but when Herschel became an adult, he chose a different path and enlisted in the army.

There Dalton discovered that many of the skills he used in music applied to heavy weapons: coordination, dexterity, and multitasking. He took to each new weapons system like a virtuoso, a talent that brought him to the G.I. JOE team under the code name Heavy Duty. At first, he served as a weapons support operative in low-security missions, but his extreme strength and grasp of advanced weapons systems moved him to a more active role. He and Roadblock operated together for a short time as part of Star Brigade. Herschel eventually saw assignment to Sigma 6, a specialist branch of G.I. JOE, where he served as the team's heavy weapons specialist. Fond of explosive power, Heavy Duty was always eager to try out the cutting-edge destructive technology engineered by Hi-Tech.

Dis the Cook

When Roadblock did not initially return to G.I. JOE after the team's temporary decommission, Heavy Duty attempted to fill in his cousin's role as a cook. Though he worked the kitchen with zeal and flair, the other G.I. JOEs weren't nearly as enthusiastic about his culinary creations. Heavy Duty tended to improvise ingredients and methods, and some G.I. JOEs swore they could taste the tang of white phosphorous on their steaks. The return of Roadblock was greatly welcomed by a hungry bunch of G.I. JOEs.

LADY JAYE
(Covert Ops)

853-71-AR49

DATA FILE
ACCESS GRANTED

File Name: Alison R. Hart-Burnett
SN: 853-71-AR49
Primary Military Specialty: Intelligence
Secondary Military Specialty: Armament repair
Other Military Specialty: Personnel clerk
Qualified Expert: M-16; M-16A2; M-1911A1 auto pistol; power javelin; reflex crossbow
Birthplace: Martha's Vineyard, Massachusetts
Grade: E-7

Alison Hart-Burnett graduated from Bryn Mawr, a highly selective women's college in Pennsylvania. A fierce competitive streak led her to excel, though it prevented her from establishing any strong friendships. She traveled abroad as part of her graduate work, studying at Trinity College in Dublin, where she picked up a faint Gaelic lilt to her speech. She was a gifted mimic, a skill she turned into a successful career as a stage actress. Following the Method approach, Alison truly sought to inhabit the skin of the characters she portrayed, submerging herself into the role. She found she could do the same in impersonating those around her.

As part of her studies, she mastered several languages, and she rolled all these skills together when she enlisted in the military. She is airborne- and Ranger-qualified, and studied at Intelligence School at Fort Holabird in Maryland. It was her expertise in covert ops that drew her to the G.I. JOE team.

Lady Jaye doesn't go in for that phony-wig-and-rubber-mask brand of disguise. She becomes the subject: body language, subtle gesture, correct shading of dialect—the right look in the eye. Cloaked and sandaled, she can squat down with a basket of oranges in any Middle Eastern marketplace and blend in perfectly.

Because of her background in working undercover on extended solo assignments, Lady Jaye came to G.I. JOE not quite ready to be a team player. In fact, her relationship with Scarlett was at first cold and antagonistic. The necessity of assignments, however, soon thawed Jaye's icy standoffish demeanor. Jaye's inability to connect with women—dating back all the way to her college years—may have been behind the protracted brawl that erupted between her and Zarana following the cessation of hostilities in the Cobra Island Civil War. The two pummeled each other for several long awkward moments while no COBRA or G.I. JOE dared to interrupt the fight.

In her role as a personnel clerk, it was often up to Lady Jaye to determine which G.I. JOEs fit which mission profiles, and prepare recommendations to General Hawk and other field commanders.

In this way, she grew to appreciate the abilities of her teammates and better connect with them. To her surprise, she found herself in a romantic relationship with Flint, a warrant officer she first dismissed as an arrogant blowhard.

The two worked exceptionally well together in the field, and spent their downtime in each other's company. When G.I. JOE was briefly decommissioned after the apparent defeat of COBRA, she married Flint. His proposal was unique: He wrote out his request to marry on a paper targeting silhouette at Lady Jaye's shooting range. She then went into semi-retirement, but returned to active duty alongside her husband when G.I. JOE was reinstated.

■ Skills and Abilities

A remarkable linguist, Lady Jaye is fluent in French, German, Russian, Polish, Afghani, Italian, and Portuguese, and able to converse in these languages with such ease that native speakers do not pick up on any accents. Though she is a qualified expert in a variety of small arms, Lady Jaye's preferred sidearm is a nickel-finish Colt Python .357 magnum revolver.

Lady Jaye's signature weapon is a set of specialized collapsible javelins that she carries within a quiver. She can hurl these unpowered projectiles over great distances with remarkable accuracy, a skill she acquired in her youth.

She has a wide variety of specialized spear tips, including explosive javelins, diamond-tipped cutting spears, and net-caster models. For greater distance and accuracy, Lady Jaye also carries a power javelin launcher.

she was rescued by Flint. G.I. JOE reinforcements soon arrived, and in the ensuing battle they leveled Doyle Manor, which proved to be Destro's ancestral home.

Though the initial letter was in part a sham—there was no solicitor, and it was in truth sent by a spiteful Baroness who wished to ruin Destro's plans—there does appear to be some ancestral connection between Lady Jaye and the nefarious weapons dealer.

Despite her often-voiced fear of heights, Lady Jaye is a qualified single-engine fixed-wing pilot and has been checked out in the "backseat" of the G.I. JOE Skystriker.

◼ Mission Report: The Destro Connection

A letter from the solicitor-at-law for the town of Loch Lomond in northern Scotland led Lady Jaye to the most surprising caper of her career. The correspondence claimed that Alison Hart-Burnett was the last living heir of Dame Agatha Doyle, and that she had inherited Doyle Manor by the loch. During a leave of absence, Jaye went to Scotland to investigate the creepy cobweb-covered mansion.

Inside, Lady Jaye found family portraits of the Doyle bloodline that bore a striking resemblance to her. Investigating the manor's dank lower chambers during the winter solstice, she found a pagan ritual under way. Among those in attendance were Destro, and the silver-masked terrorist was shocked to find a G.I. JOE agent infiltrating his most private of gatherings. Lady Jaye was nearly sacrificed by the masked pagans, but

RIPCORD
(HALO Jumper)

DATA FILE
ACCESS GRANTED

File Name: Wallace A. Weems
SN: 845-99-WA76
Primary Military Specialty: Airborne
   infantry
Secondary Military Specialty: Demoli-
   tions
Qualified Expert: M-16; M-1911A1
   auto pistol; Carl Gustav 9mm
   parabellum; Browning high-power
Birthplace: Columbus, Ohio
Grade: E-5

Wally Weems joined the Civil Air Patrol (the civilian auxiliary of the USAF) in high school and discovered his love of skydiving. The rush of free-falling was too short, though, so he sought out longer falls from higher altitudes by joining the military. His skill as a HALO (high-altitude/low-opening) jumper and paratrooper drew him to G.I. JOE, where he took the code name Ripcord.

Let's say you've got a trouble spot and you can't sail, walk, or ride into it. So you send a plane in so high that it can't be seen or heard. Ripcord jumps and drops like a rock for thousands of feet, then opens his chute at the last possible moment to avoid visual and electronic detection. What he does once he hits the ground, you don't want to hear about.

■ THE SEARCH FOR CANDY

Early in Ripcord's time with the team, he crossed paths with an undercover COBRA Crimson Guardsman during what was supposed to be a simple visit to a Staten Island shopping mall. The COBRA realized he had been identified and tried to escape by car. To give pursuit, Ripcord commandeered a colorful party delivery van belonging to "Bongo the Balloon Bear," a fur-costumed vendor. During the chase, Ripcord recklessly leaped from the van onto the Guardsman's car in an attempt to stop it, but the COBRA got away despite Ripcord's best efforts. When Ripcord returned the van to Bongo, she removed her bear head and revealed a beautiful woman underneath, a friendly all-American girl named Candace "Candy" Appel.

To make up for appropriating her van, Ripcord took Candy out for dinner. They started a romantic relationship that ended abruptly after another close call with COBRA. Since Ripcord's status as a G.I. JOE was classified, he was never able to satisfactorily explain to Candy what he did for a living, or why danger seemed to follow him. Afraid for her safety, Candy called it quits, and the two parted

ways. However, a short time later, a G.I. JOE mission uncovered that Candy was the daughter of another Crimson Guardsman. She was taken into custody and questioned.

Candy stressed her innocence and ignorance of COBRA activities. Things looked pretty damning for her when the Dreadnok Buzzer—a prisoner of G.I. JOE—escaped and took Candy with him. She died shortly afterward, killed in an explosion triggered by the COBRA agent Scrap-Iron.

Ripcord returned from assignments abroad to learn of Candy's incarceration and escape. Unaware that she was dead, he set out to find her and clear her name. He undertook a foolhardy and unauthorized airdrop into Cobra Island to find Candy's father, Professor Appel. He instead found Zartan and ended up in a fierce brawl with the master of disguise. Zartan defeated him and took his identity, leaving the unconscious Ripcord behind, dressed in Zartan's clothes. Zartan, as Ripcord, was "rescued" by a G.I. JOE team while Ripcord, as Zartan, was taken into COBRA headquarters.

Appel realized Ripcord was the G.I. JOE whom Candy had been involved with. When he learned that Candy was missing, Appel was gravely concerned for her safety, and sent Ripcord away from the island in an autopiloted Firebat jet to find her. The jet landed in Springfield, the small American town that served as a cover for COBRA operations. Ripcord had uncovered the location of COBRA's most secret domestic base of operations, and this information allowed G.I. JOE to stage a major assault on COBRA.

ROADBLOCK
(Heavy Machine Gunner)

DATA FILE

ACCESS GRANTED

G.I.JOE

File Name: Marvin F. Hinton
SN: 538-20-34MF
Primary Military Specialty: Infantry heavy
 weapons
Secondary Military Specialty: Cook
Qualified Expert: M-2 Browning
 .50-caliber heavy machine gun; all
 Warsaw Pact heavy MGs; M-16;
 M-1911A1 auto pistol
Birthplace: Biloxi, Mississippi
Grade: E-6

A one-man obstacle, Roadblock lives up to his code name for his awesome stopping power. The vision of him hoisting the heaviest of heavy machine guns onto the battlefield is intimidating enough to get COBRAs to surrender without firing a shot. Though the enemy's fear is warranted, the G.I. JOEs know Roadblock as a bit of a gentle giant—he has a light-enough touch to keep a soufflé from falling and epicurean tastes that can distinguish if a sorbet citron is made with tinned raspberry sauce.

Marvin Hinton grew up with a large extended family, cared for by a churchgoing mother. He was a Boy Scout and sang in a church choir. The Hintons were a gregarious lot, but Marvin was the shy one despite his brawn. At a young age, he developed a discriminating palate thanks to the cooking skills of his mother, as well as his aunt Sarah and uncle Caleb. A dog-eared copy of La Guide Culinaire opened him up to the world of gourmet cooking, and he dreamed of someday studying at the Escoffier School in France. To save up for his education, he worked as a bouncer.

He's the only G.I. JOE who can offer you advice on how often to baste a turkey (every 20 minutes) as well as how often to change the barrel on a Ma-Deuce .50-caliber HMG (every second belt).

A recruiter somehow convinced Marvin that the army could teach him how to be a better chef. He enlisted, but soon found army menus and preparation techniques to be appalling. Still, he connected with army life, discovering a newfound confidence. He transferred to infantry, where he found his second love: heavy machine guns. Hinton made an impression on Conrad Hauser, having served with him under fire in Trucial Abysmia and as a fellow training instructor at Ranger School in Fort Benning. When Hauser joined the G.I. JOE team as its first sergeant, Duke, he brought Hinton with him to become the team's heavy machine gunner.

◼ His Main Ax

Roadblock's preferred weapon is the M-2 HB Browning .50-caliber machine gun, a model that has been fundamentally unchanged since the 1930s. While the weapons are often found mounted on turrets as vehicle arms, Roadblock carries his by hand (though he does carry a practical, collapsible tripod as well). The "Ma-Deuce" weighs 84 pounds. Add ammunition, and it tips the scales at 134 pounds. When opened up, the heavy machine gun has a cycling firing rate of 550 rounds per minute, spitting out belt-fed ammunition with a muzzle velocity of 2,930 feet per second. With his raw firepower, Roadblock can suppress infantry and ventilate lightly armored vehicles; he has even managed to shoot down a ground-buzzing COBRA Rattler.

◼ Bon Vivant et Joie de Vivre

Roadblock is a jovial team player, beloved by his fellow G.I. JOEs for his love of living the good life. He rocks a silent rhythm in his head that often causes him to speak in impromptu rhymes ranging from clever to groan-inducing. He'll organize recreational football games for his teammates, and he's always up for preparing refreshments for any parties. At first, some of his more provincial teammates wrinkled their noses at eating dishes they couldn't pronounce, but once they got a taste, they knew better than to complain.

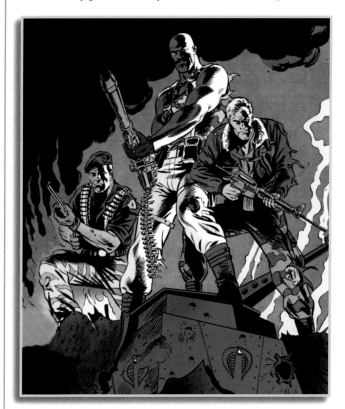

Though good-natured and patient, Roadblock can be brought to anger. Nothing riles him more than unpatriotic acts. When the American embassy in Sierro Gordo was overrun by revolutionaries, Roadblock stared down a would-be flag burner. The man with the cigarette lighter quivered as he looked at Roadblock's fierce face, enormous arms, and gigantic machine gun, and tried to defend his actions as being no worse than the looters running away with expensive office equipment. Roadblock's answer was succinct. "No one ever died for a typewriter."

On the Run and Off the Grid

During the Cobra Island Civil War, G.I. JOE fought alongside Emperor Serpentor to secure top-secret electronic hardware that had fallen into COBRA hands. Serpentor died in battle, however, and the fragmented COBRA sides struck up a new truce that effectively booted G.I. JOE off the island empty-handed. When Generals Hawk and Hollingsworth went to the Pentagon to face the music, Roadblock accompanied them. All three men were arrested by General Malthus. Malthus was looking to place blame for the botched operation squarely on G.I. JOE. Roadblock broke free from custody and disappeared into the streets of Washington, DC. A general alert made the evening news, labeling Roadblock as "a renegade and accomplice to high crimes."

Roadblock sought out an unlikely ally: Dr. Adele Burkhart, an outspoken peace activist who had crossed paths with the G.I. JOE team in the past. Using her home as a base of operations, Roadblock was able to assemble a team of G.I. JOEs not involved in the Cobra Island debacle and launch a mission that rescued Hawk and Hollingsworth, and ultimately exposed Malthus's corruption.

Service in Star Brigade

As one of the few G.I. JOEs to undergo astronaut training and emerge with flying colors, Roadblock was a founding member of Star Brigade—a short-lived aeronautic special missions group assigned to the space shuttle *Defiant*. Roadblock served on a joint Star Brigade/Oktober Guard mission dispatched to orbital space to intercept an incoming 20-mile-wide asteroid that threatened the earth. The asteroid was overrun with armed rogue robot construction drones that attempted to defend the falling rock, but the G.I. JOEs and the Russian Oktober Guard were able to destroy it, saving untold millions of lives.

The Roadblock Express

Since Roadblock regularly lifts hundreds of pounds of thundering steel, he has been used as a means of load-bearing conveyance more than once! Injured allies have leaned on Roadblock for a piggyback extraction. During the civil war on Cobra Island, Roadblock hauled a wounded Crazylegs out of a fire zone. In Sierra Gordo, a temporarily blinded Roadblock hauled the lame Oktober Guard member Misha around, in exchange for the injured Russian offering directional guidance. The same scenario also occurred during the Cobra-La incident, when Roadblock—robbed of his sight—carried a rapidly mutating Cobra Commander on his back.

Culinary Fame

When the G.I. JOE team was temporarily decommissioned following the scattering of COBRA forces, Roadblock poured his attentions into cooking, finding newfound—if short-lived—fame. He wrote several popular cookbooks, all of which reached the *New York Times* bestseller list. His smash hit *Cooking with Kung-Fu Grip* is credited with a surge in "tough guys" suddenly taking an interest in gourmet cooking, aided by a line of manly Marvin Hinton cooking products. For a time, he hosted a television show—*Kiss Your Mama Home Cooking*—out of Los Angeles, until a live broadcast was disrupted by marauding Dreadnoks. Hinton had to hang up the public chef hat when he was invited back to the reinstated G.I. JOE team.

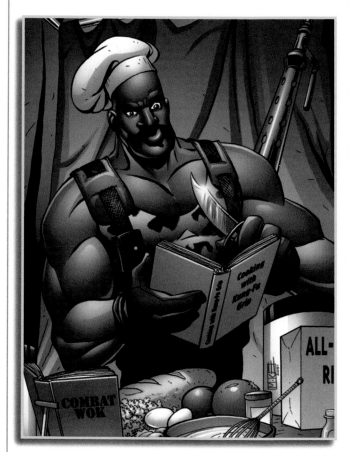

Update Your Records

Following the team's decommission, the code name Roadblock was temporarily reinstated with someone else in the role. Charles L. Griffith served as heavy machine gunner for the team for a handful of classified missions. When the original Roadblock returned to active duty, Griffith adopted the code name Double Blast.

SCARLETT
(Counterintelligence)

DATA FILE
ACCESS GRANTED

File Name: Shana M. O'Hara
SN: 624-29-SC34
Primary Military Specialty: Counter-
intelligence
Secondary Military Specialty: CLASSIFIED
Qualified Expert: M-14; M-16; M-1911A1
auto pistol; M-79; M-3A1; M-700 (Reming-
ton sniper rifle); Mac-10; XK-1 power cross-
bow; throwing stars; garotte; K-Bar knife
Birthplace: Atlanta, Georgia
Grade: E-6

The Deep South tends to cling firmly to its traditions, so when young Shana Mae O'Hara chose a path
not becoming for a young lady, it estranged her from
her mother and especially her sister, Sioban. Young
Shana instead took after her rambunctious older
brothers—Brian, Sean, and Frank—and her father,
a martial arts instructor. The O'Hara men were
skilled combatants, and Shana wanted to follow
suit. She was determined to kick down any ob-
stacles, whether they be sparring opponents or
culturally imposed gender limitations.

She began her training at age nine, and earned her first
black belt at 15. The O'Hara children worked hard to impress
their father with their prowess, but his focus was on instilling
in them a sense of confidence and self-respect. Shana exhibited a talent for immediately picking up on someone's fighting
styles and recognizing inherent weaknesses. Her insight was
so keen that her brothers would spar with her while wearing masks to conceal their identities, hoping to momentarily
break that advantage.

Beauty may be skin-deep, but lethal goes to the bone.

Young O'Hara's confidence bordered on cockiness in her teen
years, and that did not sit well with her father. When he was crippled
and confined to a wheelchair after a car accident, he used the stark
example of his injury to illustrate to Shana that no one could control
fate, no matter how tough he or she was. It was a lesson that would
take years to sink in for the stubborn Shana.

Scarlett studied at a prestigious Ivy League college then went on
to law school, passing the bar to become a lawyer. Frustrated by the
often lethargic pace of the legal system, O'Hara enlisted in the military. She underwent basic training at Fort Jackson, South Carolina,

and advanced infantry training at Fort Huachuca, Arizona. She also
went to Ranger School at Fort Benning, Georgia.

Around this time, O'Hara's abilities came to the attention of Generals Flagg and Austin at the Pentagon. A report of her defying orders
and braving intense enemy fire to rescue two of her teammates particularly caught their eye. She was shaping up to be the best
of the best, exactly the type of soldier these officers were
looking for in the developing G.I. JOE team. They surreptitiously arranged for her to receive additional training
at Quantico, where she became an FBI agent. Her
training would eventually encompass Covert Ops
School, Marine Sniper School, Special Air Service
School, and the Marine Tae Kwan Do Symposium.

One of O'Hara's first assignments was the infiltration of an IRA cell in Ireland in a bid to get closer to
a supplier distributing advanced laser weaponry. Her
investigation revealed the growing influence of Destro
and his Military Armament Research Syndicate (M.A.R.S.). It also
landed her a position on G.I. JOE, where she adopted a common
nickname, Scarlett, as her code name.

As a skilled hand-to-hand combat instructor, Scarlett put
the rest of the G.I. JOEs through their paces in training, not
finding a true challenge until Snake-Eyes joined the team.
She sensed from their sparring session that he was the
better fighter, with remarkable physical control, but Snake-
Eyes nonetheless allowed Scarlett to beat him. It was testament to his character that he lost face to save hers, and
Scarlett immediately became intrigued by this mysterious
new teammate.

Next to Snake-Eyes, Scarlett is probably the deadliest
unarmed combatant on the team. Despite this lethality,
she has a remarkably bright personality and a gener-
ous sense of humor. She and Snake-Eyes have grown
closer over the years. She often speaks for the mute
warrior, able to translate his sign language or pick up on his silent
cues for the rest of the team.

A Brush with Death

Scarlett had accompanied Snake-Eyes to the Bern Institute of Reconstructive Surgery in Switzerland, where he was to undergo a radical procedure to rebuild his ravaged face—an injury sustained years earlier when he rescued Scarlett from a helicopter crash. The surgeon, Dr. Hundtkinder, was a COBRA sympathizer who had previously operated on the Baroness. While Snake-Eyes was under the knife, Hundtkinder contacted COBRA, and the Baroness launched an attack on the institute.

Scarlett fought valiantly to protect her vulnerable lover, but she was overwhelmed and cornered by COBRA forces. In a cold and ruthless act, the Baroness shot Scarlett in the head at point-blank range. Miraculously, the bullet hit the dome of Scarlett's skull at an oblique angle and was deflected. Nonetheless, she suffered a massive fracture and concussion, and bone fragments penetrated her cortex. She was plunged into a deep coma, but was rescued by G.I. JOE medics after COBRA left her for dead.

Her condition stabilized, Scarlett was airlifted to the best-equipped surgical facility in New York, but she remained comatose for months. Snake-Eyes, meanwhile, escaped COBRA. He watched over the recovering Scarlett, but the prognosis looked grim. Doctors could not predict when or if she would recover.

Suddenly Sioban O'Hara—Scarlett's sister, who was now an attorney—appeared in Scarlett's hospital room with a court-ordered mandate to suspend her life-support systems and end her suffering. Based on recommendations from outside doctors, Sioban believed Scarlett was beyond help.

Sioban was proven wrong when Scarlett emerged from her coma. After a period of rehabilitation, she resumed active service on the G.I. JOE team.

Mission Report: Deep Undercover

Perhaps the most difficult assignment Scarlett undertook for General Hawk was posing as a traitor to G.I. JOE in order to infiltrate CO-BRA. This required her to exacerbate the growing distance between herself and Snake-Eyes caused by the latter's focus on the development of the Ninja Force special missions team. Scarlett left the team for a sabbatical in Gstaad, Switzerland, and before doing so switched her life insurance beneficiary from Snake-Eyes to Sioban. COBRA information specialists detected the change and surmised that she had grown estranged from her teammate—possibly disillusioned with the team itself. COBRA agents captured Scarlett in Switzerland and brought her to Cobra Commander in Trans-Carpathia, where he was in the midst of rebuilding COBRA and consolidating power in war-torn Eastern Europe.

Cobra Commander's plot was fiendishly multilayered and complex, and G.I. JOE required an agent on the inside gathering human intelligence in order to understand the whole scope of the operation. As part of his plot, Cobra Commander had kidnapped the brilliant scientist Dr. Sidney Biggles-Jones as well as capturing her advanced magnetic rail gun and several other experimental technologies. Both Scarlett and Biggles-Jones were admitted into the COBRA ranks, but to ensure her loyalty, Cobra Commander tasked Scarlett with assassinating General Hawk.

During a G.I. JOE weapons test in White Sands, New Mexico, COBRA attacked. Scarlett fired a sniper rifle at Hawk, and though she missed his head, her shot apparently penetrated the fuel tank of the jeep Hawk and Stalker were traveling in. The exploding tank engulfed the vehicle in flames. COBRA agents confirmed the presence of burning bodies within the fireball, and Scarlett's conversion into a COBRA agent was complete. What Scarlett did not know was that Hawk's and Stalker's apparent deaths were but a carefully crafted illusion. A rigged gas tank detonated at Hawk's command, and both he and Stalker were wearing fireproof Nonex suits covered with latex likenesses of their faces.

As a seemingly loyal COBRA agent, Scarlett provided security for COBRA's conquest of Destro's silent castle in Trans-Carpathia. She

and Biggles-Jones were ordered to ferret out Destro and the Baroness, who had escaped the Commander's captivity and were hiding within the castle's maze-like interior. At that time, Snake-Eyes and Storm Shadow were also dispatched by G.I. JOE to rescue Destro and the Baroness. General Hawk finally informed the ninjas as to Scarlett's true intentions, and ordered them to treat her as an enemy combatant should their paths cross.

Scarlett confronted Snake-Eyes as he was extricating Destro and the Baroness. In order to complete his mission and not compromise Scarlett's cover, Snake-Eyes stabbed her through the chest with his sword. It was a precision cut, one that only a ninja master could have delivered, that punctured Scarlett's body but amazingly did not perforate any major vessels or organs. Though wounded, Scarlett did not die from the stab and could be stabilized by COBRA medics in time. Despite the injury, Scarlett was silently overjoyed: It was clear to her that Snake-Eyes knew she had not truly betrayed him.

When Biggles-Jones proved to be a fellow double agent planted by a top-secret American security agency, Scarlett attempted to rescue her, blowing her cover. COBRA came to realize that Scarlett was not a loyal agent, and she escaped the group's clutches.

Scarlett and Snake-Eyes

Their relationship has weathered many hurdles and hardships, yet Scarlett and Snake-Eyes continue to depend on each other when their lives are frequently endangered. When G.I. JOE was disbanded after the apparent scattering of COBRA forces, it appeared that Scarlett and Snake-Eyes could finally enjoy a peaceful life together. They rebuilt his log cabin on Iron-Knife Ridge and planned to marry. But as often happens, tragedy intruded on Snake-Eyes's happiness and enveloped his surrounding loved ones.

Snake-Eyes was, at the time, training an apprentice to become the last Arashikage ninja, heir to the wisdom and techniques he had learned from the Arashikage clan masters in Japan decades earlier. His apprentice, Ophelia Gabriel, died on her first mission, which was to be her final test. Snake-Eyes was consumed by grief, and left Scarlett at the altar.

The O'Haras greatly resented Snake-Eyes for abandoning Scarlett, and for a time he was not welcome at their home. She would not see him for years, until G.I. JOE was reinstated to counter a renewed COBRA threat. She would eventually forgive Snake-Eyes, realizing that to him, losing Ophelia was like losing his long-mourned twin sister all over again.

Scarlett and Snake-Eyes are once again united, their love stronger than ever, and ready to face whatever challenges the future may bring. To ensure that they stay connected, each has a subcutaneous tracking device keyed to a receiver signal known only to the other.

SHIPWRECK
(Navy SEAL)

DATA FILE
ACCESS GRANTED

File Name: Hector X. Delgado
SN: 924-92-5456
Primary Military Specialty: Gunner's mate
Secondary Military Specialty: Machinist
Qualified Expert: M-16; M-14; Browning .50-caliber; 20mm Oerlikon AA gun; M-1911A1 auto pistol
Birthplace: Chula Vista, California
Grade: CPO (chief petty officer)

Although Navy SEALs specialize in Sea, Air, and Land missions, Shipwreck's loudly pronounced preference is for open waters. The saltiest of salty dogs, Shipwreck originally joined the G.I. JOE team as a sailor and gunner, but later diversified his skill set with months of intensive SEAL training, transforming an already formidable soldier into something even tougher.

Squawk! Shipwreck was a sailor/A salty dog was he/and the worstest cook that ever sailed upon the briny sea! Squawk!

A bit of a loner who never knew his true family (he was adopted), Hector Delgado grew up in the shadow of the sprawling naval yards of San Diego. Seeing service as an opportunity to get away from an impoverished and directionless childhood, he procured falsified papers that misrepresented his age and enlisted in the navy at 16. He served with distinction in the Mekong Delta, cracking down on river pirates, smugglers, insurgents, and the scum of the waterways. Such gritty service had a pronounced effect on the impressionable Delgado: He emerged a sailor through and through. His service also included stints at Gitmo (Guantanamo Bay Naval Station), US Fleet Activities Yokosuka (Japan), and a number of carrier-initiated operations in the Middle East.

Separating fact from fiction in Shipwreck's stories of his past is difficult. His tales are taller than a tall ship's masts, peppered with exploits that run the gamut from the unlikely to the obscene. Cussing and joke telling (with punch lines often punctuated by the suggestive flexing of a tattoo) are second nature to Shipwreck, who has spent more than half his life at sea. His loudmouthed pet parrot completes the image. Polly has become more than a sailor's affectation or lover's gift (where he got the bird changes with each telling), and serves almost as an unofficial mascot for all of G.I. JOE's naval operations.

Shipwreck likes being in the spotlight—when it's on his terms. If a commanding officer gives him orders he disagrees with, prepare for an earful. Shipwreck will do his duty, like a good soldier, but he will bellyache the entire time. His abrasive and difficult nature is tolerated by his fellow G.I. JOEs because, first, he is extremely effective at what he does. Second, when taken at a distance, Shipwreck keeps the team entertained. To spice up his already lively storytelling skills, Shipwreck has become a noteworthy mimic—they know him to do a dead-on impression of Cobra Commander.

During the brief decommission of the G.I. JOE team, Shipwreck ran a tour guide service for rich families all over the globe. He remained active in scuttling pirates and drug traffickers, and was one of the first brought back to the G.I. JOE team when it was reinstated.

In a development that surprised everyone, Shipwreck's scattershot and shallow flirtations with all the female G.I. JOEs have actually netted a result. The beauty of the team—Cover Girl—was actually beguiled by Shipwreck, the team's beast. The two have started a romantic relationship.

■ Mission Report: The Sailor and the Mermaid

During the search for a missing submarine, the USS *Nerka*, the G.I. JOE team uncovered an unusual COBRA escapee. Her name was Mara, and it was Shipwreck who plucked her out of the ocean and first noted her strange physiology. Mara was a volunteer in an advanced COBRA Eel program that predated the creation of the Hydro-Viper ranks. She was part of an experiment that sought to produce a squad of amphibious commandos. COBRA scientists subjected her to an experimental conversion process that altered the genetic code of certain cells in her body. Her pigment turned blue, and she developed gills, allowing her to extract oxygen from salt water. The process proved to be a failure, however—Mara was not

that held the USS *Nerka*. Mara also provided valuable intelligence on the base layout, allowing the G.I. JOEs to storm it and free the crew of the captured ship. Shipwreck and Mara ultimately parted ways, because their physiologies would not allow them to continue to be partners. He regretfully said farewell as she returned to the seas.

Mistaken Identities

COBRA had such interest in the development of the MIRC system—a mind interface remote control to operate G.I. JOE vehicles—that Zartan infiltrated G.I. JOE headquarters and incapacitated Shipwreck. Zartan then adopted Shipwreck's identity and stole the MIRC prototype, kidnapping Scarlett in the process. Shipwreck was determined to rescue her, stop COBRA, and undo the damage he had inadvertently caused.

Shipwreck and Snake-Eyes infiltrated the COBRA mountain headquarters disguised as COBRA agents. It was Shipwreck's task to acquire the security codes needed to lower the hangar doors to the COBRA citadel, allowing a follow-up G.I. JOE team entry into the fortress. While skulking around the base, Shipwreck stumbled upon a spare change of uniform for Cobra Commander and donned it. Adopting his uncannily realistic Cobra Commander persona, he began barking out orders to his underlings. The deception lasted until the real Cobra Commander discovered the imposter. Shipwreck was momentarily captured before being sprung by an undercover G.I. JOE, Agent Faces. Together they opened the hangar bay, allowing the rest of the team to infiltrate.

amphibious. She could only survive underwater and would suffocate in the air after a few minutes.

Shipwreck grew enamored with Mara, admiring her strength and beauty. He learned to appreciate how someone—*anyone*—could become a COBRA. He empathized with Mara's mean-street origins, which led her to view COBRA as a viable life choice. Shipwreck was able to coax from Mara the location of the underwater COBRA base

SNAKE-EYES
(Commando)

DATA FILE
ACCESS GRANTED

File Name: CLASSIFIED
SN: CLASSIFIED
Primary Military Specialty: Infantry
Secondary Military Specialty: Hand-to-hand combat instructor
Other Military Specialty: Covert operations
Qualified Expert: All NATO and Warsaw Pact small arms; a black belt in 12 different fighting systems and highly skilled in the use of edged weapons. He has also received extensive training in mountaineering; underwater demolitions; jungle, desert, and arctic survival; and some form of holistic medicine.
Birthplace: CLASSIFIED
Grade: E-8

If life is indeed a forge, then Snake-Eyes has played blade, anvil, and hammer, enduring hardships that would have either killed lesser men or stripped from them any compassion. Instead, his strength of character has withstood tragedy time and again, and he continues to serve his nation and his companions selflessly.

Snake-Eyes was tempered on the anvil of life until he was as dangerous as a razor-edged sword flailing in the dark. The G.I. JOE team sheathed that sword and harnessed its deadly energy, but they are wont to forget that even within the safety of its scabbard, the blade retains its cutting edge.

Very little solid information exists of Snake-Eyes's past, and what is known has been collected from firsthand accounts of those who were there. Any records of his early military career vanished in a mysterious fire at Fort Leonard Wood. A few unclassified details in his personnel file indicate that he took basic training on Tank Hill at Fort Jackson, South Carolina. He attended Infantry Advanced Individual Training, Airborne School, and Ranger School at Fort Benning, and Recondo School while abroad.

Snake-Eyes served in a reconnaissance patrol overseas alongside future G.I. JOEs Lonzo (Stalker) Wilkinson and Thomas (Storm Shadow) Arashikage. The trio were the only apparent survivors after a fierce ambush of their extraction LZ (landing zone), and Snake-Eyes was critically wounded. Storm Shadow braved a hail of enemy fire to not only rescue Snake-Eyes but also retrieve his only memento from back home, a torn and battered photo of his twin sister, Terri.

After his discharge from the service, Snake-Eyes returned home and waited at the airport to reunite with his family. It was Clayton Abernathy—the future Hawk—who had to bring the terrible news to Snake-Eyes: En route to the airport, the family car had collided with an intoxicated driver. Snake-Eyes's mother, father, and sister Terri were all killed in the resulting fire, as was the drunk.

The Path of the Ninja

After a dark period of wandering without direction and wallowing in despair and anger, Snake-Eyes left the United States at the behest of his old friend Tommy, and joined his "family business" in Japan. It was, in truth, a ninja clan, and despite being an outsider, Snake-Eyes learned the ways of the ancient Arashikage ninjas from Tommy's uncles, the Hard Master and the Soft Master. Thomas himself was dubbed the Young Master, and was poised to inherent stewardship of the clan . . . until Snake-Eyes arrived.

Snake-Eyes proved to be a remarkably quick study. The ordinarily implacable Hard Master had taken a shine to this outsider. Aside from Snake-Eyes's growing skill with the blade, there was a pronounced selflessness and humility about him. The Hard Master recognized the restraint Snake-Eyes showed when he worked to keep Storm Shadow from losing face. Before long, Snake-Eyes earned the right to wear the mark of the Arashikage clan as a tattoo on his right outer wrist.

At this time, the Arashikage clan itself was beset by enemies both inside and out. Strong leadership would be needed if the clan was to continue into the future. Storm Shadow had seen it as his life's duty to continue the tradition, but he found himself unable to measure up to Snake-Eyes in his uncle's eyes. This ignited an envy within young Storm Shadow that strained their friendship.

The animosity seemingly culminated the night the Hard Master offered Snake-Eyes inheritance of leadership within the clan. Snake-Eyes refused, not willing to take a position that was Storm Shadow's by birthright. The Hard Master continued his lesson that night, teaching the technique called Donning the Chameleon's Mantle. An exercise of intense bodily control, it altered the heartbeat, body sounds, and movements in order to fool the Ear That Sees—an equally esoteric art that granted an assassin the ability to identify targets from sound alone. The Hard Master challenged Snake-Eyes to identify whom he was impersonating, but he failed to recognize that his mentor was mimicking Snake-Eyes himself. Just then an arrow—intended for Snake-Eyes's heart—killed the Hard Master.

All evidence pointed to Storm Shadow, a master with the bow. He fled the compound that night, never to return. Snake-Eyes did the same, recognizing that the "Snake-Eyes curse"—the endless string of tragedies that seemingly dogged his every move—had shattered the generations-old ninja clan. Leaving what few worldly effects he had behind, Snake-Eyes abandoned his training and fled to America, turning his back on civilization and living an ascetic existence in a log cabin in the High Sierras.

Recruitment to G.I. JOE

The world continued to grow more dangerous, taking little note of Snake-Eyes's absence. The modern G.I. JOE team was founded to confront emergent threats to freedom. Colonel Hawk's first recruit to the team was Lonzo Wilkinson, and based on Lonzo's recommendation, they sought out Snake-Eyes.

Following the trail of the army disability checks that Snake-Eyes had earned from his service led to a rural delivery route in the High Sierras. The local loggers there had spread legends of a wolfman on Iron-Knife Ridge: a loner who bayed at the moon, with a mysterious mark on his wrist. When Hawk and Stalker arrived, they found Snake-Eyes returning from a successful rabbit-hunting trip he had apparently undertaken without a gun. The wolf rumors stemmed from Snake-Eyes's "pet," a wolf named Timber whom he had freed from a trap.

Stalker convinced Snake-Eyes that it was time to serve his country once more.

Mission Report: Charley Mike

An early example of Snake-Eyes's incredible tenacity can be found in an early G.I. JOE mission, the rescue of George Strawhacker, an American federal agent dispatched to the Middle East to investigate suspected COBRA activity. Strawhacker had been taken hostage, and the already narrow window of rescue opportunity was closing by the minute.

Snake-Eyes was part of the rescue team, riding a helicopter over the Middle Eastern desert alongside Rock 'N Roll, Grunt, and Scarlett. At this point, Snake-Eyes had already grown quite fond of Scarlett, despite his worries about the supposed "Snake-Eyes curse" ruining her life as it had for so many who'd come into contact with him.

His worst fears were nearly realized when an accompanying helicopter suffered engine failure and faltered into the flight path of his chopper. The rotor blades crossed, sending Snake-Eyes's helicopter skewing through the air. It wobbled over the ground at a low-enough altitude for Rock 'N Roll and Grunt to ditch, but as Scarlett rose to jump out of the open door, the opposite door slid shut, jamming closed on her web gear. She could not pull free, yet Snake-Eyes would not abandon her.

He began sawing through her webbing with his combat knife just as the wayward helicopters collided once more. The ruptured fuel line sprayed JP4 aviation gas, which ignited and sent a blast of fire punching through the Plexiglas window of the jammed door. The plume caught Snake-Eyes directly in the face, ravaging his features and tearing apart his larynx. He was now without a face and without a voice, but he continued cutting Scarlett free.

The helicopter crashed, knocking Scarlett out cold. Snake-Eyes emerged from the flames, carrying Scarlett to safety. The rescue mission seemingly scrubbed, a medevac helicopter arrived to carry Snake-Eyes away. But he refused to go. Unable to talk, he wrote two letters in the sand: c.m. "Charley Mike." Or "Continue mission."

With only the most perfunctory of bandages covering his scorched face, Snake-Eyes accompanied Rock 'N Roll and Grunt as they rendezvoused with Stalker, who was already undercover. They then stormed the building holding Strawhacker, with Snake-Eyes penetrating the farthest past COBRA guards. The COBRA soldiers guarding the hostage realized they were running out of options, so they stripped down to skivvies and sat in chairs flanking the captive Strawhacker. Each claimed to be Strawhacker, but in truth the two COBRAs secretly held guns behind their back.

What they could not have known was the very reason Snake-Eyes was selected for this mission. Of all the G.I. JOEs, he alone could have recognized Strawhacker, who was at one time Terri's fiancé. Had Terri not died in a car accident years before, George Strawhacker would have been Snake-Eyes's brother-in-law. Of course, Strawhacker did not recognize the bandaged soldier who freed him. He watched in amazement as the mysterious rescuer gunned down the other two COBRAs and undid his bonds.

The Path to Truth

Disfigured and mute, Snake-Eyes adopted a black mask and visor to replace his ruined features. He investigated opportunities to surgically repair his face, but those proved to be dead ends. Snake-Eyes committed himself fully to G.I. JOE, undertaking many missions against COBRAs and other threats around the world.

The past suddenly came rushing back at Snake-Eyes when he discovered that Storm Shadow was a member of COBRA, serving as a personal bodyguard to no less than Cobra Commander. Snake-Eyes would later learn that Storm Shadow had joined the terrorist organization to uncover the truth about the Hard Master's killer. As

Storm Shadow explained, he had caught a glimpse of the true killer that fateful night, an archer who had used one of Storm Shadow's recovered arrows to kill his uncle. Storm Shadow pursued the masked assailant as he escaped aboard a waiting COBRA helicopter. Armed with that scrap of information, Storm Shadow committed himself to scaling the COBRA hierarchy and discovering who was behind the shattering of the Arashikage legacy.

Though his aims were at first to clear his name and bring a murderer to justice, Storm Shadow was twisted by vengeance. When he uncovered the truth—that Zartan had pulled back the bowstring of the arrow that killed the Hard Master—there was no stopping Snake-Eyes and Storm Shadow. The two teamed up to infiltrate Cobra Island, cutting through any COBRAs who would stand in their way. In the end, Zartan had escaped and Storm Shadow nearly died in his pursuit of revenge. Snake-Eyes grew to realize that it was a hollow path, leading only to further heartbreak.

Storm Shadow did not relent. His time with COBRA had changed him, leaving him all the more susceptible to their evil. He would ultimately be captured by Cobra Commander and subjected to terrible electronic brainwashing that rendered him an enemy to Snake-Eyes once more.

■ Snake-Eyes and Scarlett

If ever there was a loving center to a life of cruel misfortune, it was the relationship between Snake-Eyes and Scarlett. At first, Scarlett did not know what to make of the laconic Ranger who had joined the G.I. JOE ranks. She was running hand-to-hand combat training at the time, and had already made short work of one of her larger male opponents. Snake-Eyes was up next, but he let himself be shoulder-thrown by Scarlett. Through the maneuver, Scarlett realized that her opponent had the skill of a high-ranking black belt, but was letting himself be defeated so she would not lose face.

She was fascinated by Snake-Eyes, and tried to learn more about him. She sensed that beneath his hard-edged exterior was a small-town boy who missed his home and was very lonely. She learned of his close bond with Terri and how Snake-Eyes wished that the good-luck talisman—Terri's photo—had protected her rather than him.

Though Scarlett had shown Snake-Eyes tenderness, she was also a deadly martial artist. The two became a formidable team, growing close both on-assignment and off. More than anyone, she reached deep into Snake-Eyes's soul, but there were still parts of him that remained closed off and unpredictable. The tempestuous relationship between him and Storm Shadow often tugged Scarlett in wayward directions and frequently into danger. She longed for the two sword brothers to find peace and finally bury the past, but such respite seemed agonizingly long in coming. She has more than once cursed the name of Thomas Arashikage, though that relationship would eventually subside into one of trust.

Scarlett accompanied Snake-Eyes when he underwent advanced cosmetic surgery to return his face to a scarred but passable facsimile of his past appearance. Around that same time, Scarlett sustained a terrible head injury when she was shot at close range by the Baroness.

Both would recover from the many injuries sustained in their fight against COBRA. In the brief interim when the G.I. JOE team was disbanded after the seeming scattering of COBRA forces, Snake-Eyes and Scarlett retired to the rebuilt cabin on Iron-Knife Ridge. Timber passed away, but a litter of wolf cubs were his heirs. Snake-Eyes and Scarlett were to be wed, but he abandoned her at the altar, once more fearful that association with him would spell heartbreak and tragedy. Luckily for him, Scarlett was not willing to give up on him.

The Silent Master

Snake-Eyes was uneasy about his Ninjutsu heritage. Though the training granted to him by the Arashikage clan gave him extraordinary abilities and strength, they came at a bloody price. For a time, he reconciled his misgivings and led a specialist team of martial arts warriors dubbed Ninja Force. When G.I. JOE briefly disbanded, Snake-Eyes turned his mountain cabin into a dojo to continue the Arashikage way, adopting the mantle of the Silent Master.

His first apprentice was a plucky young teenage girl named Ophelia Gabriel. In many ways, Ophelia reminded Snake-Eyes of his sister, Terri. During her last trial before the completion of her training—an extremely dangerous mission to stop the saboteur Firefly—Ophelia was killed by the terrorist. Snake-Eyes was distraught by the death of yet another loved one. He turned inward, for a time abandoning Scarlett and his ninja ways. Then Snake-Eyes returned to the path and instructed Sean Collins, who in turn became Kamakura, last of the Arashikage Ninjas. Though she had previously been instructed by the Blind Master, Jinx would continue to learn from Snake-Eyes as well. Another known apprentice of the Silent Master was a young ninja named Tiger Claw.

Death and Rebirth

During a rescue mission to free Scarlett from Destro's submarine, Snake-Eyes was forced to seal a flooding compartment to allow the escape of his friends. Snake-Eyes was left behind, and drowned as the cold ocean waters filled his chambers. His lifeless body was taken by the Red Ninjas—remnants of the Arashikage clan—and mystically revived to become an agent of the mercenary ninjas, at the time

under the control of an evil ninja named Sei Tin. In an uncommon reversal, it was a brainwashed Snake-Eyes who fought blade-to-blade against a G.I. JOE–loyal Storm Shadow, but ultimately the love of Scarlett snapped Snake-Eyes from the control of the Red Ninjas.

Snake-Eyes: The COBRA Connections

More than any other member of G.I. JOE, Snake-Eyes has crossed paths with former or current COBRA agents. At times, it seems the ongoing war between G.I. JOE and COBRA is merely a backdrop for the ongoing drama of Snake-Eyes's life.

Storm Shadow: The histories of Storm Shadow and Snake-Eyes are inextricably interwoven. The two served together in an overseas war. Storm Shadow, then known as Tommy Arashikage, saved Snake-Eyes's life when the latter was gunned down at an ambushed landing zone. Tommy braved enemy fire to carry Snake-Eyes to the safety of the extraction helicopter. While Snake-Eyes writhed in pain, Storm Shadow calmed him using an ancient ninja meditation technique known as the Arashikage Mind-Set. When Snake-Eyes returned stateside after the war, he took up Tommy's long-standing invitation to join the Arashikage ninja clan.

Crimson Guardsman Fred Broca II: For years, it was believed that of their six-man patrol team, only Snake-Eyes, Stalker, and Storm Shadow had survived. In truth, there was one more: Wade Collins was wounded and taken prisoner. He spent two years as a prisoner of war before returning to the United States. There Collins found himself unable to pick up the pieces of his life; his wife had divorced him, and he could not get a job. The only place he felt he belonged was with the burgeoning underground society that became COBRA. Collins became one of the first Crimson Guards, undercover COBRA agents who insinuated themselves into the fabric of American culture and business. Wade's face was surgically altered and his name changed to Fred Broca, one of a series of identical Freds active across the nation. It was as Fred Broca that he confronted Snake-Eyes and Stalker before finally turning his back on COBRA. Collins's son, Sean, would grow up to be Snake-Eyes's apprentice Kamakura.

Baroness: While Snake-Eyes was serving abroad, the Eastern European nobleman Baron Eugen Cisarovna was distributing medical supplies and other humanitarian aid to this war-torn region. His younger sister, the 15-year-old Anastasia, was there with him, on Christmas break from her Swiss boarding school. At this time, Snake-Eyes was pursuing gunmen who had ambushed him and Stalker. These same thugs had intercepted Cisarovna's aid shipment and sold it for weapons. They gunned down Cisarovna just as Snake-Eyes caught up with them and killed them. The impressionable Anastasia, not seeing who was behind the gunfire, emerged to find Eugen dead and an American soldier standing over him. She misunderstood the scenario, and when she found out years later that this soldier was Snake-Eyes, she sought vengeance against him.

Cobra Commander: After the death of his family due to the irresponsible actions of a drunk driver, Snake-Eyes wandered aimlessly, willing the mean streets of America to kill him. He tempted fate by standing before an oncoming 18-wheeler, but was saved at the last moment by a well-meaning out-of-work car salesman who tackled him out of the truck's way. The salesman was also a drifter; he had hit upon hard times, and had grown disillusioned with America. Instead of the storied promises of freedom, liberty, and prosperity, all he saw was a disaffected and forlorn populace taught lessons of selfishness by the corrupt actions of government and industry. He

was determined to turn things around, and got Snake-Eyes listening to his rhetoric.

The two traveled together for a while, chasing drug dealers away from the slums and trying to empower the disenfranchised. They adopted a Robin Hood–style existence for a while, stealing from the rich to give to the poor, but the drifter shrewdly kept some aside to pay for future endeavors. The amount skimmed mounted each day, and Snake-Eyes was increasingly put off by the growing fire in the drifter's rhetoric.

The drifter's last big act of social reform was to target Judge Mitchell Tate. Snake-Eyes did not know the details until too late, and followed his accomplice as he broke into the judge's home late at night and stirred him from a deep sleep at gunpoint. The truth began to surface.

The judge had unfairly overturned a verdict of innocence on the drifter's troubled brother, Dan, driving the latter to ruin. It was the judge's actions that had sealed the fate of two families—Dan died, drunk, in the head-on collision that had killed Snake Eyes's loved ones. The drifter had purposely sought out Snake-Eyes to bring him here, seize his destiny, and kill this judge: the first indelible step in the creation of a new order.

Snake-Eyes refused, and walked away from the salesman, who killed Judge Tate anyway. The drifter would later become Cobra Commander.

Firefly: After Snake-Eyes turned his back on the emergent vision of COBRA, Cobra Commander sought to have him killed. This was made difficult when Snake-Eyes departed America to train in a ninja compound in Japan. Cobra Commander hired Firefly, an international hit man, saboteur, and ninja of the Koga clan. Known then as the Faceless Master, Firefly was allowed entry into the Arashikage compound, where he closely watched Snake-Eyes. He came to realize that he was no match for Snake-Eyes's amazing sword talents; he would need a new approach to eliminate his mark....

Zartan: When Firefly found he could not safely kill Snake-Eyes while in the confines of the Arashikage compound, he subcontracted the job to a mysterious biker going by the unlikely name of Zartan. Zartan infiltrated the Arashikage compound by posing as a traveler needing enlightenment and purpose (which, arguably, is what Zartan *was* truly seeking at the time). He was taken in by the Iron Master, the swordsmith Onihashi. Zartan learned the mystic martial arts of the Arashikage clan, though he never truly became a member. Zartan earned Onihashi's trust, despite his duplicitous ways and his deadly business there. Using technology supplied by Firefly, Zartan homed in on a life-sign sensor reading that he mistook as Snake-Eyes's, and fired his bow. That fateful arrow instead killed the Hard Master, who had been impersonating Snake-Eyes at the time.

SNOW JOB
(Arctic Trooper)

DATA FILE
ACCESS GRANTED

File Name: Harlan W. Moore
SN: RA773-65-HM56
Primary Military Specialty: Arctic
Ski Patrol
Secondary Military Specialty: Rifle
instructor
Qualified Expert: All NATO long-
range sniper rifles; XMLR-3A laser rifle
Birthplace: Rutland, Vermont
Grade: E-7 (sergeant)

An Olympic biathlete is expected to ski a distance of 12 miles over five laps, and hit targets under two inches in diameter from more than 160 feet away. Harlan Moore was a world-class competitor, part of the US Olympic Biathlon Team. He didn't consider the requisites for a gold medal the least bit daunting, though he made it clear that he could do without the cold weather. Unfairly, the biathlon isn't the kind of sport that draws the cereal-box endorsements and media attention, so Moore didn't see it as a career choice that would guarantee a reliable income. He turned to the army for the special training and support privileges promised to Olympians, and public relations specialists with both the army and US Biathlon Association were delighted at the opportunity for media exposure. Moore surprised everyone, however, by enlisting and volunteering for service in the G.I. JOE team. He was accepted, and any publicity opportunities vanished as Moore was shuffled behind the veil of classified operations and the code name Snow Job.

You think we call him Snow Job because he does his job on skis? Negative. He's a con artist, pure and simple, except when he picks up his rifle—sure as heck, something's gonna fall down.

Unlike some of the other G.I. JOE arctic environment specialists, Snow Job doesn't thrive on the cold. Rather, he thrives on his incredible skills and accepts that the chilly environments are the best place to showcase them, though he tries not to broadcast his discomfort to his fellow arctic troopers. Snow Job can ski down steep mountains and pick off a target at 1,000 yards. The G.I. JOEs look to him as one of the best rifle instructors on the team, and while they entrust him with their lives in the thick of combat operations, they are not so ready to hand over their paychecks.

Simply put, Snow Job is a swindler. His scams are never egregious—he's not out to financially ruin anyone. He sees his chicanery as a way to keep his teammates perceptive and aware, with a week's pay typically being the biggest punishment (for the mark) or reward (for Snow Job) for a con well done. While no one wants to be on the receiving end of one of Snow Job's scams, they do bring the team together: Being conned by Snow Job has become almost a sort of hazing ritual for new recruits. No one except the newcomers will dare take a bet from him or play cards with him. Ace makes sure to avoid him on poker night, for fear of breaking his unchallenged winning streak.

"That's Why They Call Me Snow Job"

Snow Job had not been an active member of G.I. JOE more than four hours before he pulled his first scam against a teammate. Both Snow Job and Gung-Ho joined the G.I. JOE team around the same time and shared their first mission in securing the Alaskan pipeline against COBRA operations. Rock 'N Roll was also part of the team, and Snow Job began spinning a story of how Gung-Ho had a high-fashion model for a sister. He even offered to set up a date between Rock 'N Roll and Gung-Ho's sister, for a modest sum, never once telling the machine gunner that the girl was a nine-year-old child model.

SPIRIT
(Tracker)

DATA FILE

ACCESS GRANTED

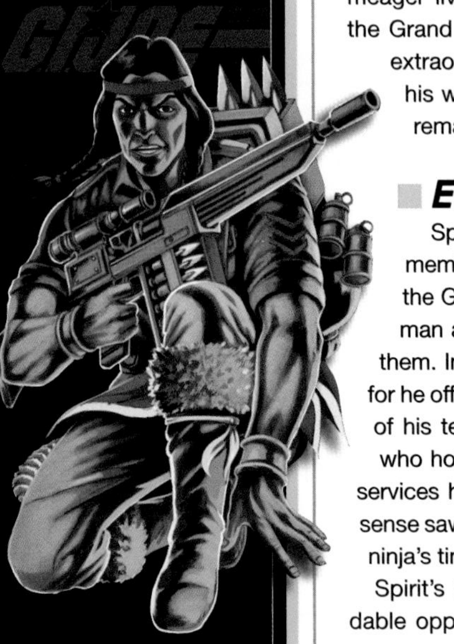

***File Name:* Charlie Iron-Knife**
***SN:* RA146-23-1009**
***Primary Military Specialty:* Infantry**
***Secondary Military Specialty:* Social services**
***Other Military Specialties:* Cartography; Air Commandos leader**
***Birthplace:* Taos, New Mexico**
***Grade:* E-6**

An unmistakable pride and presence accompany Spirit, etched into his grim features in a way that makes him seem far older than he could possibly be. He carries with him generations of pure Diné ancestry, and an acute attunement to the world around him. Census records would list the Iron-Knife family as well below the poverty line, but such distinction meant nothing to them. These Navajo had all they needed to live, ignoring the materialistic creature comforts of modern living for a way of life that better connected them to the natural world. Protecting the freedom to do so is what inspired young Charlie Iron-Knife to enlist, as well as completing an education made possible through the G.I. Bill. After serving overseas, and earning a doctoral degree in psychology, he returned to active duty, standing out as a tracker and infantryman. His exemplary record landed him placement in G.I. JOE.

You know the thousand-yard stare? Spirit has his own twist on it, but it's not from being shaken up by combat. He wills a serenity and detachment in the thick of battle that can be downright unsettling, especially once you get to know him as one of the most compassionate listeners you'll ever find.

Weapons and Specialties

An enigmatic mix of old and new, Spirit is at home with technology, since he has proven to himself that he is not dependent on it. A qualified expert with machine guns and auto pistols, he is also an expert sniper. Spirit often carries with him an automatic flechette launcher, a type of arrow-caster that pulls bolts from cassette cartridges. Spirit has a strong preference for silent and muscle-powered weaponry, such as knives and compound bows. He is also a skillful unarmed combatant, able to hold his own for short times against such foes as Storm Shadow.

A keeper of traditions that stretch back thousands of years, Spirit is a shaman and medicine man. He keeps a collection of plants and minerals gathered from the land between the four sacred mountains of the American Southwest, which he uses in ceremonies to promote healing and inner peace. His connection to the natural world has given him a respect and rapport with the ninjas within the G.I. JOE ranks, for together they share "the eye that sees the hidden world."

Spirit is the world's greatest tracker. In his youth, he earned a meager living as a hunting guide through the winding arroyos of the Grand Canyon. His harmony with nature grounds him with an extraordinary sense of direction. The man simply cannot lose his way, and is able to see paths to his objectives that would remain invisible to those less skilled.

Empathy and Psychology

Spirit's MOS of social services makes him an indispensable member of the roster when stationed at headquarters. Though the G.I. JOEs are the best of the best, they are at heart still human and the hardships they face as part of their work wear on them. In that regard, Spirit's code name takes on extra meaning, for he offers counsel and guidance to the weary and stressed. Many of his teammates have entrusted their deepest secrets to Spirit, who holds them in the strictest of confidence. His work in social services has made him uniquely attuned to suffering. This intuitive sense saw the pain and turmoil within Storm Shadow, and during the ninja's time within the COBRA ranks, the two were often at odds.

Spirit's knowledge of how the mind works makes him a formidable opponent. His grim, stoic nature is, at times, psychological armor, creating the image of an implacable imposing foe that hides a very human, warm, and compassionate listener with a downright devious sense of humor.

Brother Eagle

Spirit's most trusted confidant is a bald eagle named Freedom. During his days as a civilian guide, Iron-Knife discovered a nest left abandoned when a mother eagle died of injuries sustained from collision with power lines. Charlie safely took the egg to the Zuni Eagle Sanctuary in New Mexico, where the eaglet was hatched, tended to, and released to the wild. Freedom somehow homed in on Charlie, never straying far from his rescuer. There is an undeniable connection between Spirit and Freedom, whom he calls "brother eagle." More than once, Freedom's talons have clenched shredded blue COBRA uniform cloth. It is the spirit of the eagle that guided Iron-Knife on the wind currents when he was promoted to lead the Air Commandos, the microlight glider unit of the G.I. JOE team.

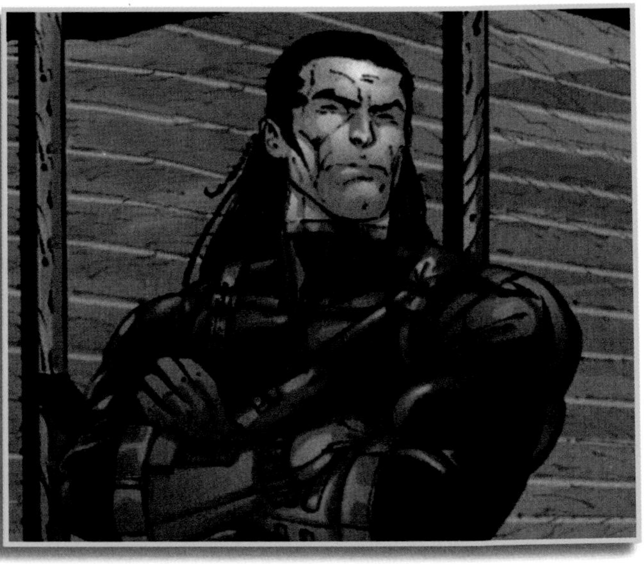

STALKER
(Ranger)

DATA FILE
ACCESS GRANTED

File Name: Lonzo R. Wilkinson
SN: 724-05-LW39
Primary Military Specialty:
   Infantry
Secondary Military Specialty:
   Medic
Other Military Specialties: Interpreter;
   explosives ordnance disposal
Qualified Expert: All NATO and Warsaw
   Pact small arms, including M-14; M-16;
   M-1911A1 auto pistol; M-3A1 grease
   gun; M-32 "Pulverizer" submachine gun
Birthplace: Detroit, Michigan
Grade: E-8

Lonzo Wilkinson grew up in some particularly mean streets of Detroit, where to survive meant mastering intimidation and violence. Alongside a young tough named Hardtop, Lonzo became the warlord of a large urban street gang, earning respect by clipping any fool who got in his way with a fast jab, a powerful uppercut, or the swing of his heavy chain. A break in ranks occurred when Hardtop tried to sidle up to bigger underworld players. He wanted the gang to peddle illicit narcotics, but Lonzo wouldn't abide selling poison to his own neighborhood. In an act of defiance, Lonzo torched a costly truckload of heroin and walked away from a criminal life that had already taken two of his brothers to an early grave. Knowing such a move would earn a price on his head, he sought a new way of living through the US Army.

We're not fighting to have everybody think the way we do. We're fighting so that people can have the right to think what they want, even if they don't agree with us. Somewhere in the middle lies an agreeable solution. That's the democractic system. It ain't perfect, but it's the best we got.
—Stalker

Basic training stripped away the street-punk attitude, revealing a smart, calculating, levelheaded soldier who graduated at the top of his class. Wilkinson went on to graduate from Ranger School at Fort Benning and Intelligence School at Fort Holabird. He is also a graduate of the Defense Language Institute in Monterey, California.

As part of his military service, Wilkinson served as sergeant for a recon patrol overseas that included the future Snake-Eyes and Storm Shadow (Thomas Arashikage). Half the patrol was wiped out by a reinforced enemy company, and only Snake-Eyes, Storm Shadow, and Stalker emerged intact. Snake-Eyes was gunned down as they approached the extraction LZ, and Wilkinson would have left him behind, but Storm Shadow risked his own life to carry his wounded comrade out alive. Wilkinson was on hand to witness the start of the inseparable bond between Snake-Eyes and Storm Shadow.

Skills and Abilities

Stalker is an expert unarmed combatant, earning a high tolerance to pain from his years in gang fights and bare-knuckle brawls. He is proficient with all NATO and Warsaw Pact small arms, with a strong preference for compact submachine guns like the MAC-10 or the M-32 Pulverizer. In addition to lining up targets through scopes, Stalker is an avid nature photographer, using his cat-like stealth to sneak up on wildlife and take some truly breathtaking shots.

Stalker is a qualified jump instructor and helicopter pilot. He loves to fly, and nothing beats the rush of strapping on a JUMP jet pack and soaring through the air. He is fluent in at least four languages aside from his native English: Spanish, Arabic, French, and Swahili.

Return to Borovia

When reporter Devlin Winchell was arrested on trumped-up espionage charges in Borovia, the Department of Defense wanted him retrieved and thus turned to G.I. JOE. Stalker led a team of undercover G.I. JOEs, including Quick Kick, Outback, and Snow Job, infiltrating the Borovian capital of Krogdnz. It was a clandestine op, and for the duration of the mission the quartet was discharged from service to allow the US government complete deniability.

The utmost secrecy in two conflicting government operations led to a disastrous mission. Though Stalker's team was able to infiltrate the State Security Building, they discovered that Winchell had already been secretly released to the US State Department in exchange for captured Borovian spies. Borovian state police closed in on the small team and Stalker ordered Outback to make a break

for it, return stateside, and let Hawk know what happened. Stalker, Quick Kick, and Snow Job were left behind and taken prisoner. They were sentenced on counts of terrorism, attempted kidnapping, grand theft auto, and a host of other inflated charges before being sent to a gulag to carry out five consecutive life sentences each.

Stalker spent five months in the deplorable conditions of Borovian Gulag 23. Through it all, he guarded his injured friends from his fellow prisoners, and attempted to lead the prisoners and remind them of any shreds of their self-respect and humanity that had not been beaten away by the guards. He earned the enmity of Sergeant Mosiev, who longed to find Stalker in the crosshairs of his rifle for any indiscretion.

Stalker, Snow Job, and Quick Kick were rescued by Snake-Eyes and Scarlett, who were operating "off the grid"—having faked their deaths to facilitate a covert infiltration of Borovia. They were joined by the ninjas Storm Shadow, Jinx, Billy, and the Blind Master. As the G.I. JOEs made their escape across the river, Mosiev finally lined up Stalker in his sights of his Dragunov SVD sniper rifle—only to find Stalker doing the same with his own captured rifle. Stalker got the shot off first, killing the Borovian sergeant.

■ Family Man

> It's one thing to battle killer androids and blast your way into underground bunkers to disarm dirty bombs and another thing to guide a young man past the temptations of easy money and the trappings that go with it. And the second part is tougher.
> —Stalker

During the G.I. JOE team's decommissioned years, Stalker married Lydia, a woman he met during an uncharacteristically cushy mission at a Mexican resort. The two had remained in contact through the years and started up their relationship anew when Lonzo at last had the time to devote to it. He became stepfather to Lydia's young son, Alvin. Lydia and Lonzo then gave Alvin a little brother, Jamal. They lived a nice, quiet family existence in the Page Manor District of Fairborn, Ohio.

G.I. JOE was reinstated, and Hawk made sure that Stalker was one of the first brought back to the team. As Alvin grew older, he came to resent the big shadow cast by his larger-than-life stepfather. While the students (and even teachers) at his school regarded Lonzo Wilkinson as a hero, all Alvin saw was a father who was frequently absent. Alvin began to fall in with the bad crowd—gangbangers called the G-Hustlers led by Mad Anthony Brown.

These toughs sought to introduce and control drugs in Fairborn, a situation that echoed Stalker's own troubled youth. Stalker took matters into his own hands and took the fight to the gangsters. Mad Anthony would have gotten the jump on Stalker if he hadn't been tackled by Alvin at the last minute. Seeing his father punch out these thugs in person, Alvin grew to appreciate and respect just what it was his father did: fiercely protect what he loved, be it family or country.

TUNNEL RAT
(EOD)

DATA FILE
—A-C-C-E-S-S—G-R-A-N-T-E-D—

File Name: *Nicky Lee*
SN: *387-87-NL90*
Primary Military Specialty: *EOD*
Secondary Military Specialty: *Combat*
  engineer
Birthplace: *Brooklyn, New York*
Grade: *E-5*

A hodgepodge of mixed racial ancestry ensured that young Nicky Lee never really fit into any of the circles in his tough Brooklyn neighborhood, so the scrappy young man learned to fend for himself as best as he could. Looking to strengthen himself against future violence, he enlisted in the army and excelled in Ranger School at Fort Benning.

Tunnel Rat is an expert at outdoor survival and, as his code name suggests, skilled at infiltrating narrow areas thanks to his small build, flexible frame, and fearlessness when it comes to dark, cramped confines. Tunnel Rat has an outrageous, gross-out sense of humor and sarcastic wit that have made him a beloved "class clown" of the G.I. JOE team.

Tunnel Rat believes that anything that doesn't kill you makes you stronger. His feelings about crawling into an enemy tunnel with a knife in one hand, a pistol in the other, and a flashlight in his mouth is simple—he can shoot straighter, bite harder, and run faster than anything he's ever encountered in a tunnel, so why worry?

■ Mission Report: To Save the Flagg

Investigating the innards of the USS *Flagg* after reports of an intruder, Tunnel Rat found evidence of a professional saboteur: plastic explosives with remote wire ignition chained in a ring series that ensured a blossoming, multisequence explosion, which could sink the G.I. JOE aircraft carrier. As Tunnel Rat worked feverishly to defuse the bombs, COBRA ninja Storm Shadow attempted to stop him. Much to Storm Shadow's surprise, Tunnel Rat held his own against Storm Shadow's repeated harassment, but the ninja's ultimate mission was one of misdirection. With much ado about the chained explosives, Storm Shadow was attempting to draw attention away from secondary explosives placed near the propeller shafts. Tunnel Rat, though, saw through the ruse when he found traces of grease left behind by the COBRA ninja. That motor lubricant led Tunnel Rat to the propeller assembly, where he was able to defuse the bomb in time.

■ Mission Report: Rat versus B.A.T.s

The ever vigilant Tunnel Rat tracked a series of suspicious shipments of Overraker-Mayle 9000 springs, industrial coils used in the manufacture of advanced robotics. His investigation pointed to consignments of the components disappearing north of Vladivostok. With the rest of the team preoccupied on other assignments, the impetuous Rat took a supersonic transport to the frigid wastes of Siberia and confirmed his suspicions: COBRA had a B.A.T. manufacturing facility concealed within the frozen wastes. Others, like Hi-Tech, dismissed Tunnel Rat's hunches since any sort of advanced robotics facility would have shown up on G.I. JOE sensors, but what Tunnel Rat discovered was a factory cleverly hidden within the heart of a glacier. Unfortunately, he was captured when he snooped too closely, and B.A.T. sentries tossed the G.I. JOE intruder into a prison cell.

Tunnel Rat's clunky motto, "Where there's a tunnel, there's a way," proved true, as he twisted his small frame into a ventilation duct and escaped his confines. The uncreative mechanicals guarding the facilities made no effort to hide Tunnel Rat's captured explosives, and he was soon reunited with his beloved shaped charges. He put them to good use in blasting apart much of the factory. Fleeing onto the windswept glacier surface, Tunnel Rat had to stare down B.A.T. commander Overkill, who was piloting an enormous battle mech. With limited explosives, Tunnel Rat fired not at the pursuing automaton, but rather at the surrounding ice shelves, collapsing the tons of frozen water onto the remains of the base and his pursuers in an avalanche. Tunnel Rat escaped with enough battered B.A.T. craniums to prove his mission's worth to any doubters back at headquarters.

WILD BILL
(Helicopter Pilot)

DATA FILE
ACCESS GRANTED

File Name: William S. Hardy
SN: 056-40-BW11
Primary Military Specialty:
   Helicopter pilot
Secondary Military Specialty:
   Fixed-wing pilot
Other Military Specialties: Aircraft
   armorer; Air Cavalry scout; tank
   driver
Qualified Expert: M-1911A1 auto
   pistol (though he prefers single-
   action .45 long Colt revolvers);
   XM-16 attack rifle
Birthplace: Brady, Texas
Grade: CW-4 (chief warrant officer 4)

Amiable, slow talking, and full of tall tales, Wild Bill is a proud, larger-than-life Texan. He developed his marksmanship and love of guns as a boy, hunting wild game on the vast open lands of his home state. He enlisted at 18 and served as a combat infantryman during overseas operations. For his distinctive roots—and preference for six-shooters—his friends and fellow soldiers nicknamed him Wild Bill. Later, wanting to get out of ground-pounding for a more liberating vantage point, Bill reenlisted for Flight Warrant Officers School, learning rotary- and fixed-wing piloting.

In an earlier age, Wild Bill's cavalry mount would have eaten oats and worn a saddle blanket, but his preferred ride now runs on jet fuel and has rotor blades. He can still make it gallop like the wind, take a turn like a thoroughbred, and stop on a dime.

In the early phases of the modern G.I. JOE team, Wild Bill served as a support member, though he wasn't actually on the roster. On Hawk's recommendations, Wild Bill was part of the first wave of expansion of the growing G.I. JOE team, becoming an essential member by piloting insertion and extraction missions around the world. Bill deflected praise and underplayed his role, demurely referring to himself as "the bus driver" who got the real soldiers onto the ground. On countless occasions, Wild Bill has shown unparalleled courage and determination in flying into some of the hairiest LZs a helicopter pilot could be expected to negotiate. He is a rescuing angel, the guns-a-blazing cavalry, and the light at the end of the tunnel all rolled into one, and the G.I. JOEs have come to regard him well for his last-minute escapes. Furthermore, Wild Bill is a man of complete integrity, brooking no deception, though he does often spin an exaggerated yarn if only to entertain his fellow soldiers.

To that end, he also fancies himself a country singer. During the decommissioned years, he pursued a recording career, and even released an album that produced a few modest hits, but he had to put this dream on hold when G.I. JOE came calling once again.

Undercover Cowboy

The hootin' and hollerin' cowpoke persona proudly worn by Wild Bill wouldn't ordinarily put him at the front of the line for undercover work, but there are occasions when he's the perfect man for the job.

The purchase of the Loco Toro dude ranch in Texas by a COBRA front company raised flags among the G.I. JOE team, and Wild Bill was one of the undercover G.I. JOEs dispatched to investigate. COBRA agents saw through their disguises and did what they could to distract the agents from their true objective: raiding a neighboring ranch that was the site of an experimental solar energy farm. Wild Bill was briefly misled by a blossoming romance with the ranch manager's daughter, Mary Belle Joe, until she proved to be the Baroness in disguise. Bill eventually snapped to the matter at hand and actually managed to defeat the COBRA plot to control the solar array by running a cattle stampede directly through their ranks.

Years later, when G.I. JOE was alerted to the suspicious buildup of a private army in Japan, Wild Bill was called in from reserve status as cover for the investigation. He and Gung-Ho posed as boisterous American investors and secured a meeting with Japanese businessman Hayatu Toba in his Tokyo headquarters. In this case, the loud and colorful temperaments of a Texan and a Cajun were an effective distraction from the stealthy efforts of Jinx, the ninja agent digging through Toba's operation. They were able to discover a link between Toba's private army and Destro's force, and put a stop to Toba's attempted uprising.

On the Ground

In addition to his legendary skills in a chopper, Wild Bill is a gifted tracker. For a time, he was also tasked with operating G.I. JOE ground vehicles, and he grew fond of piloting the advanced Patriot Grizzly tank.

The G.I. JOE C-130

When not flying a chopper like the Dragonfly, Locust, or Night Attack Helicopter, Wild Bill can most often be found behind the stick of the G.I. JOE C-130 Hercules transport plane. Not afforded a slick code name like other combat aircraft, the C-130 is an overlooked workhorse. It can carry up to 92 passengers or 45,000 pounds of cargo at a cruising speed of 336 mph. Its operational range is 2,360 miles, which can be extended by midair refueling. The G.I. JOE C-130 is the only airlifter equipped with adaptable fuel inlets to allow refueling from navy and air force tankers.

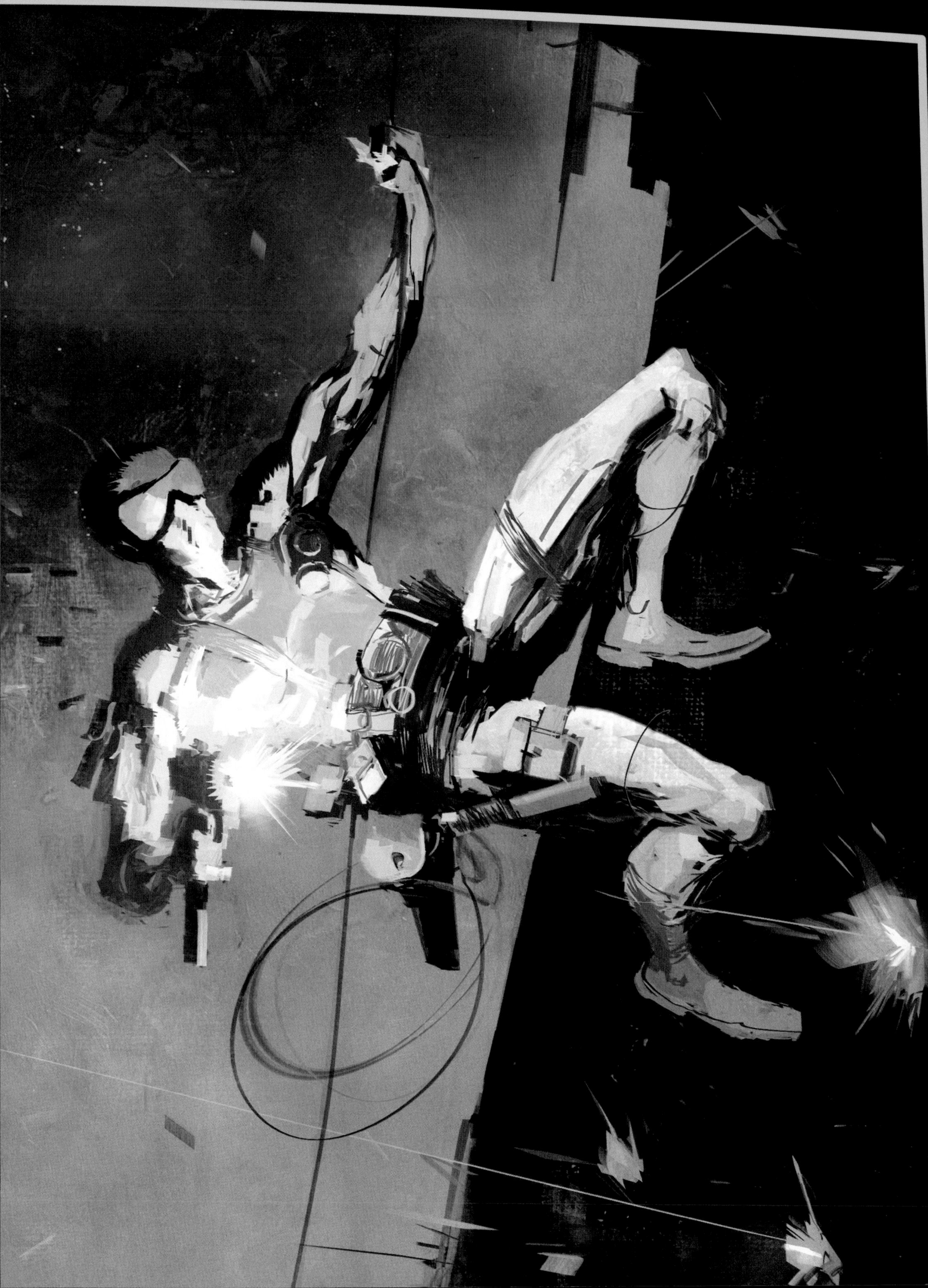

AGENT FACES
(Infiltrator)

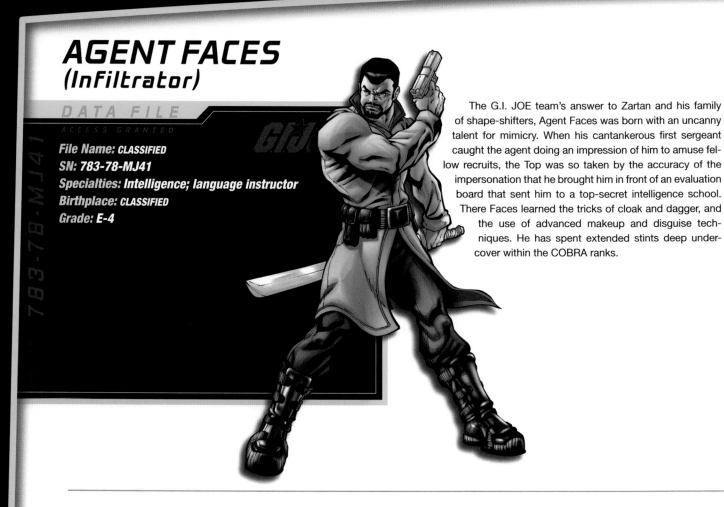

DATA FILE
ACCESS GRANTED

File Name: CLASSIFIED
SN: 783-78-MJ41
Specialties: Intelligence; language instructor
Birthplace: CLASSIFIED
Grade: E-4

The G.I. JOE team's answer to Zartan and his family of shape-shifters, Agent Faces was born with an uncanny talent for mimicry. When his cantankerous first sergeant caught the agent doing an impression of him to amuse fellow recruits, the Top was so taken by the accuracy of the impersonation that he brought him in front of an evaluation board that sent him to a top-secret intelligence school. There Faces learned the tricks of cloak and dagger, and the use of advanced makeup and disguise techniques. He has spent extended stints deep undercover within the COBRA ranks.

AIRTIGHT
(Hostile Environment)

DATA FILE
ACCESS GRANTED

File Name: Kurt Schnurr
SN: 307-42-KS83
Specialties: CBR (chemical, biological, and radiological warfare); hazardous substance control; ordnance
Birthplace: New Haven, Connecticut
Grade: E-4

Airtight was a misfit kid who grew up into the kind of adult who would readily wade into a cloud of toxic gas that could dissolve lung tissue with one whiff. He's a trained expert in chemical weaponry, able to detect, identify, neutralize, and contain whatever vile poison COBRA agents can concoct. He's also the biggest practical joker on the team. It unsettles new recruits that the G.I. JOE most likely to be handling flesh-eating viruses all day is the one also most likely to spike a drink.

ALPINE
(Mountain Trooper)

File Name: *Albert M. Pine*
SN: *237-51-HG44*
Primary Military Specialty: *Mountain trooper*
Secondary Military Specialty: *Finance clerk*
Qualified Expert: *M-16; M-14; M-60; M-1911A1*
Birthplace: *Minidoka, Idaho*
Grade: *E-4*

From his childhood home on the Snake River plain, young Al could see the rise and peaks of the Basin and Range Mountains, the Menan Buttes, and the Yellowstone Plateau blocking the horizon. Struck with wanderlust, he wanted to see what was on the other side of the mountains—but soon grew fixated with the mountains themselves. He became an expert climber, adding to the challenge by joining the military, where climbers are encumbered with weapons, armor, ammunition, and communications gear.

In his time with G.I. JOE, Alpine has forged a strong friendship with Bazooka, and their colorful personalities meld into what passes for the G.I. JOE's unofficial comedy team—though each would argue which is the joker and which is the straight man.

His secondary specialty makes good use of his other passion—accounting. Alpine sees the towering columns of numbers and dates as just more mountains to conquer. Though some on the team may tease him for his fastidious approach to bookkeeping, Alpine reminds them that the FBI has brought in more bad guys through accounting than by kicking down doors.

BARBECUE
(Firefighter)

File Name: *Gabriel A. Kelly*
SN: *321-61-4231*
Specialties: *Firefighter; infantry*
Birthplace: *Boston, Massachusetts*
Grade: *E-4*

Six generations of Kellys had previously served the Boston Fire Department, with young Gabriel slated to be the seventh. He instead joined the military, but still found a role as a firefighter for the G.I. JOE team. He does his job not out of a sense of civic duty, or even family loyalty. Barbecue is an unrepentant party animal who happens to like loud sirens, clanging bells, fire trucks, and bashing down doors with axes.

BARREL ROLL
(High-Altitude Sniper)

DATA FILE
ACCESS GRANTED

File Name: Dwight E. Stall
SN: 299-06-BR69
Primary Military Specialty: Marksmanship instructor
Secondary Military Specialty: Fixed-wing aircraft pilot
Birthplace: Cincinnati, Ohio
Grade: E-4

Bombstrike

The Stall family has no shortage of relatives to point to as examples of sterling military careers. Two of the Stall children qualified for service in G.I. JOE—Barrel Roll and his sister, Bombstrike (Alyssa Renee Stall). Thomas Stall, though, was a tragic case. Bad enough he washed out in training and failed his psychological exam, but then the disgruntled youth, tired of living in the shadow of his overachieving siblings, wound up joining the ranks of COBRA as the sniper Black Out. The ongoing struggle between G.I. JOE and COBRA is filled with many private dramas, but for Barrel Roll and Bombstrike, it's a family affair.

Barrel Roll pushes himself hard to excel, practicing daily on the sniper range. For him, the objective isn't essential—the end goal is actually quite irrelevant. It's *not failing* that matters most to him. Barrel Roll is a crack shot and a skilled HALO jumper and pilot. He can claim the high ground without being spotted, drifting in silently by glider or parachute and then disappearing in the underbrush, sitting absolutely still to align the perfect shot.

BAZOOKA
(Anti-Armor)

DATA FILE
ACCESS GRANTED

File Name: David L. Katzenbogen
SN: 112-40-DL57
Primary Military Specialty: Armor-defeating weapons systems
Secondary Military Specialty: Armored vehicle driver
Qualified Expert: Dragon anti-tank missile; Milan System; LAW rocket; recoil-less rifle; all Warsaw Pact RPG systems. Subject is also EOD (explosive ordnance disposal) qualified.
Birthplace: Hibbing, Minnesota
Grade: E-5

His slow and infrequent way of talking sometimes leads others into underestimating Bazooka's intelligence, but he's no dummy. A fast thinker, he was driving an Abrams tank in the Third Armored Division when he came to realize that a barely trained attacker armed with a $200 disposable rocket launcher could knock out a million-dollar tank. He promptly transferred to anti-armor.

Katzenbogen's training includes Advanced Infantry School (Fort Benning) and Armor School (Fort Knox). He is also an expert angler, and his fishing trips with Alpine have been the subject of many a tall tale.

After G.I. JOE was temporarily decommissioned, Bazooka retired from the military and founded a security service in his home state of Minnesota. He grew quite comfortable in civilian life, so much so that he initially failed the physical exam when he first attempted to rejoin the team.

BIG BEN
(SAS Trooper)

File Name: David J. Bennett
Primary Military Specialty: Infantry
Secondary Military Specialty: Subversive operations
Birthplace: Burford, England
Grade: Staff sergeant

Part of an exchange program between American Special Forces and the British Special Air Services, Big Ben found a home with the Yanks at G.I. JOE. His combat records are classified, but it is believed he took part in various covert operations. He received his initial training at Bradbury Lines Barracks in Hereford and was *en cadre* at the NATO LRRP School in Germany. He was once wooed by Zarana—who was disguised as a Pentagon official—in order to dupe the G.I. JOEs into entering a potentially hazardous training exercise.

BILLY
(Cobra Commander's Son)

File Name: William S. Kessler
(legal name; birth name CLASSIFIED)
Birthplace: CLASSIFIED

anyone knew his peculiar connection to the enemy. When G.I. JOE agents Zap, Scarlett, and Snake-Eyes were imprisoned in Springfield, the "friendly" small town that served as a front for COBRA headquarters, an anonymous 10-year-old boy helped them escape. That boy was Billy, who joined the anti-COBRA underground and was eventually recruited by the Baroness and Major Bludd to assassinate Cobra Commander during a COBRA Youth Brigade rally.

It was then that Billy came to the crushing realization that Cobra Commander was indeed his father. He had fooled himself into thinking that his real father had somehow been killed or otherwise replaced with the Commander. Arrested after the failed assassination, Billy was rescued from punishment by Storm Shadow, who trained him in martial arts. Becoming a highly skilled combatant, Billy would later help the ninja agents of G.I. JOE. Billy suffered extensive injuries in a car accident—losing an eye and a leg—but with an advanced prosthetic to replace his lost limb, he sprang back with a resiliency and tenacity that made his master, Storm Shadow, proud.

Later going by the name William Kessler, Billy continued to offer what aid he could to the G.I. JOE team. As a final, public act to prove he would tolerate no betrayals, Cobra Commander killed his son, and strung up William's body for all his underlings to see.

William Kessler was not an official member of G.I. JOE, but his fate was inextricably intertwined with the team. For many years, the G.I. JOEs knew him as Billy—Cobra Commander's son, though his blood ties did not make him a foe. Billy was helping G.I. JOE before

BLOWTORCH
(Flamethrower)

DATA FILE
ACCESS GRANTED

527-34-TP12

File Name: Timothy P. Hanrahan
SN: 527-34-TP12
Primary Military Specialty: Infantry special weapons
Secondary Military Specialty: Small-arms armorer; combat engineer
Birthplace: Tampa, Florida
Grade: E-4

Blowtorch knows firsthand the destructive potential of fire. As a result, he's a bit of an overbearing authority on fire safety. He can instantly eyeball whether or not a large gathering is in violation of fire codes, and instinctively knows where fire exits *should* be located. High-rises and smokers make him very nervous—especially the combination thereof. Blowtorch is also studying for advanced degrees in both structural and chemical engineering to understand, on a molecular level, what happens when fires rage out of control.

CLUTCH
(Vehicle Operator)

DATA FILE
ACCESS GRANTED

757-34-LJ82

File Name: Lance J. Steinberg
SN: 757-34-LJ82
Alternative Code Name: Double Clutch
Primary Military Specialty: Transportation engineer
Secondary Military Specialty: Infantry
Qualified Expert: M-14; M-16; M-1911A1; M-3A1; M-60
Birthplace: Asbury Park, New Jersey
Grade: E-5

Clutch is a renowned grease monkey, earning his reputation as a mechanic at Manny's Mean Machines in Asbury Park. He was sought out by Indianapolis 500 racers and NASCAR champs alike to work on their cars, to bring the unmistakable "Clutch Touch" to their vehicles. Though he could have made a comfortable living as a civilian working on cars (and chasing after girls), he enlisted.

He would dismiss his call to service as driven by a desire to see just what the army had under its hood. In truth, Steinberg believed evil did exist in the world, and needed to be effectively countered. A Jew, he grew up hearing stories of what his grandmother faced during the rise of Nazi Germany, and he was determined to be on the front line of any fight against such horrors.

His training is extensive: Advanced Infantry Training; Covert Ops School; Executive Bodyguard School; and Ranger School. Clutch instinctively gravitates to anything with a lot of horsepower. It's a long-standing wager among his G.I. JOE friends as to what he'd be drawn to first if presented with a gleaming new V-8 engine and a beautiful swimsuit model at the same time. Clutch is clever enough that he'd find a way to pursue both simultaneously.

DOC
(Medic)

DATA FILE

ACCESS GRANTED

G.I.JOE

File Name: *(original) Carl W. Greer;*
(second) Carla P. Greer
SN: *(original) RA-367-22-1097;*
(second) 521-58-CP12
Primary Military Specialty: *(original) Medical*
doctor; (second) medical corps officer
Secondary Military Specialty: *(both) chap-*
lain's assistant
Birthplace: *(both) Concord, Massachu-*
setts
Grade: *(both) O-3 (captain)*

A graduate from Harvard Medical School, Carl Greer completed his residency at Johns Hopkins University. A spiritual man, he devoted himself to alleviating suffering in the world, and greatly admired the G.I. JOE team's efforts to do the same by challenging those who would bring about violence and chaos. Greer's dedication to pacifism may seem at odds with his enlistment, but he aspired to join the G.I. JOE team. He correctly figured that military training would give him the skills he needed to survive on the most dangerous of battlefields and administer medical aid. He served as the G.I. JOE team's first medic until killed in action during a mission to Trucial Abysmia.

His niece, Carla, continued in his footsteps. She acquired her medical degree from Wayne State University and took residence at a hospital in Detroit. After enlistment, she graduated at the top of her class from the AMEDD (Army Medical Department) Officer Advanced Course, leading her into G.I. JOE. Like her late uncle, she is a pacifist. She carries a special tranquilizer gun used to help sedate patients or incapacitate enemies.

FALCON
(Green Beret)

DATA FILE

ACCESS GRANTED

G.I.JOE

File Name: *Vincent R. Falcone*
SN: *035-38-VN22*
Primary Military Specialty: *Infantry*
Secondary Military Specialty: *Medic*
Birthplace: *Fayetteville, North Carolina*
Grade: *O-2 (first lieutenant)*

A second-generation Green Beret, Lieutenant Falcon served briefly with the Fifth Special Forces Group Airborne counterterrorist unit ("Blue Light") as the executive officer of an A team prior to his service in G.I. JOE. He is proficient in Spanish, French, Arabic, and Swahili.

Specialized in training and leading native insurgents, Falcon has an overwhelming gregariousness that can sway even the staunchest isolationist into joining the fight. This excess in personality often leads to friction with commanding officers, as a little bit of Falcon goes a *long* way.

He has some undisclosed familial relationship with Duke (the term *half brother* gets bandied about, but the family tree doesn't appear to branch that way), which has more than once resulted in heated disputes. Duke has often used his good record to bail Falcon out of trouble, which has only increased the animosity between the two. The hatchet may have finally been buried after Falcon had an unfortunate run-in with the drug known as spark, a stimulant trafficked by the notorious Headman. Falcon kicked the habit and is long since clean and sober.

FIREWALL
(Computer Ops)

File Name: Michelle LaChance
SN: 555-63-ML52
Primary Military Specialty: Information
technology
Birthplace: Virginia Beach, Virginia
Grade: E-4

555-63-ML52

Time on her hands, an irresponsible rebellious streak, and elite computer-hacking skills drew unwanted Pentagon attention to LaChance. In her high school days, she figured out how to worm her way into protected school records and alter grades. This led to infantile acts of hacking into government systems in order to steal identities, shuffle about personal funds, and generally inconvenience authority figures who thought themselves untouchable by a teenage rebel.

She bit off more than she could chew, however, by slicing into classified military computers that held information about a top-secret nano-mite technology program that would later be stolen by COBRA. Her snooping was detected and landed her in a federal prison, but her handiwork impressed the brass enough that she was allocated to the G.I. JOE team, serving under Mainframe to develop a counterprogram to thwart COBRA's nanotechnology menace. Since then, she has been a loyal member of G.I. JOE, receiving basic military training in order to keep up with the rest of the team, though she is not a field operative. Since Mainframe's death in action, she has been elevated to the preeminent computer expert on the team despite her young age.

GENERAL FLAGG
(General)

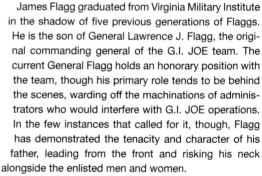

File Name: James Longstreet Flagg
SN: 212-9820-GU95
Primary Military Specialty: Chief strategic
commander
Birthplace: Alexandria, Virginia
Grade: O-7

212-9820-GU95

James Flagg graduated from Virginia Military Institute in the shadow of five previous generations of Flaggs. He is the son of General Lawrence J. Flagg, the original commanding general of the G.I. JOE team. The current General Flagg holds an honorary position with the team, though his primary role tends to be behind the scenes, warding off the machinations of administrators who would interfere with G.I. JOE operations. In the few instances that called for it, though, Flagg has demonstrated the tenacity and character of his father, leading from the front and risking his neck alongside the enlisted men and women.

FROSTBITE
(Arctic Trooper)

File Name: *Farley S. Seward*
SN: *215-58-SF36*
Specialties: *Motor vehicle driver; armor*
Birthplace: *Galena, Alaska*
Grade: *E-5*

Growing up in a tiny town set on a frozen expanse where summer was a rumor is something Frostbite wears as a badge of pride. He thrives on meteorological adversity, seeing whiteouts, blizzards, and ear-shriveling temperatures as invigorating personal challenges. He's at his best where Fahrenheit and Celsius meet. At 40 degrees below zero, survival skills are tested with no margin for error. Despite having to reach into the guts of freezing metal vehicles with shivering hands, Frostbite always manages to make sure G.I. JOE's arctic equipment performs as well as he does.

GRAND SLAM
(Laser Artillery)

File Name: *James J. Barney*
SN: *379-54-JJ44*
Specialties: *Artillery; electronic engineer; jet pack trooper*
Birthplace: *Chippewa Falls, Wisconsin*
Grade: *E-5*

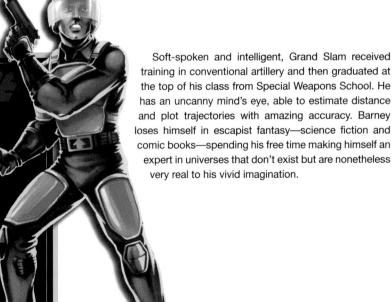

Soft-spoken and intelligent, Grand Slam received training in conventional artillery and then graduated at the top of his class from Special Weapons School. He has an uncanny mind's eye, able to estimate distance and plot trajectories with amazing accuracy. Barney loses himself in escapist fantasy—science fiction and comic books—spending his free time making himself an expert in universes that don't exist but are nonetheless very real to his vivid imagination.

GRUNT
(Infantry)

DATA FILE
ACCESS GRANTED

File Name: *Robert W. Graves*
SN: *527-79-RW96*
Specialties: *Infantry squad leader; small-arms attack specialist; artillery coordinator; glider pilot*
Birthplace: *Columbus, Ohio*
Grade: *E-5*

It fell to young Graves to support his mother when his father passed away. Unable to afford college, he gave up high school to work in construction to help make ends meet. Graves enlisted, partially to help pay for school, but also because service upheld the values instilled by his late father. During Advanced Infantry Training, Grunt so took to heart the idea of soldiers taking care of their own that he spent his leave time visiting and consoling the mother of a fellow soldier who had died in training. After serving as one of the original G.I. JOEs, Grunt left for a while to get his engineering degree at Georgia Tech. He married a fellow student, Lola, and the two have a young daughter.

HI-TECH
(Operations Support)

DATA FILE
ACCESS GRANTED

File Name: *David P. Lewinski*
SN: *711-60-KLJL*
Specialties: *Armament research and design; telecommunications*
Birthplace: *St. Paul, Minnesota*
Grade: *E-4*

A technological genius, Hi-Tech is more at home with a soldering gun than an automatic pistol, but he more than pulls his weight with the G.I. JOE team. He can be counted on to repair just about any complex computer-controlled device, enacting emergency field repairs and rewriting code on the fly to get the most out of the team's cutting-edge arsenal of 21st-century equipment. He finds COBRA innovations contemptible and makes it a hobby—even obsession—to find new ways to undo whatever contributions scientists such as Dr. Mindbender bring to the battlefield.

JINX
(Intelligence)

File Name: Kimi Arashikage
   (first name is possibly an alias)
SN: 037-42-UK83
Primary Military Specialty: Intelligence
Secondary Military Specialty: Finance clerk
Other Military Specialties: Covert operations;
   hand-to-hand combat instructor
Birthplace: Los Angeles, California
Grade: E-5

A member of the Arashikage ninja clan, Kimi is Storm Shadow's cousin. Born in the United States, she embraced her ninja heritage at a young age during a family visit to Japan, where she entered the Arashikage dojo at the same time Snake-Eyes was undergoing training. Kimi learned from the Blind Master and became extremely adept at blind fighting—often preferring to spar blindfolded without the distractions afforded by vision. Returning to the US, she studied at Bryn Mawr and is believed to have spent time serving in the CIA. She was brought into the G.I. JOE team by Snake-Eyes, whom she apprenticed with for a while. After the temporary dissolution of the G.I. JOE team, Jinx turned freelance, starting a successful bounty hunting/ bail bondsman career with fellow former G.I. JOE Budo (Kyle Jesso). The two also started an oft-tumultuous romance, despite the oil-and-water relationship of ninja and samurai.

KAMAKURA
(Ninja)

File Name: Sean M. Collins
(formerly Sean Broca)
SN: CLASSIFIED
Primary Military Specialty: Infantry
Secondary Military Specialty: Intelligence
Other Military Specialties: CLASSIFIED
Birthplace: Roseville, California
Grade: E-5

because Kamakura proved to be a dependable soldier and a formidable warrior.

Sean Collins was the son of a Crimson Guardsman killed in action and replaced by a look-alike, Fred Broca II. This doppelgänger proved to be a former ally of Snake-Eyes and Stalker—a fellow veteran from their service overseas—who would later turn his back on his COBRA allegiance, reclaim his original identity of Wade Collins, and with the support of his family enter the witness relocation program.

As a teenager looking for direction, Sean aspired to military service, despite hard-earned words of warning from his father. Sean wrote a letter to Snake-Eyes seeking advice, and Snake-Eyes sent a heartfelt reply offering an unflinching look at the gravity of service. Though Snake-Eyes's missive did give him pause, Sean eventually enlisted, and would later serve as Snake-Eyes's ninja apprentice.

The now defunct G.I. JOE Ninja Force is not remembered fondly by all, and especially not by military traditionalists such as General Hawk, who saw a dangerous predilection for rogue operations and lack of respect for chains of command. He initially rejected the notion of a new ninja in the G.I. JOE team, but later came to rescind his initial objections

LAW & ORDER
(MP & K-9)

DATA FILE

***File Name:* Christopher M. Lavigne**
***SN:* 044-5688-XI83**
***Primary Military Specialty:* Military Police**
***Secondary Military Specialty:* Intelligence**
***Other Military Specialty:* Security tactics**
***Birthplace:* Houston, Texas**
***Grade:* E-4**

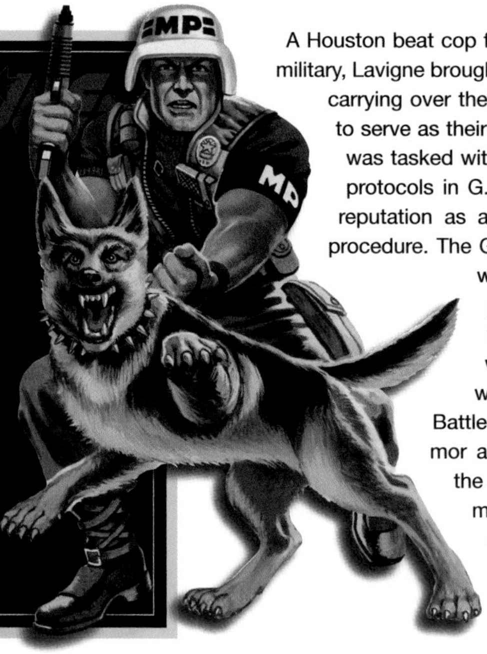

A Houston beat cop for two years prior to enlistment in the military, Lavigne brought his loyal German shepherd with him, carrying over their police nicknames of Law and Order to serve as their code names in the G.I. JOE team. He was tasked with developing and maintaining security protocols in G.I. JOE installations, quickly earning a reputation as a no-nonsense stickler for detail and procedure. The G.I. JOEs learned not to end up in the wrong part of their base without the appropriate "hall passes," or they would face the wrath of Law & Order. As the war against COBRA intensified, Law was transferred to front-line duty in the Battle Corps, donning modern Enforcer armor and equipment and reluctantly leaving the dog behind. If there's a soft spot to this mule-headed grim-jawed cop, it's Order. Law has been known to call long distance in order to get Mutt to put Junkyard on the phone so his beloved pooch could have "talkies" with his best pal.

LEATHERNECK
(Marine)

DATA FILE

***File Name:* Wendell A. Metzger**
***SN:* 368-10-WA25**
***Primary Military Specialty:* Infantry**
***Secondary Military Specialty:* Drill sergeant**
***Other Military Specialties:* Vehicle driver; marine force recon**
***Birthplace:* Stromsburg, Nebraska**
***Grade:* E-7**

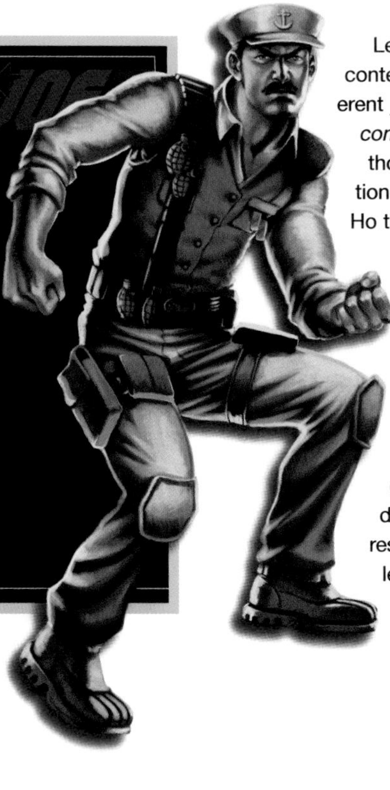

Leatherneck is not in the running for any popularity contests. He's an ill-tempered, obnoxious, and belligerent jarhead who has never had any use for the word *compromise.* He holds irrational grudges against those who have wronged him or don't fit his definition of *worthy.* He even rubs fellow marines like Gung-Ho the wrong way. The only other G.I. JOE he seems to connect with is Wet-Suit, and the two reportedly can't stand each other. Their constant bickering—rooted in storied marines-versus-navy rivalry—conceals a shared respect.

As drill sergeant, Leatherneck entrenches himself in the role of an enemy to G.I. JOEs in training—or at best, an insurmountable obstacle. It's as if he never turns the drill sergeant mode off. Though he may not have any off-duty friends among the team, he does have their respect. A capable soldier unwilling to give up or leave any man behind, Leatherneck is proof that you don't need to like your fellow soldiers to fight beside them.

LIFELINE
(Rescue Trooper)

File Name: Edwin C. Steen
SN: RA128-03-2496
Primary Military Specialty: Medic
Secondary Military Specialty: Rescue operations
Other Military Specialty: X-ray technician
Birthplace: Seattle, Washington
Grade: E-5

Growing up vulnerable to a workaholic, abusive father made young Edwin Steen reject violence and conflict of any kind—but he was determined not to be left defenseless. He found an emotional center and overriding philosophy in the study of Aikido, a martial arts discipline that sublimates an enemy's aggressive energies into defensive maneuvers. Working hard for the betterment of others, Steen attended paramedic school in Spokane and joined the Seattle Fire Department. He later enlisted, becoming a combat medic for the G.I. JOE team. His pacifist ideals frequently rub world-weary pragmatists like Leatherneck and Lift-Ticket the wrong way. They would eat any words that disparaged Lifeline's courage, though. While reluctant to pick up a weapon, Lifeline does not flinch when it comes to entering the battlefield to rescue a fallen comrade.

LOW-LIGHT
(Sniper)

File Name: Cooper G. MacBride
SN: 547-48-CG37
Primary Military Specialty: Infantry
Secondary Military Specialty: Sharpshooter
Other Military Specialties: Marksmanship instructor; night spotter
Qualified Expert: M-16A2; M-24 7.62 sniper rifle
Birthplace: Crosby, North Dakota
Grade: E-6

A childhood scarred by psychological abuse forged MacBride into the coldly effective sharpshooter he is today. He is a far cry from the timid boy who was once terrified of the dark. His father, determined to rid young Cooper of his demons, constantly derided him and locked the youth in a cellar with only a flashlight and a rifle to protect himself from rats. Cooper emerged from this house of horrors transformed.

He is grim, fatalistic, and laconic. Many of the more boisterous G.I. JOEs find Low-Light's personality chilling, as well as his effectiveness as a sniper. Low-Light has exceptional night vision, and supplements it with the latest in image-intensifier technology. He currently holds two patents in the development of nocturnal imaging devices. Where once he cowered from the darkness, Low-Light now thrives in it.

MAINFRAME
(Computer Ops)

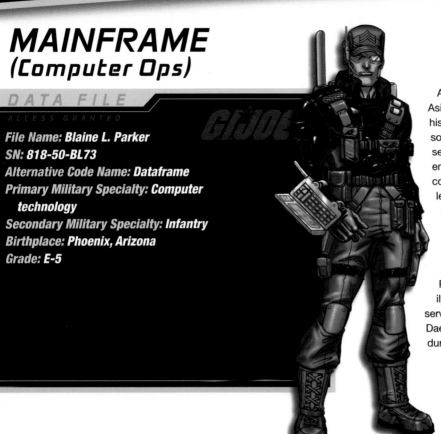

DATA FILE
ACCESS GRANTED

818-50-BL73

File Name: Blaine L. Parker
SN: 818-50-BL73
Alternative Code Name: Dataframe
Primary Military Specialty: Computer technology
Secondary Military Specialty: Infantry
Birthplace: Phoenix, Arizona
Grade: E-5

An older G.I. JOE veteran of the war in Southeast Asia, Mainframe was often underestimated due to his role in IT. He's more than earned his mark as a soldier. He was a trained airborne infantryman who served out a tour before studying computer sciences at MIT on the G.I. Bill. Parker made a very comfortable living in Silicon Valley, but grew restless until he discovered that the marines were looking for computer experts. He became the G.I. JOE team's first computer tech, a crucial yet unsung position for an organization on the bleeding edge of innovation. In a field dominated by energetic fresh faces barely out of their teens, Parker more than held his own thanks to a readily admitted geek-like passion for computers. He served as mentor to newer G.I. JOE hackers such as Daemon and Firewall until his death on Cobra Island during the battle against splinter group the Coil.

MUTT & JUNKYARD
(Dog Handler & K-9)

DATA FILE
ACCESS GRANTED

231-55-SG91

File Name: Stanley G. Perlmutter
SN: 231-55-SG91
Primary Military Specialty: Dog handler
Secondary Military Specialty: Infantry
Other Military Specialties: Animal control/ utilization technician; covert ops specialist
Qualified Expert: M-16; M-14; M-1911A1 auto pistol; MAC-11
Birthplace: Iselin, New Jersey
Grade: E-6

Mutt has always gotten along much better with animals than people. He had five pet dogs growing up and trained them exceptionally well. His skills and army record saw him join the G.I. JOE team as its K-9 officer, and he brought with him Junkyard, a mutt (fittingly) whom he had trained as a pup. Very smart, Junk once managed to lure a bunch of high-ranking COBRAs into a quicksand trap during a mission to the Florida Everglades. Some would argue that Junkyard was more popular among the G.I. JOEs than his nominal master—at least Junkyard was friendlier than the often surly Mutt. As he got older and slower, Junkyard eventually retired from service. Mutt continues as a member of the team with Junkyard II, a dog as loyal, smart, and well trained as his father.

OUTBACK
(Survival)

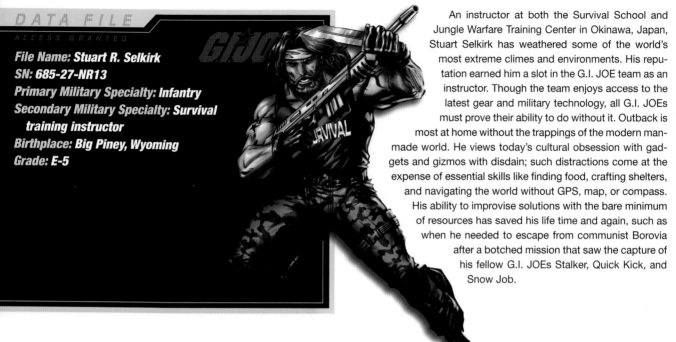

File Name: Stuart R. Selkirk
SN: 685-27-NR13
Primary Military Specialty: Infantry
Secondary Military Specialty: Survival
  training instructor
Birthplace: Big Piney, Wyoming
Grade: E-5

An instructor at both the Survival School and Jungle Warfare Training Center in Okinawa, Japan, Stuart Selkirk has weathered some of the world's most extreme climes and environments. His reputation earned him a slot in the G.I. JOE team as an instructor. Though the team enjoys access to the latest gear and military technology, all G.I. JOEs must prove their ability to do without it. Outback is most at home without the trappings of the modern man-made world. He views today's cultural obsession with gadgets and gizmos with disdain; such distractions come at the expense of essential skills like finding food, crafting shelters, and navigating the world without GPS, map, or compass. His ability to improvise solutions with the bare minimum of resources has saved his life time and again, such as when he needed to escape from communist Borovia after a botched mission that saw the capture of his fellow G.I. JOEs Stalker, Quick Kick, and Snow Job.

PSYCHE-OUT
(Deceptive Warfare)

File Name: Kenneth D. Rich
SN: 091-87-KR74
Specialties: Psy-ops; social services
counselor
Birthplace: San Francisco, California
Grade: O-2 (first lieutenant)

Psyche-Out is exactly the soldier the tinfoil-hat-wearing conspiracy nutters fear the most. After earning his psychology degree at Berkeley, he spent time researching the inducement of paranoia with low-frequency radio waves. With his specialized equipment, Psyche-Out can coax specific behavior in enemy troops with them none the wiser that their morale has been lessened, their fears heightened, and their fighting edge dulled by an unseen soldier with a parabolic transmitter. Even without the gear, Psyche-Out develops tactics that hinge on making his enemy's doubts his greatest weapon.

QUICK KICK
(Silent Weapons)

DATA FILE
ACCESS GRANTED

631-42-MS71

File Name: MacArthur S. Ito
SN: 631-42-MS71
Specialties: Infantry; intelligence
Birthplace: Los Angeles, California
Grade: E-4

Ito studied martial arts in an effort to protect his parents' Watts neighborhood grocery store from thieving thugs. He wasn't content to study just one discipline—he mastered Tae Kwan Do, Go Ju Ryu, Southern Praying Mantis Kung-Fu, Tai-Chi Sword, Zen Sword, and Wing-Chun. Of all the G.I. JOE martial arts masters, he stood out as the biggest showman. A veritable ham, Quick Kick picked up his theatricality as a stuntman in Hollywood. Tragically, he was one of several G.I. JOEs killed in Trucial Abysmia.

RECONDO
(Jungle Trooper)

DATA FILE
ACCESS GRANTED

158-24-DM87

File Name: Daniel M. LeClaire
SN: 158-24-DM87
Primary Military Specialty: Infantry
Secondary Military Specialty: Intelligence
Birthplace: Wheaton, Wisconsin
Grade: E-4

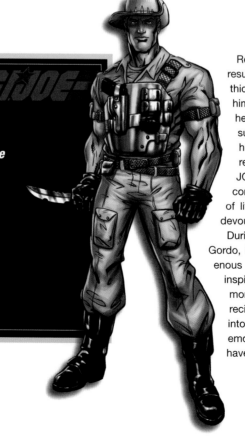

Recondo's specialty in jungle survival often results in him spending extended time in the thick of the earth's sweltering rain forests by himself. When he returns to the G.I. JOE base, he's often standoffish and aloof, not fully surfacing back to the world of face-to-face human interaction. This has led to an unfair reputation as distant and cold. A few G.I. JOEs, like Sparks, see past this veneer and connect with Recondo due to their shared love of literature. Recondo is extremely well read, devouring books of all genres.

During his lengthy stints of service in Sierra Gordo, Recondo grew to deeply admire the indigenous people known as the Tucaros. He found inspiration in their simplified society, complex morals, and respect for the land. The Tucaros reciprocated this respect by inviting Recondo into their most sacred and cherished of ceremonies. He is the only known white man to have been assimilated into their culture.

RED STAR
(Oktober Guard Officer)

DATA FILE
ACCESS GRANTED

File Name: *Anatoly Fyodorovich Krimov*
Specialties: *Commando operations; naval infantry*
Birthplace: *Odessa, Ukraine*
Grade: *Captain*

The collapse of the Soviet Union resulted in the thawing of Cold War tensions between G.I. JOE and their Russian equivalent, the Oktober Guard. After the death of longtime team leader Colonel Brekhov, Captain Krimov was promoted from service in the Black Sea Regiment of the Soviet Naval Infantry to command of the Guard. A strategic visionary with a brilliant intellect, Krimov was the youngest chess master in Odessa at age 11, and is a published scholar on the Russian poet Alexander Pushkin.

Colonel Brekhov, right, and the Oktober Guard

GENERAL REY
(Field Commander)

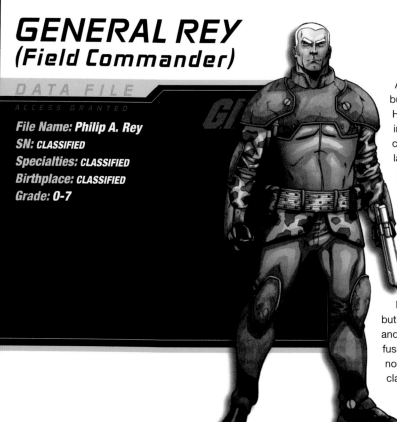

DATA FILE
ACCESS GRANTED

File Name: *Philip A. Rey*
SN: *CLASSIFIED*
Specialties: *CLASSIFIED*
Birthplace: *CLASSIFIED*
Grade: *O-7*

An organization like G.I. JOE is expected to have its secrets, but none is as shocking as the history of General Philip Rey. He emerged from seemingly nowhere to become an exceedingly effective field commander, but suspicious G.I. JOEs could find no records of Rey prior to this assignment. It was later revealed that Rey was one of the dozen original clones produced by COBRA during the development of Serpentor. Dr. Mindbender altered Rey's growth patterns and features so his connection to the COBRA Emperor would not be visibly apparent. COBRA hypnotist Crystal Ball helped construct Rey's psyche and implant in him a trigger that would activate this, the most insidious of sleeper agents. Zandar, Zartan's brother, facilitated the insertion of this genetically engineered super-soldier, sold to unscrupulous US military generals.

It was a plot that took years of meticulous planning to unfurl, but something unexpected happened. Rey's years of service, and his time with G.I. JOE, instilled in him a moral core that refused to betray his countrymen, despite deeply implanted hypnotic triggers. Rey shook off COBRA control. His past remains classified, known only to a handful of G.I. JOEs.

ROCK 'N ROLL
(Machine Gunner)

DATA FILE
ACCESS GRANTED

959-13-CM53

File Name: Craig S. McConnel
SN: 959-13-CM53
Primary Military Specialty: Infantry
Secondary Military Specialty: PT instructor
Birthplace: Malibu, California
Grade: E-7

The original G.I. JOE machine gunner, Rock 'N Roll could have easily drifted into a life of irresponsible leisure, of being a surfing beach bum whose only passions were weight lifting and playing guitar. When he was young, however, he witnessed a US Army Ranger save the life of his friend after a surfing mishap, and the event made a profound impression on McConnel. Though he still retains many of the trappings of his youth, he balances these with a devotion to civic duty and military service.

Rock 'N Roll's infectious fun-loving attitude led to an immediate and long-lasting friendship with Clutch. The two G.I. JOEs are inseparable, taking legendary road trips across the nation together during R&R leaves that made the most of their time away from active duty. The two see themselves as irrepressible lady-killers never willing to settle down, serving as each other's wingmen on the singles playing field. This friendship translates into an effective and dependable partnership when on military assignments.

SCI-FI
(Directed-Energy Expert)

DATA FILE
ACCESS GRANTED

793-2919-SF29

File Name: Seymour P. Fine
SN: 793-2919-SF29
Specialties: Infantry; electronics; laser
    weapons systems operator; starfighter
    pilot
Birthplace: Geraldine, Montana
Grade: E-4

Sci-Fi is a methodical perfectionist with endless patience. These are essential attributes for a laser rifle trooper, who must often hold still to target a pencil-thin beam across distances of two or more miles. So rock-solid is his stance, birds have been known to perch on him. Sci-Fi took a leave of absence to complete his master's degree in electrical engineering, returning with the skill set necessary to enact unparalleled enhancements to the security systems in G.I. JOE headquarters. As part of the Star Brigade aeronautical group, Sci-Fi lived up to his code name by becoming the designated pilot for the G.I. JOE starfighter.

SHORT-FUZE
(Mortar Soldier)

File Name: Eric W. Freistadt
SN: 380-22-EW32
Specialties: Artillery; infantry engineer
Birthplace: Chicago, Illinois
Grade: E-4

A volatile mix of contradictions, Short-Fuze is a logic-driven man who finds relaxation in abstract mathematics and can plot azimuths and triangulations in his head. However, when confronted with illogic, his temper frays and he blows his stack. Short-Fuze is the third generation of Freistadts in the service, though he nearly washed out of Ranger School. Eric was caught during the escape and evasion part of his training, but refused to give his captors anything beyond name, rank, and serial number even after a full week as a prisoner. This impressed the brass, particularly Hawk, who enlisted him in G.I. JOE.

SPARKS
(OPS Specialist)

File Name: Alessandro D. Verdi
SN: 101-07-0573
Primary Military Specialty: Operations manager
Secondary Military Specialty: Interpreter
Other Military Specialties: Telecommunications;
**   cryptologic operations; electronic warfare**
Birthplace: Carcare, Italy
Grade: SP-6

Though many of G.I. JOE's activities are classified top secret, they nonetheless create a mountain of paperwork and records that must be filed according to the stringent protocols of military bureaucracy. Handling this thankless task is Sparks, an avowed pacifist but essential cog in G.I. JOE operations. Sparks is not technically a G.I. JOE, but instead serves as the team's liaison to the Pentagon. Sparks was on hand during the short-listing of the original G.I. JOE recruits, helping Generals Flagg and Austin research the records of the most promising candidates.

Sparks is the son of a former US ambassador to Italy. He spent his formative years in Europe, learning many languages as well as the finer points of diplomacy. After graduating from Harvard, he hoped to become an interpreter for the military. He is fluent in 13 languages and the author of 15 bestselling books.

STEELER
(Tank Commander)

DATA FILE

ACCESS GRANTED

File Name: Ralph W. Pulaski
SN: 035-38-RW98
Specialties: Armor; artillery;
transportation
Birthplace: Pittsburgh, Pennsylvania
Grade: E-5

035-38-RW98

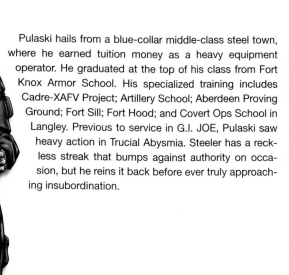

Pulaski hails from a blue-collar middle-class steel town, where he earned tuition money as a heavy equipment operator. He graduated at the top of his class from Fort Knox Armor School. His specialized training includes Cadre-XAFV Project; Artillery School; Aberdeen Proving Ground; Fort Sill; Fort Hood; and Covert Ops School in Langley. Previous to service in G.I. JOE, Pulaski saw heavy action in Trucial Abysmia. Steeler has a reckless streak that bumps against authority on occasion, but he reins it back before ever truly approaching insubordination.

TORPEDO
(SEAL)

DATA FILE

ACCESS GRANTED

File Name: Edward W. Leialoha
SN: 946-77-EL09
Specialties: Navy SEAL; underwater
demolitions; diving instructor
Birthplace: Aiea, Hawaii
Grade: CW-4 (chief warrant officer 4)

946-77-EL09

A strict vegetarian who treats his body as a temple, Torpedo is an expert diver and a master of Wu-Shu, Kenpo, Go Ju Ryu, and the balisong butterfly knife. He spends his off hours honing his physical perfection, a no-nonsense dedication that causes his teammates to think him a cold fish. He can swim underwater up to 100 yards without scuba gear and can carry half his weight in explosives. Torpedo was the first Navy SEAL in the G.I. JOE ranks and lives up to his reputation as the toughest of the tough.

TRIPWIRE
(Mine Detector)

File Name: *Tormod S. Skoog*
SN: *892-39-TS92*
Specialties: *EOD; demolitions*
Birthplace: *Hibbing, Minnesota*
Grade: *SP-4*

With the bewildering name his career military father gave him, young Tormod was destined to never quite fit in. High school was a bust, and time spent in a Zen monastery resulted in even the monks losing their temper with his clumsiness. Then the army—specifically, its grenade range—opened up a new world for Torm. He found that working with explosives, a hairbreadth away from disintegration, grounded and centered him. It's the only time he's not jittery or nervous.

WET-SUIT
(SEAL)

File Name: *Brian M. Forrest*
SN: *842-5647-LS11*
Primary Military Specialty: *Navy SEAL*
Secondary Military Specialty: *UDT (underwater demolitions)*
Birthplace: *Myrtle Beach, South Carolina*
Grade: *E-6*

It sometimes seems that Wet-Suit and Leatherneck are determined to single-handedly keep alive the tradition of long-standing rivalries between branches of service in the US military. It's a volatile mix: Wet-Suit is one of the meanest, toughest, and nastiest of the Navy SEALs, and the same can be said of Leatherneck of the USMC. Their confrontations and verbal blowups are the stuff of mess-hall legends, yet despite their constant snipes and low blows, the two are the closest that each has to a friend.

Very smart and a fast thinker, Wet-Suit is well read in both the classics and military tactics. His fierce demeanor is offset by a surprisingly tender home life. It seems that Wet-Suit channels all his energy to his sworn duty of protecting freedom as embodied in the peaceful life his wife and child enjoy.

ZAP
(Ground Artillery Soldier)

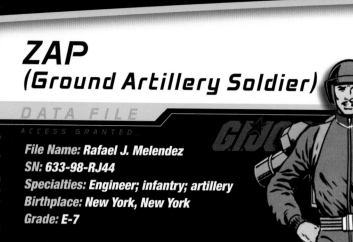

DATA FILE
ACCESS GRANTED

633-98-RJ44

File Name: Rafael J. Melendez
SN: 633-98-RJ44
Specialties: Engineer; infantry; artillery
Birthplace: New York, New York
Grade: E-7

Rafael Melendez's churchgoing parents instilled in their children the value of giving back to their community. After completing his engineering studies at MIT, Rafael chose to join the military. He graduated from Engineering School, Ordnance School, and Advanced Infantry Training before becoming the G.I. JOE team's original armor-piercing and anti-tank weapons specialist. He concentrated on demolitions later in his career, earning a reputation for being cool under fire—and a wire away from a bone-scattering explosion. Zap has most recently been involved in the training of new recruits.

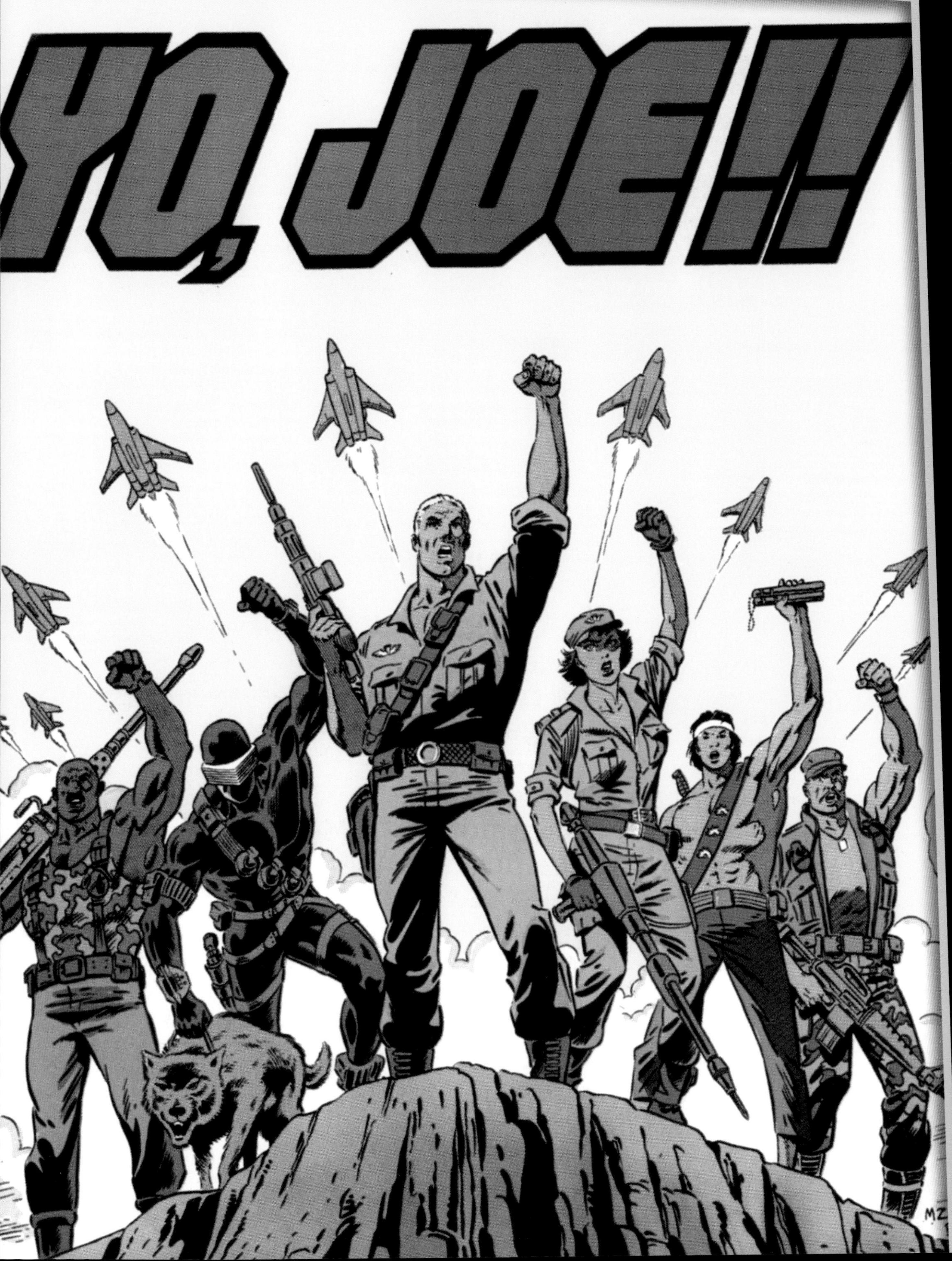
YO, JOE!!

G.I. JOE (AND ALLIES) PERSONNEL ROSTER

ACE (Brad J. Armbruster)
- Specialties: Fixed-wing pilot (single and multiple engine); intelligence ops; ordnance officer; battle copter pilot

ACTION MAN (CLASSIFIED)
- Specialties: International counter-espionage; hand-to-hand combat

AGENT FACES (CLASSIFIED)
- Specialties: Intelligence; language instructor

AIRBORNE (Franklin F. Talltree)
- Specialties: Airborne infantryman; helicopter gunship gunner

AIRBORNE (Robert M. Six)
- Specialties: Sky Patrol parachute assembler; battlefield medic

AIRTIGHT (Kurt Schnurr)
- Specialties: CBR (chemical, biological, and radiological warfare); hazardous substance control; ordnance

AIRWAVE (Cliff V. Mewett)
- Specialties: Sky Patrol audible frequency specialist; Signal Corps adjutant for Joint Chiefs of Staff (JCS)

ALPINE (Albert M. Pine)
- Specialties: Mountain trooper; finance clerk

ALTITUDE (John-Edward O. Jones)
- Specialties: Sky Patrol recon scout; combat artist

AMBUSH (Aaron McMahon)
- Specialties: Concealment specialist; infantry

ARMADILLO (Philo R. Makepeace)
- Specialties: Armored assault vehicle driver; advanced reconnaissance

AUSTIN, GENERAL AARON B. "IRON-BUTT"
- Specialties: Command

AVALANCHE (Ian M. Costello)
- Specialties: Armored vehicle driver; cold-weather survival driver

BACKBLAST (Edward J. Menninger)
- Specialties: Air Defense artillery; Signal Corps

BACKSTOP (Robert A. Levin)
- Specialties: Armor; mechanized infantry

BANZAI (Robert J. Travalino)
- Specialties: First-strike commando; nunchaku instructor

BARBECUE (Gabriel A. Kelly)
- Specialties: Firefighter; infantry

BARREL ROLL (Dwight E. Stall)
- Specialties: Marksmanship instructor; fixed-wing aircraft pilot

BARRICADE (Philip M. Holsinger)
- Specialties: Bunker buster; urban warfare; armored vehicle driver

BAZOOKA (David L. Katzenbogen)
- Specialties: Armor-defeating weapons systems; armored vehicle driver

BEACHHEAD (Wayne R. Sneeden)
- Specialties: Infantry; small-arms armorer; armored vehicle driver; special operations weapons sergeant

BIG BEAR (Grigori Ivanovich Rostoff)
- Specialties: Oktober Guard air assault; anti-armor

BIG BEN (David J. Bennett)
- Specialties: SAS infantry; subversive operations

BIG BRAWLER (Brian K. Mullholland)
- Specialties: Counterintelligence; espionage; jungle survival expert

BIG LOB (Clinton D. Sanders)
- Specialties: Infantry; PT instructor

BLASTER (Brian R. Davis)
- Specialties: Ground-effect vehicle operator; microwave technician

BLAST-OFF (Jeffrey D. Thompson)
- Specialties: Flamethrower; firefighter

BLIZZARD (Gregory M. Natale)
- Specialties: Arctic warfare training instructor; infantry

BLOCKER (David B. McCarthy)
- Specialties: Mechanized recon; special services

BLOWTORCH (Timothy P. Hanrahan)
- Specialties: Infantry special weapons; small-arms armorer; combat engineer

BOMBSTRIKE (Alyssa Renee Stall)
- Specialties: Forward air control; counterintelligence

BREAKER (Alvin R. Kibbey)
- Specialties: Infantry; radio telecommunications; computer technology

BREKHOV, COLONEL IVAN NIKOLEVICH
- Specialties: Oktober Guard command and strategy; infantry

BUDO (Kyle A. Jesso)
- Specialties: Martial artist; infantry; hand-to-hand combat instructor

BULLETPROOF (Earl S. Morris)
- Specialties: DEF leader; Battle Corps leader; federal marshal

BULLHORN (Stephen A. Ferreira)
- Specialties: Tactical intervention specialist; armor; motor transport operator

BUSHIDO (Lloyd S. Goldfine)
- Specialties: Ninja Force cold-weather specialist; strategist

CANNONBALL (John Warden)
- Specialties: Transportation; infantry

CAPTAIN GRID-IRON (Terrence Lydon)
- Specialties: Hand-to-hand combat specialties; infantry

CHAMELEON (CLASSIFIED)
- Specialties: Infiltration; intelligence; computer technologies

CHARBROIL (Carl G. Shannon)
- Specialties: Flame weapons specialist; small-arms armorer

CHECKPOINT (Jared Wade)
- Specialties: Military Police; carpenter

CHUCKLES (Philip M. Provost)
- Specialties: Criminal Investigations Division; intelligence

CLAYMORE (John Zullo)
- Specialties: Antiterrorist specialist; martial arts

CLEAN-SWEEP (Daniel W. Price)
- Specialties: Chemical operations specialist; combat engineer

CLOUDBURST (Chuck Ram)
- Specialties: Aeronautics; infantry

CLUTCH (Lance J. Steinberg)
- Specialties: Transportation engineer; infantry

COLD FRONT (Charles Donahue)
- Specialties: Armored vehicle driver; fire control technician

COLONEL COURAGE (Cliff V. Mewett)
- Specialties: Administrative strategist; armored vehicle driver

COOL BREEZE (Elijah F. Green)
- Specialties: Reconnaissance; infantry

COUNTDOWN (David D. Dubosky)
- Specialties: Astronaut/fighter pilot; electronics engineer

COVER GIRL (Courtney A. Krieger)
- Specialties: Counterintelligence; armor; AFV mechanics; recruitment

CRANKCASE (Elwood G. Indiana)
- Specialties: Motor vehicle driver; armor

CRAZYLEGS (David O. Thomas)
- Specialties: Infantry; parachute rigger

CROSS-COUNTRY (Robert M. Blais)
- Specialties: Armor; heavy equipment operator

CROSSFIRE (Bill White)
- Specialties: Heavy weapons operator; demolitions

CROSS HAIR (Don G. Fardie)
- Specialties: Infantry; marksmanship instructor

CUTTER (Skip A. Stone)
- Specialties: Hovercraft captain; special services; vehicle operations specialist; Coast Guard officer

DAEMON (Jeff M. Lacefield)
- Specialties: Information technology; electronic countermeasures

DART (Jimmy Tall Elk)
- Specialties: Recon; infantry; refrigeration repair technician

D-DAY (David D. Brewl)
- Specialties: Heavy artillery; hand-to-hand combat

DEE-JAY (Thomas R. Rossi III)
- Specialties: Radio telecommunications; infantry

DEEP SIX (Malcolm R. Willoughby)
- Specialties: Diver; small craft pilot; underwater demolitions instructor

DEPTH CHARGE (Nick H. Langdon)
- Specialties: Underwater demolitions; bandsman (glockenspiel)

DESERT WOLF (Lance M. Mitchner)
- Specialties: Combat and reconnaissance; desert survival

DIAL-TONE (Jack S. Morelli)
- Specialties: Radio telecommunications; infantry

DOC (Carl W. Greer)
- Specialties: Medical doctor; chaplain's assistant

DOC (Carla P. Greer)
- Specialties: Medical corps officer; chaplain's assistant

DODGER (Richard Renwick)
- Specialties: Armored vehicle maintenance; electronics maintenance

DOGFIGHT (James R. King)
- Specialties: Mudfighter pilot; electronics technician

DOJO (Michael P. Russo)
- Specialties: Ninja Force martial arts weapons specialist; Kung-Fu instructor

DOUBLE BLAST (Charles L. Griffith)
- Specialties: Heavy machine gunner; electrical engineer

DOWNTOWN (Thomas P. Riley)
- Specialties: Mortar soldier; infantry; special operations

DRAGONSKY (Andrei Freisov)
- Specialties: Oktober Guard incendiary weapons; armored vehicle specialist

DROP ZONE (Samuel C. Delisi)
- Specialties: Sky Patrol weapons specialist; Special Forces adviser

DUKE (Conrad S. Hauser)
- Specialties: Airborne infantryman; military intelligence; Ranger; Star Brigade battle commander; artillery; small-arms armorer

DUSTY (Jeffrey Paquette)
- Specialties: Infantry; equipment maintenance

DUSTY (Ronald W. Tadur)
- Specialties: Infantry; refrigeration and air-conditioning

DYNAMITE (Hector J. Garrido)
- Specialties: Demolitions expert

EFFECTS (Aron Beck)
- Specialties: Explosives/munitions ordnance; special effects coordinator/deceptive warfare

FALCON (Vincent R. Falcone)
- Specialties: Infantry; medic

FAST DRAW (Eliot Brown)
- Specialties: Ordnance; clerk typist

FIREWALL (Michelle LaChance)
- Specialties: Information technology

FLAGG, GENERAL JAMES LONG-STREET
- Specialties: Chief strategic command

FLAGG, GENERAL LAWRENCE J.
- Specialties: Command

FLASH (Anthony S. Gambello)
- Specialties: Infantry; electronics CBR

FLINT (Dashiell R. Faireborn)
- Specialties: Infantry; helicopter pilot; demolitions; paratrooper operations; commando; LAV operator

FOOTLOOSE (Andrew D. Meyers)
- Specialties: Infantry; special services

FREE FALL (Philip W. Ardnt)
- Specialties: Paratrooper; Infantry

FRIDGE, THE (William Perry)
- Specialties: Physical training instructor; special services

FROSTBITE (Farley S. Seward)
- Specialties: Motor vehicle driver; armor

GEARS (Joseph A. Morrone)
- Specialties: Chief engineer, Star Brigade special projects; research and development

G.I. JANE (Jane Ann Martelle-Colton)
- Specialties: Particle physics; combat medic

G.I. JOE (Joseph B. Colton)
- Specialties: Executive officer; combat infantry—training and intelligence

GHOSTRIDER (Jonas Jeffries)
- Specialties: Stealth fighter pilot; aeronautical engineer

GLENDA (Jane Mullighan)
- Specialties: Test pilot; intelligence

GORKY, LIEUTENANT MIKHAIL P.
- Specialties: Oktober Guard naval commando; infantry

GRAND SLAM (James J. Barney)
- Specialties: Artillery; electronic engineer; jet pack trooper

GRILL (Darren K. Filbert)
- Specialties: Infantry

GRUNT (Robert W. Graves)
- Specialties: Infantry; small-arms attack specialist; artillery coordinator; glider pilot

GUNG-HO (Ettienne R. LaFitte)
- Specialties: Recondo instructor; jungle warfare training instructor; reconnaissance; battle wagon driver; anti-armor; bio-military expert (Mega Marines)

HARDBALL (Wilmer S. Duggleby)
- Specialties: Infantry; special services

HARD DRIVE (Martin A. Pidel)
- Specialties: Combat computer technology; special services

HARDTOP (Nicholas D. Klas)
- Specialties: Heavy equipment operator; electronics

HAWK (Clayton M. Abernathy)
- Specialties: Strategic command operations; artillery; radar; Star Brigade Armor Bot command

HEADBANGER (Kevin M. Kaye)
- Specialties: Infantry

HEAVY DUTY (Herschel Dalton)
- Specialties: Heavy ordnance; laser weapons systems operator; indirect fire infantryman; tank commander

HEAVY METAL (Sherman R. Guderian)
- Specialties: Armor; finance

HIT & RUN (Brent Scott)
- Specialties: Infantry; mountaineering

HI-TECH (David P. Lewinski)
- Specialties: Armament research and design; telecommunications

HOLLINGSWORTH, GENERAL SAMUEL J.
- Specialties: Command

HOLLOW POINT (Max V. Corey)
- Specialties: Marksmanship instructor; helicopter recon

HORROR SHOW (Stepan Drukersky)
- Specialties: Oktober Guard anti-armor; infantry

HOT SEAT (Michael A. Provost)
- Specialties: Raider driver; drill instructor

ICEBERG (Clifton L. Nash)
- Specialties: Infantry; cold-weather survival instructor

ICE CREAM SOLDIER (Tom-Henry Ragan)
- Specialties: Fire operations expert; barbecue chef

INFERNO (Sean L. Brownson)
- Specialties: Firefighter

JINX (Kimi Arashikage)
- Specialties: Intelligence; finance clerk; covert operations; hand-to-hand combat instructor

KAMAKURA (Sean M. Collins)
- Specialties: Infantry; intelligence

KEEL-HAUL (Everett P. Colby)
- Specialties: Command; pilot

KNOCKDOWN (Blaine M. Gonsalves)
Specialties: Infantry; microwave technician

KWINN (Jesse Kwinn)
- Specialties: Freelance special ops enforcer; tracker

LADY JAYE (Alison R. Hart-Burnett)
- Specialties: Intelligence; personnel clerk; armament repair

LAW (Christopher M. Lavigne)
Specialties: Military Police; intelligence; security tactics

LEATHERNECK (Wendell A. Metzger)
Specialties: Infantry; drill sergeant; vehicle driver; marine force recon

LEDGER, ADMIRAL WARREN D.
Specialties: Naval officer; nautical ops

LIEUTENANT STONE (Cederic D. Stone)
Specialties: Pilot; intelligence; covert ops

LIFELINE (Edwin C. Steen)
Specialties: Medic; rescue operations; X-ray technician

LIFELINE (Greg Scott)
Specialties: Medic; rescue operations

LIFT-TICKET (Victor W. Sikorski)
Specialties: Rotary-wing aircraft pilot; fixed-wing aircraft pilot

LIGHTFOOT (Cory R. Owens)
Specialties: Demolitions; artillery coordinator

LOCKDOWN (Peter J. Handley)
Specialties: Police weapons and tactics; law enforcement

LONG ARM (Thomas P. Mangiaratti)
Specialties: Initial attack; offensive tactician; bomb disposal robotic systems operator; EOD

LONG RANGE (Karl W. Fritz)
Specialties: Thunderclap driver; artillery

LONG RANGE (Alejandro Garcia)
Specialties: Transportation; infantry

LOW-LIGHT (Cooper G. MacBride)
Specialties: Infantry; marksmanship instructor; night spotter

MACE (Thomas S. Bowman)
Specialties: Undercover surveillance; intelligence

MAINFRAME (Blaine L. Parker)
Specialties: Computer technology; infantry

MAJOR ALTITUDE (Robert D. Owens)
Specialties: Battle copter pilot; fuselage art designer

MAJOR BARRAGE (David Vennemeyer)
Specialties: Artillery; physical fitness instructor

MAJOR STORM (Robert G. Swanson)
Specialties: Mobile headquarters commander; long-range artillery officer

MANGLER (Michael S. Hickey)
Specialties: Infantry

MARINER (David O. Adcox)
Specialties: Nautical ops

MAVERICK (Thomas P. Kiley)
Specialties: Pilot

MAYDAY (Paige I. Adams)
Specialties: Sharpshooter; urban warfare

MED ALERT (Kirk Bacus)
Specialties: Medic; Tai Chi Chuan instructor

MERCER (Felix P. Stratton)
Specialties: Small-arms armorer; explosives

MIRAGE (Joseph R. Balkun)
Specialties: Rocket-fire assault; heavy artillery

MOUSE (Morris L. Sanderson)
Specialties: Infantry

MUSKRAT (Ross A. Williams)
Specialties: Infantry; social services

MUTT (Stanley G. Perlmutter)
Specialties: Dog handler; infantry; animal control/utilization technician; covert ops specialist

NUNCHUK (Ralph Badducci)
Specialties: Self-defense instructor; ordnance

OUTBACK (Stuart R. Selkirk)
Specialties: Infantry; survival training instructor

OZONE (David P. Kunitz)
Specialties: Environmental health specialist; chemical laboratory specialist; aeronautical ops

PATHFINDER (Willian V. Iannotti)
Specialties: Jungle assault specialist; forward observer; recon

PAYLOAD (Mark Morgan Jr.)
Specialties: Astronaut; fixed-wing pilot

PSYCHE-OUT (Kenneth D. Rich)
Specialties: Psy-ops; social services counselor

QUICK KICK (MacArthur S. Ito)
Specialties: Infantry; intelligence

RAMPAGE (Walter A. McDaniel)
Specialties: Infantry; vehicle driver; counterintelligence

RAMPART (Dwayne A. Felix)
Specialties: Shoreline defender; Air Defense artillery missile specialist

RAPID FIRE (Robbie London)
Specialties: Fast attack; sabotage

RECOIL (Joseph Felton)
Specialties: Infantry; radio telecommunications

RECONDO (Daniel M. LeClaire)
Specialties: Infantry; intelligence

RED DOG (David Taputapu)
Specialties: Infantry

RED SPOT (Michael P. Ritchie)
Specialties: Laser weapons systems operator

RED STAR (Anatoly Fyodorovich Krimov)
Specialties: Oktober Guard commando operations; naval infantry

RED ZONE (Luke Ellison)
Specialties: Steel Brigade urban warfare; rotary-wing pilot

REPEATER (Jeffrey R. Therien)
Specialties: Infantry; heavy weapons

REY, GENERAL PHILIP A.
Specialties: CLASSIFIED

RIPCORD (Wallace A. Weems)
Specialties: Airborne infantry; demolitions

ROADBLOCK (Marvin F. Hinton)
Specialties: Infantry heavy weapons; cook

ROBO-JOE (Greg D. Scott)
Specialties: Information technology; technology ops

ROCK 'N ROLL (Craig S. McConnel)
Specialties: Infantry; PT instructor

ROLLBAR (Robert D. Dubé)
Specialties: Assault vehicle driver; mechanic

ROOK (Andy Lombardi)
Specialties: Lie detection; Steel Brigade interpreter

RUMBLER (Earl-Bob Swilley)
Specialties: Fast-attack vehicle driver; small-arms armorer

SALVO (David K. Hasle)
Specialties: Anti-armor trooper; weapons repair technician

SCANNER (Scott E. Sturgis)
Specialties: Information technology

SCARLETT (Shana M. O'Hara)
Specialties: Counterintelligence

SCI-FI (Seymour P. Fine)
Specialties: Infantry; electronics; laser weapons systems operator; starfighter pilot

SCOOP (Leonard Michaels)
Specialties: Journalist; microwave transmission specialist

SGT. BOULDER (Greg M. Donahue)
Specialties: Mountain climbing; reconnaissance

SGT. HACKER (Jesse E. Jordan)
Specialties: Computer technology; radio telecommunications

SGT. SAVAGE (Robert S. Savage)
Specialties: Combat mission leader; infantry

SHARPE, COLONEL DEXTER
Specialties: Command

SHIPWRECK (Hector X. Delgado)
Specialties: Gunner's mate; machinist

SHOCKWAVE (Jason A. Faria)
Specialties: Special weapons and tactics; Military Police officer; choir

SHOOTER (Jodie F. Craig)
Specialties: Infantry; chaplain's assistant

SHORT-FUZE (Eric W. Freistadt)
Specialties: Artillery; infantry engineer

SHRAGE (CLASSIFIED)
Specialties: Oktober Guard infantry; battle technician

SIDE TRACK (Sean C. McLaughlin)
- Specialties: Wilderness survival specialist; demolitions expert

SIDETRACK (John Boyce)
- Specialties: Infantry; medic; interpreter

SKIDMARK (Cyril Colombani)
- Specialties: Fast-attack vehicle driver; infantry

SKYDIVE (Felix N. Lynton)
- Specialties: Sky Patrol leader; personnel administration

SKYMATE (Daniel T. Toner)
- Specialties: Glider trooper; infantry

SKYSTRIKER (Alexander P. Russo)
- Specialties: Tiger Rat pilot; combat technician

SLIP-STREAM (Gregory B. Boyajian)
- Specialties: Fighter pilot; computer technology

SNAKE-EYES (CLASSIFIED)
- Specialties: Infantry; hand-to-hand combat instructor

SNEAK PEEK (Anthony Bueke)
- Specialties: Infantry

SNEAK PEEK (Owen King)
- Specialties: Infantry; radio telecommunications

SNOW JOB (Harlan W. Moore)
- Specialties: Arctic ski patrol; rifle instructor

SNOW STORM (Guillermo "Willie" Suarez)
- Specialties: Arctic warfare; cold-weather survival instructor

SPACE SHOT (George A. Roberts)
- Specialties: Astronaut; combat operations engineer

SPARKS (Alessandro D. Verdi)
- Specialties: Operations manager; interpreter; telecommunications; cryptologic operations; electronic warfare

SPEARHEAD (Peter R. Millman)
- Specialties: Infantry; finance

SPIRIT (Charlie Iron-Knife)
- Specialties: Infantry; social services

STALKER (Lonzo R. Wilkinson)
- Specialties: Infantry; medic; interpreter; EOD

STARDUSTER (Edward J. Skylar)
- Specialties: Infantry transportable air recon; helicopter assault

STATIC LINE (Wallace J. Badducci)
- Specialties: Sky Patrol demolitions expert; aircraft maintenance

STEAM ROLLER (Averill B. Whitcomb)
- Specialties: Heavy equipment operator; armor

STEEL BRIGADE COMMANDER (CLASSIFIED)
- Specialties: Counterintelligence; helicopter pilot

STEELER (Ralph W. Pulaski)
- Specialties: Armor; artillery; transportation

STORMAVIK (CLASSIFIED)
- Specialties: Oktober Guard airborne forces; infantry

STORM SHADOW (Thomas S. Arashikage)
- Specialties: Covert operations; sabotage; demolitions

STRETCHER (Thomas J. Larivee)
- Specialties: Medical specialist; troop transportation

SUB-ZERO (Mark Habershaw)
- Specialties: Winter operations specialist; field artillery

SUPER TROOPER (Joe DeNiro)
- Specialties: Infantry; covert operations

SUPER TROOPER (Paul Latimer)
- Specialties: Infantry; public relations

SURE FIRE (David S. Lane)
- Specialties: Criminal Investigation Division; telecommunications

SWITCH GEARS (Jerome T. Jivoin)
- Specialties: Armored vehicle driver; intelligence field operative

TALBOT, DR. LINCOLN B.
- Specialties: Veterinarian; scientist; special operations

TANK (Dwight M. Prudence)
- Specialties: Infantry

TAURUS (Varujan Ayvazyan)
- Specialties: Demolitions

TEIKO (Teiko Sasaki)
- Specialties: Martial arts

T'GIN-ZU (Joseph R. Pamore)
- Specialties: Vehicle operator; sword master

THUNDER (Matthew Harris Breckinridge)
- Specialties: Artillery; bandsman (drummer)

THUNDERWING (Spencer D. Crecelius)
- Specialties: Armor; heavy equipment operator

TIGER CLAW (Chad M. Johnson)
- Specialties: Infantry; ninja weapons instructor

T'JBANG (Sam LaQuale)
- Specialties: Martial arts swordsman; infantry

TOLLBOOTH (Chuck X. Goren)
- Specialties: Combat engineer; transportation

TOPSIDE (John Blanchet)
- Specialties: Navy assault seaman; telecommunications specialist

TORPEDO (Edward W. Leialoha)
- Specialties: Navy SEAL; underwater demolitions; diving instructor

TRACKER (Christopher R. Green)
- Specialties: Navy SEAL; underwater arms developer

TRAKKER, SPECIALIST MATT
- Specialties: MASK vehicle designer; advanced technology

TRIPWIRE (Tormod S. Skoog)
- Specialties: Explosive ordnance disposal; demolitions

TUNNEL RAT (Nicky Lee)
- Specialties: EOD; combat engineer

UPDRAFT (Matthew W. Smithers)
- Specialties: Retaliator pilot; weapons systems officer

VORONA (Daina L. Janak)
- Specialties: Oktober Guard small-arms specialist; helicopter pilot; marksman; infantry

WET DOWN (Daniel R. Alexander)
- Specialist: Covert naval operations; martial arts instructor

WET-SUIT (Brian M. Forrest)
- Specialties: Navy SEAL; UDT

WHITEOUT (Leonard J. Lee III)
- Specialties: Arctic Ski Patrol; communications

WIDE SCOPE (Larry M. Kranseler)
- Specialties: Infantry; negotiations

WILD BILL (William S. Hardy)
- Specialties: Helicopter pilot; fixed-wing pilot; aircraft armorer; air cavalry scout; tank driver

WILDCARD (Eric U. Scott)
- Specialties: Armored vehicle operator; chaplain's assistant

WINDCHILL (Jim Steel)
- Specialties: Armored vehicle driver; cold-weather survival instructor

WINDMILL (Edward J. Roth)
- Specialties: Stopped-rotor aircraft operator; attack helicopter pilot

WRECKAGE (Dillon L. Moreno)
- Specialties: Demolitions; jungle warfare instructor

ZAP (Rafael J. Melendez)
- Specialties: Engineer; infantry; artillery

ZUBENKOV, SERGEANT MISHA
- Specialties: Oktober Guard artillery; infantry

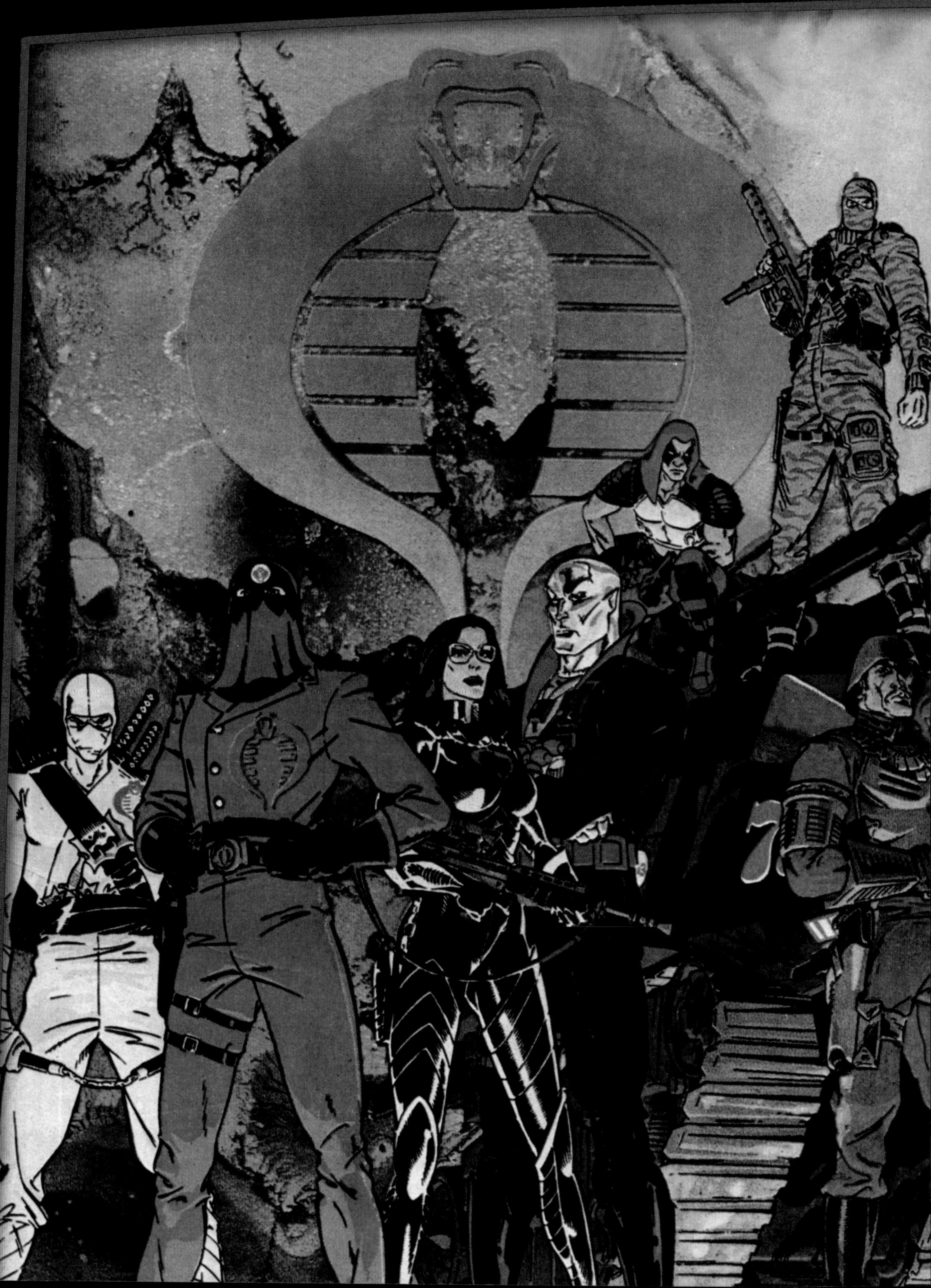

CHAPTER 2
THREAT FORCES

BARONESS
(COBRA Intelligence)

DATA FILE

File Name: **Anastasia Cisarovna**
Aliases: **Anastasia DeCobray; Coverta Fatale; Ana Lewis; Anna von Stromberg**
Specialties: **Intelligence; disguise; fixed-wing pilot**
Qualified Expert: **M-16; AK-47; RPG7; Uzi; H.I.S.S. tank**

The aristocratic Cisarovna family was known throughout Europe for its philanthropy. The young, spoiled Anastasia was afforded any luxury in the world. She greatly admired her elder brother Eugen, who cared nothing for such material trappings but instead carried out what charity he could, distributing food and medical supplies to the third world and nations racked by war. Fifteen-year-old Ana accompanied Eugen on one such humanitarian mission to a war-torn nation. Eugen was gunned down in cold blood by thieving murderers, a tragic death that shattered Anastasia's faith in humanity. She forever changed that day, turning her life down a cold, dark path quite counter to the world her parents had hoped to build.

I promise you will regret this day. You will look back on it with gnashing teeth, and then you will die.
—Baroness

In boarding schools in Prague and elsewhere in Eastern Europe, Anastasia turned to student radicalism to sow discontent and discord. She soon graduated from placards and pamphlets to improvised explosives and arson. Violent radicals sought her out for her family fortune, but later learned she was an effective operative on the ground as well. She demonstrated a callous disregard for innocent life and uncanny skills at disguise and deception that put her very much in demand among criminal operatives. Absconding with what was left of the family fortune, she buried her name and went by a host of aliases, finally settling on the Baroness. It was under this name that she was brought into COBRA, bringing with her capital and European connections that helped grow COBRA from an American underground operation into an international organization.

■ A New Face

Such global scope allowed Cobra Commander to bring Destro and his M.A.R.S. Industries into the fold, but he was dismayed to discover that the Baroness and Destro already had some past association. Recognizing that the Baroness's loyalties were split between the Commander and Destro, the enemy leader sought to eliminate the weapons supplier as a potential threat. To that end, he hired mercenary Major Bludd to eliminate Destro in the thick of battle, but the Baroness saw the plan unfurl. Desperate to save her beloved, she drove her H.I.S.S. tank into a nearby truck to throw off Bludd's shot. Her ploy succeeded, but she was trapped in the wrecked H.I.S.S. when a gas tank explosion engulfed her in flames. The Baroness suffered third-degree burns over her body and was plunged into a deep coma. Ironically, it was Bludd who saved her, absconding with the unconscious Baroness and taking her to an advanced surgical clinic in Switzerland.

Under the ministrations of Dr. Hundtkinder, the Baroness underwent extensive reconstructive surgery. She emerged far more beautiful than before. The ravishing femme fatale then rejoined COBRA. She continued to be a key player in the COBRA command structure, despite the sniping rivalries of the terrorist organization's upper echelons. When Cobra Commander was replaced by Fred Broca VII, a Crimson Guard imposter, it was up to the Baroness to vouch for his identity—she was one of the few COBRAs who could indentify the Commander without his mask. The Baroness lied, confirming that Fred was indeed the Commander, all the while manipulating the inexperienced leader from behind the scenes.

When Destro departed from the COBRA ranks, he would return to take the Baroness with him. The two retired from active involvement in COBRA for a time, but before long their fates were wrapped up with the continued machinations of the real Cobra Commander, who had returned to retake his rightful position as head of COBRA.

CHAMELEON

For a time after the Baroness's incapacitation in the H.I.S.S. fire, an independent agent code-named Chameleon infiltrated the ranks of COBRA posing as the Baroness. The illegitimate half sister of Anastasia Cisarovna, this woman was the adopted daughter of French revolutionaries. She bribed Hundtkinder to reconstruct her face to match the Baroness's new look, and led a kidnap mission to capture the Baroness. Who Chameleon was working for, and whatever became of her, remains unknown.

■ Motherhood

Years later, the Baroness and Destro secretly wed, and she became pregnant with his child. In such a vulnerable state, she receded from the front lines and remained protected within the armored fortresses of Cobra Island. When Destro tried to transport her to safety within a Night Raven, he watched in horror as Cobra Commander detonated an explosive aboard the plane, destroying it and seemingly killing the Baroness and her unborn child. In truth, the Baroness had avoided the explosion in an escape craft, and ended up in US custody.

She was secretly held deep within the G.I. JOE headquarters facility code-named the Rock. She had given birth to a son, Eugen, who was taken from her. She demanded to know the whereabouts of her child, but the few G.I. JOEs aware of her presence were using her infant child as leverage against her to discover intel against COBRA. She refused to divulge anything; she did not want the first lesson her son to witness to be one of surrender.

Baby Eugen was taken to a hospital in Lincoln, Nebraska, whose whereabouts were uncovered by Cobra Commander. He dispatched an elite team of COBRA agents to kidnap the child. The Baroness later escaped G.I. JOE custody and made it her quest to find Eugen. Nothing could stop her. She tortured and gunned down COBRA operatives in her search. She would eventually find her son in the custody of Cobra Commander, who returned Eugen to his parents in return for control of M.A.R.S. Industries.

ATHENA

Though Anastasia took great pains to keep her Cisarovna roots hidden under such aliases as DeCobray, she still maintained some of her family's trappings. She secretly transformed the Cisarovna family guard into a private army code-named Athena. She kept this unit separate from Destro's Iron Grenadiers even after she wed McCullen.

B.A.T.S
(Battle Android Troopers)

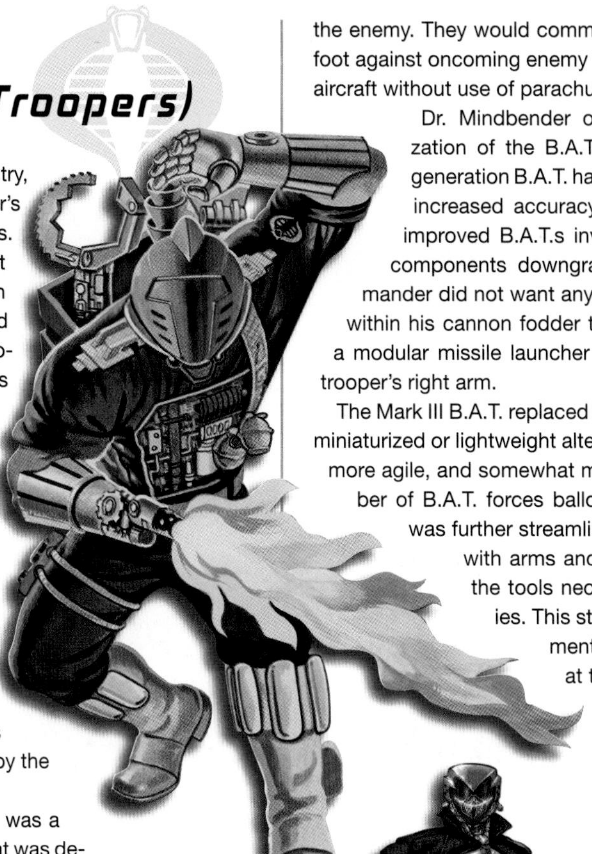

■ The soul-less legions of robotic infantry, the B.A.T.s are, to Cobra Commander's skewed ways of thinking, perfect soldiers. Continuous innovation and refinement have made their creation comparable in expense to the training, equipping, and care of live troops—but with B.A.T.s, Cobra Commander is assured of mindless loyalty and fearless obedience. They are tireless servants, willing to sacrifice themselves to achieve their preprogrammed objectives.

Cobra Commander overlooks their manifold shortcomings. A B.A.T.'s ability to distinguish between friend and foe can be overwhelmed in the thick of changing battlefield conditions. This tendency for a B.A.T. to continue pumping destructive fire ahead of itself regardless of who crosses its line of fire has made them despised by the organic troops in COBRA Command.

The first-generation prototype B.A.T. was a much larger, hulking humanoid figure that was deliberately left behind at a COBRA facility for capture by G.I. JOE. The robot was transported to G.I. JOE headquarters in fragments. Security scans of the pieces revealed them to be electromagnetically inert, so the G.I. JOEs mistakenly believed the automaton to be dead. But a chemical timer built into the robot's right hand activated it remotely, and the animated manipulator then began reactivating the rest of the components; in effect, the robot reassembled itself. Its objective was to achieve radio contact with the rest of COBRA Command and thus reveal the location of G.I. JOE headquarters. The vigilant G.I. JOEs, however, were able to destroy the robot's various independent components before it could clamber its way into broadcast range.

The next prototypes were cheaply produced remote-controlled humanoid robots intended primarily for training exercises. A cache of these automata and similarly robot-controlled H.I.S.S. tanks were discovered near Zartan's swamp compound in the Florida Everglades.

The first mainline production-series B.A.T. was developed by Dr. Mindbender. These models had exposed electronics in their chest cavity to allow for ease of battlefield maintenance, though such visible wiring and componentry did present a tempting target for enemy fire. There was no single critical system left open to the elements, so while the G.I. JOEs would whittle away at the center of the B.A.T.'s mass, the B.A.T. would continue clawing its way toward its objectives.

These B.A.T.s had a humanoid form covered in combat fatigues to keep dirt and water out of the servomechanisms that animated them. The right forearm had a swappable weapons carriage, which could be equipped with a flame projector, laser cannon, gripper claw, or standard robotic hand. B.A.T. power cells could be recharged through a common household electrical outlet.

Cobra Commander and his officers deployed the B.A.T. troops to the battlefield in perverse ways designed specifically to demoralize the enemy. They would command the B.A.T. troopers to charge on foot against oncoming enemy vehicles or drop them from low-flying aircraft without use of parachutes.

Dr. Mindbender oversaw modifications and customization of the B.A.T. infantry over the years. The next-generation B.A.T. had a more streamlined appearance and increased accuracy to its targeting sensors. Curiously, improved B.A.T.s invariably had their logic and memory components downgraded. This is because Cobra Commander did not want anything approaching individual initiative within his cannon fodder troops. This model of B.A.T. featured a modular missile launcher system that could be affixed to the trooper's right arm.

The Mark III B.A.T. replaced some of the heavier components with miniaturized or lightweight alternatives, making these models faster, more agile, and somewhat more vulnerable to damage. The number of B.A.T. forces ballooned as the manufacturing process was further streamlined. Once the B.A.T.s were equipped with arms and logic centers, they were then given the tools necessary to build the rest of their bodies. This stepped up the pace of B.A.T. development, with additional subseries appearing at this point with only a casual regard to nomenclature protocol.

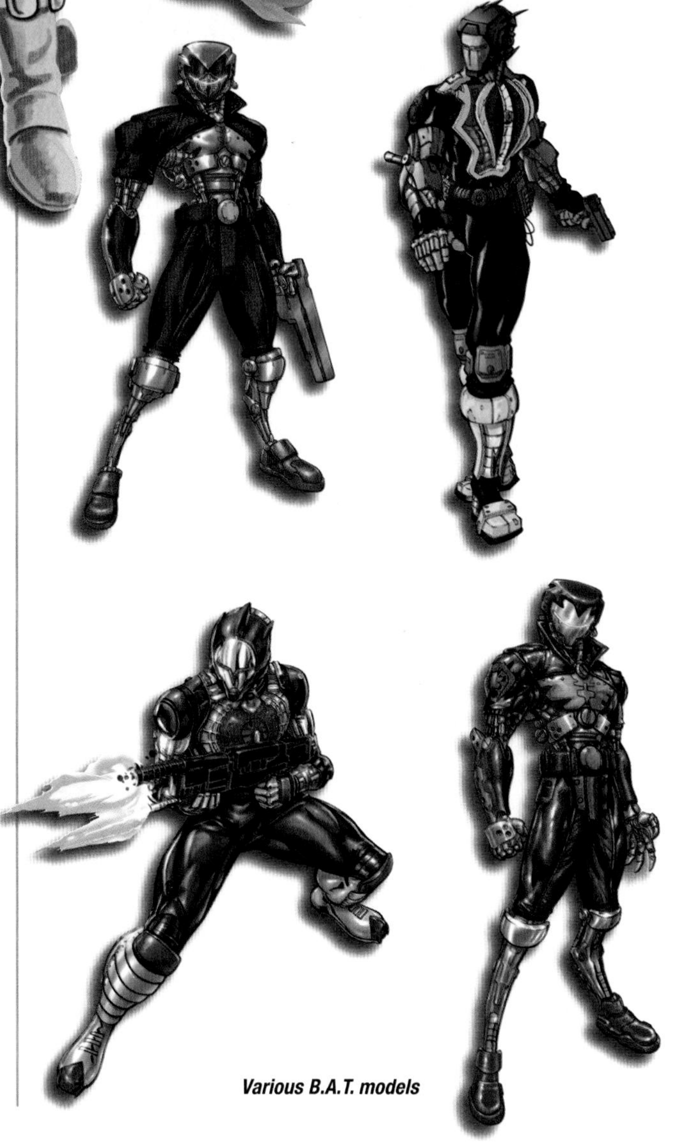

Various B.A.T. models

COBRA COMMANDER AND COBRA
(COBRA Supreme Leader)

DATA FILE

File Name: CLASSIFIED

Specialties: Intelligence; ordnance;
  experimental weaponry

Birth Place: CLASSIFIED

Rank: Commander in Chief of COBRA
  forces

He has been branded the most dangerous man alive. His past remains shrouded in mystery and conflicting accounts that make it difficult to discern his true origins. The most despicable and deadly of homegrown terrorists to arise from American soil, Cobra Commander transformed his boundless ambitions and a militia of similarly disaffected countrymen into a worldwide terrorist organization. By merging cutting-edge technology and venomous ideology, he has made COBRA a threat that has overshadowed all others, necessitating the elevation of G.I. JOE from a small, top-secret team of special operatives to a world-renowned military force to be reckoned with. Though the G.I. JOE mission statement describes its purpose as countering any and all threats to human freedom, it's commonly accepted that it exists to fight COBRA. The struggle between G.I. JOE and COBRA is a silent war that has played out around the globe for years, erupting into public consciousness when Cobra Commander's most diabolical plots threaten millions. Until Cobra Commander's campaigns of global domination are brought to an end, G.I. JOE will be there.

I, Cobra Commander, have seen fit to bring the blessing of COBRA domination to your pathetic little run-down municipality! We are going to bring you a new prosperity! New jobs, new industry, new commerce! All this, coupled with an end to crime and immorality! Of course, this will mean curtailing a few insignificant personal freedoms that you won't even miss much!

—Cobra Commander

■ Dangerously destabilized, Cobra Commander's persona runs the gamut from fiendishly charismatic to terrifyingly sociopathic. He brandishes a strange form of charm that can twist intentions and morals so that his rhetoric actually reads as plausible and relatable to his minions. When things run counter to his plans, though, he erupts with a shrieking temper that can frighten even the most hardened soldiers. Failure means spilled blood, and Cobra Commander ensures loyalty by instilling fear in his underlings, making highly visible examples of those who disappoint him. Among the core of COBRA Command, the august leader is equally admired and despised. The upper echelon of COBRA is indeed a nest of vipers, requiring an overseer as ruthless as the Commander to keep them in line.

Fairness and *honor* are but mere euphemisms for "weakness" and "cowardice" to Cobra Commander. He has adapted his message and aims to fit the times and nature of his recruitment efforts. Cobra Commander lures the young, angry, and downtrodden with promises of empowerment and stirring words about seizing fate and destiny. In truth, he cares little for the troops that make up the Viper ranks. They are but the disposable means to his glorious ends. It is little wonder that when the technology became available, he embraced the notion of a fully mechanical infantry. To Cobra Commander, his android troopers are the ideal, for he trusts no man. He knows firsthand what treachery the human heart is capable of, for he is the paragon of deception and betrayal.

Psychoanalysts who have remotely studied Cobra Commander's case files describe him as an ingenious hustler and junk-bond salesman with visions of grandeur. This makes him all the more dangerous. Most dictators and would-be Napoleon types are hampered by the need to pretend they are pursuing a noble and just cause. Cobra Commander doesn't have that problem. He is in it for the money and power, and believes he can achieve both by uprooting the existing power structures across the globe. Cobra Commander hopes to fray the fabric of society, using terrorism, social tyranny, and economic slavery as his pathway toward standing high atop the ruins of a world he views as too imperfect to continue.

■ Possible and Tragic Origins

The man who would be Cobra Commander once did play by the rules. He was a used-car salesman attempting to make a life for himself in order to raise a family, as per the American dream. He wanted no handouts or favors, just a day's pay for a day's work. What he found instead was a bureaucratic morass that frowned upon the advancement of the "little guy." It was an impenetrable system built on cronyism and corruption, where corporate greed and government complicity coiled together to choke the life out of the everyman. As the debts piled up, and his marriage strained under such burdens, the man looked for someone to blame. He saw no idols, no sterling examples to follow.

The only person this man respected was his older brother Dan, who exemplified the ideal of selfless sacrifice only to find cruel

his brother. Truly, he believed, this survivor would share and empathize with the man's increasingly skewed worldview. The survivor was an army veteran who went by the nickname of Snake-Eyes. Alone in the world, Snake-Eyes had become an aimless, suicidal drifter. The salesman turned Snake-Eyes's life around.

Keeping their shared history a secret, he befriended Snake-Eyes, recruiting him on a wave of vigilantism meant to bring back power and purpose to the everyday citizen. Targeting destitute neighborhoods, Snake-Eyes and his newfound partner spent months kicking over rocks and chasing out the vermin that hid underneath. Slumlords, drug dealers, and other social parasites were their targets, and with Robin Hood–like flair the man and Snake-Eyes would turn illicit profits back to the neighborhoods. But the man wasn't doing this altruistically; he was *buying* the loyalty of the rescued. The man cynically saw how easy it was to gain followers when the cash was flowing. He saw how the worst parts of human nature were the easiest to exploit.

Snake-Eyes eventually grew wary of the salesman's methods. Their differences came to a head when the man finally revealed the connection of fate that tied the two of them together. Their last "errand" saw them break into Judge Mitchell Tate's home and surprise the sleeping magistrate at gunpoint. The man revealed that it was his brother, Dan, who had died in that fateful car accident, driven to that low ebb by Tate's verdict. Tate, reasoned the man, was the thread that tied their destinies together, and was a symptom of a sickened justice system that crushed the working man. The man sought to deliver a cure, and offered Snake-Eyes the first chance to kill the helpless judge. Snake-Eyes refused, so he carried out the deed himself, firing a single shot that killed Tate. The salesman swore vengeance on Snake-Eyes as they parted ways. That vengeance would wait, for the man was just at the start of building his empire.

Slithering Fronts

I won't stop with Springfield. I won't stop until my organization coils around the whole world like a giant cobra.
—Cobra Commander

Cobra Commander had the will, but he still needed to amass the way—the financial means to make his vision of restructuring societal order a reality. No longer restricted by scruples, he used his natural charm and persuasiveness to hoodwink investors as he traveled across America, carefully covering his tracks so the bilked would not

abandonment. Dan was a soldier who served his country overseas. When he returned home, Dan was unfortunately cast aside by a system not prepared to treat its veterans with the respect they deserved. Nonetheless, Dan sought to give back, opening a halfway house for vets seeking guidance through the murk of bankruptcy, divorce, and unemployment that awaited them stateside. Dan went into deep debt keeping the place running, and the bank stood poised to seize the property after one too many missed payments. The place accidentally burned down, but the bank branded Dan as a culprit looking to escape his financial responsibility. The dispute went to court, and a strict judge, Mitchell Tate, sided with the creditors, handing down a sentence that financially ruined Dan. This hardship drove Dan to drink. On a cold February night, while driving under the influence, Dan was killed in a head-on car collision that also wiped out the family of three in the other vehicle.

Dan's death was the weightiest of the tragedies piled upon his brother. Pressured by ruinous circumstance, the man underwent a transformation. While driving in a car from his repossessed lot, he nearly hit an upwardly mobile professional crossing the street. This stranger erupted in a spout of anger against him, claiming that his shoes alone were probably of greater worth than the man and his car. The salesman snapped. He emerged from his vehicle and forced the pedestrian into an alley. With his life's every unfair blow and disadvantage weighing on his mind, the salesman killed the pedestrian.

He took a life. He made an indelible impact. He enacted change with his bare, newly bloodied hands. It was easy, far easier than succeeding on the terms dictated by society. Those who had succeeded in a corrupt system must have realized similar epiphanies. From that day forth, he abandoned the precepts of society and sought to make his own fate. He would be a victim no longer.

Vigilante Justice

Estranged from his wife for a time, the man sought out the sole surviving member of the family killed in the same collision that took be able to locate him once they saw through his false promises. His travels landed him in Springfield, a small planned community of tract housing in the Appalachian highlands. As an outsider with a lot of money, he was welcomed, despite his outlandish and fiery ideas. The townsfolk accepted his radical concepts because he appealed to their greed, offering a quick solution during troubled economic times.

Backed with the profits of several Ponzi schemes, he formed Arbco, a front company to accrue even more wealth by selling cleaning supplies, beauty products, and magazine subscriptions in pyramid schemes. Burgeoning information technologies allowed Arbco to sell across the nation, and more and more money poured into Springfield. It became a gated community, with privatized security and essential services. No one outside Springfield suspected what was happening behind closed doors at community centers, police stations, or fire halls.

Well-informed on national affairs, Cobra Commander had seen radical movements fail before. Too often they took the forms of misguided backwoods militias, easily quelled by law enforcement when they became troublesome. He instead patterned COBRA to be far more insidious. Rather than reject society through isolation, Cobra Commander found a way to weave his threads into the American tapestry. The Crimson Guardsmen ranks were instrumental in this effort, beginning as a twist on American upward mobility. Cobra Commander even subverted the cloying image of the nuclear family to be the front for the suburban professional CGs, COBRA's most destabilizing corps.

The cash flow allowed international networking, and Cobra Commander's vision and persuasive ways drew the attention of foreign investors. Baroness Anastasia Cisarovna, a wealthy European noble, was drawn to the movement and adopted the alias of Anastasia De-Cobray. Soon COBRA money was bankrolling private armies in third-

world nations. Their business fronts allowed for legitimate real estate purchases, corporate takeovers, and capital investments. Cobra Commander targeted countries with shaky leadership and overthrew governments, installing despots loyal to COBRA. He personally led uprisings in the Middle East, Southeast Asia, and other trouble spots around the world. When M.A.R.S. Industries became COBRA's primary weapons supplier, the organization turned into an undeniable global threat.

> *War is an extension of politics and politics is an extension of economics. If the government says that an honest man can't work as much as he wants to and earn as much as he wants to—it's wrong. And we have a right to fight back if we want to.*
> —Cobra Commander

■ Mission Report: The Birth of Cobra Island

One of Cobra Commander's most ambitious plots resulted in his terrorist organization being granted legitimacy on the world stage.

Masterminded by the Crimson Guardsman Professor Appel, the plot began with a fortified COBRA bunker on the ocean floor of the Gulf of Mexico. Equipped with ultrasonic transmission gear, the bunker began broadcasting signals that killed aquatic life in the region. With the future of the lucrative fishing industry at stake, G.I. JOE needed to respond quickly. The bunker could only be cracked with thousands of tons of conventional explosives—the destructive equivalent of a small tactical nuke, but without the radioactive fallout. The resulting titanic blast triggered an aggravation of a fault line, pushing an entire section of the gulf floor above sea level.

COBRA had created a new landmass within the Gulf of Mexico, well beyond the three-mile limit of any neighboring state. Crimson Guardsmen lawyers in Washington, DC, New York City, Mexico City, and Havana pounced, pushing their paperwork through and buying Cobra Island sovereignty. The nascent landmass was recognized as a nation with COBRA as its legal government.

■ Family Ties

When founding his organization, Cobra Commander left his wife and took custody of his young son, taking him to Springfield. With little time for him, Cobra Commander left young Billy to be raised by the COBRA Youth Brigade. Billy did not fully realize the scope of what his father was up to. The child grew to reject the notion that the hooded man leading hateful rallies was his father. The boy tried to run away from Springfield but was caught by COBRA security. He then fell in with a resistance

movement in underground Springfield, and was ultimately recruited by the scheming Baroness and Major Bludd to serve as an assassin. The two elder COBRAs planned to have Billy pose as a Cobra Youth who, during a ceremony, would pull a gun on the Commander and shoot him. The conspirators did not know the true connection between Billy and Cobra Commander—a connection revealed by Destro, who put a stop to the attempted patricide.

Later, Billy was taken in by the rogue ninja Storm Shadow and underwent extensive martial arts training. He sustained grievous injuries in a car accident, resulting in the loss of a leg and eye.

THE CLOTHES MAKE THE MAN

In the earliest days of COBRA rallies in Springfield, Cobra Commander was simply a man in a business suit, albeit one who also wore a cowl over his head. The simple blue mask had two eyeholes and bore a COBRA sigil on its forehead. As COBRA expanded, and the Commander grew comfortable in his role as military leader, his uniform became more ornate, with gilded sashes and epaulets. A more practical version was a double-breasted suit with a charged backpack in which he carried an experimental laser pistol.

As Cobra Commander became the target of more dangerous enemies, he supplemented his cowl with a chrome-faced battle helmet. The armored mask hid any eyeholes behind a mirrored finish, and contained a small port to allow him to drink through a straw. The helmet was lined with plastic explosives keyed to a coded locking mechanism. If anyone attempted to remove the mask without the proper authorization, the resulting explosion would kill both the Commander and the assaulter. This helmet also was equipped with short-range radio receivers built into the earpieces.

Later, the best technical minds from M.A.R.S. forged a special suit of body armor that combined flexible bulletproof polymer fabrics with beryllium steel plate components. The incredibly expensive battle armor—which reportedly cost as much as a jet fighter—was air-conditioned, solvent-resistant, and ray-shielded. The helmet was fitted with an integral commo-system, internal readouts for environmental quality, and a miniaturized computer display. The armored plates could withstand a direct hit from a heavy machine gun, while the flex parts could stop a .357 magnum.

These systems were later miniaturized and streamlined by Dr. Mindbender to become a powered bodysuit that could fit beneath more traditional garb. The advanced motive systems increased the Commander's reflexes and strength, granting him the ability to hold his own in hand-to-hand combat, even against highly trained ninjas such as Snake-Eyes.

Cobra Commander discovered an ailing Billy recovering under the care of one of his Crimson Guardsmen, Fred Broca VII, in Denver. Perhaps reminded of his brother's fate, the Commander was overcome by regret and his failure as a father. For a time, it appeared the Commander was ready to hang up his cowl for good and turn over a new leaf. But Fred, who had devoted his life to COBRA, grew incensed and shot the wavering Commander in the back. Thinking him dead, Fred buried Cobra Commander. Billy awoke from his coma and went on to assist the G.I. JOE team.

■ Imposter Under the Hood

Fred Broca VII assumed the role of the Commander, taking advantage of the secrecy afforded by Cobra Commander's anonymity. Only a small handful of COBRA agents had ever seen him unmasked. Among that select cadre was the Baroness, who saw through Fred's deception but viewed it as an opportunity to pull the strings of COBRA with the inexperienced Fred as her puppet. Fred grew in the role, making a series of strategic decisions that were a mix of blunders and fortuitous windfalls. In the Cobra Civil War, Fred challenged the Emperor Serpentor for supremacy over COBRA, a mismanaged military campaign that ultimately proved victorious when Serpentor was assassinated.

Fred's stint as leader would come to an end when the real Cobra Commander surfaced years later. The gunshot clearly had not killed the COBRA leader. He was rescued from a shallow grave by loyal Crimson Guardsmen, who rehabilitated him. He then clawed his way back to the top just as he had when he founded COBRA: through greed, cunning, and deception. The sting of betrayal reminded him of what had set him on this path so many years ago, and he forgot the momentary compassion he had felt toward his son. He would describe it as an irrational decision that had resulted in him getting shot. He would not make that mistake again.

■ The Endless Snake

Like the fabled snake that would eat its tail and perpetually grow, Cobra Commander and his plots seemed endless. Though he was thwarted time and again, he would shed his skin and resurface. A joint military effort so effectively scattered COBRA that it resulted in the temporary decommissioning of G.I. JOE—the Pentagon mistakenly believed the COBRA threat permanently neutralized. It was the rise of the Red Shadows that led to the most convincing defeat of Cobra Commander, and for a time many in the US military truly believed the terrorist leader to be dead.

Instead, it was far worse. Cobra Commander not only was alive but had slithered into the White House. Cobra Commander killed and replaced Garret Freedlowe as the US chief of staff, adopting his identity by using some of Zartan's masking technology. In this position of influence and authority, the Commander uncovered secrets of the G.I. JOE team. He nearly had the team replaced by an elite organization of his own design. This violation of the deepest levels of American security precipitated the largest, most diabolical operation Cobra Commander had ever mounted, an activation of COBRA sleeper cells worldwide that touched off trouble spots around the globe. It was a conflagration large enough to earn the label World War III, and it was all one man's vision.

■ Conflicting Intelligence: Cobra-La

A very different tale of COBRA origins is told within the classified incident reports filed concerning Cobra-La. These outlandish stories describe an ancient society hidden within the most inaccessible reaches of the Himalayas, a strange cult more than 40,000 years old that built technology not from inert machinery, but from living tissue. Cobra-La was sequestered in the mountains, witnessing the rise of man from afar since the Ice Age. Human civilization and its technological trappings were anathema to Cobra-La, and its leader, Golobulus, sought to put an end to it. He selected one of his most brilliant noblemen to spearhead a push to reclaim Cobra-La dominance. This man, disfigured in a laboratory accident, was to become Cobra Commander. But his repeated failures led Golobulus to cause the creation of Serpentor as his replacement. As punishment, Golobulus subjected Cobra Commander to mutation spores that devolved the former leader into a cobra. The Commander stayed trapped in this form for years until he was returned to humanoid form by shamanistic magical rituals.

■ COBRA Command

COBRA is a ruthless organization determined to extend the will of its leaders through military force, terrorism, social subversion, and economic pressures. COBRA has matured far beyond local militia forces to become a worldwide threat. The history of COBRA is kept purposely mercurial and obscured, to not only allow the organic growth of whispered legends as to its origins, but also to confound investigators trying to unravel COBRA from its roots. For example, conflicting yet baseless tales describe ancient mystical origins for COBRA, while others reveal it to be a Freemason-like secret society, the Cryptic Order of Benevolent Reptilian Apostates.

Through a bewildering array of front companies in the United States and abroad, COBRA has insinuated its way into the everyday life of many unsuspecting citizens. The COBRA model of growth fueled by greed, corruption, and insurgency has proven appallingly successful around the globe, and COBRA has secured footholds throughout the third world, giving its agents remarkable freedom of travel, resources, and haven. Its wealth grants it legitimacy and operational sway in the borderless arenas of multinational corporations.

The COBRA ranks are international, though a dismaying number of troopers are disaffected American militiamen who have turned against the laws of their nation. COBRA infantry is dominated by the ranks of the Vipers, multitudes of anonymous masked soldiers with ultramodern equipment. There exists a wide variety of specialized Vipers with gear and uniforms customized to their occupational focus.

By kidnapping, coercing, or outrightly buying the greatest scientific minds of the world, COBRA has acquired cutting-edge technology. Their ranks are bolstered by Battle Android Troopers—fully robotic soldiers that can suffer copious amounts of damage yet continue unabated. COBRA scientists have tampered with genetic and biological agents to produce vile toxic weapons and mutated soldiers that can no longer be labeled humans. COBRA has advanced aeronautical programs that can launch not only surveillance and armed satellites into orbit, but troops as well.

Much of the technological infrastructure comes to COBRA by means of M.A.R.S., the Military Armament Research Syndicate that is ostensibly a neutral party simply doing business with a wealthy client.

In truth, the interests of M.A.R.S.'s chairman, Destro, are inextricably linked with Cobra Commander's campaign of worldwide terror.

COBRA's headquarters are scattered and varied. Domestically, its founding headquarters was secreted within the gated town of Springfield, USA. COBRA later established similar hamlets on Broca Beach, New Jersey, and Millville, New York, as well as Delhi Hills, Ohio. Internationally, the organization had strategic headquarters in Trans-Carpathia, Borovia, Trucial Abysmia, Badhikstan, and of course its own sovereign nation of Cobra Island.

DATA FILE

FRONTS AND FEINTS

The following is a sampling of some of the known COBRA front operations, with notes about how COBRA uses them to cover their activities. This is but a partial list. The true extent of worldwide COBRA operations remains unknown.

Arbco Industries: A varied corporate conglomerate with subsidiaries that include health and beauty products, magazine publishing, and shipping and moving services. Arbco trucks help transport COBRA heavy armor and equipment around the nation.

Extensive Enterprises: A wealth management and investment firm that also includes legal counsel and intellectual property development. It is owned and operated by Tomax and Xamot, the leaders of the Crimson Guardsmen.

Swan Airlines: A legitimate passenger and freight carrier service that facilitates the international and domestic travel of COBRA agents.

Naja Hanna Video Corporation: A video game and electronics firm attached to the Naja Trading Corporation, which allows for worldwide distribution of secret technological components.

CRIMSON TWINS
TOMAX & XAMOT
(Crimson Guard Command)

DATA FILE

File Names: **CLASSIFIED**
Specialties: **Infiltration; espionage; sabotage; propaganda; corporate law**
Birthplace: **Ajaccio, Corsica**

The bond that connects the twin brothers Tomax and Xamot goes well beyond any comfortably explained by science. Since childhood, their connection could only be described as psychic. One twin would frequently be able to complete the other's sentences and thoughts. When one twin felt pain or distress, the other would echo similar feelings. In quiet moments of concentration—or sudden moments of surprise—one twin could even see out of the other's eyes, gaining fleeting images of the other's surroundings regardless of where they were. This asset also grew to be a vulnerability. One twin could be used against the other if captured or tortured. As such, Tomax and Xamot (assumed names) took great care never to separate far from each other. Each is the mirror image of the other, a biological reality enhanced by stylistic choices—they part their hair on opposite sides and wear mirrored asymmetrical clothing. The main distinguishing feature between the twins is a large scar on Xamot's face.

Both twins were discontented with the pace of life and dearth of opportunities that their parents made available to them, so to strike out into the world on their own, they joined the French Foreign Legion, serving as paratroopers in Algeria. Attracted by the double promise of conflict and gold, they became mercenaries in the bush wars of Africa and South America, serving as highly skilled operatives for very high price tags. Tiring of actually putting their necks on the line, and recognizing the inherent risk of physically dangerous operations while sharing a psychic connection, the twins eventually gravitated to more behind-the-scenes roles.

They channeled their cutthroat demeanors and two-faced charisma into the business world and became bankers in Zurich. Despite their wealth, they found the ins and outs of international finance too unpredictable and hard to control . . . at least, when playing by the rules of international law and regulatory oversight. They founded Extensive Enterprises, a multinational firm of diverse investments, to better launder their ill-gotten gains through scores of front companies and subsidiaries. It was their deep pockets that magnetically attracted the ambitious Cobra Commander, who invited the twins into the COBRA fold as leaders of the Crimson Guard.

■ The Crimson Guard

Though much has been said of Cobra Commander's nefarious plots involving chemical, biological, or advanced technological warfare, it is his Crimson Guardsmen that are possibly his most powerful and insidious weapon. They are highly trained and physically capable, but it is not in their role as traditional soldiers that

DATA FILE

EXTENSIVE ENTERPRISES

With Crimson Guard serving as the agents of legal and financial subversion, branches of Extensive Enterprises specialize in social operations. Among the EE subsidiaries are television production companies, publishing houses, and media distribution channels that pump out a steady stream of value-eroding propaganda disguised as pop-culture entertainment, all the while reaping enormous revenue. EE's intellectual property divisions have been gradually weakening the fiber of American culture by presenting an endless stream of polarizing rhetoric, tabloid journalism, bloviating cable news punditry, and mindless sitcoms and reality television meant to keep the citizenry from paying too much attention to the world beyond their diversions.

they prove the greatest danger. The real threat is that the Siegies (CGs) have insinuated themselves into everyday American lives, as bankers, stockholders, accountants, businessmen, and lawyers. The mover and shaker with the wireless headset constantly tapping away into a PDA may look respectable in his three-piece Italian suit, but he may also be concealing a red military suit in the deepest corner of his personal closet.

With the Crimson Guardsmen spreading their controlling tendrils throughout the business world, Cobra Commander effectively controls weapons of mass economic destruction. Siegie agents on Wall Street have been promulgating doctrines of greed and irresponsible lending practices for years, effectively pivoting the world economy to the brink of collapse. While COBRA Vipers and Snow Serpents may fight with steel and claw, the Crimson Guards can financially wipe out entire innocent communities with paper, law, and money. It should never be forgotten that it was Crimson Guardsmen lawyers who made it possible for COBRA—a world-renowned terrorist organization—to become a legitimate foreign state.

DESTRO
(Enemy Weapons Supplier)

DATA FILE

File Name: *James McCullen Destro XXIV*
Specialties: *Weapons manufacture;*
terrorism
Birthplace: *Callander, Scotland*

A man of seeming contradictions who follows his own quiet code, Destro is a fascinating foil to Cobra Commander's unabated megalomania. To call a terrorist like Destro honorable is a strain on the word, but compared with other nihilists who wish the world to burn, Destro exhibits respect for his enemies and for the engagement of war.

I see no shame in my profession. For most of history the right to bear a weapon was the only distinction between a free man and a slave.
—Destro

Destro hails from a long line of war profiteers. During the 17th century, James McCullen I was captured by enforcers of King Louis XIII of France for selling armaments to both the king and his enemies. As punishment, McCullen was incarcerated within the Bastille, and affixed with a searing-hot metal mask to make him a highly visible example. Or so the tale goes, which suggests that Destro's ancestor was the original man in the iron mask of legend.

The mist-shrouded banks of the River Teith in Scotland are home to many whispered legends of the McCullen clan, and many follow the same arc. Another tale says James McCullen was forced to wear the mask after being captured by Lord Cromwell's men for supplying arms to both sides in the English Civil War. Others posit that it was John McCullen in the 13th century who gained the ire of the English king for refusing to pay his taxes. Yet another tale credits suspicion of witchcraft for the gruesome fate that befell the McCullen ancestor. Destro allows the propagation of such conflicting tales, for they all share in common the central tenet that the McCullens will not be betrayed, prosecuted, or punished without consequence.

Destro sees war as inevitable and conflict as man's natural state. He has a Malthusian philosophy that war cleanses society of its deadweight, and shifts priorities from the trivial to the essential. War drives technology forward and is a catalyst for a better civilization.

To that end, the McCullens have found ways to develop a vast array of refined weaponry to reshape the modern battlefield. To Destro's thinking, war can and should be startlingly efficient, effective, and profitable. Unlike Cobra Commander, who places himself above all in his quest for world domination, Destro sees family as paramount. His bloodline has coursed through world history for generations, and he surrounds himself with trappings of history, including the silver mask he wears and the red medallion on his chest.

Should his family line or ancestry be targeted, Destro will not hold back in defending what is his or obliterating the offender.

■ Career with COBRA

As COBRA grew into international ventures, it drew the attention of McCullen. The organization soon became M.A.R.S. Industries' biggest client, drawing Destro into its coils. Cobra Commander demanded technological perfection and, at no small expense, hired Destro to become an on-staff adviser and part of the COBRA command chain. It was an incredibly profitable venture, structured in such a way to allow Destro to continue to hold the patents on technological innovations co-designed by COBRA. In this way, COBRA could kidnap scientists and engineers, and develop weapons systems, with complete disregard to ethics and law; M.A.R.S. would reap the benefits.

Within the COBRA ranks, Destro grew enamored with the Baroness, and the two developed a relationship that was, at first, veiled from the rest of COBRA rank and file before becoming more open. Cobra Commander grew suspicious of Destro's motives and focus. The Commander was more content with spineless lackeys and easily moldable underlings; Destro had too much initiative and too much independence for his tastes. That the Commander could no longer count on the primary loyalty of the Baroness, effectively one of the co-founders of COBRA, troubled him. Cobra Commander hired Major Bludd to assassinate Destro in the thick of battle, but such a move was thwarted by the Baroness.

After repeated internal conflict and disagreements, COBRA and Destro finally parted ways. Destro had made all the profit he required, and by this point Cobra Commander had scientific geniuses on his payroll; he did not need the M.A.R.S. think tank to fill his weapons stores. COBRA had entered the weapons market, supplying such technologies as their prefabricated Terror Dromes to third-world dictatorships and other trouble spots around the world. To collect his thoughts and rethink his direction, Destro retired from COBRA, returning to his ancestral lands in Callendar, Scotland.

■ Iron Independence

Castle Destro has stood near Loch Lomond since the 11th century, bordered by lands owned by Lord Malaprop. Destro maintained a private army with uniforms resembling the Scots Guard—an affectation of his grandfather, who fancied the kilts and glengarries. Despite its antiquated appearance, the castle was fitted with radar, infrared detectors, motion sensors, and passive listening devices, making it exceedingly difficult to infiltrate.

When Destro returned from COBRA, he discovered that an imposter had taken over the castle. With the help of Lady Jaye and Flint—who struck a temporary allegiance with Destro to secure intelligence on M.A.R.S. technology—McCullen reclaimed his title of laird, discovering that the imposter was Major Bludd.

Realizing that he would never truly be free of his past connections with COBRA, Destro concentrated on eliminating any vulnerabilities M.A.R.S. and his ancestral lands may have developed in his absence. He reorganized his private guard and did away with the archaic uniforms, replacing them with modern fighting equipment and gear. His soldiers were reforged as the Iron Grenadiers. Destro began applying his private weapons contracts to bolster his own army, developing unique weapons and vehicles such as the AGP, D.E.M.O.N. tanks, the Dominator tank/helicopter hybrid, and his own personal Despoiler flight craft. He supplemented his Grenadier ranks with Nullifier pilots, Annihilator elite troops, Ferret vehicle drivers, and T.A.R.G.A.T. aerial troopers. He hired lieutenants including General Voltar, Metal Head, and Darklon.

But Destro was not bent on world domination like COBRA. Instead, he used his forces to protect his markets from COBRA weapons programs and guard his lands from enemy incursions. Despite the high-tech trappings of his infantry, he retained numerous arcane traditions. Every Iron Grenadier was trained and equipped with a

sword. Also, teatime was a near-sacred custom. Even in the thick of battle, Destro would pull back troops from the front line and rotate them to ensure that the tradition of elevens was observed.

Destro tried to remain apart from the ongoing conflict between G.I. JOE and COBRA. During the heated COBRA Civil War, an Iron Grenadier army invaded the beaches of Cobra Island but did not fire a single shot. Their objective was simple: Secure the Baroness. With his beloved safely removed from COBRA, Destro attempted to retire with the Baroness, but inevitably they were dragged back into the intrigue.

M.A.R.S. INDUSTRIES

The result of more than 20 generations of McCullen family investments, M.A.R.S. is the modern incarnation of the clan's for-hire armorer ancestry. The Military Armament Research Syndicate is the world's leading private developer of weapons technology, with clients around the globe. It was founded in 1752 as a Naval Gun Foundry by the then-current James McCullen Destro. Well-guarded research labs in various nations allow M.A.R.S. to bypass regulations and oversight. In this manner, M.A.R.S. broke technological barriers far ahead of the next leading developers. Their product line has moved beyond machine guns and tanks, and now includes next-generation nano-scale technology, advanced robotics, directed-energy weapons, and force barrier defenses.

Some of M.A.R.S.'s past breakthroughs and prototypes include:

AGP (Anti-Gravity Pods): The power plant for this small, one-man flying vehicle effectively cracks the gravity barrier by isolating and implementing a form of energy that pushes against the pull of the planet. Destro incorporated the technology to propel this agile attack craft and its STUNG (silent-running titanium under-radar negative gravity) missiles.

Cloaking Technology: The ultimate in electronic countermeasures, this combination of holographic imagery and sensor shroud technology essentially renders a vessel—such as a Cobra Night Raven—invisible to both radar and the naked eye.

M.A.S.S. Device: Resembling an immense cannon with an industrially-forged gem tip, the experimental molecular assembly, scrambling, and sending array device can teleport matter—even living subjects—across huge distances. The matter transference field is fueled by three essential catalytic elements: radioactive crystals from the Sea of Ice, heavy water from the Ocean's depths, and meteorite fragment from the Ring of Fire.

Molecular Reducer/Enlarger: A decade of research went into this unpredictable device capable of expanding or contracting subatomic particle spacing to shrink or expand its targets.

Parasite Matrix: A complex energy-based net launched at enemy vehicles; upon enveloping its target, the netting bleeds all power from devices trapped within.

Suborbital Tractor Beam: An advanced harmonics transmission device that can disrupt the positioning of orbital satellites and drag them down from the heavens; in the hands of the terrorist Vance Wingfield, this device became a threat to the entire world.

Weather Dominator: A high-energy targetable device capable of disrupting weather patterns and creating dangerously inclement weather. It consisted of three primary components: the laser core, ion correlator, and hydromaster.

Wrist Rockets: An example of cutting-edge miniaturization, the small bracket of rockets that Destro wears on his wrist contain the type of guidance and flight systems typically found on full-scale ground-to-air missile systems. Carried aloft on compressed catalytic decomposition propellants, these rockets are capable of traversing hundreds of feet in seconds and pack enough punch to knock out a combat helicopter.

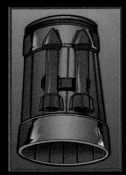

BEHIND THE MASK

Destro maintains a number of masks that symbolize his family lineage. In the most secure vaults, he even has the first mask applied by French torturers in the Bastille four hundred years ago.

Destro's first mask was made of polished beryllium with a hinged jaw to allow his mouth to move. This was replaced by one with a platinum-enriched finish, giving the mask a distinctive golden sheen. He later combined cutting-edge M.A.R.S. technology into both his mask and armor, giving him enormous advantages in one-on-one combat.

The current mask is made of a flexible metallic compound composed of intricately machined sections. A quarter mile of intricate circuitry lines the inner sections of the mask, powering such high-tech functions as enhanced optics with night-vision and infrared view modes. The mask's crown has a brainwave scanning function keyed specifically to Destro, and a voice sampler and modulator that can simulate any voice recorded into its memory.

■ Blood Ties

As important as family is to Destro, it has made him vulnerable—as proven by the rise of his illegitimate son, Alexander McCullen. Completely unknown to Destro until Alexander reached adulthood, the younger McCullen was the offspring of a single mother who lived in near poverty in the Midland Valley of Scotland. The result of a dalliance well below Destro's class, Alexander grew obsessed with his father when he discovered he was the heir to such a world-renowned aristocracy. Teamed with the ambitious Lilian Osborne, Alexander incapacitated Destro with stolen COBRA nano-mite technology and assumed his identity, returning to the COBRA hierarchy to usurp control of the organization from Cobra Commander.

The ersatz Destro then unleashed the nano-mite weaponry on the world in a bid to make a name for himself on the global stage and prove his worth to his father. But the undermining, scheming, and sheer undisciplined destructive swath cut by Alexander only disgusted Destro, who was cured of his nano-mite infection and resumed his identity.

Iron Grenadier

A man of integrity, Destro did not sweep Alexander under some rug of convenience but instead took responsibility for the misguided youth. He kept Alexander as a lieutenant of sorts, hoping to mold the man into a proper McCullen. But too often, Alexander displayed an impulsiveness that disappointed his father, especially when coerced into ill-advised ventures and power plays by his beloved Lilian, who had joined COBRA operations under the code name Mistress Armada.

Alexander's connection with his father was further eroded when Destro produced a legitimate heir with the Baroness. The Baroness seemingly died in an explosion, however, devastating Destro. The weapons baron adopted a much more dangerous, recklessly aggressive streak in his mourning, selling weaponry to such maniacal terrorists as Vance Wingfield. In truth, the Baroness lived, and she was eventually reunited with Destro. However, her son—Eugen McCullen—was kidnapped by Cobra Commander. With Eugen's life in his hands, Cobra Commander issued an unthinkable ultimatum: Turn over control of M.A.R.S. to COBRA in exchange for Eugen's life. This was Destro's Achilles' heel, and he could not deny Cobra Commander what he wanted.

Although the infant Eugen was reunited with his parents, the world became a far more dangerous place as Cobra Commander proliferated cutting-edge M.A.R.S. technology around the globe, exacerbating existing world conflicts and ushering in a wave of chaos that could only fittingly be described as World War III. Realizing his role in the devastation that followed, Destro allied with the G.I. JOE team to provide whatever advantage he could from his knowledge of M.A.R.S. weapons systems.

THE SILENT CASTLE

A long-standing point of contention between Destro and COBRA has been ownership of the Silent Castle. Destro originally built the impressive edifice for COBRA in the stark mountains of Trans-Carpathia. A single, winding road leads to the harsh, trapezoidal structure. With unknown technologies, Destro devised an intricate structural scheme that allowed the castle to transform into a secondary appearance, that of a re-creation of the Castle Destro from Scotland.

DR. MINDBENDER
(Master of Mind Control)

DATA FILE

File Name: Dr. Brian Binder (possible alias)
Other Aliases: Dr. Brainwave
Specialties: Genetic engineer;
interrogation; orthodontist
Birthplace: Unknown

Dr. Binder was an orthodontist who maintained a practice at the Broca Medical Complex in Springfield. Aside from the odd affectation of a monocle, Binder was a friendly, unremarkable man who hated the pain his work would often cause, particularly in his younger patients. Binder also happened to be an expert in brainwave electronics (it seems Dr. Venom, COBRA's first scientific genius, was also one of his patients, suggesting a possible intellectual connection). Binder explored radical techniques to cancel the neural signals that transmitted pain from the jaw to the brain. Knowing he couldn't experiment on his patients, Binder selflessly subjected himself to his helmet-like contraption. The device scrambled his brain, utterly transforming his personality. The meek, amiable orthodontist was changed into an unscrupulous, domineering mastermind.

All these people running around willy-nilly, having their own opinions and making up their own minds! It's hideously chaotic and totally unacceptable!
—Dr. Mindbender

dard practice to kidnap leading scientists and extort their services on pain of death. This led to staggered advances in COBRA technology. Mindbender's constant tinkering and development created a rapid series of startling innovations. Even Destro, whose engineers had been supplying COBRA with weaponry, was taken aback by Mindbender's contributions. It would eventually lead to Destro breaking ties with COBRA as the organization became more self-sufficient in weapons research and actively became a competitor to Destro's M.A.R.S. Industries.

Mindbender's projects included the development of mutant creeper plant spores, humanoid synthoid duplicates, Battle Android Troopers, and a revamped brainwave scanner device that allowed for the seamless implantation of false memories. His most challenging and astounding breakthrough was the ability to extract viable genetic material from long-dead bodily remains for the purposes of creating clone hybrids. This directly led to the creation of Serpentor, the COBRA Emperor that was the genetic amalgam of some of history's most effective military leaders. Mindbender's brainwave-guided mental programming supplied Serpentor with several lifetimes' worth of historical texts inside his synthetic brain, ensuring that the artificial man that emerged from Mindbender's cloning vat was truly the best-schooled military expert in existence.

Mindbender himself was no combatant. Though he kept in peak shape (the result of myoelectric muscle stimulant devices rather than any true physical discipline), he was a coward at heart. He preferred to send endless legions of B.A.T.s into combat rather than face danger himself. Where he ruled supreme was lording over a victim strapped to an interrogation chair. Mindbender twisted his original intentions as an orthodontist, and instead devised means of transmitting false pain signals to the brain without the need for actually injuring a patient. This would result in torturous sessions without any risk of the subject dying.

The brainwave device had a peculiar side effect. Binder's brain became a sponge, able to absorb and retain vast amounts of knowledge. The initial kernel of genius that had allowed him to build the device led to a process that expanded that genius. In a short time, Binder became an expert in advanced genetics, robotics, electronics, and more. Cobra Commander knew of Binder (he was the Commander's dentist), and witnessed the transformation and creation of a new scientific genius. Since his previous scientist, Venom, had died, the Commander recruited Binder to lead COBRA technological research. Binder accepted, adopting the colorful moniker of Dr. Mindbender.

The addition of Mindbender to the COBRA ranks had pronounced effects on the organization. In the past, COBRA had made it stan-

When Serpentor's unbridled ambition clashed with Cobra Commander's iron-fisted rule of Cobra Island, Mindbender loyally sided with his creation in the civil war that followed. The conflict ended when Serpentor was killed by an assassin, and Mindbender signed a truce with the Commander, but the damage to his perceived loyalty was done. In truth, the Cobra Commander of the civil war era was an imposter, but when the original Cobra Commander returned, he readily lumped Mindbender in with all the various traitors he found objectionable. In a cold-blooded housecleaning of his ranks, the Commander threw Mindbender along with several other offenders into a landlocked freighter, which he then trapped under a collapsed volcano on Cobra Island. Mindbender perished after being stranded for months, ultimately succumbing to food poisoning from eating botulism-contaminated food rations.

■ *Resurrection*

Life and death do not have their traditional starting points within the confines of Mindbender's advanced laboratories. During his brainwave experimentations, he made an exact digital duplicate of his brain, programmed to download its parameters into a cloned brain and body in the event of his demise. In this manner, Mindbender was re-created after his death in the freighter, emerging as an artificial duplicate. Mindbender began to biologically enhance his body, making him more formidable in combat than his pre-cloned self. He continued to serve Cobra Commander until COBRA was apparently disbanded after a joint US military effort scattered the core of its leadership from its entrenchment in Eastern Europe. Like Mindbender himself, however, COBRA refused to stay dead.

■ *The Clone Contingencies*

The process that resulted in Serpentor created a number of intriguing by-products, chief among them 11 preliminary clones. These clones served as biological test beds, to ensure that the final Emperor was as close to perfection as possible. These clones were not age-accelerated to adult maturity as the 12th one was, and instead remained children when Serpentor took command. Cobra Commander, fearful of the clones falling into the wrong hands, ordered them exterminated. Mindbender, though, secreted the clones, still in their nutrient vats, to a laboratory whose location on Cobra Island was known only to Mindbender himself.

Shortly after the creation of Serpentor, Mindbender continued to examine and refine the techniques that gave birth to the Emperor. He decanted one of the prototype clones and altered it sufficiently so its relation to Serpentor would not be so visibly apparent. He accelerated its growth process so that it, like Serpentor, would emerge as a grown man. After the death of Serpentor in the Cobra Island Civil War, Mindbender used a disguised Zandar to broker a deal with corrupt US generals for the transfer of the clone to US custody. The generals hoped that the clone would jumpstart a long-stalled American super-soldier program. This clone would emerge years later as a COBRA sleeper agent, General Philip Rey.

■ *The Return of Serpentor*

Mindbender returned to COBRA as the organization arose again. He soon was plagued with strange dreams and visions, the result of the original 10 clones of Serpentor being active. Mindbender possessed a psychic connection with these children, probably a side effect of him being reanimated through the same processes that gave them life. The children were taken into US custody after COBRA lost stewardship of their island nation, and secretly distributed to foster families by the Jugglers, who closely monitored their growth. A COBRA splinter group called the Coil resuscitated Mindbender's long-dormant cloning technology and created a new, 13th clone—a resurrected COBRA Emperor, the second coming of Serpentor.

Mindbender and the children were inexorably drawn to Cobra Island to be with their Emperor. The doctor managed to find one of the children, Hannibal, and accelerated his age to late adolescence. The fit and brilliant Hannibal then secured two more clones, Julius and Alexander. In short order, all 10 children were brought together, and Mindbender was once again loyally serving at Serpentor's side. Despite his burning visions of global conquest, Serpentor was defeated, and Mindbender attempted to flee Cobra Commander's wrath. The Commander wrested from Mindbender details about the Coil's failed plot to capture the secret weapon known as the Tempest, a cloud-seeding weather-dominating satellite. The Commander intended to use the device to spread the Death Angel virus across huge distances, resulting in the deaths of millions.

Cobra Commander needed Mindbender to activate the Tempest, but once the project was under way, he coldly shot Mindbender in the back to prevent further treachery. Mindbender lay dying on the laboratory floor, where he was found by G.I. JOE agents determined to stop the Tempest device. Mindbender's last act was to help the G.I. JOEs destroy the Tempest before he finally bled to death.

THE DREADNOKS
(Shock Troops)

The Dreadnoks are motorized mayhem, a rampaging motorcycle gang that has spread from the Outback of Australia and now has chapters throughout the United States. Its rise in power began when the Dreadnoks defeated and absorbed the rival Melbourne Maulers into their ranks. When Dreadnok leader Zartan offered his unique mercenary services to COBRA Command, he brought the Dreadnoks with him. At first, only a handful of the 'noks were allowed into COBRA's secret citadels. Over the years, more Dreadnoks were given clearance. The more traditional military-minded types—nobles like Destro and the Baroness—found the Dreadnoks barbaric and offensive. Cobra Commander tolerated their raucous nature, for they did deliver spectacular—if unpredictable—results. Dreadnok raids on air force bases or other military installations resulted in millions of dollars in destruction for the costs of keeping the Dreadnoks supplied with gasoline, grape soda, and chocolate donuts. It just made good business sense to keep them on COBRA payrolls.

The following are only some of the Dreadnoks whom G.I. JOE has faced in the past. The Dreadnok ranks are constantly in flux, due to the high attrition rate incurred by their hard-living, hard-fighting lifestyle.

BUZZER

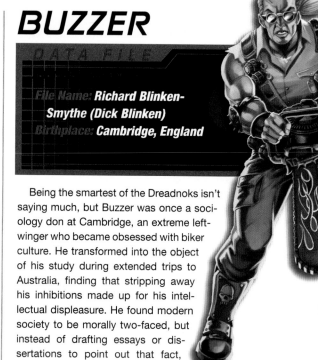

DATA FILE

File Name: **Richard Blinken-Smythe (Dick Blinken)**
Birthplace: **Cambridge, England**

Being the smartest of the Dreadnoks isn't saying much, but Buzzer was once a sociology don at Cambridge, an extreme left-winger who became obsessed with biker culture. He transformed into the object of his study during extended trips to Australia, finding that stripping away his inhibitions made up for his intellectual displeasure. He found modern society to be morally two-faced, but instead of drafting essays or dissertations to point out that fact, Blinken-Smythe turned to hacking through expensive technology with a high-powered diamond-toothed chain saw. That at least was pure, honest, and intensely liberating.

It is believed that Buzzer is in some way connected to Zartan's acquiring of his chameleon abilities. The two share a history that predates their involvement with the Dreadnoks, and as such, Buzzer maintains a position of some security within the gang. He is smart enough to lead, but still frequently exhibits poor judgment—like the time he "borrowed" Zartan's hologram-equipped motorcycle for a spree of mayhem as a lark. Though frequently reprimanded by Zartan and Zarana for his various foul-ups, he is still allowed to ride with the Dreadnoks, indicating that some past history makes up for such transgressions.

Buzzer hates animals. He holds a particular animosity toward Mutt and Junkyard from the G.I. JOE team, with whom he's tangled on repeated occasions.

RIPPER

DATA FILE

File Name: **Harry Nod**
Birthplace: **Grim Cape, Tasmania**

Arguably the most destructive of the Dreadnoks, Ripper was born with a mean streak. Legend has it he was kicked out of nursery school for aggravated assault and running a candy extortion racket. His childhood was a blur of junior correctional facilities, each one a vain effort to scare young Nod straight. Instead, they made him tougher and cockier. It got so that even Tasmanian biker gangs kicked him out for being too nasty. He found a home with the Dreadnoks, who disregarded his profound lack of hygiene in favor of his destructive talents. It is possible Ripper has some military experience in his checkered past, and it most likely ended with him being discharged. Ripper particularly hates G.I. JOE for being clean-cut and organized. The more squeaky-clean the soldier, the more he wants to bloody him up.

Ripper specializes in unorthodox edged weaponry, like the enormous case-hardened bayonet he carries secured to a rifle he rarely fires. He is also known to carry a gas-powered pile driver. Of surprise to his fellow Dreadnoks is that Ripper appears to have some sort of business sense. His greed led him to learn basic accounting, and he regularly pockets dividends from business ventures both legal and otherwise. If this doesn't meet his financial needs, he can always fall back on his safecracking skills.

THRASHER

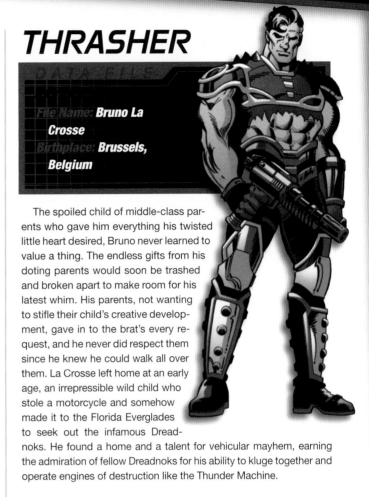

File Name: Bruno La Crosse
Birthplace: Brussels, Belgium

The spoiled child of middle-class parents who gave him everything his twisted little heart desired, Bruno never learned to value a thing. The endless gifts from his doting parents would soon be trashed and broken apart to make room for his latest whim. His parents, not wanting to stifle their child's creative development, gave in to the brat's every request, and he never did respect them since he knew he could walk all over them. La Crosse left home at an early age, an irrepressible wild child who stole a motorcycle and somehow made it to the Florida Everglades to seek out the infamous Dreadnoks. He found a home and a talent for vehicular mayhem, earning the admiration of fellow Dreadnoks for his ability to kluge together and operate engines of destruction like the Thunder Machine.

TORCH

File Name: Tom Winken
Birthplace: Botany Bay, New South Wales, Australia

Winken was a juvenile delinquent who joined the Merchant Marine and became a sure hand with an oxyacetylene cutting torch. With that knowledge, he began running chop shops, gutting and remodeling stolen cars. He'd often get carried away with his work, transforming a hot car into a smoldering scrap pile. A former member of the Melbourne Maulers, he joined with the Dreadnoks when the latter gang absorbed the former. A stupid, unrepentant thug, he is tolerated by the other Dreadnoks for his skill in motorcycle repair. Torch inherited his uncle's business, Uncle Winken's Hard Grape Soda Company, which he somehow runs surprisingly well despite being illiterate.

MONKEY WRENCH

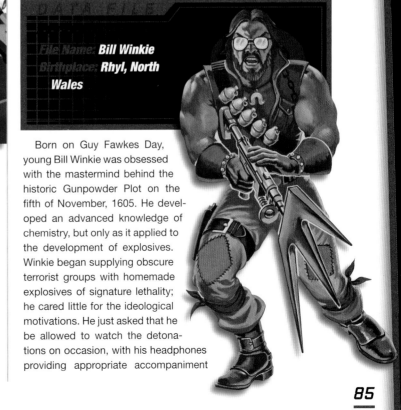

File Name: Bill Winkie
Birthplace: Rhyl, North Wales

Born on Guy Fawkes Day, young Bill Winkie was obsessed with the mastermind behind the historic Gunpowder Plot on the fifth of November, 1605. He developed an advanced knowledge of chemistry, but only as it applied to the development of explosives. Winkie began supplying obscure terrorist groups with homemade explosives of signature lethality; he cared little for the ideological motivations. He just asked that he be allowed to watch the detonations on occasion, with his headphones providing appropriate accompaniment such as the 1812 Overture, the Anvil Chorus, or "Wipeout." Ostracized by the North Wales community once his pastime became public knowledge, 16-year-old Winkie fled to London's East End, becoming part of the New Wave punk movement that stripped away any last vestiges of civility he might have possessed. He eventually fled to Australia ahead of authorities, finding a new life as the Dreadnok nicknamed Monkey Wrench.

ZANZIBAR

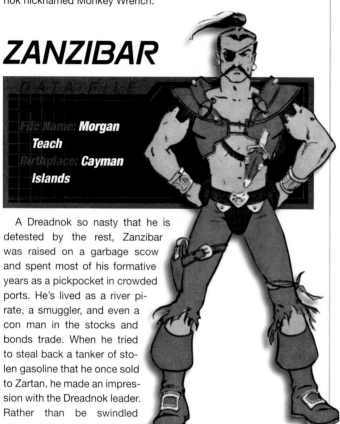

File Name: Morgan Teach
Birthplace: Cayman Islands

A Dreadnok so nasty that he is detested by the rest, Zanzibar was raised on a garbage scow and spent most of his formative years as a pickpocket in crowded ports. He's lived as a river pirate, a smuggler, and even a con man in the stocks and bonds trade. When he tried to steal back a tanker of stolen gasoline that he once sold to Zartan, he made an impression with the Dreadnok leader. Rather than be swindled

again, Zartan decided to place him on retainer so that he could at least keep an eye on him. Zanzibar overplays the role of the pirate to the letter (typically, the letter *"Arrrr..."*), raiding waterways aboard his nimble air skiff with a surplus of bluster. Many suspect the eye patch is simply an affectation.

ROAD PIG

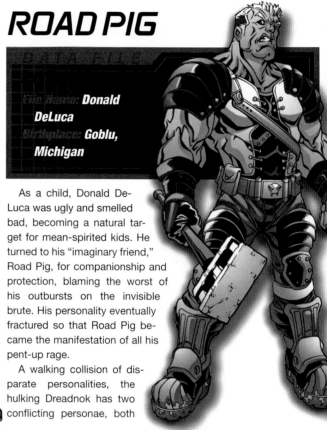

File Name: Donald DeLuca
Birthplace: Goblu, Michigan

As a child, Donald De-Luca was ugly and smelled bad, becoming a natural target for mean-spirited kids. He turned to his "imaginary friend," Road Pig, for companionship and protection, blaming the worst of his outbursts on the invisible brute. His personality eventually fractured so that Road Pig became the manifestation of all his pent-up rage.

A walking collision of disparate personalities, the hulking Dreadnok has two conflicting personae, both

of them in love with Zarana. As Donald, he seems almost erudite, able to construct sentences with proper form and diction. As Road Pig, all he is capable of is brutish violence, doled out by a cinder block attached to a pipe and wielded as a makeshift hammer. As he pounds the object of his rage into dust, he peppers his destructive streak with stuttered fragments—the only speech Road Pig seems capable of when this personality is in control. He has declared himself Zarana's protector—she herself has little say in the manner—and though it is clear he loves her, Donald is far too chivalrous to make any advances on her, and Road Pig, too simple-minded. Zarana does not reciprocate these emotions, but she does appreciate having such a titan wrapped around her finger. If pressed, she'll admit to liking the brutish Road Pig more than the brainy Donald.

GNAWGAHYDE

File Name: **Unknown**
Birthplace: **Unknown**

The fact that other poachers couldn't stand Gnawgahyde and chased him out of Africa is some indication of just how detestable this Dreadnok can be. He is a belligerent hunter who is convinced that all animals are lesser life-forms suitable for skinning, eating, or stuffing. Somehow, his beloved pet warthog Clyde is an exception to this outlook. Gnawgahyde believes in living off the land and finds the artifice of civilization a sign of weakness. As such, he adjures deodorants or cosmetics of any kind, refuses to eat processed food, and will not wear synthetic fibers. This eccentric naturalism isn't exactly out of respect for Mother Earth—he believes such man-made affectations would warn the animal kingdom of his murderous presence.

BURN OUT

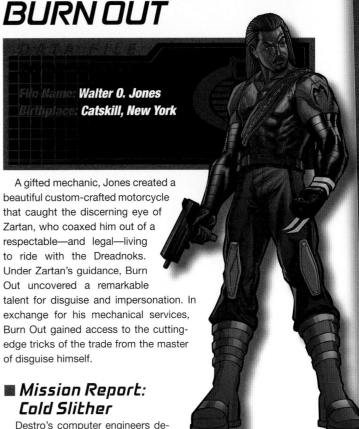

File Name: **Walter O. Jones**
Birthplace: **Catskill, New York**

A gifted mechanic, Jones created a beautiful custom-crafted motorcycle that caught the discerning eye of Zartan, who coaxed him out of a respectable—and legal—living to ride with the Dreadnoks. Under Zartan's guidance, Burn Out uncovered a remarkable talent for disguise and impersonation. In exchange for his mechanical services, Burn Out gained access to the cutting-edge tricks of the trade from the master of disguise himself.

■ Mission Report: Cold Slither

Destro's computer engineers developed a program that composed rock music that concealed subliminal messages; those messages could lull people into a trance-like state and make them subject to COBRA's will. COBRA bankrolled a plot for Zartan and his trio of primary Dreadnoks—Buzzer, Torch, and Ripper—to record a single as the band Cold Slither. The eponymous tune, complete with a loud and crass music video, broke the Top 20 immediately, earning COBRA even more riches, eventually reaching number 1. Millions were enthralled with COBRA propaganda. Before the organization was able to extort billions of dollars, G.I. JOE uncovered the subliminal program and exposed COBRA's scheme.

We're Cold Slither, you'll be joining us soon
A band of Vipers playing a tune
With an iron fist and a reptile's hiss
We shall rule

We're tired of words, we've heard it before
We're not going to play the game no more
Don't tell us what's right, don't tell us what's wrong
Too late to resist 'cause COBRA is strong

We're Cold Slither, heavy metal machine
Through the eyes of a lizard, in you will dream!
When the venom stings, a new order brings
Our control!

We're tired of words, we've heard it before
We're not going to play the game no more

FIREFLY
(Saboteur)

File Name: *Unknown*
Specialties: *Sabotage; demolitions; terror*
Qualifications: *An expert in all NATO and Warsaw Pact explosives and detonators*

Firefly has a talent for discerning and exploiting flaws or fracture points in structures, be they bridges, bunkers, or relationships. With expertly applied pressure, he derives great satisfaction in bringing down his target. Cobra Commander has nicknamed him "the Rembrandt of plastic explosives," but unlike famed artists, Firefly does not sign his work. He has rarely ever been spotted entering or leaving a target area. It's the anonymity of the destruction that ironically serves as his signature. If the devastation is complete and there are no possible culprits, then that is the mark of Firefly.

Firefly's career as an international saboteur predates the rise of COBRA, and it is not known how Cobra Commander came to hire him. Firefly's preferred mode of operation is to keep as much distance from his clients as possible. His fees are paid into a numbered Swiss bank account, always in advance, with no guarantees or refunds.

I'm a person of infinite practicality and one not overburdened by useless sentiment.

—Firefly

■ Secret Ninja Origins

Firefly's father was a plantation owner and anti-Japanese guerrilla in French Indochina. He spared the life of a young Japanese officer who turned out to be the son of the Grand Master of the Koga ninjas. After the Vietminh betrayed Firefly's father and murdered him, the Koga ninja clan took the young boy in and trained him in their ways. He became the first outlander to become the full master of any ninja style.

This status, combined with a peculiar hypnotic ability to keep others from properly remembering his features, allowed him to take on the title Faceless Master. It was under this guise that he interacted with the Arashikage ninja clan in Japan, working in the forge of the Arishikage swordsmith, Master Onihashi.

The Faceless Master had been hired by Cobra Commander to assassinate Snake-Eyes, the result of a deranged personal vendetta that the commander had been nursing for years. Seeing firsthand Snake-Eyes's combat abilities, the Faceless Master reneged on the deal, but not before subcontracting the hit to another operative: a mysterious drifter by the name of Zartan. Faceless would not be the triggerman, but he nonetheless supplied Zartan with the weapons and intelligence he needed to pull the job off. In his last days at the Arashikage dojo, Faceless Master fanned the flames of revolt, goading isolationists such as Master Sato—who objected to Snake-Eyes' presence within the clan—into open revolt.

It was this confusion that allowed Zartan such access to the clan. Zartan's attempt to kill Snake-Eyes, however, resulted in the death of the Hard Master instead. Firefly piloted Zartan's extraction helicopter, and they fled the compound. Though their assignment was a failure—Snake-Eyes lived—the repercussions of that fateful night would shape the destinies of Snake-Eyes, Storm Shadow, and Cobra Commander for years to come.

The Faceless Master put behind him his identity as a ninja, deliberately keeping his martial arts skills as a deadly surprise to those who would underestimate him. He instead built his reputation as a master of explosives. Firefly's handiwork was known to be notoriously difficult to defuse, filled with confusing cross-wired anti-tamper devices that would confound the world's most skilled experts. Though Firefly continues, to this day, to work for COBRA, his loyalty is anything but assured. He simply follows the highest bidder.

■ Mission Report: Rise of the Firefly

After being presumed dead by both G.I. JOE and COBRA for months, Firefly reclaimed his ninja heritage and took control of the Red Ninja clan—a loose-knit organization of Arashikage renegades. He combined his knowledge of technology and esoteric martial arts to reinvent himself as a new kind of threat. Firefly gassed unconscious the members of the G.I. JOE Ninja Force—including its leader, Storm Shadow—and used an appropriated brainwave scanner to turn them into his loyal minions. He then set his sights on Cobra Island, the former COBRA nation that had been all but abandoned by the terrorist organization as its operations spread to Eastern Europe. Firefly set up a stronghold on the vacant island, guarded by modified B.A.T. soldiers and his corrupted Ninja Force guard. Snake-Eyes used the Arashikage Mind-Set to break his fellow Ninja Force members free of Firefly's mental hold.

FACELESS

Firefly maintained his anonymity for years with a specialized form of hypnosis that made subjects forget his features the instant they saw him. A viewer's brain could not keep up with Firefly's hypnotic commands, resulting in a "signal cancellation" between the optic nerves and cerebral cortex. As a result, those looking directly at an unmasked Firefly would see an unsettling blur rather than a face. Such a technique required intense concentration from Firefly, and he instead later opted to use masks to preserve his identity. Of course, hypnotism would have no effect on cameras, so when he knew his photo was being taken, the Faceless Master would simply move his head in such a way as to cause the picture to be blurred.

MAJOR BLUDD
(Mercenary)

File Name: **Sebastian Bludd**
Specialties: **Covert operations;**
weapons and tactics
Birthplace: **Sydney, Australia**

When you're feeling low and woozy/
Slap a fresh clip in your Uzi!/
Assume the proper firing stance/
And make the suckers jump and dance!
—Major Bludd

A loathsome enemy, Major Bludd is quite possibly the villain most hated by G.I. JOEs, second only to Cobra Commander himself. Bludd's despicable deeds are not done for any larger ideaology; he is simply a murderer for hire.

Bludd was once a serviceman in the Australian Special Air Services, and spent time honing his combat skills and tactical mind as part of the French Foreign Legion. He worked as a military adviser in numerous third-world countries, offering tactical expertise in some of the bloodiest campaigns in modern history. For his rampant disregard of human rights in the waging of war, Bludd has earned warrants for capture in Zimbabwe, Libya, and the United States.

Bludd possesses not a shred of loyalty. He's been hired by Cobra Commander to kill Destro, and then by the Baroness to kill the Commander. Strangely, the knowledge that his complicity can simply be purchased has made him a desired lackey within COBRA's ranks. Cobra Commander knows exactly where Bludd stands, and should the mercenary once again try to threaten the Commander's life, he knows he can simply purchase his way out of any attempted plot. Even shadowy elements of the US government are known to have Bludd on retainer; the Jugglers have at least twice hired him to eliminate inconvenient loose ends.

Bludd is proficient in plastic explosives, long-range sniper rifles, garrotes, blunt and edged arms, and just about anything that can be used as a weapon. He often carries a missile-firing pistol that requires him to wear at least partial armor to protect his arm from the rocket's back-blast. It is not known how Bludd lost his left eye. Though he favors an eye patch, he does on occasion don a glass eye. He has a brilliant tactical mind, able to improvise effectively when the larger strategic picture proves ineffective.

Bludd's vanity often runs counter to best practices as a killer for hire. Though he would benefit more from keeping a low profile and disappearing from the attention of law enforcement authorities, Bludd fancies himself a poet, and regularly reaches out to journals and fine literary publications to ensure that his latest works get published. It is assumed he is somehow extorting the editors of such journals, given the quality of the work that makes it to print.

SERPENTOR
(COBRA Emperor)

Dr. Mindbender's most fiendishly inspired plot was the creation of the ultimate military mastermind. Cobra Commander shortsightedly approved the development of a genetic super-soldier, thinking incorrectly that he could control the genetic amalgam of history's greatest leaders.

Per Dr. Mindbender's decree, Destro dispatched teams of CO-BRA scientists and operatives to comb the tombs, sarcophagi, and relics of long-dead leaders for any usable DNA traces. These genetic fragments were then combined to create a composite clone, which could be coupled with a digital mind constructed by the COBRA brainwave scanner, loaded with historical records and extensive strategic texts.

This I command!
—Serpentor

After a period of experimentation and biological incubation, a fully grown man emerged from a saline tank within Dr. Mindbender's laboratory. He was dubbed Serpentor, COBRA Emperor, and he immediately took command of COBRA forces during the evacuation of Springfield. Much to Cobra Commander's dismay, Serpentor proved exceedingly popular with the troops he commanded, and he fostered a strong following among the upper echelons of COBRA as well. Cobra Commander considered assassinating Serpentor, but the Emperor proved far too effective.

Some time later, the real Cobra Commander was replaced by an imposter unknown to virtually everyone within COBRA Command. This masquerader, Fred Broca VII, was not nearly as disciplined or experienced as Cobra Commander, so when tensions between him and Serpentor came to a boil, the result was a civil war on Cobra Island.

The schism split COBRA into two sides. Loyal to Cobra Commander were the Baroness, Zartan, his Dreadnoks, and the Viper infantry. Loyal to Serpentor were Dr. Mindbender, the Crimson Twins, and the B.A.T. infantry. Because Serpentor was in possession of stolen technology valued by the US military, G.I. JOE was assigned by the Pentagon to serve in an advisory capacity to Serpentor in overthrowing Cobra Commander's rule. Though Serpentor and the G.I. JOE team

waged the better war, surrounding Cobra Commander on all sides, Serpentor fell in combat, killed by an arrow launched by Zartan.

Dr. Mindbender kept Serpentor's body in deep-cold storage, not wanting such prime genetic material to go to waste. Little did anyone suspect he had developed a number of surprising contingencies based on the creation of Serpentor.

■ Return of Serpentor

When the US government took possession of Cobra Island, they discovered the cloned children hidden in Dr. Mindbender's secret laboratory. These children were studied for a while and deemed healthy, intelligent, normal boys. They were then scattered among foster families across the United States, though remotely monitored. Meanwhile, a COBRA splinter group called the Coil uncovered Mindbender's old cloning apparatus and created a 13th clone from the Serpentor templates. They, in effect, resurrected Serpentor, and installed him as leader of the Coil. Due to a strange empathic connection shared by Serpentor and his 10 child clones, he was able to summon the children to Cobra Island to be with him. Likewise, Dr. Mindbender—himself a clone of the long-since-dead original—heeded this

THE OTHER CLONES

During the development of Serpentor, Dr. Mindbender created 10 other clones as biological test beds for his experimental processes. These clones were, at first, not age-accelerated, and remained infants by the time Mindbender was content with the results. The clones were named for the genetic sample templates culled from history's leaders: Alexander, Hannibal, Attila, Genghis, Ivan, Julius, Napoleon, Philip, Thomas, and Vlad.

Wanting to ensure the secrecy of the project, Cobra Commander ordered Mindbender to destroy the infant clones. Mindbender instead hid them in a secret laboratory on Cobra Island and continued his experimentation, age-accelerating Hannibal to a slight degree.

Mindbender also created an 11th clone, altered in appearance so its origins as a Serpentor duplicate would not be visibly apparent. This clone was age-accelerated to adulthood and sold to the US military to become the sleeper agent General Philip Rey.

call. He was possibly sensitive to it due to being born of the same cloning process.

Serpentor led the Coil in a far-reaching attack on countries around the world, including the United States. He reclaimed Cobra Island as a headquarters, and battled Cobra Commander in hand-to-hand combat. Though Serpentor was the more capable fighter, Cobra Commander was far more devious. He handed over his battle helmet to the Emperor, and then triggered it to explode in Serpentor's hands. Wounded, the Emperor stumbled enough so Cobra Commander kicked him off a perilous precipice. Serpentor was killed in the fall.

Serpentor's body was recovered by General Gibbs of the secret cabal of US military commanders known as the Jugglers. Whatever plans the general had for the clone disappeared when he and the body were destroyed by the Red Shadows.

HISTORICAL RECIPE

The complete list of DNA "donors" who formed the composite genetic template for Serpentor may never be known—Dr. Mindbender took this secret with him to the grave. But based on records and admittedly conflicting accounts, here is a list of figures believed to be involved in the process.

Amon-Toth (circa 1441–1425 BC) A powerful Egyptian military general serving Pharaoh Thutmose III.

Solomon (circa 1000–922 BC) The first king of the unified Jewish kingdom.

Cyrus the Great (circa 600–529 BC) Founder of the Persian Empire.

Sun Tzu (circa 400–320 BC) Chinese author of *The Art of War*.

Philip II of Macedon (382–336 BC) Ancient Greek king, father of Alexander the Great.

Alexander the Great (356–323 BC) The ancient Greek king of Macedon who conquered the known world by the age of 33.

Hannibal (circa 248–183 BC) The Carthaginian military commander who nearly toppled Rome.

Julius Caesar (100–44 BC) Roman dictator.

Attila the Hun (406–453 BC) Leader of the Hunnic Empire, enemy of the Roman Empire.

Erik the Red (circa 950–103 BC) Viking lord, founder of the first Nordic settlement in Greenland.

Genghis Khan (circa 1162–1227) Mongolian warlord and ruler of the Mongol Empire.

Vlad Tepes Dracula (1431–1476) Wallachian warlord and monarch.

Moctezuma II (circa 1466–1520) The last Aztec ruler of Tenochtitlan.

Ivan the Terrible (1530–1584) A cruel Russian monarch.

Napoleon Bonaparte (1769–1821) French emperor and military leader.

GENGHIS KHAN

Dr. Mindbender (contemporary) Mindbender used a digital model of his mind to help populate Serpentor's memories with modern information about COBRA and G.I. JOE.

Storm Shadow (contemporary) The COBRA ninja, believed dead but in actuality within a sleeping trance, was placed in a biological reactant tank to offer "fresh" genetic material to the process.

STORM SHADOW
(COBRA Ninja)

File Name: Tomisaburo "Thomas"
S. Arashikage
Specialties: Assassination;
intelligence
Birthplace: San Francisco, California

Storm Shadow's heart does not know true evil, but he is guilty of the sins of pride and vengeance. His honor has been shadowed by his association with COBRA, which began with intentions of justice. Poisoned by COBRA's ideology, and subjected to brutal mind control techniques, the good man who was Storm Shadow was almost completely obscured by villainy. Yet despite his wavering loyalties, the bond that exists between Snake-Eyes and Storm Shadow is unbreakable. It is a bond of blood and sword, which has seen them turn from allies to enemies time and again.

Thomas Arashikage and Snake-Eyes both served together as part of a patrol unit stationed overseas. His fellow patrolmen could not correctly pronounce his surname, so Arashikage insisted on simply being called "Tommy." He had the odd habit of favoring a compound bow over his standard firearm, and proved extremely adept with this perfectly silent weapon. Tommy and Snake-Eyes became friends, and Tommy extended an open invitation to join his "family business" in Japan after their service.

Experience, study, and the slow passage of time polish the patina of a Master, but the core and essence is internal, like the heart of an uncut diamond.
—Storm Shadow

■ Fall of the Young Master

The business was a front for the Arashikage ninja clan, a line of highly trained assassins and operatives whose history stretched back centuries, into the time of feudal Japan. Known as the Young Master, Thomas studied under his uncles, the Hard Master and the Soft Master. Thomas was poised to continue the family business and inherit stewardship of the clan, but Snake-Eyes proved to be an amazingly quick study. Within months, Snake-Eyes was mastering the demanding katas of the Arashikage, becoming nearly the equal of Storm Shadow. The outsider quickly gained the Hard Master's favor, much to Storm Shadow's chagrin. Tommy could not see that it was his pride

the Hard Master objected to—in practice duels Snake-Eyes would lose face so as to allow Storm Shadow to keep his, a selflessness that only enamored him to the Hard Master even more.

This competitive streak in Storm Shadow and the toxin of jealousy drove a wedge in their friendship. That the Hard Master was considering offering Snake-Eyes the future of the clan came as a blow to Thomas. Had he not been so self-centered and envious, he might have seen the deadly conspiracy brewing in the Arashikage compound. An assassin had infiltrated the ranks, posing as a fellow student. This hired killer sought to murder Snake-Eyes, and used an arrow carelessly discarded by Storm Shadow as his weapon. He fired his bow and the arrow pierced the heart of his target—but the assassin had mistakenly killed the Hard Master instead.

Thomas saw the shadowy killer leaving the compound, but the evidence he left behind was damning: Storm Shadow's blood-covered arrow, and the undeniable resentfulness felt by the Young Master, painted the picture of Storm Shadow's guilt. Storm Shadow fled, for he alone knew the truth of his innocence. That night, he also witnessed his uncle's murderer climbing aboard a helicopter with an unmistakable sigil painted on its side: that of a cobra.

■ Into the COBRA Ranks

Determined to find his uncle's killer and ostracized from the Arashikage clan, Storm Shadow became a blade for hire, joining the COBRA ranks as an assassin. He was determined to work his way through the organization to find the information he needed to clear his name. Cobra Commander knew what Storm Shadow was after—and he knew far more about the circumstances surrounding the Hard Master's death than Storm Shadow would ever believe—but he cynically strung Storm Shadow along, keeping the information from him in order to ensure his loyalty.

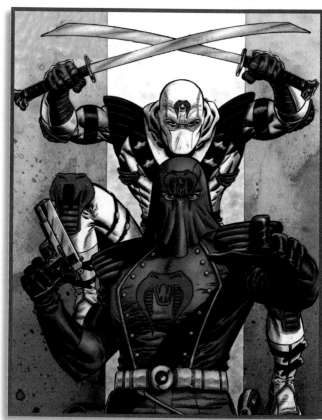

DATA FILE

KUJI-NO-IN

As a versatile practitioner of esoteric martial arts, Storm Shadow performs the *kuji-no-in* as a meditative technique meant to harness and channel inner energies. There are nine *mudras*, or symbols, represented through the weaving of fingers in complex positions. The first symbol, *Rin*, begins with the channeling of *ki* energy; *Pyo* is the second, as the adept progresses along the path of mastering all nine; *To* is the third, as the adept ponders the aspects of reality; *Sho* is the fourth, banishing illusion; *Kai* is the fifth, wherein the adept strives for the cessation of desire; the sixth, *Jin*, allows for *ki* to flow unhindered; *Retsu*, the seventh, is like the wind through the great Bodhisattva Pass; the eighth, *Zai*, is the wind that scatters the leaves of memory; and the ninth is *Zen*, a reflexive catching of a scattered leaf. On this one must write the 10th symbol, a combined effect of the previous nine.

The conflict between G.I. JOE and COBRA brought Snake-Eyes and Storm Shadow face-to-face once more. Their teammates recognized the obvious connection between the two—both incredibly skilled ninjas, each with a hexagram clan symbol tattooed to his forearm—but neither divulged their true connection. During one encounter, Storm Shadow was finally able to tell his tale of the terrible night the Hard Master died to Snake-Eyes, revealing his motive behind joining COBRA.

But the quest for vengeance was consuming Storm Shadow, and his former friends had difficulty recognizing the man who was Thomas Arashikage. Upon uncovering the proof he had sought for years—that Zartan was the killer who had pulled the bowstring—Storm Shadow went on a rampage, determined to slice through anyone who would attempt to stop him from claiming his pound of flesh. Snake-Eyes accompanied him to Cobra Island, where Storm Shadow cut his way through dozens of COBRA soldiers in his search for the master of disguise. But Zartan eluded him, and Storm Shadow's vendetta merely left the ninja vulnerable to the heartless recriminations of COBRA. The Baroness deemed Storm Shadow too dangerous and treacherous to live, and she gunned him down in cold blood.

■ Risen From the Ashes

The bullets tore into Storm Shadow's chest. His strength oozed out of him along with the blood that stained the sands. COBRA geneticist Dr. Mindbender, not willing to sacrifice such a prime biologi-

cal specimen, had Storm Shadow's body preserved. But the ninja was not quite dead. In his waning moments, Storm Shadow had entered the Sleeping Phoenix, a trance-like state that was one of the many mystical techniques known to the Arashikage. Storm Shadow's life signs were slowed and dimmed to be nearly unreadable. He would have certainly died had not Mindbender used his body as part of the genetic stew to create the new COBRA Emperor, Serpentor.

> I have the memories of a dead man. They are cold and dark, like black icicles … I remember Carthage, Tyre and Sumer! I remember the splendor of Rome's Legions! The golden horde of the Great Khan! The smell of death at Ypres, Waterloo, Hastings and Thermopylae! What have you done to me?
> —Storm Shadow

Storm Shadow awoke from his trance with fragments of memories torn from the pages of history, the result of Serpentor being the genetic amalgam of the past's greatest military minds. Given a second lease on life, he came to realize how hollow and destructive the pursuit of vengeance truly was. Given access to Snake-Eyes's cabin retreat, Storm Shadow convalesced in the High Sierras for some time, healing his body and his spirit. He would eventually return and assist the G.I. JOE team, being offered full membership. Along with his cousin Jinx and Snake-Eyes, Storm Shadow became one of the founding members—and eventual leader—of Ninja Force, an elite team of G.I. JOE martial arts operatives. It seemed Storm Shadow had finally found a place, but it would not last.

■ Relapse

While on a mission to Trans-Carpathia, Storm Shadow was captured by COBRA agents and subjected to the insidious brainwave scanner, an advanced technological nightmare capable of painfully tearing through and altering a subject's memories. A torturous form of brainwashing, the latest iteration of the diabolical contraption caused addiction in its victims—those forced to undergo the scanner's probes would become dependent on the process. So it was with Storm Shadow, and repeated brainwave scanning broke his spirit and left him within COBRA's folds for far too long. When COBRA seemingly scattered after a resounding defeat by a combined US military force, Storm Shadow spent much time trying to piece together his life, his identity, and his sanity.

■ *Path of the Ronin*

Walking away from his nefarious affiliations of the past, Storm Shadow found a new lease on life as an independent operative claiming no allegiance but still available to help various security agencies across borders. He moved to Hong Kong and tried to pick up the fragments of his life, and actually found love with his apprentice, Junko Akita. It was to end in tragedy, however, as COBRA once again intruded into what passed for tranquility in Arashikage's life. Sei Tin, leader of the Red Ninja clan, kidnapped and corrupted Junko, turning her into Storm Shadow's mortal enemy. It was a potent reminder of how often tragedy and pain touched the lives of those closest to Storm Shadow. The cold clarity of having to face and defeat his beloved as an enemy shook loose the last of the cobwebs on his mind left by COBRA brainwashing.

Tommy became entangled with a bizarre array of powerful and dangerous enemies in a globe-spanning hunt for a lost Arashikage treasure, the sword known as Morning Light. Storm Shadow confronted Russian gangsters, Spetsnaz, the Yakuza, and a mercenary bankrolled by the International Research Institute of Zurich—an organization of modern ninjas led by the former Night Creeper leader. All were in some way connected to a mysterious Russian benefactor known as "the client."

It was a caper warped by deception and illusion. When the smoke and mirrors cleared, Morning Light was revealed to be both an ancient katana forged by the original Master Onihashi and a duplicate created by Onihashi XXIII. The client was Zartan, who was seeking to ensure the safety of the ancient blade. Strangest of all, Storm Shadow's "niece," Tiff—who was kidnapped to exert leverage on Tommy—was in truth a 27-year-old assassin and little person covert operative.

THE ARASHIKAGE CLAN

Centuries ago, during the time of the Kemmu restoration, the emperor of Japan asked his general to protect the mystical Jewel of Amaterasu, a gem said to allow those who wielded it to control their *ki*. The gem was so well concealed that its location was lost with the ascendency of subsequent emperors. The general's family eventually lost its standing, reduced to simple farmers who would later become the Arashikage. For 30 generations, the Arashikage worked as shadowy assassins, using deception as the foundation of their deadly trade. They were ninjas, earning a keep through their kills, as well as a whispered reputation for being able to perform impossible tasks.

In modern times, the Arashikage continued the deception—financing front businesses that hid their true work as covert operatives, bounty hunters, thieves, and contract killers. Their remote compound was hidden in the mountains of Japan. For years, they perfected katas and disciplines known solely to their members. Only those who had truly proven their worth and commitment to the Arashikage way were allowed full membership in the clan, denoted by the tattooing of the clan symbol upon the forearm.

The symbol of the Arashikage is a hexagram taken from the I-Ching. A stack of six lines alternating as broken and unbroken, the symbol was open to interpretation as "after completion" or "success in small matters." The three lines at the core of the hexagram denote an abyss, while the upper three in comparison with the last three denote water over fire (*k'an li*).

■ *The Masters*

At the top of the modern Arashikage hierarchy was the board of masters. Those who were true-blood Arashikage directed the business dealings of the clan.

The Hard Master: Storm Shadow's uncle, the president and lifetime chairman of the board. The Hard Master, as his name implied, was the most difficult of instructors, teaching the most challenging lessons. He was adept at the most demanding of katas and techniques. Ironically, it was his mastery of the Cloak of the Chameleon that led to his death: So perfect was he at mimicking the life signs of another, the Hard Master was killed by an assassin who mistook him for Snake-Eyes.

The Soft Master: Younger brother to the Hard Master, vice-president in charge of finance of the clan. More lenient and approachable than his implacable brother, the Soft Master concerned himself more with matters of the mind and spirit than with physical perfection in his tutelage. Indeed, his rotund features hardly seemed threatening, but the Soft Master was nonetheless a deadly ninja, possessing incredible reflexes. After the dissolution of the clan following his brother's death, the Soft Master eventually gravitated to New York City, operating a simple diner called Comidas China in Spanish Harlem. He was killed by COBRA agents during the search for the Hard Master's murderer.

The Iron Master: The swordsmith of the Arashikage clan, the Iron Master spent an extended absence in parts unknown before returning to Japan following the death of his replacement, Professor Onihashi. He was responsible for the creation of the Dragon's Eye, one of the most powerful and revered blades in the Arashikage arsenal. During his days as a student, his sword brother was Black Dragon, who fell from the honorable path and became a mortal enemy of the Arashikage. The Iron Master is now a grizzled veteran, his skin toughened by the forge and his right eye lost to an enemy. He is full of wisdom, offering tales of the past to new students of the ninja way.

The Blind Master: A rare example of an outsider who ascended to the board, the Blind Master was an African American ninja. It is not known how he lost his vision, but this was not all that was stolen from him—his wrist, too, bore the scars of skin long removed that would have once held the Arashikage hexagram tattoo. After the clan dissolved, he opened a dojo in Denver, where he was known by his students as Sensei Moore. Among his past protégés is the ninja Jinx. The Blind Master was killed by Zartan.

The Faceless Master: A visiting foreigner, not actually a true member of the Arashikage, he was nonetheless a respected guest from the Koga ninja clan. He was, in truth, an agent hired by Cobra Commander to infiltrate the clan on a mission to assassinate Snake-Eyes. The Faceless Master would later subcontract this assignment to Zartan. The Faceless Master is named for his unsettling ability to use hypnotic suggestion to prevent anyone from truly remembering his features. He is now known as the international terrorist Firefly.

Master Sato: A conservative hardliner who had serious misgivings with the way the Hard Master was running the Arashikage, Master Sato led a revolt that would unravel the clan. He objected to the presence of a westerner—Snake-Eyes—within the clan. Spurred on by the Faceless Master, Sato rallied like-minded clan members in an attempted coup that was put down by the Hard Master and Soft Master. Sato was expelled, taking his dissenters with him.

Onihashi: The Arashikage clan swordsmith during the Iron Master's lengthy absence, Onihashi was a 23rd-generation forger of mystic blades. Not truly part of the Arashikage bloodline, the Onihashi family has nonetheless produced some of the most revered weapons used by the clan. Professor Onihashi XXIII's last act for the clan was to take on the teaching of a mysterious outsider who proved to be the Hard Master's murderer. For the shame of this failure, Onihashi committed seppuku.

Obake-Obaason: The Hard Master's widow, she took the fragments of the Arashikage clan and pieced them together for operation in the 21st century. Eschewing the ninja dojos of past generations, the clan now has computer hackers, molecular biologists, chemists, and electrical engineers on retainer. Gone are the hexagram and blade; the Arashikage name graces only the front business for clandestine operations—the Arashikage Novelty Company.

■ Contemporaries

After Storm Shadow's return from Southeast Asia, the Hard Master required him to resume training, to compensate for such an extended absence outside the walls of the Arashikage compound. What follows is a sampling of other students of the Arashikage ways.

Snake-Eyes: Storm Shadow's friend and former platoon mate, Snake-Eyes's presence within the clan had a polarizing effect. The outsider ushered in tragedy when an assassin targeted him but killed the Hard Master instead.

Zartan: An apprentice swordsmith to Professor Onihashi, the nameless drifter who would later be revealed as Zartan infiltrated the clan on assignment to assassinate Snake-Eyes. Zartan was moved by Onihashi's teachings, and his act of murder devastated Onihashi.

Dojo (Michael F. Russo): The secret pupil of a ninja master in hiding, Russo proved to be an exceptional combatant with chain and sickle. He was invited by the reformed Storm Shadow to join the ranks of the Ninja Force, and helped establish a new training academy in Spanish Harlem, New York.

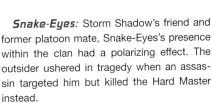

T'Jbang (Samuel LaQuale): A distant cousin of Storm Shadow, LaQuale spent some time studying under a master swordsman at the Arashikage compound. He carries a sword of his own forging and is the sole master of a secretive technique called the Silent Backhand. For years, he observed a strict oath of silence, but that has since subsided. T'Jbang was a member of the Ninja Force, and later helped in the training of Kamakura.

Anibal Alcazar: An older student of the Hard Master, Anibal Alcazar studied the way of the ninja and learned enough to survive both the sodden battlefields of Southeast Asia and the criminal mean streets of Lithuania. Advancing in age, Alcazar hired Storm Shadow for the strangest of assignments: He wanted the ninja to kill him. Anibal had been diagnosed with inoperable terminal cancer, and wished a death that befit a warrior. Storm Shadow refused the assignment and offered an alternative: retreating to Japan for additional training and meditation before death took Alcazar.

■ The New Generation

Though the clan was scattered following the Hard Master's murder, the various Arashikage followers sought to continue the methods taught by their forebears. The Arashikage dojo still sits empty, though the knowledge of centuries flows through a new generation of highly trained acolytes.

Jinx (Kimi Arashikage): A disciple of the Blind Master and cousin to Storm Shadow, Jinx followed the path of the ninja directly to G.I. JOE, becoming a covert operations specialist.

Nunchuk (Ralph Badducci): A student of the Blind Master in Denver, he later studied under Storm Shadow in San Francisco, becoming a key member of the Ninja Force.

T'Gin-Zu (Joseph R. Pamore): As a student, Pamore traveled the world, learning a variety of martial arts techniques before becoming one of Storm Shadow's most gifted apprentices. He briefly served with the Ninja Force.

Billy (William S. Kessler): The son of Cobra Commander, Billy was Storm Shadow's first apprentice, taken by the ninja from the COBRA ranks and trained in his secret New York dojo.

Tiger Claw (Chad M. Johnson): Inspired by the martial arts movies that fascinated him as a child, Johnson sought out training from the best, earning a placement on G.I. JOE as a weapons instructor and becoming an apprentice to both the Iron Master and Snake-Eyes.

Ophelia Gabriel: A favored apprentice to Snake-Eyes. The Silent Master saw Ophelia Gabriel as a younger sister and was devastated by her untimely death during her final trial.

Kamakura (Sean Collins): Snake-Eyes's last apprentice, Kamakura is both a member of G.I. JOE and the future of the Arashikage clan.

■ Enemies

For 600 years, the Arashikage clan has been beset by rivals and enemies, looking to pry from its members the secrets of its most powerful techniques. Despite this endless cycle of adversity and betrayal, the clan has survived.

The Red Ninja Clan: The scattered remnants of the Arashikage clan that fled following Master Sato's failed coup. Many still bear the mark of the clan hexagram on their forearms. The Red Ninjas fell into league with COBRA, often under the leadership of former clan members such as Storm Shadow, Zartan, or Firefly. After the seeming defeat of COBRA, the Red Ninjas retreated to a remote mountain dojo in Tibet, where they were led by Sei Tin.

Black Dragon: The former sword brother of the Iron Master, Black Dragon turned his back on the ancient art of swordsmanship in favor of high-tech weaponry. He adopted the mantle of a defunct spy organization defeated by Joseph Colton years ago—the Black Dragon—and revitalized the organization, teaming it with COBRA to become a renewed threat.

Night Creepers: A new enemy, the Night Creepers are a bizarre modern incarnation of the ninja. A syndicate of Swiss bankers highly trained in martial arts and equipped with cutting-edge technology, the high-priced mercenaries handle COBRA's bankroll as well as their most dangerous assassination missions.

■ *Secrets of the Arashikage*

The techniques of the Arashikage clan defy documentation; no scrolls or textbooks describe how these ancient katas or practices are performed. They have instead been passed on from generation to generation through hands-on training and oral history.

Arashikage Mind-Set: Requiring concentration beyond concentration, focus beyond focus, the Mind-Set is perhaps the most powerful and dangerous of the Arashikage secrets. It is a form of hypnotism that imbues the spirit and consciousness with impenetrable armor, collapsing all trivialities and distractions into a pinpoint singularity of attention, granting an Arashikage warrior unshakable resolve and tenacity. A Mind-Set warrior will ignore pain, fear, or, distressingly, any moral compunction, turning into a deadly berserker until the condition is removed. The Mind-Set has also proven capable of sloughing off the effects of brainwashing.

Sleeping Phoenix: This technique mimics the cessation of all life signs by extreme physical control of otherwise involuntary bodily processes. To the untrained examiner, a ninja entering the Sleeping Phoenix appears dead. This technique has proven valuable both in fooling enemies and in extending survival when faced with limited provisions.

The Ear That Sees: An exercise that concentrates hearing to compensate for the loss of sight (or the unreliability of sight), the Ear That Sees homes in on other cues—such as heartbeat, the sound of cloth against cloth, and the patterns of breathing and other movement—to identify a foe through sound alone.

The Cloak of the Chameleon: An effective yet difficult counter to the Ear That Sees, the Cloak of the Chameleon uses extreme physical control to alter breathing and circulatory patterns in order to perfectly mimic the sounds of another person.

The Four Trials: Students of Arashikage study must undergo four trials before ascending beyond the rank of apprentice. The first, *Misu,* is the trial of water, and is meant to teach how to take the "shape" of a "container" as water does. In practice, a student is judged on how he or she adapts to tasks or situations with rigid boundaries or rules. The second trial, *Tsuchi,* is the trial of earth. It is opposite of *Misu,* for the earth is solid and supportive, resisting change and giving strength. *Kaze,* the trial of wind, is an exercise in swordsmanship. The last trial, *Hi,* the trial of fire, is a deadly test that serves as a crucible to finally forge a true Arashikage ninja.

VIPER LEGIONS

The rank and file of COBRA infantry is designed to appear largely anonymous. The faces of individual soldiers are concealed behind masks or full wraparound helmets. This is to reinforce the philosophy that COBRA's strength lies in the vast number of troops that can be wielded as an extension of Cobra Commander's will.

The first COBRA soldiers were disaffected Americans, often ex-military or unemployed workers left with few options. They were trained in paramilitary militia compounds like the ones run by Vance Wingfield as part of his Strike First organization. These COBRA soldiers wore simple blue military uniforms and half-face masks beneath their helmets. Later, as COBRA grew in power and resources, their military underwent a significant organizational overhaul, with the Viper becoming the basic unit of COBRA infantry.

The COBRA Viper is the lowest rung in the COBRA organization. The original Viper uniform consisted of basic blue-and-black combat fatigues with a red-and-black armored vest, as well as a silver-faced wraparound combat helmet that resembled that of Cobra Commander. The basic Viper uniform would undergo some revisions over the years, but would eventually return to this standard.

Vipers can then opt for additional training that sees them transferred to specialized units focusing on distinct military occupational specialties. Some of these units are considered elite—drawing command benefits, better equipment, or higher pay. These units are constantly undergoing scrutiny for effectiveness, with some being renamed and reorganized, absorbed into other units, or sometimes completely phased out. It should also be noted that some localized COBRA cells customize their chain of command and order of battle, allowing for the creation of wholly distinct and unique Viper designations. What follows is a partial list of known COBRA Viper units.

■ Aero-Vipers
(Fixed-Wing Pilots): COBRA Air-Vipers that do not undergo surgical alteration like the elite Strato- or Star Viper ranks. These are often assigned to pilot crafts such as the Condor Z25.

■ Air-Vipers
(Air Force Trainees): Pilots that largely consist of military and civilian flight school washouts. Qualified candidates must log more than 1,500 hours of flight and be familiar with the vast arsenal of COBRA aircrafts before advancing to a more specialized position.

■ Alley Vipers
(Urban Assault Troopers): The COBRA equivalent of police SWAT or British SAS units, specializing in inner-city warfare.

■ Astro-Vipers
(Cobranauts): COBRA's high-altitude and space aeronautical pilots, elevated from the Strato-Viper ranks. They have already undergone surgical alterations to better withstand acceleration strains.

■ A.V.A.C.s
(Air-Vipers; Advanced Class): COBRA pilots that meet the exceptional piloting and navigation prerequisites to fly the Firebat jet.

■ Bio-Vipers
(Bio-Genetic Mutants): Monstrously mutated COBRA Eels whose genetic makeup has been cross-pollinated with that of some of the ocean's most fearsome predators.

■ Cyber-Vipers
(Cybernetic Officers): Cybernetically enhanced COBRA soldiers with robotic and computer-enhanced cerebral componentry. They serve as guardians and keepers for the Bio-Vipers and Monstro-Vipers.

■ Desert Scorpions
(Desert Troopers): COBRA Vipers demoted from service as punishment and forced to serve a year as Scorpions. After a year of unblemished service, a Desert Scorpion *might* be promoted to a Toxo-Viper.

COBRA Eels

■ Eels

(COBRA Frogmen): The underwater demolitions specialists of COBRA, manning and operating marine outposts.

■ Electric Eels

(V-Troop Underwater Specialists): Genetically modified Moray and Eel troops who are biologically capable of creating an electrical discharge.

■ Fast Blast Vipers

(Anti-Tank Specialists): COBRA infantry equipped with specially designed battlefield bazookas. Fast Blast Vipers have also had implanted within their skulls a mood-altering computer chip that can neutralize fear while enhancing aggression.

■ Flak-Vipers

(Anti-Aircraft Troopers): These troops have advanced targeting systems built into their helmets and carry electronic-firing dual missile launcher backpacks.

■ Frag-Vipers

(Grenade Throwers): COBRA troops with cesta-like bomb-throwers that accurately can lob framentation grenades over long distances without the report or muzzle blast of a launcher.

■ Gyro-Vipers

(Rotary-Wing Pilots): Fast-thinking pilots capable of flying some of the most complicated COBRA contraptions, like the double-rotored COBRA Mamba helicopter.

■ H.E.A.T. Vipers

(High-Explosive Anti-Tank): COBRA soldiers equipped with the latest generation of hyperkinetic high-speed wire-guided armor-piercing technology.

■ Heli-Vipers

(Battle Copter Troopers): Elite COBRA aviators personally screened by Cobra Commander himself. They are permitted to test-fly experimental one-man combat vehicles.

■ H.I.S.S. Drivers

(H.I.S.S. Tank Operators): Graduates of COBRA battle school and advanced weapons system testing, they are selected from the best of COBRA infantry.

■ Hydro-Vipers

(Demons of the Deep): Surgically altered Eels who can withstand nitrogen narcosis and other side effects of deep-sea diving. They've had synthetic webbing implanted between their fingers and toes, and are altered to have greater natural insulation.

■ Ice Vipers

(Cold-Weather Vehicle Drivers): The mechanized branch of Snow Serpents. They start off as COBRA Eels; additional Techno-Viper training enables them to repair their vehicles in adverse weather conditions.

■ Imperial Guard

(Elite Guard): The handpicked personal guards for Cobra Commander. They may come from any branch of the COBRA military, and undergo biomechanical "adjustment" to ensure that their sole focus is the protection of their august leader.

■ Incinerators

(COBRA Flamethrowers): The flame-weapon and arson specialists of the COBRA ranks, encased in fire-resistant, air-conditioned fighting suits.

■ Jungle Vipers

(Jungle Assault Troopers): Trained in guerrilla fighting techniques and extended survival in harsh environmental conditions.

■ Kitchen Vipers

(Food Services): The unsung heroes of KP duty, these COBRAs prepare meals for the rest of the military.

■ Lampreys

(Hydrofoil Pilots): The elite of the COBRA sea arms, they start off as COBRA Eels.

■ Laser Vipers

(Laser Troopers): These COBRAs are primarily tasked with painting specific targets with laser light so artillery strikes or air attacks can home in on them.

■ Medi-Vipers

(Medical Troopers): COBRA battlefield medics recruited from any branch of the military.

■ Mega-Vipers

(Monster Trainers): Tough and well-equipped soldiers tasked with training the horribly mutated Bio-Vipers and Monstro-Vipers.

■ Monstro-Vipers

(Biogenetic Mutants): Mutated COBRA Range-Vipers transformed into brutal battle beasts. They have computer-controlled implants in their bodies and minds that allow Mega- and Cyber-Vipers some modicum of control over the savages.

■ Morays

(Underwater Elite): The elite of the COBRA Eels, they continue to serve in underwater demolitions capacity.

■ Motor-Vipers

(Vehicle Drivers): The COBRA recon and perimeter defense forces tasked with operating and maintaining COBRA's ground vehicle motor pool.

■ Neo-Vipers

(Infantry Officers): Genetically enhanced COBRA Vipers who are stronger and faster with greater endurance, than unequipped regular infantry.

■ Night Vipers

(Night Fighters): Infantry equipped with image-intensification and other sensor-enhancement units allowing them to see in absolute darkness.

■ Ninja Vipers

(Martial Arts): Recruited from the highest ranks of the COBRA Vipers, they are trained in karate, jujitsu, kung-fu, and other martial arts forms.

■ Nitro-Vipers

(Detonator Drivers): The most elite of the COBRA Track Vipers, selected to pilot Detonator tanks.

■ Para-Vipers

(Airborne Infantry): Picked from the best of the Eel troopers, these COBRAs specialize in HALO jumps and covert insertions.

■ Pit Vipers

(Infiltration Troopers): Equipped with magnetically shielded padded uniforms that allow them to disappear from all sensor scopes, these troopers are trained to silently enter deep behind enemy lines for intelligence gathering or sabotage.

■ Range-Vipers

(Wilderness Troopers): These troopers are committed to long-term operations deep within hostile territory cut off from communications or supplies. They are expected to live off the land like hardened survivalists.

■ Razor Troopers

(V-Troop Infantry): Biologically altered Alley Vipers whose pain tolerance and combat skills have been artificially heightened. They have wild tiger DNA spliced into their genetic makeup.

■ Rock Vipers

(Mountain Troopers): Specialized infantry outfitted with nonslip camo-traction suits and equipped with rocket-assisted, tungsten-steel grappling hooks and mega-tensile-strength rappelling rope.

■ Sand Scorpions

(Elite Desert Troopers): Handpicked Sand Vipers subjected to genetic alteration that adds arachnid scorpion DNA into their biological makeup, resulting in heightened combat reflexes and scales that allow them to breathe while submerged in the sand.

■ Sand Vipers

(Desert Infiltrators): The next generation of Desert Scorpions, these are COBRA infantry troops dedicated to desert combat, as opposed to those forced to undergo training as punishment. They wear combat armor that not only deflects incoming fire but also preserves water and recycles body moisture.

■ S.A.W. Vipers

(Heavy Machine Gunners): Armed with a gyro-stabilized, cryogenically cooled mini-chain gun scoped with an infrared night-vision, autoranging optical sighting system.

■ Sea Slugs

(Sea Navigators): Elite COBRA Eels chosen to operate the Sea Ray tactical submersible and its variants.

■ Secto-Vipers

(BUGG drivers): The vehicle operators dedicated to shoreline defense of Cobra Island.

■ Shadow Vipers

(Counterintelligence): These COBRAs are expert computer hackers and skilled in every means of camouflage, disguise, and concealment.

■ Shock Vipers

(Fire Assault Troopers): Incendiary and explosive assault troopers well equipped with fireproof suits.

■ Sludge Vipers

(Hazardous Waste Troopers): These COBRA soldiers are trained in weaponizing industrial waste.

■ Snow Serpents

(Polar Assault): The arctic specialist branch of the COBRA Eels, which must undergo a six-month cold-weather course somewhere above the Arctic Circle.

■ Star Vipers

(Stellar Stiletto Pilots): Qualified COBRA Strato-Vipers surgically altered with electromagnetic shunts leading directly into the right side of their brains. Electronic impulses delivered via the shunt increase a Star Viper's reflexes and awareness to superhuman levels.

■ Strato-Vipers

(Night Raven Pilots): To qualify as a Strato-Viper, an Air-Viper must log 1,500 hours of flight time, be rated to fly up to four engines, have combat experience, and enjoy an impeccable security clearance. These Vipers undergo a surgical procedure that reinforces their circulatory systems, making them more resistant to hypoxia, hyperventilation, and other decompression sicknesses that result from high altitudes.

■ Sub Vipers

(Underwater Demolitions): These are the deepest of the deep-sea COBRA divers.

■ Swamp-Vipers

(Amphibious Assault Troopers): The primary coastal defenders of Cobra Island.

■ Techno-Vipers

(Battlefield Technicians): These Vipers provide field maintenance support and combat-engineering capability to COBRA frontline troops.

■ Tele-Vipers

(Communications): The RTOs (radio telecommunications operators) of the COBRA ground forces.

■ Terra Vipers

(Demolitions): These troops are experts in combat engineering and specialize in undermining and damaging large fortified structures.

■ Toxo-Vipers

(Hostile Environment Troopers): Assignment to the so-called leaky-suit brigade is meted out as punishment for major offenses among the COBRA ranks.

■ Track Vipers

(HISS II Drivers): Track Vipers tend to be physically larger and more muscular than most COBRA infantry divisions.

■ W.O.R.M.S.

(Weapon Ordnance Rugged Machine Specialists): These are the self-propelled artillery specialists of the COBRA ground forces, piloting such vehicles as the COBRA Maggot.

ZARTAN
(Master of Disguise)

DATA FILE

File Name: *Unknown*
Specialties: *Infiltration; intelligence; counterintelligence*
Aliases: *Far too numerous to list*

Zartan's tale is a confounding web told by the most unreliable narrator. His true identity has been so buried under a lifetime of lies and deception, it is nearly impossible to piece together a cogent history that accurately describes how he came to be. He remains an enigma to even his closest relatives. The only consistency in his background is unpredictable change.

Zartan has remarkable abilities, both natural and artificial. He is fluent in more than 20 languages and dialects, and is an accomplished ventriloquist, able to throw his voice. He is a master of makeup and practical special effects (blood packs, squibs, and other theatrical sleights of hand). Coupling his natural mimicry and acting skills with cutting-edge holographic technology and suspected genetic enhancement has turned Zartan into the ultimate master of disguise. He has contortionist and acrobatic skills that rival the world's best escape artists, and his proficiency in a number of mystic martial arts makes him a deadly unarmed opponent.

I am never what I appear to be, and I am always something other than what I am expected to be. Those who think they know me are deluded.
—Zartan

■ Troubled Youth

Though Zartan is certainly an alias, it is believed to be not too dissimilar to his given name. Young Zartan and his siblings, Zoe and Zachary, were placed in Our Lady of Valour Orphanage in Florida after the untimely death of their parents at the hands of loan sharks. As a boy, Zartan exhibited psychological problems that made it difficult for him to focus. Prescription medication allowed him to concentrate, but he often rebelled at having to take it. While at the orphanage, Zartan came to the rescue of his bullied little brother and killed a fellow student. The youth then ran away, taking to a life in the streets, stealing and lying to survive under a host of aliases. Using the name Luke McKinney, he enlisted in the US Army at Fort Benning, Georgia. After that, the trail goes cold.

■ European Intrigue

Most security agencies around the world theorize that Zartan must have had some sort of European military academy training. Recently declassified Rusnian documents point to a suspicious French soldier by the name of Amaury Sanderson, out of the St. Cyr Special Military School. Sanderson was a traitor who sold the Rusnians French military secrets. Sanderson uncovered a super-soldier project, dubbed Project: Chameleon, being developed by the French, which he compromised for his Rusnian benefactors. However, rather than deliver usable intelligence on the operation, an insider helped Sanderson destroy the Project: Chameleon test facility in Paris. What pointed to a Zartan connection was the insider: an English professor named Richard Blinken-Smythe, who would later be known as the Dreadnok Buzzer.

■ The Other Zartan

Concurrent with the stories of Amaury Sanderson was the rise of the Dreadnok motorcycle gang in Australia. The gang's leader was a hooded tough who went by the name Zartan, an Aborigine term that defies translation. It is believed that Sanderson would later adopt this Zartan's identity, a theory that plausibly collapses all the various convergent threads into a single history that tracks Zartan from a troubled youth in Florida to the modern leader of the Dreadnoks and recipient of cutting-edge European bio-mimetic technology.

Apparently Sanderson had stolen information about Project: Chameleon and sold it to a third party rather than turn it over to the Rusnians. With that money, he purchased the land in Florida that housed Our Lady of Valour Orphanage and had the building razed. While living in Chicago, he appropriated the alias Zartan while the *real* Zartan was operating the Dreadnoks on the other side of the world. As the American Zartan, he began traveling across the United States doing mercenary work and building a reputation for himself as a cutthroat for hire.

■ Arashikage Infiltration

I understand that Zartan is a very talented individual and is currently available. I have a very interesting business proposition....
—Cobra Commander

It was at a biker dive, the Don't Fall Inn, in Daytona that the ersatz Zartan was approached by a man looking to hire a killer. The future Cobra Commander had his targets set on Snake-Eyes and had previously hired Firefly to do the job to little effect. Firefly subcontracted the hit and brought Zartan to the Commander's attention. Zartan still had his riches from selling Project: Chameleon, and he initially declined payment. He took the hit for the challenge of infiltrating a ninja compound and killing an Airborne Ranger.

Zartan arrived in Japan and camped out in front of the tradesman's entrance to the Arashikage compound for six months, claiming to want to apply for apprenticeship to the clan's swordsmith, Professor Onihashi. Onihashi immediately sensed deception in Zartan, but nonetheless took on his training as a challenge. He sought to temper Zartan's soul and hammer out the impurities, making an honest and keen sword out of the outlander.

Despite his deadly intentions, Zartan grew to respect Onihashi's teachings. Creating elegant swords was, at long last, a moment of fulfillment for the often-distracted, restless drifter. But he nonetheless had a task to complete. Outfitted with specialized gear by Firefly, Zartan used sound-enhancing equipment to home in on Snake-Eyes's life signs from a distance. Using one of Storm Shadow's discarded arrows, Zartan fired blindly into the dojo, knowing that technology would allow his arrow to find its mark. But he killed the Hard Master and not Snake-Eyes.

Onihashi was shamed by this murder and his failure to prevent it. The swordsmith committed seppuku. Zartan, for whom bloodshed had always come easy, was pained by regret at this loss of life. Zartan fled the compound with his accomplice, Firefly. Returning stateside, he once again tried to make a break from his past, and once again the trail of Zartan's history disappears into shadows.

Project: Chameleon

Some time later, Rusnian agents took great interest in the American soldier Raymond Hoffman, which evidence suggests was Zartan's next long-running alias. The Rusnians captured Hoffman and subjected him to experimentation derived from Project: Chameleon. Rusnian general Moskin had purchased the Project: Chameleon data from the third party that Sanderson had sold it to: M.A.R.S. Industries. Exacting vengeance, Moskin used Hoffman as his guinea pig, having pieced together enough evidence that Sanderson and Hoffman were one and the same. Rusnian scientists had plugged in gaps from the original French experimental data with untested genetic material.

After a lengthy operation including a complex regimen of micro-implants and gene splicing, Hoffman's immune system surprisingly did not reject the foreign additions. In fact, upon awakening, he exhibited marginal control of his ability to shift the color of his skin to blend into his surroundings. What was supposed to be Rusnian vengeance instead granted Zartan the abilities of natural camouflage.

Hoffman escaped Rusnian custody and returned to Florida, joining with his former partner Blinken-Smythe, who now ran with the Dreadnok motorcycle gang under the alias Buzzer. Hoffman used his mimicking abilities and his martial arts prowess to replace the Dreadnok gang leader, Zartan, and essentially stole his identity. He would later be reunited with his brother and sister, Zachary and Zoe—who, following his suggestion, adopted the aliases Zandar and Zarana, respectively. Years later, he would also discover his daughter, Zanya, born from a tryst he had during his time in Chicago.

COBRA Agent

It was Cobra Commander who sold out Hoffman to the Rusnians, and as such the Commander was responsible for his ultimate trans-

formation into Zartan. Nonetheless, the new leader of the Dreadnoks approached the Commander with an offer to serve, because he had heard whispers of the growing COBRA organization. The Commander accepted, for the two had elements of leverage over each other. The Commander knew that Zartan was culpable for the Hard Master's death—knowledge that would surely set Storm Shadow after the human chameleon. Likewise, Zartan knew that Cobra Commander was the benefactor who had hired him to do the job, information that also would not sit well with the COBRA ninja. This stalemate resulted in a workable business relationship, and Zartan proved remarkably loyal to Cobra Commander. The Dreadnoks were allied to the COBRA organization, though the unruly lot resisted formal integration into its ranks. With COBRA technology at his disposal, Zartan supplemented his camouflage abilities with compact holographic equipment that allowed him to alter his features and his surroundings to suit his needs.

Health, Mental and Physical

Since childhood, Zartan has been haunted by dissociative identity disorder. When medicated, he maintains control over his various personalities, as well as over rampant paranoia. But separated from his anti-psychotics, Zartan becomes wildly unpredictable. No one knows of this weakness, except for his brother, sister, and daughter. Ironically, it was this ability that helped Zartan become the famed mimic that he is. He truly creates new personalities to such a degree that they bury the old. Without medical assistance, the original Zartan—whoever that may be—was lost under a blur of new identities.

As Zartan aged, his physiology began to reject the genetic tampering that he withstood in his prime. Sunlight became painful to his skin, and it was feared that his immune system would ravage itself trying to eject the foreign biology introduced to his system. He became increasingly reclusive, turning over more active operations of the Dreadnoks to his sister, Zarana, and his daughter, Zanya. Exposure to COBRA nano-mite technology corrected the flaws in his genetic makeup, and Zartan eventually made a full recovery.

THE ZARTAN FAMILY (ZARANA, ZANDAR & ZANYA)

The blood ties of the Zartan family are enduring despite the often contradictory nature of their relationships. They will fight fiercely to defend one another, yet each is filled with dangerous secrets and the bond of family not does necessarily include a bond of trust. Case in point: Zartan—the central figure and head of the family—remains a stranger to them all. Yet his siblings and daughter alone know of his psychological weaknesses, and work to protect him and maintain his fragile sanity.

Family remains important to Zartan, though he spent years separated from his siblings. Hailing from Florida, Zarana and Zandar were adopted by a family that soon moved to England, and the two grew up abroad unaware of what their brother was up to. In an example sure to give the nature-versus-nurture debate more fuel, Zandar and Zarana both ended up riding with the Dreadnoks, independent of Zartan's involvement. Reunited in the criminal underworld, Zartan took his siblings into the ranks of the COBRA organization.

ZARANA

File Name: *Zoe (real last name unknown)*
Specialties: *Infiltration; sabotage; espionage; disguise; business management; intelligence; assassination*
Qualified Expert: *A variety of small arms, explosives, and edged weapons*
Birthplace: *Believed to be somewhere in Florida*

Like a method actress, Zarana closely monitors her would-be identities, memorizing traits and hypothesizing their origins so as to build a plausible, if unspoken, history behind the role she is about to play. She can lie with ease, for she is able to formulate an internal truth to that lie, one that can defy any mechanical method of detection. The most outwardly ambitious of the family, Zarana deftly maneuvered herself to a strong position of leadership among the Dreadnoks. True, nepotism means that few would question her, but her skills ensure that there is rarely ever reason to.

Zarana drapes herself in punk styles and surrounds herself with brutish oafs in a calculated bid to have others misjudge her. The Baroness often took this bait, branding Zarana as little more than biker trash. She is far more, and has proven to have exceptional managerial skills and strategic judgment, earning her visible roles of command responsibility within COBRA, often at the *expense*

of the Baroness. To Zartan's dismay, Zarana soon began spending more time within the upper echelons of COBRA, managing the Commander's business, than dealing with Dreadnok concerns.

This led to an unspoken estrangement that Zarana especially felt when she returned to Dreadnok activities after the seeming dissolution of COBRA. Rather than the lofty perch she had left behind, she instead found Zartan's attentions and ambitions projected upon his newly discovered daughter, Zanya. The teenage girl was being groomed to be second in command of the now nationwide motorcycle gang, and Zarana left the Florida command compound to take over control of the Chicago chapter of the Dreadnoks. Zarana would further alienate Zartan by appropriating his disguising technologies for Cobra Commander's use in creating the Phoenix Guard, an American elite special missions force meant to rival G.I. JOE that was actually made up of undercover COBRA agents.

■ *Mission Report: Forbidden Love*

At the behest of Cobra Commander, Zarana infiltrated G.I. JOE headquarters posing as Sergeant Carol Weidler, a computer specialist. Her mission was to facilitate COBRA's overriding of the computer-controlled submarines G.I. JOE was using to secure a downed space probe from the ocean's floor. An unexpected complication to the assignment was a burgeoning romance between Weidler and Mainframe, the G.I. JOE computer specialist. At first, Zarana coldly rebuffed Mainframe's flirtations, but then she came to genuinely appreciate them and reciprocate them in kind. It was not a viable relationship, given their incompatible allegiances. Zarana ultimately was forced to betray Mainframe, completing her mission, but she did spare his life when her brother Zartan intended to kill him with an explosive.

ZANDAR

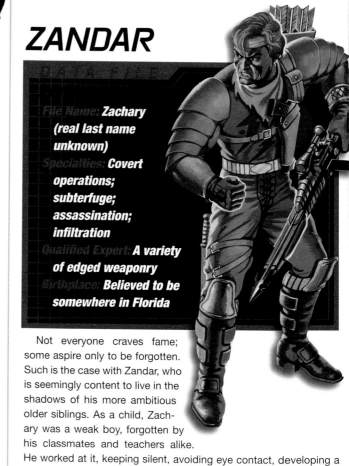

File Name: *Zachary (real last name unknown)*
Specialties: *Covert operations; subterfuge; assassination; infiltration*
Qualified Expert: *A variety of edged weaponry*
Birthplace: *Believed to be somewhere in Florida*

Not everyone craves fame; some aspire only to be forgotten. Such is the case with Zandar, who is seemingly content to live in the shadows of his more ambitious older siblings. As a child, Zachary was a weak boy, forgotten by his classmates and teachers alike. He worked at it, keeping silent, avoiding eye contact, developing a *social* form of invisibility. This developed hand in hand with feelings of entitlement and poorly developed scruples. People would notice that things went missing; no one would notice that Zach stole them.

In the seedier and more dangerous avenues of London, Zachary and his sister, Zoe, carved out a living as grifters and thieves. His sister's performance skills made her the embodiment of misdirection, while Zachary moved in to lift a wallet, pick a purse, or shove a shiv. Their underworld activities landed them in the United States as part of the Dreadnoks, reunited with their long-lost brother, Zartan. Zachary adopted the alias Zandar.

Not that many would ever remember to call him any name at all.

■ *Mission Report: Coil Betrayal*

Though Zandar would have others believe he shunned the spotlight by choice, his reclusion over time fomented a secret animosity toward his brother. Never one to vocalize his disdain, Zandar stewed as his brother accrued riches and underworld notoriety, and his sister advanced up the COBRA chain of command. No success or accolades ever fell his way. He vanished from sight, but no one thought it odd; it was his modus operandi, after all.

Zandar resurfaced as an agent of the Coil, a COBRA splinter group that resurrected Serpentor in a plot to unseat Cobra Commander and conquer the world. Zandar was the agent tasked with kidnapping the commander, an act that sparked another civil war on Cobra Island. Zartan, ostensibly still loyal to the Commander, was one of the many combatants brought to the island. In a fistfight with a Coil trooper, Zartan plunged a knife into his enemy's chest, only to realize he had stabbed his brother. Shaken by this turn of events, Zartan collected his wounded brother and called off his Dreadnoks from supporting COBRA, retreating from the war to mend not only his brother's health, but their relationship as well.

ZANYA

File Name: *Zanya*
(real last name unknown)
Birthplace: *Chicago, Illinois*

As Zartan's daughter, Zanya has big shoes to fill, and she exhibits the tenacity and toughness to do so. That she could earn the respect of so raucous and dangerous a lot as the Dreadnoks is testament enough to her fierceness.

Zanya was born as a result of a fling Zartan had while living in Chicago. Drifting through life with more ambition than responsibility, Zartan unknowingly left the single mother behind to raise young Zanya on her own. The impoverished mother and cruel circumstances resulted in a terrible childhood for Zanya. She was witness to a parade of would-be "fathers" who treated her mother like dirt, an esteem-withering cycle that led her mother to treat Zanya horribly. It never broke Zanya, though; it just fostered

in her an acute anger, and a desire to control her own fate. Her first act exercising such control was to stop her mother's hand in mid-slap. The next was to torch their apartment to cinders.

Zanya then lived her early teenage years in the streets of Chicago, panhandling and stealing to earn a meal a day. She was more than scrappy; she was dangerous in hand-to-hand combat, using her small size and agility to unbalance larger opponents. When she was 14, her older boyfriend, Kevin Shulte, would arrange bets on fights between Zanya and anyone who would underestimate her—which proved to be lucrative enough for the young couple to travel the country. Shulte, envisioning himself as a tough-as-nails gangster (though it was Zanya who did all the real physical work), aspired to join the Dreadnoks. Zanya did, too, but for reasons Kevin would never suspect.

While in the Everglades, an exhibition of Zanya's fighting prowess impressed some Dreadnoks enough for them to invite Zanya and Kevin to their compound. There, Zanya surprised them all by confronting Zartan about her parentage. Her age fit with Zartan's past in Chicago, and he realized she was telling the truth. He gave her an opportunity to join the Dreadnoks.

Kevin hoped to make the most of it; Zanya was now his ticket to the big league. Seeing her as heir apparent to the Dreadnok leadership, Kevin conspired to have Zanya kill Zarana while on an assignment, an act that could easily be pinned on someone else, leaving Zanya and Kevin to climb up the ranks with no visible blood on their hands. Zanya instead savagely beat Kevin. Zarana and Zartan saw that the girl had proven herself—blood was thicker than any aspirations of power and leadership.

COPPERHEAD
(Swamp Fighter)

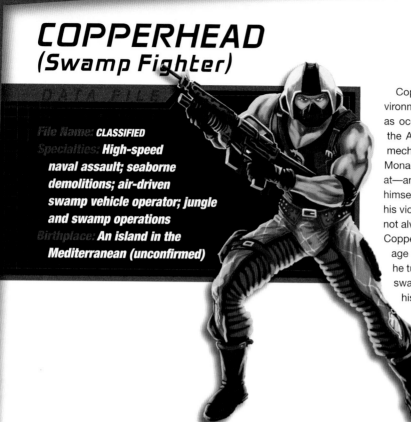

Copperhead is extremely comfortable and capable in swamp environments. Conflicting intelligence reports peg his formative years as occurring in either the Florida Everglades or the rain forests of the Amazon basin. He is also believed to have gathered valuable mechanical experience racing speedboats in high-stakes races in Monaco and Japan. This is likely where he also picked up his skill at—and addiction to—gambling. Copperhead would place bets on himself under false identities, then sabotage other racers to ensure his victories and a healthy payout. However, his luck in the races did not always translate to luck in the cards and other games of chance. Copperhead offered his services to COBRA in exchange for coverage of his debts. When his combat skills proved formidable, and he turned out to be a capable pilot for the COBRA Water Moccasin swamp boat, COBRA gladly paid off—or otherwise eliminated—his bookies.

Copperhead is a gifted mechanic. He spends much time elbow-deep in the transmissions of various COBRA watercraft, tuning and customizing them for maximum performance to match his taste for speed and power.

CRYSTAL BALL
(Hypnotist)

Crystal Ball wraps himself in an impenetrable mythos that claims his origins are steeped in the dark and mysterious power of the occult. None of his creepy tales has borne any evidence of truthfulness, but Crystal Ball's repeated tellings, and his preternaturally compelling delivery, have caused them to gain weight and worth among the more superstitious of COBRA and G.I. JOE ranks. He is supposedly the seventh son of a seventh son, born of a Romalian father and American mother, and granted supernatural powers of telepathy and mind control.

Independent research taken on by Psyche-Out has uncovered another possible origin, tied to an unnatural spike in encyclopedia sales in a specific time and place in Maine. A theatrical hypnotist known as the Trance-Master operated out of Maine and moonlighted as an encyclopedia salesman before traveling abroad to gain new knowledge of hypnotic techniques. His disappearance from the lecture and sideshow circuit corresponded with the appearance of Crystal Ball as part of COBRA.

Whatever the true story behind Crystal Ball's past, and how he came to join COBRA, he has proven to be an effective agent, helping Dr. Mindbender perfect modifications to the brainwave scanner and using his unusual talent at hypnosis to bend the will of prisoners.

DARKLON
(Mercenary)

File Name: *Unknown*
Specialty: *Mercenary*
Birthplace: *Castle Darklon, Darklonia*

A distant cousin to the Destro/McCullen clan, Darklon was the last in a long line of privateers, mercenaries, and investment bankers. He unscrupulously offered his private armies to the highest bidder. His soldiers marched his for-hire banner on the battlefields of some of the most reprehensible conflicts in Eastern Europe. Darklon served as the ruler of the tiny nation of Darklonia, lording from a cast-iron castle in the Alps.

Darklon's military motor pool consisted of surplus from both G.I. JOE and COBRA inventories. He sold these cast-offs to COBRA as test vehicles for the "pythonization" process that rendered them invisible to radar. To prove their effectiveness, these stealth vehicles were surreptitiously launched from Darklonia into neighboring Wolkekuck-uckland. Later, as Destro effectively retired from frontline conflict, Darklon became the leader of the Iron Grenadiers. When Cobra Commander resumed control of COBRA and began expanding operations into Eastern Europe, he targeted Darklon as a potential threat. Darklon died when a COBRA missile launched from Trans-Carpathia destroyed his castle.

NIGHT CREEPERS
(High-Tech Ninjas)

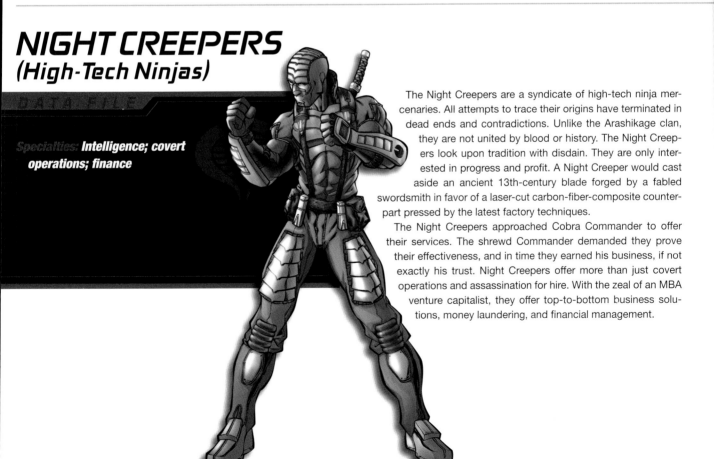

Specialties: *Intelligence; covert operations; finance*

The Night Creepers are a syndicate of high-tech ninja mercenaries. All attempts to trace their origins have terminated in dead ends and contradictions. Unlike the Arashikage clan, they are not united by blood or history. The Night Creepers look upon tradition with disdain. They are only interested in progress and profit. A Night Creeper would cast aside an ancient 13th-century blade forged by a fabled swordsmith in favor of a laser-cut carbon-fiber-composite counterpart pressed by the latest factory techniques.

The Night Creepers approached Cobra Commander to offer their services. The shrewd Commander demanded they prove their effectiveness, and in time they earned his business, if not exactly his trust. Night Creepers offer more than just covert operations and assassination for hire. With the zeal of an MBA venture capitalist, they offer top-to-bottom business solutions, money laundering, and financial management.

OVERKILL
(B.A.T. Leader)

File Name: **Robert Skelton (deceased)**
Specialty: **Infantry leader**
Birthplace: **Unknown**

The first soldier named Overkill began as an experimental prototype for a new generation of B.A.T. troopers. The prototype proved too costly to mass-produce, but enough finances had been sunk into it that it would be considered wasteful to shelve the product indefinitely. The terrifyingly independent B.A.T. was marched onto the battlefield as a type of unit commander, using his cyber-cerebral communication signals to instantly transmit orders to vast numbers of mechanical soldiers.

Like his less intelligent underlings, Overkill could be blasted apart and put back together again, but one disassembly too many eventually taxed his cognitive units. COBRA engineers were unable to re-create the original Overkill, but they did save much of the machinery that drove him. COBRA surgeons next took the mutilated body of a dying organic soldier, the S.A.W. Viper Robert Skelton, and fused it with Overkill's mechanical frame. Thus a new Overkill was created, part organic, part mechanical.

This indefatigable soldier had integral body armor, a self-contained breathing unit, and a wireless network connection ported into his brain. His psyche became forever warped by stripping away the last vestiges of his humanity. Overkill came to favor mechanicals far more than organic company. This psychosis eventually proved to be Overkill's undoing, however, because Skelton longed for the release of death. After he was killed, another organic soldier was fused to the Overkill frame to take over his role as B.A.T. commander.

RAPTOR
(COBRA Falconer)

File Name: **Unknown**
Specialties: **Falconry; finance**
Birthplace: **Somewhere in the United States**

Raptor was once an upwardly mobile tax consultant who took up falconry as an appropriately blue-blooded pastime to impress his richer clients. He discovered an unmistakable kinship with birds of prey, and began breeding falcons, hawks, and ospreys for the avian blood sport. He learned how to breed bigger, stronger birds and equip them with steel-tipped talons. Becoming too obsessed with his feathered minions, Raptor took to dressing like a giant bird in order to put his birds at ease. At first, he supplemented his income by training his falcons to steal jewels or attack profitable game. When he was caught poaching on a COBRA mink ranch by Destro, Raptor's bizarre modus operandi was intriguing enough that Destro allowed him to continue, but only in the service of COBRA.

Raptor was one of the few COBRAs who knew that Fred Broca VII had murdered and replaced the original Cobra Commander. He attempted to divulge this knowledge to Dr. Mindbender, bringing the COBRA scientist to the Commander's supposed burial site. They found an empty grave, for Cobra Commander was in fact not dead. His life had been saved by loyal Crimson Guardsmen, and he slowly rebuilt his power base while Fred Broca VII masqueraded as the leader. Cobra Commander, in an act of cold vengeance, then gathered together the various COBRA agents who had wronged him in the past and tossed them into a landlocked freighter on Cobra Island, which he buried under thousands of tons of rubble. Raptor was among those who perished in the freighter.

RED SHADOWS

The Red Shadows were a paramilitary organization of terrorists devoted to unseating the current world order via advanced technological means. They saw the future of humanity as being strictly controlled by a technocratic order, shaped by science and technology. Among their membership were scientific and artistic visionaries; among their innovations, advanced combat armor and neural accelerants that granted superhuman strength and reflexes.

In their first major public campaign, the Red Shadows were responsible for the deaths of multiple world leaders and key COBRA and G.I. JOE agents. To the Red Shadows, the ongoing struggle between COBRA and G.I. JOE was simply symptomatic of a global system that needed upheaval. Led by Wilder Vaughn, a former MI-5 special agent who, years before, had served alongside Joseph Colton, the Red Shadows proved a lethal threat until their plot was disrupted by the efforts of the G.I. JOE team. Vaughn and other Red Shadow agents disappeared. It is unknown what nefarious plans they may be developing next, but one of their most dangerous aspects is that their actions caused G.I. JOE to lose track of Cobra Commander prior to COBRA's most ambitious global plot.

Dela Eden

Wilder Vaughn

Artur Kulik

SCRAP-IRON
(Anti-Armor Specialist)

File Name: **CLASSIFIED**
Specialties: **Armored vehicle destroyer; weapons designer**
Birthplace: **CLASSIFIED**

A methodical engineer and designer employed by Destro, Scrap-Iron detests imperfection. In his nihilistic view, the world itself is the greatest imperfect blemish on creation, and he strives to develop more sophisticated and elegant instruments of destruction to pound it into order. In service to M.A.R.S. Industries, Scrap-Iron carries out initial field tests on all new armor-piercing munitions and submunitions. He is an expert in a wide variety of remote-launched, laser-guided rocket-propelled piezo-electric fused anti-tank weapons.

His keen analytical nature makes him an amazing strategist. He is able to predict the moves of the enemy well in advance and prepare all the appropriate countermoves along various chains of possibility. His overriding perfectionism makes him nearly intolerable to other COBRA troops, though they put up with his endless demands because he consistently delivers explosive results.

SKULL BUSTER
(Range-Viper Commander)

File Name: **Unknown**
Specialties: **Survival; infantry command**
Birthplace: **Unknown**

The COBRA Range-Vipers were a mean-spirited and tough brigade of survivalists, and one of them rose from the ranks by being twice as mean and three times as nasty as the rest. Dubbed Skull Buster, this Range-Viper embraced the hard life of inhospitable wilderness with zeal, cheerfully dining on any animal that offered enough protein to be worth killing for. Skull Buster imagined himself as the ultimate alpha predator. While he would dine on carrion as a last resort, he was more likely to kill a scavenger such as a vulture or jackal first.

When G.I. JOE was actively pursuing any and all known COBRA operatives around the world, Skull Buster was listed as "at large." He had attempted to leave his past with COBRA behind him and disappear into the wilderness, sequestering himself on a deserted island. G.I. JOE agents Cover Girl and Shipwreck tried to apprehend Skull Buster, but he would not go quietly, finding the notion of spending the rest of his life confined to a small cement room as a fate worse than death.

WILD WEASEL
(COBRA Pilot)

File Name: **CLASSIFIED**
Specialty: **Ground support pilot**
Birthplace: **CLASSIFIED**

As a pilot for hire, Wild Weasel honed his talents in a variety of scattered bush wars in South America and Africa, flying close support aircrafts over the heads of friendly and enemy infantry. A mouth injury sustained during a strafing run resulted in a characteristic sibilance in his speech. In swooping down from the skies to tear apart armored vehicles and squads of soldiers, Wild Weasel developed an arrogant personality; he reviles anything that can't fly. He'll even buzz COBRA troops just for his own sick amusement. This has led many ground-pounders and fellow COBRAs to hate Wild Weasel, but conversely, other pilots—even G.I. JOEs—respect him for his amazing skill behind the stick. Wild Weasel has an unerring eye for judging distance and speed, making him a crack shot with airborne weaponry.

VANCE WINGFIELD
(Militia Leader)

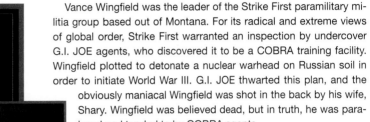

Vance Wingfield was the leader of the Strike First paramilitary militia group based out of Montana. For its radical and extreme views of global order, Strike First warranted an inspection by undercover G.I. JOE agents, who discovered it to be a COBRA training facility. Wingfield plotted to detonate a nuclear warhead on Russian soil in order to initiate World War III. G.I. JOE thwarted this plan, and the obviously maniacal Wingfield was shot in the back by his wife, Shary. Wingfield was believed dead, but in truth, he was paralyzed and tended to by COBRA agents.

His son, Tyler, tried to follow in his father's footsteps in order to avenge his father's (presumed) death. Tyler hatched a similar diabolical plot, attempting to spread the lethal Death Angel virus by means of a commandeered missile base. Tyler, though, was also stopped by G.I. JOE. Shary Wingfield shot him in the back as well, as history seemingly repeated itself in a most dramatic way.

Vance surfaced a short time later as the mastermind behind an incredibly destructive plot that used M.A.R.S. technology to tug satellites from orbit and have them collide with cities on earth. Tens of thousands of innocent civilians were killed when Wingfield unleashed devastation on Chicago and Silicon Valley. G.I. JOE agents were able to stop Wingfield and take him into custody before he could cause more chaos.

WRAITH
(Counterintelligence)

Charles Halifax was an extremely skilled mercenary whose loyalty was up for grabs by those who could offer the most intriguing—not necessarily the most valuable—prize for his services. Destro lured Halifax with an opportunity to become nearly indestructible by offering him a stolen stealth suit, reportedly designed by the Red Shadows for use by the Chinese. Wraith readily accepted, becoming the ultimate infiltration agent.

As the Wraith, Halifax could turn practically invisible thanks to light-warping technology built into his high-tech suit. Its reinforced ceramic plates were impenetrable, and its forearm cannon yielded much destructive potential. The stealth suit's only drawback was that rapid movement negated some of the imaging technology, causing a partial outline to appear around his body. However, if Wraith was close enough for this outline to be seen, he had likely already targeted his would-be spotter.

Despite the advanced hardware and a cunning intellect, Wraith could not outrun a vengeful Baroness looking to eliminate all who had wronged her in the past. The Baroness killed the Wraith, and the suit fell back into the hands of the Red Shadows.

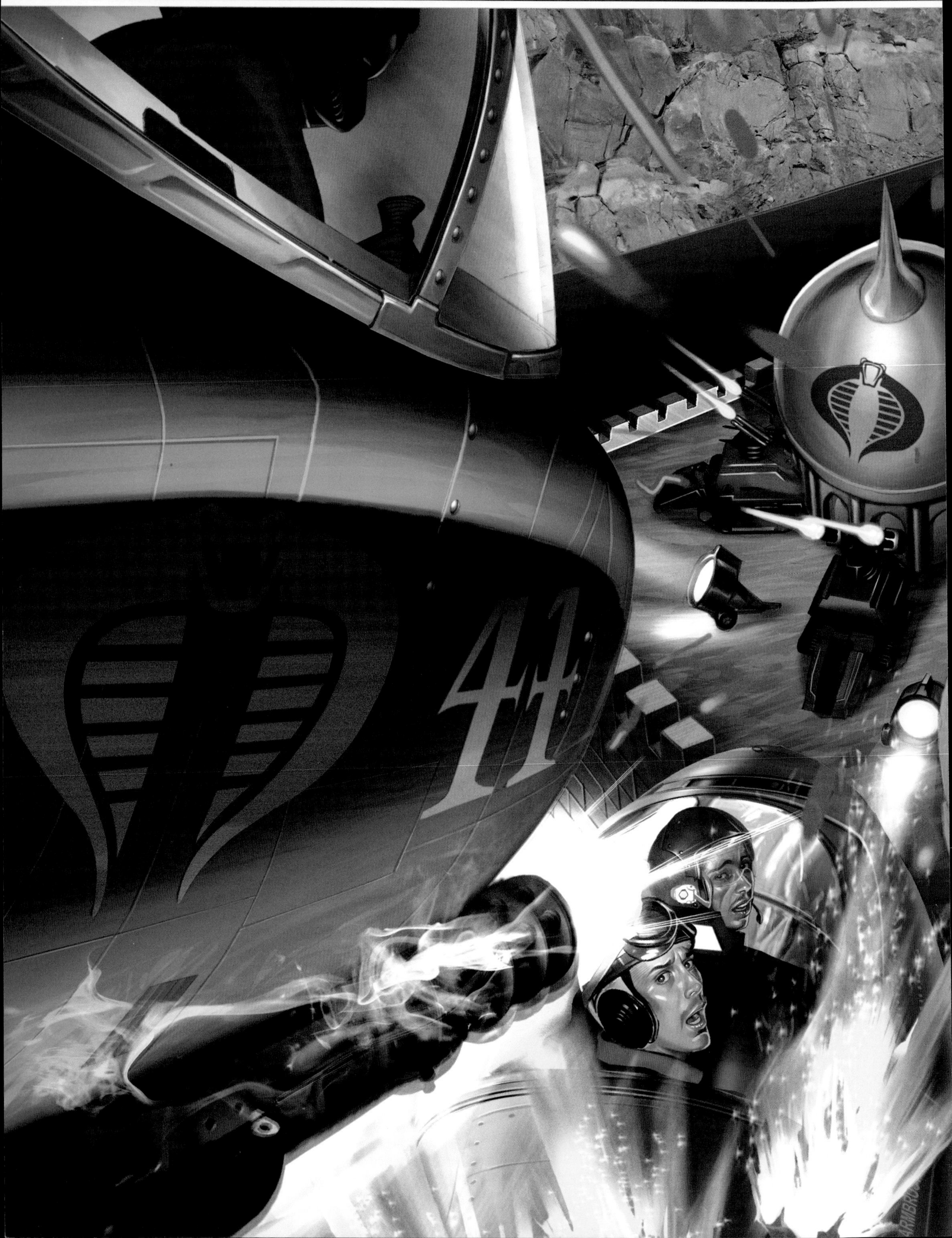
41

CHAPTER 3

MOTOR POOL: VEHICLES & HARDWARE

OVER LAND...

G.I. JOE VAMP

One of the most versatile and proven vehicles in the G.I. JOE motor pool is the VAMP, a multipurpose attack vehicle that has served the team for years. G.I. JOE's king grease monkey, Clutch, flexes his automotive muscles maintaining and improving the team's fleet of VAMPs, keeping the vehicles shipshape and cutting-edge with his constant tinkering beneath the hoods. Off the assembly line, the original VAMP sported a 4.8-liter fuel-injected turbocharged V-12 engine, which could kick the vehicle to speeds up to 95 mph. Its operational range was 550 miles, though its rear cradle and other storage bins could extend that range to 850 miles when filled with self-sealing, ruggedized gas cans.

The VAMP's lightweight construction assures its battlefield agility, especially with a lead-foot like Clutch behind the wheel. Should a near-miss flip the vehicle, its sturdy roll cage keeps driver and passenger from being flattened by the vehicle's 2.25-ton weight... as Clutch found out when he rolled a VAMP down a steep grade in the Swiss Alps without suffering a scratch.

Earning the *MP* at the end of its acronym, the VAMP is truly multipurpose and ruggedized for operation across varied terrain. Its four-wheel drive and independent suspension allow it to venture into the wilds cross-country. Self-sealing off-road flotation tires let the VAMP brave the muck of wetlands; should it ever get really stuck, its grille houses a heavy-duty winch. Piercing the darkness are quartz-halogen headlamps with electric defrost settings. The vehicle's back end features a tow hook capable of hauling such heavy loads as a HAL laser cannon into combat.

The first-issue VAMPs came standard with a 7.62mm hood-mounted machine gun. The vehicle's rear-mounted turret first featured a .50-caliber twin-mount computer-synchronized machine gun controlled via a removable remote panel on the dashboard. The Mark II VAMP and the subsequent Tiger Sting variant featured a four-bay box missile launcher, which housed various short- and medium-range surface-to-surface fragmentation, demolition, fire, and smoke missiles. Later models included a dash-mounted 60mm machine gun and a laser cannon affixed to the roll cage crossbars.

Proving the maxim that imitation is the highest form of flattery, COBRA Command found the VAMP so effective that it reverse-engineered captured samples to become the basis of their Stinger and Rattler 4WD assault vehicles. The Dreadnoks were also known to use captured VAMPs.

AWE Striker

Its abbreviated sandrail-like chassis, integrated roll cage, and large 175/70/VR15 Pirelli off-road tires give the AWE Striker the appearance of a dune buggy, but this vehicle is designed to handle a wide variety of weather and terrain conditions. This versatility is the source of its name, the All Weather & Environment Striker.

A rear-mounted 200-horsepower inner-cooled six-cylinder fuel-injected transverse engine grants the light strike vehicle an off-road speed of about 60 miles per hour, dependent on terrain conditions. The AWE Striker can work its way through the densest of underbrush or most unstable of dunes, and carry on through blinding storms. Its lightweight construction—an aluminum-alloy engine and fiberglass frame—and a fully adjustable nitrogen-dampened independent suspension grant it breakneck mobility.

The AWE Striker seats two in an exposed carriage—the vehicle sheds any sort of armored protection in exchange for its speed and maneuverability. For weaponry, it boasts a top-mounted modified 7.62mm six-barreled mini-gun with 6,000 rounds of ammunition in a tandem magazine on a linkless feed mechanism. The spinning barrels of the gun are housed within a flash suppressor. A counterweight at the end of the cannon helps alleviate torque pull from the rotation of the barrels. The weapon mounts on an auto-tracking platform that follows a dashboard-mounted laser target designator. Some models of the AWE Striker featured instead a 10-round recoilless rifle, but the blast of the weapon was still enough to upset the nimble vehicle on particularly uncertain terrain.

In its support of extended special missions, the AWE Striker carries a complex yet rugged suite of communications equipment. A pair of tall, two-way communications antennas extend from the vehicle fairing, offering gigahertz-range frequency wobbling to keep enemies from intercepting vital transmissions.

LCV Recon Sled

The LCV Recon Sled is a low crawl vehicle intended for stealthy insertion of a single soldier deep behind enemy lines. Its peculiar ground-hugging frame has a height of less than three feet off the ground, allowing the sled to slink beneath the detection umbrella of most radar systems. Its odd configuration—with the driver lying on his or her belly—may look uncomfortable at first glance, but the operator rests atop an ergonomically designed bio-fit saddle, adjusting steering and acceleration with variable-select knee and leg controls.

An array of electronic detection equipment crowds the forward section of the sled, serving the vehicle well in reconnaissance duty. The screen displays are further enhanced by holographic HUD projection along the inner canopy, and a digital-zoom periscope pokes from the upper frame of the sled, capturing and recording imagery for later analysis or transmitting it directly to other operatives.

The sled is lightweight and lightly armored, though its forward profile completely conceals the rider behind an armored shroud that protects against small-arms fire. A side-mounted auto-loading 9mm machine gun provides anti-personnel fire to cover fast escapes. The sled relies more on its near-silent 96-horsepower epoxy-sleeved aluminum engine to avoid detection than on any offensive systems to get out of a jam.

G.I. JOE Mauler M.B.T.

The Main Battle Tank of the G.I. JOE ground forces, the Mauler M.B.T. was originally intended to replace the older MOBAT, but thanks to innovations and lessons learned, the original MOBAT was upgraded to serve alongside its newer cousin on the battlefield.

The Mauler's heavy-duty skin consists of lightweight nylon micromesh titanium armor, able to withstand all but the most direct anti-tank fire. The tank's speed and horsepower have led it to be nicknamed the "iron steamroller," especially after the disconcerting sight of the Mauler plowing down phalanxes of COBRA B.A.T.s without shedding any momentum.

Tank commanders such as Steeler and Heavy Metal remain well connected to the outside world despite this thick armored shell. A vehicle-to-vehicle coded transmitter keeps the Mauler's onboard computer systems in touch with other friendly vessels via synchronized-scrambling [G.I. JOE code] protocols, while twin shortwave transmitters connect it to any and all receivers in range. For direct communications without fear of interception, a vehicle-to-ground personnel two-way comm-link extends from the turret assembly, allowing contact via a traditional handset.

The tank crew—consisting of a commander, a gunner, a loader, and a driver—gets a wraparound view of the battlefield with multiple layers of data that can be toggled on and off. A thermal viewer that rotates independently of the tank chassis provides one level of information, while a holographic imager translates data from the computerized battle management systems into a virtual landscape relayed to goggles worn by the crew. At the time such systems were rolled out, they were cutting-edge, but subsequent tank generations—such as the Persuader and the Patriot Grizzly—have since rendered these advancements commonplace. Even the MOBATs still in use by the G.I. JOE team sport such tech.

A gas-guzzling supercharged Avco-Lycoming A.G.T. 1500C multi-

Representative G.I. JOE Multipurpose Vehicles

VAMP

- **Primary Armament:** Mk I: turret-mounted .50-cal twin-mount machine-gun turret; Mk II: four-bay box missile launchers; Later models: laser cannons
- **Secondary Armament:** Hood-mounted 7.62 mm machine gun; optional dash-mounted 60mm machine gun
- **Special Equipment:** Radar scanner and multiband radio frequency jammers
- **Maximum Speed:** 140 mph with Clutch's modifications; 95 mph standard; 48 mph off-road
- **Maximum Range:** 550 miles; 850 miles extended

Desert Fox 6WD

- **Primary Armament:** 20mm automatic anti-aircraft cannon
- **Secondary Armament:** "Scorpion" SS-12 anti-tank missiles
- **Special Equipment:** 327 CID/350 BHP supercharged engine; dual transaxle/pivoting real-wheel-drive unit
- **Maximum Speed:** 150 mph; 65 mph off-road
- **Maximum Range:** 500 miles

Hammer/Brawler Humvee

- **Primary Armament:** Multideployable, twin-barreled side gun stations; high-impact pulse cannon with mega tracer round capacity (Brawler variant includes rotating multi-rocket launcher)

- **Secondary Armament:** Long-range guided missile system
- **Special Equipment:** Fully rotational computer-controlled gun turret
- **Maximum Speed:** 65 mph
- **Maximum Range:** 350 miles

AWE Striker

- **Primary Armament:** 7.62mm mini-gun with 6,000 rounds of ammunition, with dash-mounted laser target designator
- **Special Equipment:** Heavy-duty all-terrain tires; gigahertz-range frequency wobbler clandestine ops radio
- **Maximum Speed:** 105 mph road; 60 mph off-road
- **Maximum Range:** 520 miles

LCV Recon Sled

- **Primary Armament:** 9mm machine gun with 900 rounds
- **Special Equipment:** Array of thermal imaging sensor systems; digital video recorder and transmitter; self-sealing gas tank
- **Maximum Speed:** 65 mph road; 40 mph off-road
- **Maximum Range:** 180 miles

Representative G.I. JOE AFVs

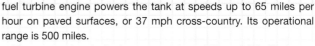

MOBAT

- **Primary Armament:**
  90mm anti-tank cannon
  with 105 rounds; variant:
  130mm cannon
- **Secondary Armament:**
  .50-cal machine gun
- **Special Equipment:**
  Halon fire suppression system; dual-action hydraulic shock
  absorbers
- **Maximum Speed:** 44 mph; 34 mph off-road
- **Maximum Range:** 340 miles

Mauler M.B.T.

- **Primary Armament:**
  105mm M68 rifled gun;
  variant: MXZ 125mm Earthquake cannon
- **Secondary Armament:**
  .50-cal M2HB machine gun;
  two M240 7.62mm machine
  guns
- **Special Equipment:** Lightweight titanium armor; lead-
  lined weapons storage compartment
- **Maximum Speed:** 65 mph; 37 mph off-road
- **Maximum Range:** 500 miles

Wolverine

- **Primary Armament:**
  12 anti-tank or anti-personnel
  medium-range, optically sighted,
  laser-designated missiles
- **Maximum Speed:** 33 mph; 20
  mph off-road
- **Maximum Range:** 450 miles

Armadillo M2710 Mini-Tank

- **Primary Armament:**
  4x60mm synchronized
  variable-range cluster
  cannon
- **Special Equipment:**
  Welded aluminum
  laminate hull armor;
  quick-repair high-speed track assemblies; rear roll bar
- **Maximum Speed:** 70 mph; 45 mph cross-country
- **Maximum Range:** 250 miles

fuel turbine engine powers the tank at speeds up to 65 miles per hour on paved surfaces, or 37 mph cross-country. Its operational range is 500 miles.

The cannon's principal armament is a 105mm M68 rifled gun, capable of lobbing up to 75 rounds of high-explosive warheads. A costlier M.B.T.-A1 variant sports an MXZ 125mm "Earthquake" cannon that can fire HEAT (high-explosive anti-tank), MPAT (multi-purpose anti-tank), HE-FS (high-explosive fin-stabilized), and APFSDS (armor-piercing fin-stabilized discarding sabot) rounds. Should long-range bombardment turn into a close-range brawl, the tank features top-mounted smoke dispensers and anti-personnel charges.

Secondary armament varies among a mix of easily swappable machine-gun additions on standard mounts. A common configuration includes a .50-caliber M2HB heavy machine gun supplemented by two M240 7.62mm machine guns.

G.I. JOE R.O.C.C.

After their headquarters was compromised by COBRA, the scaled-down G.I. JOE team code-named Sigma 6 operated out of a mobile fortress code-named the R.O.C.C.—Rolling Operation Command Center. Unlike previous incarnations of a mobile HQ, the R.O.C.C. relies on an element of surprise and duplicity. The oversized transport isn't exactly stealthy, but it does boast nested holographic imaging arrays that allow for the projection of false "skins" along its surface. These can cause the R.O.C.C. to resemble a big-rig truck or civilian transport, concealing its military function. As such, the R.O.C.C. can travel unobtrusively over interstate highways.

The R.O.C.C. is essentially an armored articulated truck, with two primary components—the towing engine, or tractor, and the semi-trailer containing the command center. Durable data linkages keep both components in constant communication, relaying important motion, stress, and performance data to an onboard computer that "housekeeps" all driving and maintenance functions. The cab-over-engine (COE) tractor is a two-axle design, with super single tires distributing weight and grabbing traction, allowing it to haul more than 70 tons. The streamlined fairing above the sleeper cab includes a retractable missile launcher with eight ground-to-air Shockblast HE-35 missiles.

The craft's trailer section contains all the systems expected of a modern command center, including heavily encrypted wireless network connections to national defense computer systems. The R.O.C.C. has clearance to serve as a field command post (serving under a major to colonel) and, with Pentagon authorization, flag command level (such as when General Hawk takes command). Its own dedicated relay satellite keeps the R.O.C.C. tied in with more permanent command centers around the world.

The trailer has slots for two modular 30mm turret machine guns that can be remote-operated from the cab or specifically manned from the command center. The R.O.C.C. also includes a compact escape and recon jet using reverse-engineered M.A.R.S. A.G.P. technology that allows for it to "cold launch" from the trailer launchpad before its combustion chambers fire and the jet engines flare to life.

Bridge Layer

The concept of a vehicle-launched bridge to span trenches, rivers, or other impassable gaps on the battlefield has been around

R.O.C.C.

- **Primary Armament:** Shockblast HE-35 missiles
- **Secondary Armament:** Two 30mm turret cannons
- **Special Equipment:** 327 CID/350 BHP supercharged engine; dual transaxle/ pivoting rear-wheel-drive unit
- **Maximum Speed:** 65 mph; 30 mph off-road
- **Maximum Range:** 500 miles

Rolling Thunder

- **Primary Armament:** Turreted 50mm mortar cannon; deployable twin six-stage missile launchers
- **Secondary Armament:** 15 short- and long-range air-to-ground and air-to-air tactical missiles; four wing-mounted gunner stations
- **Special Equipment:** Fully armed one-man scout vehicle; armored all-terrain tires; ground ordnance loading capabilities; radar-guided weapons systems
- **Maximum Speed:** 160 mph; 75 mph off-road
- **Maximum Range:** 400 miles

General

- **Primary Armament:** Four 30mm dual-barreled corner cannons for flank defense; long-range, positionable mortar cannon enclosure with munitions stockpile
- **Secondary Armament:** Four tri-barreled 30mm machine-gun defensive armament stations; ground-hugging heat-sensitive surface-to-surface missile launchers
- **Special Equipment:** Recoiling front tow hook with 50,000-pound test cable; crushproof, titanium-plated protective cockpit shields; landing platform; bombardment shield
- **Maximum Speed:** 50 mph; 20 mph off-road
- **Maximum Range:** 400 miles

Mobile Command Center

- **Primary Armament:** Two reflex coaxial computer-operated .50-cal cannons
- **Secondary Armament:** Two four-pod Shockwave electronic HE-27 250-pound missile launchers; "Swinger" sidewinder-mounted missile launcher
- **Special Equipment:** Nonclogging "Heavy Hauler" steel-plated tracks; 2,000-kilowatt/2,700-horsepower diesel engine; "Barrage" phased array targeting computer
- **Maximum Speed:** 45 mph; 15 mph off-road
- **Maximum Range:** 500 miles

Bridge Layer

- **Primary Armament:** Two 152mm anti-tank cannons
- **Secondary Armament:** Two 2.75-inch anti-tank/ anti-personnel rocket launchers
- **Special Equipment:** Magnesium alloy road plate extendable bridge; laser target designation system
- **Maximum Speed:** 44 mph road; 25 mph off-road
- **Maximum Range:** 550 miles

H.A.V.O.C.

- **Primary Armament:** Twin 75mm recoil-less Leveler cannons with 20 rounds of ammunition each
- **Secondary Armament:** Dual 9mm Repeater auto-load machine guns with 500 rounds of ammunition each
- **Ordnance:** Four Lancer rear-mounted anti-armor heat-seeking missiles
- **Special Equipment:** Rear-launched anti-personnel hovercraft; distributed control system; heavy armor
- **Maximum Speed:** 40 mph road; 15 mph off-road
- **Maximum Range:** 175 miles

since the First World War. The G.I. JOE incarnation, the MIAB5367D Bridge Layer, is code-named the Toss 'N Cross. It consists of a re-purposed tank chassis with a top-mounted, folding bridge on an extendible hydraulic cradle. In typical operation, the Toss 'N Cross deploys its bridge across spans measuring up to 23 feet, then detaches its hydraulic arms. Armored infantry crosses the bridge; the Bridge Layer itself is the last vehicle to cross. It reconnects its arms to lift the bridge, folding it back to its stowed configuration. The magnesium-alloy road plate bridge can support more than 60 tons of weight.

The tank chassis features a titanium alloy/nylon micromesh bonded hull. An HTS-T2 forced-induction 1,700-horsepower turbine engine provides a top speed of 44 miles per hour, and the Bridge Layer has an operational range of 550 miles.

Armament consists of a pair of 152mm anti-tank "Rap" (rocket-assisted projectile) cannons with six rounds each. Both are paired to a 2.75-inch anti-tank or anti-personnel rocket launcher with 40 rounds. The weapons systems share a digital ballistics computer-aided firing system, with precision data supplied by dedicated laser target designators on each cannon.

H.A.V.O.C.

The product of advanced military design explorations and experimentation, the H.A.V.O.C. is unlike any other armored fighting vehicle on the battlefield. Specifically engineered for the G.I. JOE team, the Heavy Articulated Vehicle Ordnance Carrier is ideally suited for short, heavy-fire campaigns.

The armored carrier's hunchback design accentuates its primary armament: twin massive recoil-less 75mm Leveler cannons for long-range assault. Both are mounted on articulated hydraulic arms that stabilize and elevate the twin weapons systems. These forward-facing cannons carry 20 rounds of ammunition each, and can be operated from a dorsally mounted gunnery chair. The exposed nature of the chair limits its use in the thick of close combat, though the cannons can be fired from the armored cabin as well.

The front of the H.A.V.O.C. features dual 9mm Repeater auto-load machine guns, each with 500 rounds of ammo. The H.A.V.O.C. also lugs a quartet of rear-mounted anti-armor heat-seeking Lancer missiles. As impressive as these armaments are, the H.A.V.O.C. requires a near-constant resupply of ammunition, limiting its role in extended operations. Should the H.A.V.O.C. expend all its weaponry, its thick armor will keep it protected as it moves off the battlefield.

A nine-liter, 900-horsepower diesel engine drives the four sets of nonclogging epoxy caterpillar tracks, granting the H.A.V.O.C. a top speed of 40 miles per hour when fully loaded. The H.A.V.O.C. boasts a distributed control system that allows the vehicle to be piloted from its armored forward cabin, the gunnery command chair, or even remotely.

Launched from a reinforced liftoff pad is a small, one-person hovercraft pod, used for anti-personnel or recon operations. Twin lifting fans driven by a 115-horsepower direct-drive Blower engine carry the sled-like conveyance to altitudes of 400 feet and speeds of up to 60 miles per hour. The hovercraft comes equipped with two 7.62mm computer-synchronized machine guns with 300 rounds of ammunition each.

G.I. JOE Snow Cat

Able to withstand merciless polar weather conditions, the stalwart Snow Cat may have been eclipsed by newer, more advanced arctic AFVs, but this two-man half-track mobilization unit is still capable of holding its own against a host of COBRA cold-weather threats. The lack of onboard electronics arguably make the Snow Cat more reliable in extreme conditions, where glitches during subzero whiteouts cannot be tolerated.

The Snow Cat's rear missile rack can rotate 360 degrees and elevate 45 degrees. Its four bays can each hold a 250-pound Shockwave HE-27 electronic missile, though different payloads can be swapped out depending on mission requirements. Bracketing the vehicle are a pair of low-pressure, high-speed Avalanche ski missiles that launch from the Snow Cat's track fairing. When its onboard propellant ignites, these explosives can ski across an icy surface at

Representative G.I. JOE Cold-Weather Assault Vehicles

Snow Cat EB-884

- **Primary Armament:** Four launcher-based fire-by-wire Shockwave HE-27 missiles
- **Secondary Armament:** Two low-pressure ski-mounted Avalanche missiles
- **Special Equipment:** Titanium-belted tracker treads; canopy ejection mechanism; thermal-insulated cockpit; long-range weapons guidance system; long-range radio transmitter
- **Maximum Speed:** 80 mph road; 50 mph off-road
- **Maximum Range:** 200 miles

Polar Battle Bear

- **Primary Armament:** Two .50-cal machine guns with 250 rounds each
- **Secondary Armament:** Two skid-mounted heat-seeking missiles
- **Special Equipment:** Independently suspended floating bogey system; bulletproof acrylic windscreen; 160-horsepower rear-mounted V-6 engine
- **Maximum Speed:** 42 mph off-road
- **Maximum Range:** 325 miles

better than 100 miles per hour and be triggered by proximity fuses. Later models did away with the ski-mounted ordnance, replacing it with electrically heated machine guns or laser cannons.

A nine-liter 680-horsepower direct-ignition engine mounted on a transaxle assembly makes the Snow Cat purr, plowing its half-track drive through the thickest of snowdrifts. The Cat's low front face and apron panel serve as a rudimentary snowplow, though a more dedicated plow-front can be affixed if need be. The wheel arches sport snow and mud deflectors, while the rims and track sprocket plates feature nonclogging assemblies.

Forward xenon spotlamps illuminate the path ahead, especially helpful in environments where nights can stretch on for months. Because the forward lamps are often submerged in deep snow, a secondary set of auxiliary lamps shine from a mount atop the cabin. These can be powered by an independent generator to serve as lifesaving beacons in case of a breakdown. Heavy-duty dual-blade canopy wipers keep the snow from building up on the windscreen, while impregnated filaments serve to defrost the windows from ice buildup.

The interior insulated cabin can be heated to a comfortable temperature and carry a driver, plus a passenger who serves as the weapons operator. A third passenger can squeeze in if necessary, and additional crew can hold on to grab bars on the rear skirt, though given the Snow Cat's typical operating temperatures, few would opt to ride outside if given a choice.

COBRA H.I.S.S. Tank

Prior to COBRA entering into an exclusive business arrangement with M.A.R.S. Industries, the organization made do with Warsaw Pact surplus armored fighting vehicles painted dark blue and sporting COBRA sigils. While capable of successful combat engagements in third-world arenas, these outdated designs were simply no match for G.I. JOE's modern tanks. Therefore, one of the first orders Cobra Commander placed with the weapons development firm was for a new generation of unique combat tanks that could not only hold their own on today's battlefield, but also be distinctive enough to be uniquely COBRA. The result was the High-Speed Sentry—the COBRA H.I.S.S. tank.

Representative Threat Assault Vehicles

COBRA H.I.S.S. High-Speed Sentry

- **Primary Armament:** Dorsal-mounted twin "Diablo" 30mm area fire automatic guns with 2,000 rounds each
- **Special Equipment:** Low-level light and infrared scanners plus micro-resolution radar for high-speed vehicle maneuvering and personnel motion detection
- **Maximum Speed:** 75 mph road; 60 mph cross-country
- **Maximum Range:** 275 miles

COBRA STUN

- **Primary Armament:** Four 3.5-inch high-explosive rocket launchers with 400 drum-fired rounds each
- **Secondary Armament:** 9mm circular-magazine machine gun with 300 rounds
- **Special Equipment:** Battle-armored wheel shields; separating boron/epoxy battle shells
- **Maximum Speed:** 75 mph road; 44 mph cross-country
- **Maximum Range:** 340 miles

Iron Grenadier D.E.M.O.N. (Dual Elevating Multi-Ordnance Neutralizer)

- **Primary Armament:** Roof-mounted magnetic array triple-lens laser; variable energy pivoting triple-barreled laser
- **Secondary Armament:** Six computer-assisted anti-aircraft/anti-personnel missiles
- **Special Equipment:** High-intensity solar power gather panel; angled ballistic-resistant windscreens; thermal imaging optical scanner; reconfigurable chassis for battlefield elevation
- **Maximum Speed:** 40 mph road; 25 mph cross-country
- **Maximum Range:** 75 miles

Maggot

- **Primary Armament:** 155mm RAP long-range gun howitzer
- **Secondary Armament:** Forward 40mm cannon; turret-mounted HEAT anti-tank laser cannon
- **Special Equipment:** Forward armored anti-tank vehicle; rear armored recon vehicle
- **Maximum Speed:** Total assembly: 40 mph road, 15 mph off-road; ATV: 75 mph road, 45 mph off-road; ARV: 50 mph road, 25 mph off-road
- **Maximum Range:** 200 miles

At 9.75 tons, the H.I.S.S. tank is lightweight and speedy, using titanium alloy laminate composite hull armor to lessen overall vehicle mass. Its compact custom M.A.R.S. GH7c power plant can propel the tank at top speeds of 75 miles per hour. Fully loaded, the H.I.S.S. tank has an operational range of 275 miles. Integral fuel canisters feature self-sealing skins to minimize fuel leakage from enemy bullet penetration.

The original, more robust prototype H.I.S.S.—the GH5a model—featured an armored roll cage over the driver's chamber, with entrance and egress provided by a lowering hydraulic jaw. This was eventually phased out because damage sustained to the vehicle could lead to hydraulic failure, essentially trapping the driver within the tank, a grim situation experienced by the Baroness firsthand during a COBRA night attack on the US Treasury.

The H.I.S.S. tank's sole armament rests on a dorsal turret, which can be operated by a dedicated gunner, or less effectively from the driver's compartment. The original prototype H.I.S.S. tanks sported 90mm anti-tank and anti-aircraft ammunition; however, low fire rate and limited ammunition storage space caused this to be phased out and replaced by twin Diablo 30mm area fire automatic guns with 2,000 rounds of ammunition. Other variants carry twin synchronized EER-8 laser-seeking anti-tank launchers.

The H.I.S.S. tank has a tall profile, its trapezoidal shape making a tempting target—though its speed makes it difficult to hit. Its front silhouette is very thin. Its height and the shallow angle of depression of its dorsal cannon mean that a H.I.S.S. tank cannot target enemies immediately flanking it. This has led to a weakness to sappers who attempt to mine the tank's tall track assembly. To counter this flaw, H.I.S.S. tanks often operate in tandem, or have infantry or small scout vehicles running on each side to pick off would-be saboteurs. At the rear end of the tank is an abbreviated personnel apron to carry additional infantry, and a tow hook for hauling equipment.

Onboard electronics include low-level light and infrared scanners plus micro-resolution radar for high-speed vehicle maneuvering and personnel motion detection. These tend to make the H.I.S.S. tank fairly visible to EM scanners, and thus far the H.I.S.S. has resisted attempts at successful pythonization stealth modification.

The success of the original H.I.S.S. Mk I GH7c has spawned several subsequent series and variants, including the Mk II JVK585, the Mk III SM8a, the Mk IV S66-4, and the Toxo-Viper specialized biohazard combat vehicle known as the Septic Tank.

COBRA Maggot

A long-range artillery tank developed during the reign of Serpentor, the COBRA Maggot is a combination anti-armor vehicle, artillery piece, and versatile command post—a three-in-one segmented tank. The two main bodies of the Maggot are connected by an articulated hydropneumatic joint.

The forward treaded unit—dubbed a high-speed armored anti-tank vehicle (ATV)—is built around a Spin-Up 1,000-horsepower turbo diesel engine that provides propulsion enough for it to tow the remainder of the Maggot. When unencumbered from the tail section, the ATV is capable of speeds up to 75 miles per hour. The ATV includes a forward-mounted sweeping 40mm cannon capable of firing 240 rounds per minute. The ATV's primary armament is a top gyro-turret-mounted HEAT (high-explosive anti-tank) laser cannon that is patched into a rotating MAG-61 radar system.

The tail section of the Maggot further subdivides into two battlefield components. The turret assembly disconnects from the towing

cradle by battlefield technicians (often Techno-Vipers), who then lock it into position with a quartet of sturdy support legs. The enormous gun howitzer is a 155mm RAP (rocket-assisted projectile) long-range cannon supported by four hydropneumatic variable recoil supports. The cannon can lob shells over distances of approximately 18 miles.

The treaded cradle that supports the turret, once freed of its load, can operate as either an armored reconnaissance vehicle (ARV) or a central fire control vehicle. This boxy, open-carriage tracked vehicle has no weaponry, but is equipped with long-range scanners and telemetric equipment that can connect to multiple Maggots across a battlefield, forming a coordinated artillery battery.

The COBRA soldiers tasked with maintaining and operating the Maggots are W.O.R.M.S.—weapon ordnance rugged machine specialists.They are cross-trained with specialties that cover all aspects of self-propelled artillery. W.O.R.M.S. serve as drivers, gunners, loaders, combat engineers, and diesel mechanics in the field.

Dreadnok Thunder Machine

Howling its way onto the battlefield like a postapocalyptic nightmare, the Dreadnok Thunder Machine is one of the most hideous combat vehicles to enter a fray. A manic patchwork of military surplus and the spoils of grand theft auto, it is an armored crazy quilt suitable only to Dreadnok sensibilities. And it is Thrasher's pride and joy.

Cataloging the Thunder Machine's capabilities is largely futile, because the vehicle is notoriously unpredictable. The Dreadnoks' constant tinkering with their beloved heavy strike vehicle means that it is never the same threat twice. By all rights, it shouldn't even move, but once it does, it is nearly unstoppable. Somewhere buried beneath all the armor is a stock car frame, heavily reinforced with tubular roll cages and other assemblies to protect the driver from collision. Armor plates cobbled together from a variety of sources—tanks and jet fighters included—surround the Thunder Machine, making its vital compartments impenetrable to bullet fire.

The 4.2-ton vehicle can achieve speeds of 115 miles per hour, hugging the road with 205/50 vr15 racing tires. Its unmuffled engine lets out a deafening racket when fully gunned, but that is nothing compared with the roar emitted by the rear-mounted Knockdead 21K thrust turbojet engine.

The Thunder Machine has only one primary armament, but it's enough to dissuade almost all head-on attacks. A pair of 20mm chain guns with a linked ammo system can fire 2,500 rounds of explosive dual-purpose ammunition. This hail of metal can chew up oncoming traffic like paper, leaving Thrasher to plow through the smoking scraps, knowing he is perfectly safe within his armored cocoon.

...AND SEA

G.I. JOE Killer W.H.A.L.E. Hovercraft

The US Navy maintains a number of hovercraft in service, but primarily in the capacity of landing craft launched from larger vessels to bring supplies and troops ashore. The G.I. JOE Killer W.H.A.L.E. (Warrior: Hovering Assault Launch Envoy) hovercraft is distinct from these in that it is an assault, patrol, and liaison vessel.

Armaments aboard the W.H.A.L.E. include two massive forward-firing 105mm Pounder cannons mounted starboard and port side. These are fired from the navigator's station next to the pilot's command post. On the craft's forward section are two paired "Thrasher" .50-caliber machine guns with 1,800 rounds of ammunition each, affixed to "Crow's Nest" ring turrets. Completing its surface armaments are a pair of four-bay box missile launchers with various short-range anti-ship/anti-armor missiles.

For anti-submersible defense, the W.H.A.L.E. has two depth-charge deployment racks—one on each side. These drop 100-pound SD-30 high-explosive depth charges that are triggered by pressure-sensitive firing mechanisms.

Two gas turbine engines propel the internal fans to generate the air cushion beneath a flexible puncture-resistant steel mesh/nylon composite skirt. This raises the 8.5-ton hovercraft off the surface, affording it a speed of 35 knots over water or 25 miles per hour on land. The W.H.A.L.E. has an operational range of 240 miles, though it is capable of refueling on either land or sea. Its forward hold, if kept clear of troops or cargo, can be stocked with additional fuel bladders.

The W.H.A.L.E. requires a crew of four for optimum performance—a pilot, navigator/gunner, and two machine gunners. It can carry a six-man team aboard, with two serving topside in "shotgun" positions.

The Killer W.H.A.L.E. carries two auxiliary craft. Its nose section launches a high-speed reconnaissance sled, a compact one-man craft with a top speed of 25 knots and a range of 30 miles. The sled carries a mini-watt highly directional radio to maintain contact with the W.H.A.L.E. The second vehicle is a collapsible MOTO-1 HL-66 lightweight surveillance motorcycle for overland recon.

G.I. JOE S.H.A.R.C.

One of the most sophisticated weapons in the G.I. JOE arsenal is the Submersible High-Speed Attack and Recon Craft, known more simply as the S.H.A.R.C. flying submarine. Advanced engineering offers a unique tactical solution for deep-sea- and air-based operations: a small, one-pilot craft capable of descending hundreds of feet beneath the ocean's surface, or striking from the skies above. Transition from water to air is facilitated by extendable hydrofoil legs that allow for high-speed surface takeoffs attainable with twin turbo-fan jet engines. When submerged, the same modular jet assemblies and ceramic laminate exhaust nozzles that generate thrust in the air propel the S.H.A.R.C. through the water.

Its stabilizers and rudders are rigid enough to steer the vessel through both air and water. A boron-epoxy skin over a titanium frame provides strong yet lightweight armor for the S.H.A.R.C., allowing

---

Killer W.H.A.L.E. Hovercraft

- **Primary Armament:** Two 105mm Pounder port and starboard cannons; two paired .50-cal "Thrasher" anti-aircraft machine guns
- **Secondary Armament:** Two four-bay box missile launchers with various surface-to-air missiles; two SD-30 depth-charge racks
- **Special Equipment:** Fully armored cabin; one-man high-speed recon sled; HL-66 lightweight surveillance motorcycle
- **Maximum Speed:** 35 knots over seas; 25 mph cross-country
- **Maximum Range:** 240 miles

DevilFish

- **Primary Armament:** Two hull-mounted .50-cal chain guns with 3,000 rounds each
- **Secondary Armament:** Four short-range spring-launched/solid rocket fuel "Sea Phoenix" anti-armor missiles; wire-guided Mk 78 "Captor" torpedoes
- **Special Equipment:** Twin 110-horsepower water-jet motors; automatic engine kick-up system; semi-active monopulse guidance system
- **Maximum Speed:** 43 knots
- **Maximum Range:** 125 miles

Shark 9000

- **Primary Armament:** Top-mounted compressed water cannon with direct-feed ammo tubes and secondary water reservoirs for land-based assaults; two deck-mounted H20-X1 machine guns
- **Secondary Armament:** "Aqua-Attack" variable-payload missile launcher; "Shark-Pedo" wire-guided torpedo
- **Special Equipment:** Flip-down front boarding ramp; sure-grip external supports for additional troops; high-speed turboprop with two-position direct-drive propeller shaft
- **Maximum Speed:** 45 knots
- **Maximum Range:** 300 nautical miles

USS Flagg (CVN-99)

Named for General Lawrence J. Flagg, the majestic USS *Flagg* is effectively the G.I. JOE operational headquarters at sea. A veritable floating city, the immense craft is a *Nimitz*-class supercarrier extending 1,115 feet in length, with a beam of 257 feet. Twin Westinghouse A4W nuclear reactors coupled with four steam turbines and four shafts propel the craft at better than 30 knots.

The USS *Flagg* is in service to the US Navy, but can be allocated to G.I. JOE operations by presidential decree. Since the rise of Cobra Island, the *Flagg* has been considered an active G.I. JOE command asset, but not all the 3,200 ship's company nor 2,500 air wing personnel are considered G.I. JOE members. Its commander, Admiral Everett P. Colby, is a G.I. JOE operative, code-named Keel-Haul.

The ship's expansive full-deck design accommodates both fixed- and rotary-wing crafts. Angled runways facilitate simultaneous launch and land operations. Four catapults, driven by steam from the ship's reactors, originally aided in takeoffs by providing extra acceleration (up to 180 miles per hour in three seconds) to the launching craft, though these were later replaced by a linear induction electromagnetic launch system. A corollary device, the greased arrestor cable, helps decelerate forward momentum on incoming craft by snagging an aircraft's tailhook. The USS *Flagg* can launch up to four aircraft per minute.

The USS *Flagg*'s decks can support 85 aircraft, though it typically carries 48 fighter and 16 support craft. The *Flagg* also maintains a fleet of repair and support vehicles, typical of an active airfield.

The *Flagg* is armed with four eight-bay RIM-7 Sea Sparrow missiles, three Phalanx CIWS 20mm cannons, and four RIM-116 rolling airframe missile launchers, each with a 21-missile configuration.

it to sustain the pressures of extended dives. Sophisticated sonar-damping gear prevents it from being detected by enemy submersibles.

The S.H.A.R.C. is constantly undergoing design reviews and electronics upgrades, ensuring that it stays at the forefront of advanced weapons technology. The S.H.A.R.C. carries two pairs of wing-mounted retractable .30-caliber "Tidal Wave" machine guns, each with 1,000 rounds of ammunition. It also comes equipped with either a S.H.A.R.C. series-1 ASW, Honeywell Mk 46 Mod 1, or Night Shade Series-5 acoustic homing torpedo.

Though the S.H.A.R.C. can fly at speeds of 850 miles per hour, pilots are advised not to engage in air combat, as the craft is nowhere near as maneuverable in the air as it is in the water, where it can attain speeds of 25 knots when fully submerged. The S.H.A.R.C. has an operational range of 210 nautical miles in water, or 350 nautical miles in air.

COBRA Moray Hydrofoil

A high-speed water demon of a craft, the COBRA Moray hydrofoil slices through the sea in a blur, leaving a curtain of spray in its wake. While COBRA has experimented with more outlandish aquatic craft, the Moray remains one of the more dependable weapons in their

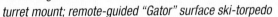

COBRA Moray HydroFoil

- **Primary Armament:** Two 20mm enclosed Vulcan guns, variable rate of fire; two 40mm grenade launchers; top-mounted 60mm cannon or high-explosive charged mortar; four-bay missile launcher with HE-J-180 surface-to-surface missiles
- **Secondary Armament:** Synchronized .50-cal machine gun in ring turret; four .30-cal machine guns; two short-range surface-to-surface HE-07A missiles; two hull-mount acoustic torpedoes; depth-charge canisters
- **Special Equipment:** High-flow 775-horsepower V-12 gasoline engine; carbon-fiber-reinforced laminated single-V hull; extendable hydrofoils
- **Maximum Speed:** 48 knots hullborne; 100 knots foilborne
- **Maximum Range:** 425 nautical miles

COBRA Water Moccasin

- **Primary Armament:** Two variable-rate-of-fire 40mm "Destructor" chain guns
- **Secondary Armament:** Two synchronized .50-cal DES-20B machine guns on a turret mount; remote-guided "Gator" surface ski-torpedo
- **Special Equipment:** Boron-epoxy composite military-grade hull; anti-glare shellproof windscreen; twin supercharged M.A.R.S. Industries V-12 engines (580 horsepower; 9,250 rpm redline); high-pitch high-speed glass-fiber fan
- **Maximum Speed:** 28 knots
- **Maximum Range:** 370 nautical miles

arsenal. A high-flow 775-horsepower V-12 gasoline engine custom-designed by M.A.R.S. Industries powers the craft. This gas turbine engine powers water-jet propulsors that generate thrust, pushing the Moray along its planing boat hull for a speed of 48 knots. With its aft and forward hydrofoil struts extended and submerged, the Moray can accelerate to a sufficient velocity that the foils create lift, raising the attack boat off the water's surface to unmatched speeds of up to 110 knots.

The Moray is extremely well armed. Most of its weapons systems face forward, though the command post—typically manned by a Lamprey officer—maintains a synchronized pair of .50-caliber coaxial machine guns with 3,000 rounds of ammunition each. Additional armaments include four lateral .30-caliber machine guns, two to each flank at the aft end of the boat. The primary cannons are a pair of 20mm enclosed Vulcan guns with variable rate of fire and 4,500 rounds of ammunition apiece. Each is coupled to a 40mm grenade launcher with 300 rounds. A top-mounted 60mm cannon is remote-activated by the pilot, and carries lightweight armor-piercing rounds. Some Morays replace this with a high-explosive charged mortar with 275 rounds.

For ASW (anti-submarine warfare) actions, the Moray carries a stock of 75-pound eight-inch depth-charge canisters deployed from aft dispensers. Other ordnance includes two short-range surface-to-surface electro-optically guided anti-ship HE-07A missiles, along with two hull-mounted acoustic-homing "Black Ray" torpedoes with 225-pound warheads. These projectiles have a range of 6,400 yards before they exhaust their propellant. The forward hull has a retractable four-bay missile launcher carrying HE-J-180 "Jumpstart" surface-to-surface missiles.

...AND AIR

Skystriker XP-14F Air Superiority Fighter

Renowned as a defender of the skies, the XP-14F Skystriker is still in active service as the most storied and venerable of G.I. JOE's air superiority fighters. Based on the airframe of a Grumman F-14 Tomcat, the Skystriker boasts sophisticated—and highly classified—avionics and control systems that allow it to edge into performance territory claimed by such 21st-century fighter planes as the F-22 Raptor, the Storm Eagle, and Sky Sweeper jets. New-generation hotshot pilots know better than to bad-mouth the Skystriker as outdated or antiquated; instead they show the supersonic fighter the respect it has richly earned.

The Skystriker is a variable-sweep wing aircraft, with titanium wings that fold back to allow high-speed pursuit or intercept, or fold out for better maneuverability and sharper turns. An onboard flight computer automatically configures the wings to maximize performance.

Propulsion is provided by Pratt & Whitney TF30-P-412-A axial-flow turbofan engines; each develops up to 25,100 pounds of thrust with afterburner, though some later models opt instead for the General Electric F110 afterburning engine, adding 50 more inches of tailpipe to the craft. With a maximum wing sweep of 68 degrees, the Skystriker can achieve speeds of up to 1,544 miles per hour (or Mach 2.3 at 60,000 feet). In the less rarefied altitudes of sea level, this performance degrades to 910 miles per hour (Mach 1.36). Fully loaded, the Skystriker has an operational range of 2,200 miles and a flight ceiling of more than 53,000 feet.

Standard advanced onboard avionics during the Skystriker's initial manufacture included an AN/AWG-9 fire control radar, an AN/5400-B weapons control computer, an AN/ALR-45 radar warning system, and an AN/ALQ-100 deception electronic countermeasure (ECM) system. Many of these systems have since been upgraded or wholly swapped out with classified block box electronics and ECM pods. The standard targeting package could track 24 targets independently; current units can achieve reliable tracking data on even more targets, though the exact specifications remain classified.

Armament for the Skystriker consists of a portside nose-mounted M61A1 Vulcan 20mm cannon with 800 rounds of ammunition. Standard ordnance includes two AIM-54A Phoenix radar-guided long-range, two AIM-7 Sparrow medium-range, and two AIM-9 Sidewinder short-range air-to-air missiles. More modern ordnance load-outs consist of two AIM-120 AMRAAM Slammers, two AIM-7M Sparrows, and two AIM-9X Sidewinders. The aft section of the Skystriker includes infrared flare launchers and rapid blooming chaff (RBC) dispensers that spread out radar-reflective foil to neutralize the tracking systems of incoming ordnance.

The cockpit seats two in tandem—a pilot and radar intercept officer—with each afforded a full 360-degree view of the sky. Each seat is equipped with ejection capability, with automatically deploying parachutes.

Dragonfly XH-1 Attack Helicopter

An all-weather multipurpose attack helicopter, the twin-engine G.I. JOE Dragonfly finds its design origins in the reliable Bell Huey AH-1 SuperCobra attack helicopter. The Dragonfly builds upon the standard gunship design with improved-efficiency twin General Electric T700 turboshaft engines, as well as advanced electronics such as a 317-A high-resolution radar system.

Beneath the diffusion-bonded canopy is an armored two-seat cockpit in tandem configuration. The co-pilot/gunner sits in the forward position while the pilot sits in the rear. The Dragonfly can achieve speeds of 220 miles per hour with an operational range of 510 miles.

Armaments for the Dragonfly include a rotating chin turret with an M-134 7.62mm mini-gun that has 2,500 rounds of ammunition, plus an airborne flame gun with three minutes of fuel. Variant chin turret configurations equip the Dragonfly with an M197 three-barreled 20mm Gatling gun and M-34 grenade launcher instead. An integral weapons pod located on the port side forward fuselage typically holds a 20mm cannon, though some Dragonflies instead equip this slot with reconnaissance gear such as precision telephoto camera equipment.

The standard pylon armament includes four medium-range air-to-surface wire-guided Scorpion anti-tank rockets, two short-range "fire-and-forget" air-to-air Dragonfire anti-aircraft missiles, and a Hughes XM-230 chain gun with variable rate of fire and 1,200 rounds of aluminum-cased ammunition.

The Dragonfly was successful enough to spawn two notable variants, even in the face of newer, more advanced competing models. The Tiger Fly includes a recoil-less rifle on its pylon mount as well as a smoke grenade launcher. The Locust XH-1 is largely identical to the Dragonfly, save for improved weapons targeting systems and more advanced electronics.

JUMP Jet Pack

One of the first specialized pieces of equipment that really set the G.I. JOE team apart from the conventional military was the JUMP jet pack. Seemingly borrowed from the pulp pages of science fiction, the jet pack transforms a single soldier into an armed high-speed projectile, capable of achieving a velocity of up to 210 miles per hour in short bursts.

The jet mobile propulsion unit (JPU81G-P) is built around a classified liquid rocket fuel turbo-injection system, fed by twin tankages that then lead to a reinforced combustion chamber. From there, the reaction creates a relatively cool-temperature thrust through a pair of articulated exhaust nozzles. Directional control of the pack is facilitated through a wand-like board built into the stalk of an XMLR-2JA laser rifle. First-generation JUMP packs incorporated directional switches on the control wand, while current versions are driven by a multi-axis accelerometer that translates specific movements into flight maneuvers. The XMLR-2JA rifle is a solid-state laser weapon with a high rate of fire and a maximum effective range of 100 yards.

Piloting a JUMP jet pack is difficult; extensive training is required to master the precision acceleration and attitude control. Among the most qualified pilots on the team are Stalker, Starduster, and Grand Slam. Though the JUMP jet pack can operate independent of any launch or monitoring systems, military doctrine stipulates initial launch be carried out on a dedicated pad that includes a diagnostics system status monitor and laser blaster recharge station.

Sky Hawk

Conceived by Lieutenant Frederick Bama of the US Air Force Research Laboratory at the Wright-Patterson Air Force Base in Ohio, the Sky Hawk began as an advanced ground-support aircraft concept. While the USAF passed on the development of such a craft—its primary function in ground support did not afford it any prioritization—G.I. JOE planners saw potential in Bama's pet project.

The Sky Hawk's vertical/short takeoff and landing (V/STOL) feature neutralizes the need for conventional airfields, giving the Sky Hawk enormous deployment versatility. It is compact, lightweight (weighing 3.7 tons), low-maintenance, and inexpensive. Its basic construction allows for it to be shipped within a modular storage container and quickly assembled and fueled at its destination point.

Despite its avian name, the Sky Hawk has a streamlined titanium-alloy chassis and flitting, hovering motions that give it an almost insectile appearance. Its profile is dominated by a forward control cabin that rests in front of two large tubular SK34-series 1 High Bypass turbofan engines. These thrusters rest within an articulated cradle that can tilt 90 degrees, granting the Sky Hawk hover capability. The engines are flanked by vertical stabilizer side planes and capped with a top horizontal tail fin. An air control stabilization intake above the cockpit frame directs airflow to a set of variable-pitch waste gates that work in tandem to give the Sky Hawk remarkable agility.

Its redline speed of 510 miles per hour does not put it in contention with air superiority fighters, but it can harass helicopters and devastate ground emplacements. G.I. JOE infantry troops greatly praise having Sky Hawks for aerial support. The twin 20mm Thunderclap chain guns slung in a sweeping front-arc turret beneath the cockpit can expend 2,400 rounds of withering fire. Add to that a pair of 20mm Vulcan cannons set into recessed nacelles on either side of the cockpit, which each carries 1,100 rounds. Some models of Sky Hawk are fitted instead with 30mm cannons in these slots. Mounted on support pylons extending from the landing skids are two signal-processing air-to-surface rockets, nicknamed SPATS.

The Sky Hawk proved successful enough to spawn multiple generations with improvements and variants. The Sky Patrol version upgraded the engines with GX-3902 Jet Thrusters for increased speed, though at limited range. The latest variation, the Ghost H.A.W.K., includes an advanced suite of electronic countermeasure systems.

Representative G.I. JOE Fighter Craft

Skystriker XP-14F Air Superiority Fighter

- **Ordnance:** *Two long-range, two medium-range, two short-range air-to-air missiles (variable mix, though typically two Phoenixes, two Sparrows, two Sidewinders)*
- **Armament:** *20mm Vulcan cannon*
- **Special Equipment:** *Ejection seats; swing-wing configuration; inertial navigation unit, tactical air navigation system; IFF/UHF/data link and hydraulic reservoir flight system*
- **Maximum Speed:** *Mach 2.3 (1,518 mph)*
- **Maximum Range:** *2,200 miles*

Conquest X-30 Multi-Role High-Performance Fighter

- **Ordnance:** *Eleven external hardpoints accommodating 7,000 pounds of ordnance or equipment (typical configuration: four anti-tank cluster bombs plus two underwing 300-pound fuel tanks that increase operational range by 40 percent)*
- **Armament:** *Two "Double Blast" 20mm Vulcan cannons*
- **Special Equipment:** *Micro-adjust inertial navigation computer; forward-swept wing design; classified electro-optic sensors and avionics*
- **Maximum Speed:** *Mach 2.42 (1,597.2 mph)*
- **Maximum Range:** *1,200 miles*

G.I. JOE Dragonhawk Dropship

Inspired by the versatility and effectiveness of the Sky Hawk VTOL, the top brass commissioned a new vehicle built around the same fundamental airframe characteristics of the smaller vessel, but scaled up for greater operational range, transport duty, and aggressive power. The final Dragonhawk design, initially rolled out as a limited run prototype, proved to be a superior air strike vehicle, ground support, and troop/cargo dropship

The Dragonhawk defies easy categorization, as it straddles both

Phantom X-19 Stealth Fighter

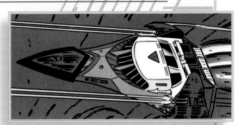

- **Ordnance:** *Two BY-106 "Little Guy" long-range air-to-air missiles; one Bullseye III air-launched cruise missile*
- **Armament:** *Twin energy-diverting pulse-fire laser cannons (for anti-satellite ops; not for air-to-air or air-to-surface combat)*
- **Special Equipment:** *Radar-absorbing "Blackball" paint; rear-mounted "early warning" radome; low IR profile ramjet intakes; titanium-finned air induction directors*
- **Maximum Speed:** *Mach 3.6 (2,375 mph)*
- **Maximum Range:** *3,200 miles*

Storm Eagle ATF (Advanced Tactical Fighter)

- **Ordnance:** *Four air-to-surface electro-optical laser guided tactical missiles*
- **Armament:** *Nose-mounted "Liquid Fire" tactical laser cannon*
- **Special Equipment:** *Programmable radar data scan convertor with multimode display of terrain conditions; double-slotted aeroflo wings with supercritical alloy-reinforced multidirectional flaps*
- **Maximum Speed:** *Mach 2.25 (1,500 mph)*
- **Maximum Range:** *1,600 miles*

fixed-wing and rotary-wing aircraft definitions. Twin reinforced outrigger arms suspend disc-shaped turbo-fan engines that provide lift and thrust. When the arms are flat, the Dragonhawk floats about like a helicopter with true VTOL and hover capability. The arms rotate the discs up to 90 degrees in either direction (for a total 180-degree sweep), providing both forward and reverse thrust, granting the Dragonhawk remarkable agility.

Suspended via a magnetic interface connector (M.I.C.), under the Dragonhawk's frame is a drop cage that deploys troops or small vehicles. To cover its deployment of payload, the Dragonhawk is formidably armed. Its chin turret carries a massive 30mm Gatling gun, while two weapons pods have modular armament bays typically filled with a total of six surface-to-air missiles. There are hard point mounts on either side of the main fuselage and the outward facing sides of the weapon pods for the addition of weapons, often 60mm mortar cannons.

Defiant *Space Shuttle*

A space race emerged between G.I. JOE and COBRA during the height of their conflict, one that remained largely unknown to the rest of the world. The sovereignty afforded to COBRA by the creation of their own island nation allowed the terrorist organization unprecedented and unhindered access to matériel, technology, and scientific research, resulting in a rapidly advancing space program. Though all public-facing aeronautical initiatives were steeply couched as benign missions—the launch of weather, communications, and observation satellites—the brass at the Pentagon prepared for the ramifications of COBRA having unfettered access to the heavens. In the past, G.I. JOE had piggybacked on NASA space shuttle missions for classified operations; the time came for G.I. JOE to have control of its own orbital launches. The result was the *Defiant* space shuttle, a multiuse spaceflight conveyance like no other.

The *Defiant* encompasses three main vehicular modules, all of them custom-engineered and unique to G.I. JOE operations. Launch procedure begins with the transit of an armed and armored crawler gantry, which transports the shuttle from its classified desert base to its launch site. The booster rocket module then blasts off, carrying

Representative G.I. JOE Helicopters

Dragonfly XH-1 Attack Helicopter

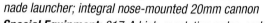

- **Ordnance:** *Standard pylon configuration includes four medium-range air-to-surface wire-guided anti-tank rockets; two short-range air-to-air anti-aircraft missiles*
- **Armament:** *Turret-mount M-134 7.62mm mini-gun; turret-mount airborne flame gun or M-34 grenade launcher; integral nose-mounted 20mm cannon*
- **Special Equipment:** *317-A high-resolution radar; carbon-reinforced rotor; twin turboshaft engines; offset V-tail; rescue hook and winch*
- **Maximum Speed:** *220 mph*
- **Maximum Range:** *510 miles*

Tomahawk Heavy Lift Assault Helicopter

- **Ordnance:** *Six 250-pound wing-mounted general-purpose bombs; two short-range air-to-air radio-controlled visually sighted missiles*
- **Armament:** *Six-barreled XM-197 20mm cannon; door .50-cal machine gun*
- **Special Equipment:** *Motor-driven winch with 2.5 ton-capacity; cockpit ejection mechanism; folding rear loading ramp*
- **Maximum Speed:** *175 mph fully loaded; 240 mph minimal load*
- **Maximum Range:** *320 miles fully loaded; 1,750 miles ferry range*

Night Attack Helicopter

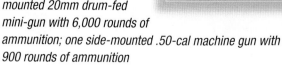

- **Ordnance:** *10 medium-range air-to-air Wildfire missiles*
- **Armament:** *Turret-mounted 20mm mini-gun with 3,500 rounds of ammunition; side-mounted 20mm drum-fed mini-gun with 6,000 rounds of ammunition; one side-mounted .50-cal machine gun with 900 rounds of ammunition*
- **Special Equipment:** *Composite-armor plating; top-of-the-line communications gear; nearly soundproof engine casing*
- **Maximum Speed:** *400 mph*
- **Maximum Range:** *475 miles*

Representative G.I. JOE Air Vehicles

JUMP Jet Pack

- **Primary Armament:** Computer-assisted rapid-pulse laser blaster
- **Special Equipment:** Rocket fuel turbo-injection system; reinforced combustion chamber
- **Maximum Speed:** 210 mph in short bursts; typical speeds average 150 mph
- **Maximum Range:** 300 miles

Sky Hawk

- **Primary Armament:** Two paired 20mm Thunderclap single-barreled chain guns with 1,200 rounds each
- **Secondary Armament:** Two Vulcan 20mm or 30mm single-barreled chain guns on lateral, recessed nacelles with 1,100 rounds each
- **Ordnance:** Two signal-processing air-to-surface rockets
- **Special Equipment:** Rotating thruster assembly affording true V/STOL capability
- **Maximum Speed:** 510 mph
- **Maximum Range:** 275 miles

G.I. JOE Dragonhawk Dropship

- **Primary Armament:** Chin-mounted 30mm Gatling gun
- **Secondary Armament:** Two sets of surface-to-air missile launchers with a payload of three missiles each; optional two 60mm mortar cannons
- **Special Equipment:** Rotating turbofan assembly affording true V/STOL capability; M.I.C.-connected drop cage
- **Maximum Speed:** 375 mph
- **Maximum Range:** 1,200 miles

Crusader 0107W Spaceplane

- **Primary Armament:** None
- **Secondary Armament:** None
- **Special Equipment:** Remote manipulator system; classified avionics bay
- **Maximum Speed:** 17,321 mph (Mach 26.2)
- **Maximum Range:** 1,500 nautical miles

the final component: one of two orbiter spaceplanes that G.I. JOE maintains (the *Defiant* 1010X or the *Crusader* 0107W). It is from the spaceplane that the mission commander operates.

Within the gantry crawler, an enormous 2,750-horsepower/2,050-kilowatt "Plough-Boy" engine drives a quartet of 1,000-kilowatt generator/traction motors, providing propulsion to four sets of four extra-plated super-traction bogeys. This rumbling churn of outsized mechanisms moves the enormous vehicle at a lethargic pace of 10 miles per hour. Atop the crawler's dorsal surface, the gantry rests in its horizontal, stowed configuration along with the spaceplane orbiter and booster.

Only upon reaching its designated launch point—precisely positioned via independent GPS navigators located in each of the four bogey wheel collections—does the gantry begin elevation. Precision-machined servos erect the gantry at a slow and steady pace, also driving the mechanisms that open the armored shuttle launch doors. Quadruple-redundant laser-calibrated levelers confirm the shuttle's position and alignment before launch countdown can begin.

A series of frangible bolt-ties connect the shuttle to the gantry. The booster sits atop an armored black deflector ramp intended to protect the crawler from the worst of the rocket backwash. In addition to dedicated water tanks that douse the gantry prior to launch, the surrounding structure is lined with calibrated sound-dampening technology. A cluster of dozens of powerful emitters shriek an adaptive feedback cancellation wave. This serves to eliminate the acoustic shock wave blast that would otherwise accompany the explosive launch of the shuttle.

The gantry crawler is armed with a variety of laser weaponry, intended to eliminate the risk of ricochets or projectile backfire harming the shuttle itself. *Surge*-class dual repeating self-generating laser cannons, *Countdown*-series auto-load auto-fire surface-clearing laser cannons, and *Protector*-class forward-facing pulse laser cannons can create a web of defensive fire around the gantry, although launch protocol strongly recommends launch delays until all threat forces are eliminated.

The Launch Control Center and Electronics Control Unit (ECU) is the armored drive cabin of the crawler, where G.I. JOE heavy ve-

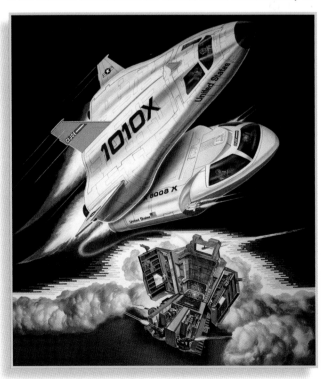

hicle operator Hardtop sits. This control center is protected from the elements and rocket blast by a layered tempered alum-silicate blast-proof windshield. The ECU is further protected by a recessed 7.62mm machine gun.

The booster component comes in two varieties: a disposable version (LRB-D9121) meant to be jettisoned in orbit, and the X 8008 X version that incorporates a crewable space station module. Safety protocols recommended that the booster module not be crewed during liftoff—only after launch does the station crew transfer from the spaceplane orbiter.

The booster component contains two main propulsion engines fueled by a mixture of liquid hydrogen and liquid oxygen oxidizer. Each is flanked by a pair of primary reaction control thrusters that help position the space station module during docking maneuvers. These smaller modules are fueled by a mixture of monomethylhydrazine and nitrogen tetroxide.

The space station module includes a 65,000-pound payload area and operations bay. A control cockpit complete with TACtical Air Navigation (TACAN) guidance systems allow for the module to adjust position for station-keeping. These limited space station modules have standard interlinkages that allow for multiple units to be chained together. This means that repeated *Defiant* launches can add to a growing space station complex. The modules are not designed for orbital reentry. These X 8008 X features a trio of laser systems—two forward and one rearward—for defense.

The individual vehicular assembly that could solely carry the name *Defiant* separate from the other two is the spaceplane orbiter. The shuttle typically forms the command platform for all *Defiant* missions, as it is from here that Colonel Mark Morgan Jr. (code name: Payload) is based, serving as mission lead and pilot for the spaceplane. The shuttle includes a payload bay equipped with a remote manipulator system for satellite placement and repair. The *Defiant* is, in standard configuration, unarmed, although weapons systems can be included in its payload bay.

The *Defiant* 1010X spaceplane is designed for orbital reentry. Its surface is covered with high-temperature ablative ceramic tiles meant to absorb the heat from atmospheric friction. The delta-winged flier has extending stabilizer fins with tilting rudders and elevons for control during reentry and landing. A trio of quad-wheeled landing gear deploy for standard runway landings and taxiing.

COBRA Rattler

COBRA's tank-smashing ground attack jet is M.A.R.S. Industries' radical retooling of a Fairchild A-10 Thunderbolt II. The engine systems have been majorly altered to grant the Rattler VTOL (vertical takeoff and landing) capability, which makes the craft incredibly versatile. Without need of a runway, Rattlers can be stowed in strategic locations unthinkable for standard fixed-wing aircraft. Across the United States, COBRA maintained a number of hidden Rattler hangars within enormous water storage tanks and dummy silos, able to launch and land the craft with minimal visibility.

A pair of wing-mounted COBRACo high-bypass continuous-ratio turbofan engines rest atop articulated cradles that tilt 90 degrees, providing a cushion of thrust that can lift the Rattler vertically. A Rattler can hover or loiter over ground operations for an hour and a half before exhausting its fuel supplies. A rear-mounted low-thrust turbofan tripak engine provides stabilization amid a fixed triblade tail. In standard flight, the Rattler can achieve speeds of 450 miles per hour. While this is slow compared with air superiority fighters,

it's sufficient for the Rattler to carry out its role of close air support for ground forces.

The Rattler pilot sits within a reinforced shell of titanium armor—900 pounds' worth that varies in thickness from half an inch to one and a half inches. Affectionately nicknamed the "bathtub," this armor can protect the pilot from cannon fire and fragmented shrapnel. Overall, the Rattler is far more durable than higher-performance jet fighters. It is a glutton for punishment, able to brave the retaliatory fire of its intended ground targets thanks to its armor and multiple redundant systems.

Another radical alteration to the standard Thunderbolt design was the addition of a tailgunner within a shellproof molded turret with self-seal barrier in its dorsal midline. The rear turret has twin 20mm armor-piercing automatic guns with 2,000 rounds of ammunition each. Gunner and pilot maintain constant communication through shared readout displays and headset comm-links.

The forward armament is a seven-barreled Kerry CDY-9B Jawbreaker 30mm nose cannon, an anti-tank weapon with 1,400 rounds of ammunition. The onboard SK-5 laser targeting system allows the Rattler to home in on laser targets painted by ground crews—typically, Laser Vipers.

The 10 wing-mounted hardpoints can carry 14,000 pounds of ordnance. Though mission-specific payloads vary greatly, one common configuration consists of two sets total of the following (one set per wing): three 750-pound high-explosive aerial mines on triple ejector bomb racks; one pilot-selectable air-to-air or air-to-ground missile; one air-to-surface armor-piercing torpedo; one radiation-seeking air-to-air missile.

COBRA Night Raven

The stealth flier of the COBRA forces, the Night Raven can reach speeds exceeding three times that of sound, enabling it to infiltrate a field of operation within seconds. During COBRA's control of its own island nation in the Gulf of Mexico, the Night Raven was often scrambled for recon sorties over North American soil at speeds and altitudes so extreme that it was able to evade detection and pursuit. To survive the grueling physiological pressures attained at the Night Raven's maximum velocity, its dedicated crew of Strato-Vipers have had to undergo surgical alterations to reinforce their circulatory systems.

The extended lines of the Night Raven's lengthy fuselage have a symmetrical grace, causing pilots—regardless of their allegiance—to remark with awe upon the aircraft's beauty. The aerodynamic form is also shaped to better befuddle radar, and to dissipate the excess heat built up by atmospheric friction at the phenomenal speeds the Raven is designed to achieve.

At an altitude of 86,000 feet, the Raven's dual Viper turbojet engines can reach Mach 3.32 (2,189 miles per hour). It can squeeze past that limit, reaching Mach 3.5 for short bursts. The aircraft has an operational range of 3,250 miles.

Though the Night Raven is well armed, its primary role is recon and not air superiority. These planes are simply too expensive to be risked in combat missions. A dorsal hatch contains two 30mm chain guns, each with 900 rounds of ammunition. An internal rotary launcher supports up to eight short-range air-to-air missiles.

The crew of two consists of a forward-facing pilot and a rearward-facing intelligence and weapons specialist officer. The Night Raven also supports a deployable short-range craft for launches. The small one-man flight pod has a low radar-reflective surface and is armed with two 20mm MK12 machine guns.

Representative COBRA Fixed-Wing Aircraft

COBRA Rattler

- **Ordnance:** 14,000 pounds on 10 external hardpoints; common configuration: six 750-pound high-exposive aerial mines; two air-to-air or air-to-ground missiles; two air-to-surface armor-piercing torpedoes; two radar-seeking air-to-air missiles
- **Armament:** Nose-mounted seven-barreled Kerry CDY-9B Jawbreaker 30mm anti-tank gun; two paired turret-mounted 20mm armor-piercing automatic guns
- **Special Equipment:** Pivoting VTOL engines; DEC-5 infrared air defense jamming system; SK-5 laser target indentification system
- **Maximum Speed:** 450 mph
- **Maximum Range:** 300 miles with one and a half hours over target

COBRA Night Raven

- **Ordnance:** Internal rotary launcher can hold up to eight short-range air-to-air missiles
- **Armament:** Two 30mm chain guns
- **Special Equipment:** Launchable fully armed one-man piggyback flight pod; radar-absorbing lift canards; electronic countermeasure scramblers; airborne early warning rear radome
- **Maximum Speed:** Mach 3.5 short sprint (2,310 mph)
- **Maximum Range:** 3,250 miles

COBRA Flight Pod

- **Ordnance:** Two Warlock laser-seeking missiles; some models also feature a solid-propellant SNK-7 aerial mine
- **Armament:** XM-97 .30-caliber machine gun
- **Special Equipment:** Infrared targeting sensors; high-reflex synchronized steering rudders
- **Maximum Speed:** 80 mph
- **Maximum Range:** 120 miles

COBRA Firebat

- **Ordnance:** Four aerial mines
- **Armament:** One 7.62mm variable-rate-of-fire mini-gun with 2,000 rounds
- **Special Equipment:** Collapsible wing struts for compact stowage; advanced autopilot systems
- **Maximum Speed:** 470 mph
- **Maximum Range:** 1,400 miles

COBRA Condor Z25

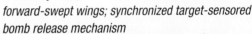

- **Ordnance:** Two air-to-surface missiles; seven incendiary bombs
- **Armament:** Dual laser support cannons
- **Special Equipment:** Separating fuselage secondary craft; forward-swept wings; synchronized target-sensored bomb release mechanism
- **Maximum Speed:** Mach 2.6 (1,716 mph)
- **Maximum Range:** 1,400 miles

COBRA Stellar Stiletto

- **Ordnance:** Two SLICE laser-firing interceptor missiles; two DK-87 strike rockets
- **Armament:** Nose-mounted Stiletto plasma laser cannon
- **Special Equipment:** High-altitude atmospheric containment system
- **Maximum Speed:** Mach 20 (13,200 mph)
- **Maximum Range:** CLASSIFIED

COBRA Stellar Stiletto

The Stellar Stiletto is the most advanced aircraft within the COBRA arsenal. The sleek, overpowered dart-shaped plane can achieve a phenomenal rate of acceleration exceeding Mach 20 for short bursts. This allows it to break the pull of earth's gravity and achieve low orbit. By launching into a high parabolic arc and raking the upper atmosphere, the Stiletto can conserve fuel and power-dive through a rapid descent, flying around the world in a matter of hours—a Stellar Stiletto instantly extends COBRA's reach around the globe. A reinforced carbon-carbon (RCC) heat-resistance nose cone sloughs off the high temperatures of atmospheric friction.

Bloated liquid fuel tanks dominate the lower airframe of the Stiletto, and they are vulnerable to enemy weapons fire. This is why standard operation is for a Stiletto not to engage in hostilities during launch. It is free to do so once maximum altitude has been achieved as well as during reentry, for by then it has expended its most volatile fuel mixtures.

In upper atmosphere, the Stiletto has few enemies—only a handful of G.I. JOE craft can achieve comparable heights. At these rarefied altitudes, a Stiletto can inflict enormous damage on unprotected satellite systems. Among the spaceplane's armaments are a pair of wing-mounted SLICE (supersonic laser-firing interceptor) dual-purpose missiles. This ordnance is armed with straight line-of-sight laser systems that activate upon locking on a target. These high-intensity low-bore beams instantly burn holes in the target. While the beams themselves may not be enough to outright destroy the target craft, they usually impair performance and maneuverability long enough for the missile to close in and detonate. The SLICE missiles are extremely expensive, and tend to be used only on high-value targets.

In addition to this exotic ordnance, the Stiletto carries more conventional DK-87 strike rockets with telemetric data link. The Stiletto's onboard targeting equipment can connect to a satellite network that extends its operational parameters by getting real-time position data from a variety of COBRA "eye in the sky" satellites. The Stiletto also carries a plasma laser that draws power from its main engines.

The extremely high cost of its onboard technologies and precision engineering is not the only limiting factor in the Stellar Stiletto's effectiveness. Only a select few COBRA pilots are physically capable of piloting the fighter. The best of the best Strato-Vipers undergo extensive physiological modification, strengthening their circulatory systems to withstand the extremes of gravity, atmosphere, and acceleration. Furthermore, their neurological systems are "spiked" with electronic interfaces that increase sensory input while minimizing reaction time. These technological hybrid pilots become the elite known as the Star Vipers.

COBRA Mamba

An enormous combat helicopter that dwarfs others within the COBRA arsenal, the Mamba is one of the most powerful weapons to emerge during Serpentor's reign over COBRA. Its unique twin-rotor design incorporates a syncopated spin system that creates an eye-bending optical illusion. It looks like the two layered-epoxy counter-rotating rotor blades *should* collide or intersect in flight, but they are spun in precise sequence by the Servo-Tox NT-58 tur-

Representative COBRA Rotary-Wing Aircraft

COBRA F.A.N.G. (Fully Armed Negator Gyrocopter)

- **Ordnance:** *Four landing strut-mounted short-range air-to-air missiles*
- **Armament:** *Nose-turret-mounted 20mm grenade launcher with 100 rounds*
- **Special Equipment:** *High-speed reinforced rotor; LCD/analog instrumentation; nose-mounted "bubble" ball-joint turret*
- **Maximum Speed:** *175 mph*
- **Maximum Range:** *320 miles*

COBRA FANG II

- **Ordnance:** *Six air-to-air missiles*
- **Armament:** *Nose-turret-mounted 20mm grenade launcher*
- **Special Equipment:** *Variable air-intake modulator; induct nozzle equalizer; flak-proof stabilizer winglets; dual triblade turbofan rotors; thermo-shield cockpit*
- **Maximum Speed:** *200 mph*
- **Maximum Range:** *310 miles*

COBRA Mamba

- **Ordnance:** *Four laser-guided anti-tank missiles; four supersonic air-to-air missiles; one cluster bomb*
- **Armament:** *Two paired .50-cal machine guns*
- **Special Equipment:** *Launchable MOLT pods; synchronized counter-rotating rotors; SMASH noise elimination system*
- **Maximum Speed:** *210 mph*
- **Maximum Range:** *450 miles*

boshaft engine. The Mamba can achieve speeds of 210 miles per hour, with an operational range of 450 miles.

The triple-cockpit design creates a unique operational hierarchy during Mamba flights. The central cockpit carries the primary pilot, the Gyro-Viper, with the flanking MOLT (Mamba Offensive Light Tactical) pods devoted to weapons systems and sensor operators. However, at any point the Gyro-Viper can override command of the secondary pods. He can also initiate launch sequences that fire off the individual flight pods. The reclined and compact interior of the MOLT pod design has caused some in the COBRA ranks to nickname it the "coffin." A high-resolution laser-enhanced projected heads-up display more than makes up for any visibility limitations.

Each MOLT pod carries a pair of .50-caliber machine guns and two Nemesis laser-seeking anti-tank missiles. The pods can reach speeds of 200 miles per hour, and are fairly maneuverable with a "lifting body" aerodynamic fuselage. Landing a pod is typically handled by onboard computers, requiring a precise firing of retro-rockets and drag chutes. A Mamba cannot recover a launch pod in flight. A MOLT pod can only be reattached to the main helicopter hull at an appropriately equipped launch facility or airstrip.

Despite its size, the Mamba's shape has a low side and front silhouette. Its engine section is shrouded with the COBRA-designed SMASH system (sensor system: Mamba air suppression and heat reduction) noise eliminator. The main body of the helicopter carries four supersonic air-to-air missiles as well as one large cluster bomb.

COBRA Flight Pod

An unusual aerial conveyance found flitting through the skies of Cobra Island and around other COBRA facilities, the flight pod's ubiquity, persistent patrols, and potent anti-personnel weapons have earned it the not-so-affectionate nickname of the "trouble bubble."

Unlike the G.I. JOE jet pack, this small one-man flight conveyance is extremely easy to operate; most COBRA troopers get the hang of it quickly and have logged in some time aboard a pod performing basic aerial security or scouting operations. Twin vertical-thrust high bypass ratio turbofan engines elevate the craft up to altitudes of 400 feet, while forward thrust is generated through redirecting vector ducts, pushing the pod to speeds of up to 80 miles per hour.

A reinforced domed flight canopy gives the pod its bubble-like appearance. Some models feature a fully enclosed canopy; others have a half dome. While this protects against small-arms fire for a short time, the pods are notoriously fragile. They typically only hang out long enough to spot and report intruders before moving back out of range of small-arms fire. Slung below the pod's frame is a long-barreled XM-97 .30-caliber machine gun. Bracketing the sides of the pods are two Warlock LR-3.7 laser/IR-seeking anti-tank missiles that can follow a path painted by the handlebar-mounted infrared targeting sensors.

HARDWARE

JOE-COM Gauntlet

Connectivity to command has never been more important than in modern operations scattered across the globe. To facilitate constant contact with G.I. JOE headquarters, field agents tested a wrist communicator that came to be adopted by the Sigma 6 subunit. The JOE-COM gauntlet is a compact, lightweight, feature-laden piece of complex electronics. Resembling a metallic vambrace, the JOE-COM is powered by a laminated paper-thin copper chloride battery. Features include GPS tracking, heart monitor, and video-audio comm-link. An advanced ferritin protein-based memory core can hold up to a terabyte of data. The gauntlet is voice-activated and sensitive to vocal patterns, allowing a user to voice-lock command and functions. Snake-Eyes's gauntlet was keyed to his fingerprints and other biometric data. The JOE-COM also included a nutrient dispenser that served as a programmable transdermal delivery method of vitamins or other medicines.

PAC/RATs

The PAC/RATs (Rapid All Terrain Programmed Assault Computers) represented the G.I. JOE team's first foray into robotic combat equipment. These small automata featured rugged locomotion systems that could handle a wide variety of uneven terrain. They could operate independently or via remote control. They are now considered primitive compared with COBRA B.A.T.s or the more sophisticated robotics developed by Star Brigade engineers, such as the Armor Bot and Robo-JOE's cybernetic enhancements.

The flamethrower PAC/RAT moves along a triple-tread assembly with hydraulic suspension system. Its primary armament is the EX-

556 flame projector. As a result, it includes many related systems that monitor and moderate internal temperatures. A pair of armored and articulated deflector shields protects the fuel canisters. This PAC/RAT also has a pair of underslung 7.62mm machine guns.

The PAC/RAT K0-80 machine gunner is a mobile quartet of 20mm machine guns, two fixed and two articulated. It moves along on four self-sealing soft-terrain tires atop a multidirectional pivoting all-terrain carriage.

A four-point drive bogey track system moves the missile launcher PAC/RAT about. It is armed with four twin-stage boosted anti-tank missiles in a two-stage rack configuration.

Transportable Tactical Battle Platform

On those occasions when you can't take the high ground, there sometimes comes the opportunity to *make* it. The Transportable Tactical Battle Platform is a G.I. JOE combat asset that allows for the quick implementation of a prefabricated battleground command center. It is typically carried into target sites via multiple helicopters hoisting it on chains or cables. The platform's adjustable, reinforced telescoping legs allow it to secure level purchase in a variety of terrain. It can even be stationed in the sea, through a tension-leg platform model deployed along with a flotation collar. This grants the platform high axial stiffness, eliminating the vertical motion of the waves, and giving an offshore mooring the stability of an oil platform.

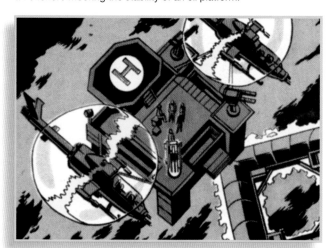

The Tactical Battle Platform has four corner stations. One holds a surface-to-air missile emplacement. Some older models carry a quartet of Chaparall MIM-72A surface-to-air warheads with an effective range of just under four miles, but these have largely been updated with more modern warheads. The next corner clockwise from this houses a control station that features communications gear, computer systems, tracking systems, and fire control monitors. It is shrouded by a reinforced composite-grid windscreen and includes a powerful searchlight.

In between this and the next corner is an elevated aluminum-alloy octagonal helipad, with a short set of stairs leading down to the main platform deck. Past the helipad is a hydraulic-assisted cargo winch crane, which abuts a series of storage lockers. The next corner clockwise hosts a double-barreled recoil-less 75mm "Defender" cannon, driven by a multimode computer system.

The PIT

G.I. JOE has maintained a number of headquarters during its operational history, many of them christened with the code name "the PIT" for their subterranean construction. The PIT locations are highly classified, and while most have been located on (or rather, *in*) American soil, others have been situated abroad.

All PIT bases consist of multiple underground levels of steel-reinforced radiation-shielded concrete and alloy armor. They are designed as complete, self-contained environments capable of withstanding a five-megaton direct hit and remaining sealed and

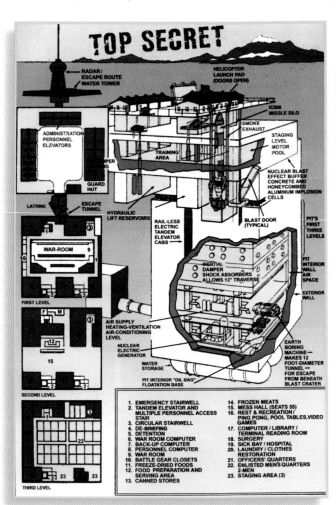

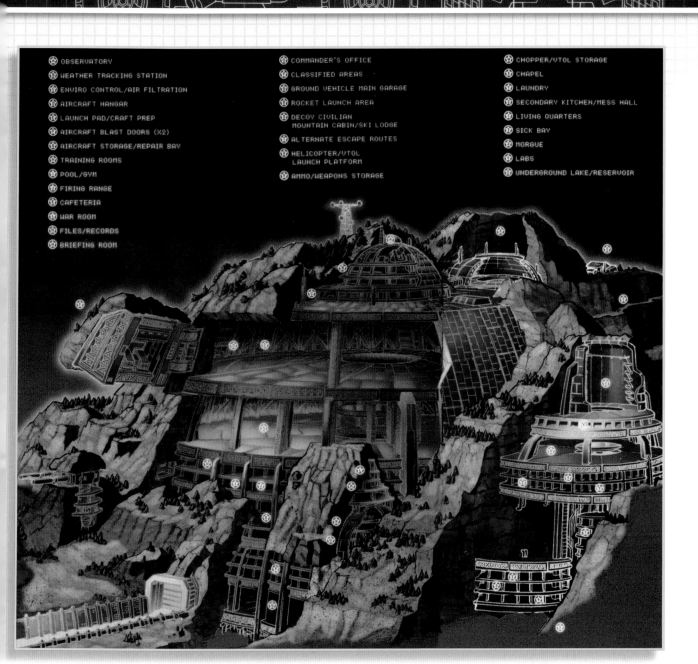

- ① OBSERVATORY
- ② WEATHER TRACKING STATION
- ③ ENVIRO CONTROL/AIR FILTRATION
- ④ AIRCRAFT HANGAR
- ⑤ LAUNCH PAD/CRAFT PREP
- ⑥ AIRCRAFT BLAST DOORS (X2)
- ⑦ AIRCRAFT STORAGE/REPAIR BAY
- ⑧ TRAINING ROOMS
- ⑨ POOL/GYM
- ⑩ FIRING RANGE
- ⑪ CAFETERIA
- ⑫ WAR ROOM
- ⑬ FILES/RECORDS
- ⑭ BRIEFING ROOM

- ⑮ COMMANDER'S OFFICE
- ⑯ CLASSIFIED AREAS
- ⑰ GROUND VEHICLE MAIN GARAGE
- ⑱ ROCKET LAUNCH AREA
- ⑲ DECOY CIVILIAN MOUNTAIN CABIN/SKI LODGE
- ⑳ ALTERNATE ESCAPE ROUTES
- ㉑ HELICOPTER/VTOL LAUNCH PLATFORM
- ㉒ AMMO/WEAPONS STORAGE

- ㉓ CHOPPER/VTOL STORAGE
- ㉔ CHAPEL
- ㉕ LAUNDRY
- ㉖ SECONDARY KITCHEN/MESS HALL
- ㉗ LIVING QUARTERS
- ㉘ SICK BAY
- ㉙ MORGUE
- ㉚ LABS
- ㉛ UNDERGROUND LAKE/RESERVOIR

self-sufficient while the radiation fallout subsides. All utilities are self-contained, from generators to relay batteries to atmospheric recycling gear and food stores. The first PIT had enough supplies for six months of isolated operation. Subsequent bases extended this span to levels that remain classified.

For security measures, the various levels of the PIT can be sealed hermetically. This not only helps isolate intruders or escaped prisoners, but serves as effective quarantine measures should a biological attack target the interior of the base.

For structural integrity, the early PIT bases featured flexibility systems in their architectural designs. For instance, an "oil bag" flotation base and inertial dampener shock absorbers built into the structural substrate gave the PIT up to 13 feet of traverse before any of its major load-bearing members would buckle.

A standard emergency feature found in the PIT is an earth-boring machine meant to create a tunnel should a catastrophic collapse cave-in the PIT. Soldiers trapped in the reinforced lower levels could carve out their own escape route by commandeering the earth borer.

Some incarnations of the PIT were "hidden in plain sight"—beneath a military motor pool or ski lodge cabin, for example. Great care was given to make the surface decoy facilities absolutely convincing and fully functional. Other versions were instead remotely located under harsh or forbidding terrain that would never welcome any trespassers who might tempt accidental discovery.

One of the later iterations of the PIT, dubbed the ROCK, had the most sophisticated computer infrastructure of any organization on earth, with more than 200 networked supercomputers forming the information foundation of modern worldwide G.I. JOE operations.

COBRA Brainwave Scanner

One of the most diabolical interrogation devices ever developed, the COBRA brainwave scanner can subvert a victim's own sanity and turn his or her most precious memories into painful constructs. Through careful use of the scanner, a malicious tormentor such as Cobra Commander can alter a subject's very perceptions so that reality itself becomes questionable. Most pernicious of all, somewhere deep in the psyche a kernel of free will remains, looking on in terror as the higher consciousness and active motor abilities become completely subservient to COBRA machinations.

The very first brainwave scanner was developed by Dr. Venom. As an interrogation device, it involved a two-step procedure. The first was the establishment of a visual "language" between the scanner and the subject. The scanner would flash a series of sensory stimuli to the subject, recording the resulting brainwave signature until it amassed a personalized vocabulary of the subject's thinking patterns reduced to an extensive digital database. With enough of this language established, the process was reversed, and the brainwave information could be translated to computer-generated visual and auditory reconstructions, essentially *reading* a subject's mind and projecting the results on an attached monitor. Both processes were extremely painful and strenuous to the subject, and the brainwave scanner also incorporated a variety of life-sign monitors to ensure that a victim did not die during either procedure.

Venom built upon his initial innovation to miniaturize some of the

technology involved and include it in the S.N.A.K.E. robotic armor—a heavy power suit that could enclose a prisoner and force him or her to march into combat as part of COBRA infantry. Dr. Mindbender used the original scanner as an essential device in the development of a digital simulacrum of a brain during the creation of Serpentor. He then redesigned the scanner, making it more compact and giving it a much more frightening appearance.

The brainwave scanner could also be used to implant and alter memories. This process was even more painful and potentially lethal. High-resolution virtual-reality interfaces allowed COBRA agents to walk through dimensionalized constructs of a subject's memories and thoughts and directly interact with the environs, altering the past or implanting suggestions and commands. These alterations were then "sealed" in place with a painful jolt of electricity, while any memories of the process itself were erased. The erasure was not without its telltale signatures of tampering. A victim would experience nausea or headaches when exposed to anything that would have otherwise reminded him or her of the procedure.

Cobra Commander and Dr. Mindbender's refinement of this process created a sensation of addiction within the user. The painful memory alterations could be used to ensure the loyalty of even the most rebellious subject. Further eroding a subject's free will was a pronounced and overriding desire to undergo repeated brainwashing sessions.

S.N.A.K.E. (System: Neutralizer—Armed Kloaking Equipment)

Before COBRA developed its battle android troopers, one of its earliest forays into the creation of automated soldiers dovetailed into experiments in armored powersuits that enhanced the strength and battlefield power of a standard infantry soldier. Engineered by Dr. Venom, the powersuit was driven by a soldier's body, enhancing gross muscle movement with an array of micromotors. Brainwave scanners built into the helmet of the armor further translated impulses into electrical signals, eliminating the need for complex, abstract controls within the suit.

The S.N.A.K.E. armor's thick shell could easily withstand small-arms fire, and was even able to resist light missile strikes. A full communications array kept the soldier in constant contact with battlefield commanders. An oxygen canister maintained its own internal atmosphere, allowing the armored soldier to operate in toxic environments. Predating the modular arm weaponry of the B.A.T. soldier, the S.N.A.K.E. also featured a weapons socket in its right arm that could be affixed with a variety of attachments, including a reinforced claw, a flamethrower, a 5.56mm machine gun, and an anti-personnel rocket launcher.

Attempts to fully automate the S.N.A.K.E. met with limited success; it was far more effective as armor around a living soldier. Venom's twisted genius found a way to exploit prisoners who were capable warriors and transform them into COBRA combat assets. Using a downsized variant of his sinister brainwave scanner, Venom could override the loyalty of his prisoners and force them to carry out orders on behalf of COBRA.

A precautionary move meant to enforce control over these prisoners backfired on Venom. The weapons systems aboard the S.N.A.K.E. were color-coded to ignore the distinct dark hues of

COBRA vehicles of the era, but he painted the S.N.A.K.E. armor itself a bright white. Venom had thought that should a S.N.A.K.E. prove defective, he could use others to destroy it. This is not what occurred when prisoners Snake-Eyes and Kwinn were forced to march as S.N.A.K.E. soldiers. Snake-Eyes shook off the thrall of the brainwave device and used his weapons systems to crack open the armor that contained his fellow captive, Kwinn. Freed from the mind-altering armor, Kwinn was able to kill Dr. Venom.

MASTER G.I. JOE MOTOR POOL VEHICLE ROSTER

1.0 Land

1.1 General-Purpose/Multipurpose Vehicles
AWE Striker
Badger
Battle Wagon
Brawler GP (Hammer variant)
Crossfire
Desert Coyote
Desert Fox
Desert Humvee (Hammer variant)
Desert Striker
Dune Runner
Eco Striker (AWE Striker variant)
Eliminator Jeep (BF2K)
Forest Fox
Grizzly SS-1
Ground Striker
Hammer
Mudbuster
MUV
Night Ops Humvee (Hammer variant)
Night Ops VAMP
Panther Rail
Sand Razor
Smoke Screen Transport
Split Fire
Tiger Sting (VAMP Mk II variant)
VAMP
VAMP Mark II

1.2 Tanks
Armadillo mini-missile-tank variant
Armadillo mini-tank
Armored Panther mini-tank variant
Brawler
Equalizer
H.A.V.O.C.
Lynx
Mauler M.B.T.
MOBAT
Night Blaster (COBRA Maggot variant)
Night Raider (Triple T variant)
Night Rhino (Warthog variant)
Night Storm (Persuader variant)
Patriot
Patriot Grizzly Tank
Persuader
Pulverizer (BF2K)
Raider
Sky Havoc (H.A.V.O.C. variant)
Sky Sweeper (BF2K)

Sledgehammer
Tiger Cat (Snow Cat variant)
Triple T
Warthog A.I.F.V.
Wolverine

1.3 Heavy Mobile Armor
Armadillo assault vehicle
General
Mean Dog
Mobile Battle Bunker
Mobile Command Center
Monster Blaster APC
Blockbuster
R.H.I.N.O.
R.O.C.C.
Rolling Thunder
Slugger

1.4 Cold-Weather Vehicles
Arctic Blast
Arctic VAMP
Avalanche
Dominator Snow Tank (BF2K)
Ice Saber
Polar Battle Bear
Rock Slide
Snow Cat

1.5 Motorcyles and Small Vehicles
Assault Quad
ATV
Battle Blitz
Desert Blast Attack Quad
L.C.V. Recon Sled
Marauder Motorcycle Tank (BF2K)
Night Ranger Quad
Ninja Hovercycle
Ninja Lightning
Ninja Tracker ATV
RAM
Road Rebel
Rock Crusher ATV
Silver Mirage
Swampmasher
Tiger Paw (COBRA Ferret variant)

1.6 Support Vehicles
APC
'CUDA (APC variant)
Night Scrambler (APC variant)
Road Toad
Toss 'N Cross Bridge Layer

1.7 Artillery
Air defense missile station (ATX-30 platform)
Coastal Defender
FLAK
Gun station
HAL

MMS
S.L.A.M.
Thunderclap
Whirlwind

2.0 SEA

2.1 Sea Craft
Barracuda mini-sub
Depth Ray
G.I. JANE
Ghostshark
Hover Strike
Killer W.H.A.L.E.
Moray Hydrofoil (G.I. JOE variant)
Night Ray (Moray variant)
Night Shade (S.H.A.R.C. variant)
Night Striker (W.H.A.L.E. variant)
Raging Typhoon
S.H.A.R.C.
Shark 9000
Sky Sharc (S.H.A.R.C. variant)
Thunderwave Jet Boat
Tiger Shark (Water Moccasin variant)
USS Flagg
Vindicator hovercraft (BF2K)

2.2 Aquatic Support
Devilfish
M.A.N.T.A.
Manta Ray
Rapid Runner
Rising Tide
Tiger Fish (Devilfish variant)
Wave Crusher

3.0 AIR

3.1 Air Support
Air assault glider
Falcon glider
G.I. JOE air commando glider
JUMP jet pack
Mudfighter

3.2 Rotary-Wing Vehicles
Battle Copter
Desert Apache AH-74
Dragonfly
Dragonhawk Dropship
Locust
Locust XH-1 helicopter
Missile Storm
Mudbuster
Night Attack Helicopter
Razor Blade
Retaliator
Skystorm X-wing chopper

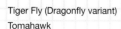

Tiger Fly (Dragonfly variant)
Tomahawk
Winged Fury

3.3 Fixed-Wing Aircraft
A-10 Thunderbolt
C-130 Hercules
Conquest X-30
Ghost H.A.W.K.
Ghost Striker
Night Boomer (Skystriker variant)
P-40 Warhawk
Phantom X-19 stealth fighter
Sky Hawk
Sky Raven (Night Raven variant)
Sky Sweeper
Skystriker
Storm Eagle ATF
Tiger Rat (Rattler variant)
Vector (BF2K)

3.4 Space Operations
Armor Bot
Avenger Scout
Crusader 0107W Spaceplane
Defiant Complex
Starfighter

4.0 Battlefield Technology
Anti-aircraft action pack
Armor Bot
Atlas Mech
Iron Hammer Mech
JOE-COM gauntlet
Metal Mayhem Mech
Ninja Battle Axe
PAC/RATs
Radar Rat battlefield robot
R.P.V.
Transportable Tactical Battle Platform
Tri-Blaster battlefield robot

MASTER COBRA/ THREAT FORCES VEHICLE ROSTER

1.0 Land

1.1 General-Purpose/ Multipurpose Vehicles
COBRA attack cruiser
COBRA Rage
COBRA Scorpion
COBRA Stinger
COBRA STUN
Dreadnok Thunder Machine
Python Patrol STUN (STUN variant)
Steel Crusher APV

1.2 Tanks
COBRA CAT
COBRA H.I.S.S.
COBRA HIS II
COBRA H.I.S.S. III
COBRA Hiss IV
COBRA Imp
COBRA Maggot
COBRA Paralyzer
COBRA Tread Fire
D.E.M.O.N.
Dominator
I.R.O.N. Panther
Razorback
Septic Tank (H.I.S.S. tank variant)

1.3 Heavy Mobile Armor
COBRA Detonator
COBRA Earthquake
COBRA Hammerhead
COBRA Parasite
COBRA Ringneck

1.4 Cold-Weather Vehicles
COBRA WOLF
Ice Sabre
Ice Dagger
Ice Snake
Polar Blast

1.5 Motorcycles and Small Vehicles
COBRA Buzz Boar
COBRA Ferret
COBRA Mole Pod
COBRA Night Prowler
COBRA Ninja Hovercycle
COBRA Pogo Ballistic Battle Ball
COBRA Rat
COBRA Sand Snake
COBRA Snake Trax (Ferret variant)
COBRA Venom Cycle
COBRA Venom Striker ATV
Darklon's Evader
Dictator
Dreadnok Cycle

1.6 Artillery
COBRA Adder missile system
COBRA A.S.P. gunpod
Python Patrol ASP (A.S.P. variant)

2.0 SEA

2.1 Sea Craft
COBRA BUGG
COBRA Man-O-War
COBRA Mantis Submarine
COBRA Moray hydrofoil
COBRA Piranha

COBRA Sea Ray
COBRA Water Moccasin
Wave Crusher (S.H.A.R.C. variant)

2.2 Aquatic Support
Chameleon swamp-skier
COBRA battle barge
COBRA Night Landing

3.0 AIR

3.1 Air Support
COBRA Air Chariot
COBRA air commando glider
COBRA C.L.A.W.
COBRA Flight Pod (Trouble Bubble)
COBRA gunship
COBRA jet pack
COBRA Viper glider
Destro's Despoiler
Dreadnok air skiff

3.2 Rotary-Wing Vehicles
COBRA Battle Copter
COBRA F.A.N.G.
COBRA Fang II
COBRA Fang III
COBRA Mamba
Crimson Command Copter
Dreadnok Swampfire

3.3 Fixed-Wing Aircraft
A.G.P. (anti-gravity pod)
COBRA Condor Z25
COBRA Firebat
COBRA Hurricane
COBRA Liquidator
COBRA Night Adder
COBRA Night Raven
COBRA Rattler
Python Patrol Conquest (X-30 variant)

3.4 Space Operations
COBRA Invader
COBRA Stellar Stiletto

4.0 Battlefield Technology
COBRA Brainwave Scanner
COBRA Devastator battlefield robot
COBRA hovercraft battlefield robot
S.N.A.K.E.
Iron Mech

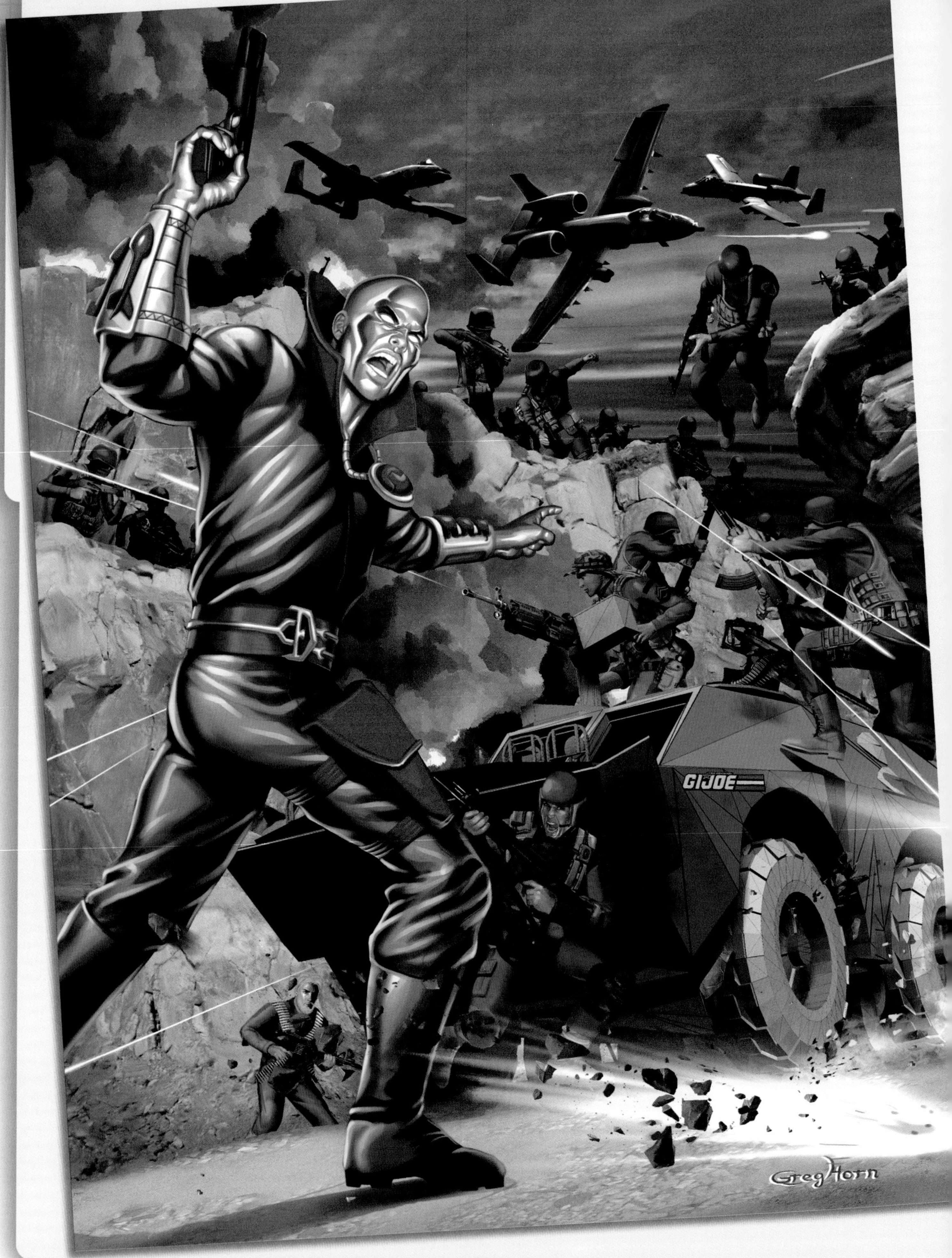
GIJOE
Greg Horn

CHAPTER 4

MISSION REPORTS

OPERATION: LADY DOOMSDAY

Background: One of the earliest G.I. JOE operations on file was the rescue of Dr. Adele Burkhart, a nuclear physicist involved in a top-secret government program that she came to reject and protest against when she discovered her innovations would be used in the development of nuclear retaliation. She dubbed the program "A Doomsday Project," and garnered much media attention as "Lady Doomsday." Her stance against the military was polarizing; some saw her as a hero for her "whistle-blowing"; others dubbed her a traitor for potentially jeopardizing national security.

Day 1: 0830 Hours

While en route between New York City and Washington, D.C., Dr. Burkhart prepares to give a press conference aboard Amtrak Train 840. The commuter train is attacked by COBRA airborne infantry, and Dr. Burkhart is captured by the Baroness, who escapes the train and is airlifted away. The Baroness leaves behind a warning, painted in lipstick on the ladies' room mirror: TRY TO RESCUE HER, AND SHE DIES.

Day 1: 1100 Hours

Generals Lawrence J. Flagg and Aaron B. Austin assign the G.I. JOE team the mission of rescuing Dr. Burkhart. Although she has proven to be a national security embarrassment, she retains knowledge that is too dangerous to allow to fall into COBRA hands.

Day 1: 1920 Hours

Cobra Commander holds Dr. Burkhart captive within a fort converted into a headquarters on a small Caribbean island. Radar detects a submarine 20 miles off the northern coast of the island. Cobra Commander orders two heavy weapons platoons to cover the north beach, and to eliminate the island's small civilian population.

Day 1: 2015 Hours

An insertion team of G.I. JOEs (Force One) is deposited into the ocean beyond radar range of COBRA's island stronghold. The team rafts toward the north beach, where Stalker blasts off with a JUMP jet pack and destroys the island coastal defenses. Upon reaching the beach, the G.I. JOE team splits up to follow individual mission objectives.

Day 1: 2045 Hours

Breaker and Flash arrive at the unmanned radar dome on the island, and dig through the ground to expose the communications lines between the radar and fort headquarters. Flash uses his laser rifle to pierce the quarter-inch steel pipe containing the cable. Breaker then splices a top-secret electronic black box into the cable, transmitting a false "all clear" to the fort command center, facilitating the undetected arrival of armor reinforcements by sea (Force Two).

Day 1: 2100 Hours

Grunt, Stalker, and Short-Fuze wipe out the island's airfield with a mortar attack, leaving one small aircraft intact per orders. Unbeknownst to the G.I. JOEs, the airfield is made up of dummy planes.

Day 1: 2110 Hours

Scarlett and Snake-Eyes infiltrate the fort.

Day 1: 2130 Hours

Force Two arrives on a high-speed hydrofoil LCT, which unloads an armored strike force consisting of Rock 'N Roll on the RAM motorcycle; the MOBAT tank carrying Steeler, Zap, and Hawk; and the VAMP with Clutch and Grand Slam towing the HAL laser cannon.

Day 1: 2140 Hours

Snake-Eyes and Scarlett use grenades to disable the fort's generator room.

Day 1: 2155 Hours

Cobra Commander orders the Baroness to disguise herself as Dr. Burkhart and leave the fort in an armed motorcade.

Day 1: 2230 Hours

Stalker rescues Dr. Burkhart, only to discover it is in fact the Baroness. The G.I. JOEs realize their true objective is still within the fort. COBRA has been stalling them. Cobra Commander's true intention is to draw together the one force that can stop him from properly interrogating Dr. Burkhart. He is purposely luring them into the fortress headquarters so that he can detonate a huge explosive that will wipe out the G.I. JOE team.

Day 1: 2245 Hours

The G.I. JOE team raids the fort to find Cobra Commander holding Burkhart at gunpoint as he attempts to make his escape in a helicopter. Burkhart warns the G.I. JOEs about his explosive plans and tries to stop him, only to be shot by the Commander. The Commander and

the Baroness (brought to the fort with the G.I. JOEs) escape through a hidden hatchway. The G.I. JOEs, tipped off by the wounded Burkhart, pile aboard the Commander's escape helicopter. Zap flies them to safety as the fort explodes. Burkhart will recover from the gunshot wound.

Day 2: 0030 Hours

Cobra Commander and the Baroness flee the island aboard a small aircraft.

THE M.A.S.S. DEVICE

Background: From the COBRA mountain citadel, Destro and Cobra Commander plot to unleash the M.A.S.S. device, an experimental teleporter. With this weapon, they plan to conquer the planet.

Day 1: 1945 Hours

General Flagg and Major Juanita Hooper task the G.I. JOE team with testing the security measures in place around the RelayStar, an advanced energy broadcast satellite scheduled for launch the next day. Snake-Eyes, Stalker, and Scarlett manage to infiltrate the top-secret installation, but despite their success Flagg mistakenly considers security adequate, since to actually steal the satellite would require a much larger force than three infiltrators.

Day 1: 2000 Hours

Juanita Hooper is, in truth, the Baroness in disguise. During a tour of the RelayStar, she affixes a special COBRA homing beacon on its surface. Upon receipt of the signal, Destro attempts to teleport the RelayStar to the COBRA citadel, but the experimental M.A.S.S. device fails to

energize. As an alternative plan, Destro orders COBRA troops to the sending grid to transmit them to the homing beacon's location.

Day 1: 2006 Hours

COBRA forces led by Major Bludd materialize next to the Relay-Star, forcing the G.I. JOE security team into retreat. Major Hooper reveals her true identity as the Baroness and joins Bludd. The G.I. JOEs use the gantry elevators that lifted the RelayStar into launch position to pry open its silo doors, allowing them to counterattack.

Day 1: 2012 Hours

Just as the COBRA insertion team prepares to surrender, the M.A.S.S. field begins to energize around the RelayStar; Destro has perfected the teleportation technique. The COBRA forces dematerialize along with the satellite, but Duke gets caught in the field as well. Transported to the COBRA citadel, Duke is overwhelmed by COBRA guards and taken captive.

Day 1: 2030 Hours

COBRA launches the primed RelayStar satellite into orbit.

Day 2: 0911 Hours

COBRA agents affix a homing beacon to the Eiffel Tower in Paris, France. COBRA then broadcasts a worldwide signal, facilitated by the RelayStar, to issue a 24-hour ultimatum to the world: Surrender to COBRA or else. Using M.A.S.S., they cause the famous French landmark to disappear.

Day 2: 1015 Hours

A G.I. JOE task force is dispatched to New England to contact Dr. Lazlo Vandemeer, a leading scientific genius who is knowledgeable about molecular transference devices. COBRA has arrived ahead of JOE, however, and is holding Vandemeer captive. A battle ensues, but G.I. JOE Dragonfly helicopter air support succeeds in chasing the COBRAs away. Major Bludd issues a retreat, and Scarlett and Stalker's team frees Vandemeer. The scientist agrees to construct a second M.A.S.S. device to counter the one used by COBRA.

Day 2: 1032 Hours

The captive Duke is forced to fight in gladiatorial combat within the COBRA Arena of Sport, made sub-servient by a neurological override headband controlled by Destro. The match is cut short when COBRA learns that the United Nations has rejected their ultimatum. Meanwhile, Duke disrupts the neurological headband with the help of fellow slave Selena.

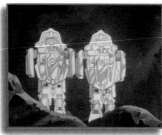

Day 2: 1435 Hours

A G.I. JOE team led by Scarlett and Snow Job is sent to a glacial expanse in the Arctic Circle known as the Sea of Ice to recover radioactive crystals used to fuel the M.A.S.S. device. COBRA left the crystal mine booby-trapped with S.N.A.K.E. robots.

Day 2: 1500 Hours

COBRA makes a second worldwide address, this time specifically singling out Soviet premier Ivan Velenkov with their demand for surrender. When he refuses to comply, COBRA teleports the entire Red Square Battalion into their citadel; the Russians surrender when they are surrounded by COBRA. Cobra Commander issues his next ultimatum: All world leaders must gather at Tanu Island at noon tomorrow.

Day 2: 1517 Hours

With the help of Selena, Duke escapes captivity and steals a Viper glider. He leaves Selena his ring as a keepsake and promises to return to rescue her. He eventually limps his way to the nearest US embassy, exhausted.

Day 2: 1532 Hours

COBRA forces led by Major Bludd arrive at the crystal mine and attack. Bludd triggers a booby trap that releases a deadly radioactive cloud into the mine. Snake-Eyes lowers a radiation shield, cutting himself off from the rest of the JOE team, but allowing them to escape.

142

Day 3: 1200 Hours

At Tanu Island, world leaders convene—General Flagg is the presidentially appointed American representative. COBRA targets them with their M.A.S.S. device, teleporting the leaders into the COBRA citadel, where they are fitted with neurological bands. The Commander issues another ultimatum: The rest of the world must surrender by noon tomorrow.

Day 3: 1202 Hours

Duke, now back at the G.I. JOE base, recovers but cannot remember his experiences within the COBRA citadel.

Day 3: 1218 Hours

Major Bludd and COBRA combat engineers dispatch a repair robot into the mine to capture their store of crystals. The radioactive Snake-Eyes has emerged carrying a canister of crystals, apparently a doomed man. Despite his radiation poisoning, he rescues an injured wolf from a fur trap, earning its loyalty.

Day 3: 1312 Hours

Aboard the *G.I. JANE* frigate, the G.I. JOEs arrive at the point in the ocean above the Challenger Deep, the deepest point of the Marianas Trench. This is where the second of the catalytic elements lies, a pool of heavy water. Duke and Torpedo lead the diving team aboard prototype S.H.A.R.C. submarines.

Day 3: 1539 Hours

A blind woodsman finds Snake-Eyes's collapsed form in the snow and takes him back to his cabin. There he applies holistic medicines to cure the G.I. JOE of his radiation poisoning.

Day 3: 1600 Hours

Immense tube worms emerge from their monolithic stone cylinders on the ocean floor and attack the G.I. JOEs just as COBRA agents led by the Baroness also make a play for the heavy water pool. The dangers posed by the worms force G.I. JOE and COBRA to agree to a temporary truce. They work together to kill the worms by blasting their anchors and letting them float to zones of lesser pressure. COBRA and G.I. JOE agents then split their haul of heavy water.

Day 3: 1800 Hours

Cobra Commander issues another ultimatum: G.I. JOE must surrender or else he'll disintegrate New York City with the M.A.S.S. device.

Day 4: 0611 Hours

Based on an idea by Short-Fuze, Steeler, and Clutch, G.I. JOE launches a killer satellite into orbit to take out the RelayStar, but COBRA counters by using M.A.S.S. to teleport shock troopers into space and destroys the G.I. JOE device. This move nearly exhausts the COBRA supply of the final catalytic element.

Day 4: 0712 Hours

Snake-Eyes returns to G.I. JOE headquarters with the canister of radioactive crystal. Cover Girl helps the team narrowly avoid a deadly booby trap secreted within the canister.

Day 4: 0745 Hours

Dr. Vandemeer fails in his attempt to synthesize the final element. As such, the G.I. JOE team must head to a volcanic ridge in South America where an ancient meteor rests in the so-called Devil's Cauldron.

The G.I. JOEs, meanwhile, transmit a falsified surrender on an internal frequency known to be monitored by COBRA.

Day 4: 1143 Hours

G.I. JOE forces arrive in South America to extract ore from the

meteorite. Dragonfly helicopters attempt to lift the 10-ton alien rock from the lava. A COBRA force led by Destro attacks, triggering a volcanic eruption that launches the meteor skyward, where it is caught by an immense COBRA air transport.

Day 4: 1200 Hours

Cobra Commander, angered at the slow pace of the G.I. JOE surrender, targets New York City with a M.A.S.S. blast that finally depletes the stores of catalytic element. The slave Selena tampers with the device before its destructive cycle is completed, thus saving millions in New York.

Day 4: 1209 Hours

Gung-Ho, Wild Bill, and Scarlett lead a jet pack assault on the COBRA air transport. Destro hammers off a fragment of the metal meteor and then attempts to flee aboard an escape jet. Scarlett, in an attempt to stop him, becomes his captive.

Day 4: 1823 Hours

Destro arrives at the COBRA citadel and reprimands Cobra Commander for his bungled attempt on New York. Destro then assumes control over the operation.

Day 4: 1841 Hours

Scarlett, incarcerated, meets Selena in the dungeons. When she recognizes Duke's ring on Selena's finger, she realizes she has an ally.

Day 5: 0805 Hours

Dr. Vandemeer's M.A.S.S. device is operational at G.I. JOE headquarters.

Day 5: 0900 Hours

The kidnapped world leaders are addressed by Destro, who orders them to force their representative countries to comply with COBRA's demand and surrender. The multitude of nations refuse to capitulate to COBRA pressures. Destro, angered, orders New York City destroyed in order to make good on Cobra Commander's failed threats. Vandemeer uses the G.I. JOE M.A.S.S. device to counter this attempt; the two energy beams cancel each other out.

Day 5: 0931 Hours

Frustrated, Destro issues a broadcast ultimatum that he will assassinate the world's leaders every half hour starting with General Flagg.

Day 5: 0933 Hours

Selena and Scarlett stage a prison break, freeing the slave captives and engineering an uprising. Though they storm the COBRA headquarters, the uprising is quelled and they are recaptured.

Meanwhile, Duke, in a sensory deprivation tank at G.I. JOE headquarters, remembers that he has given his ring to Selena. The ring includes custom electronics that serve as a homing beacon for Vandemeer to track; he begins M.A.S.S.-transmitting G.I. JOE forces to the COBRA citadel.

Day 5: 0950 Hours

Teleported G.I. JOE forces include MOBAT tanks equipped with mountain-climbing articulated cradles, with which the G.I. JOEs scale the steep grade to the COBRA citadel. Duke leads the infantry attack wearing a JUMP jet pack. Air support comes via Skystriker jets. Cobra Commander tries to counter the assault with massive combat robots.

Day 5: 1000 Hours

The G.I. JOEs infiltrate the citadel just as Destro is about to shoot General Flagg. They free Selena and Scarlett from the dungeons as Destro flees to the M.A.S.S. device. In a last-ditch effort, he triggers the device to overload in an apocalyptic explosion. G.I. JOE disables it before it does any damage.

Day 5: 1025 Hours

The last of the fighting is mopped up. Destro flees the COBRA citadel in a F.A.N.G. helicopter. Cobra Commander is a G.I. JOE captive.

Day 5: 1211 Hours

G.I. JOE Breaker attempts to use the M.A.S.S. device one last time to send the Eiffel Tower back to its original location, but he accidentally deposits it in London.

THE WEATHER DOMINATOR

Background: The latest M.A.R.S. innovation nears completion—the Weather Dominator, a complex energy device that can alter the natural weather conditions of localized areas around the world. It consists of key components such as the water controlling mechanisms of the hydromaster and the electromagnetic capabilities of the ion correlator. It requires one more vital component—an extremely energetic power supply—for it to be most effective.

Day 1: 1004 Hours

COBRA forces attack a G.I. JOE convoy that escorts a new laser cannon powered by an inexhaustible laser core source. Though COBRA secures the laser core and in the process captures Duke and Snake-Eyes, G.I. JOE manages to capture Cobra Commander in the assault.

Day 1: 1012 Hours

The colossal COBRA air transport soars away with its laser core and prisoners. In Duke's absence, Flint assumes command and orders Gung-Ho, Short-Fuze, and Breaker to form a guard detail and transport Cobra Commander to Blackwater Prison in Florida. The rest of the team is devoted to following the transport.

Day 1: 1312 Hours

Colonel Sharpe receives word of Cobra Commander's capture and arrival at Blackwater. He hightails it through the Everglades only to be captured and replaced by Zartan.

Day 1: 1423 Hours

A squadron of Skystrikers follow the COBRA air transport as it flies over desert terrain.

Day 1: 1435 Hours

The Baroness and Zartan use disguises to infiltrate Blackwater and free Cobra Commander. Gung-Ho and the rest of the prison detail give pursuit, but the COBRAs escape into the swamps.

Day 1: 1525 Hours

The jets soar over the Pit of Chaos, an immense chasm in the desert landscape. From the nearby Cobra Temple, Destro uses his new Weather Dominator to create a sudden storm that tosses the Skystrikers about like toys. Roadblock, Mutt, and Flint are knocked from the sky into the canyon while the rest of the squadron falls back.

Day 1: 1548 Hours

The COBRA transport jet arrives, delivering Duke and Snake-Eyes as prisoners. COBRA engineers begin installing the laser core to power the Weather Dominator.

Day 1: 1913 Hours

Cobra Commander arrives at the base, transported by Zartan and the Dreadnoks.

Day 1: 1921 Hours

Cobra Commander addresses the world in a global broadcast. With the laser core powering the Weather Dominator, he can now take the whole planet hostage by controlling its weather, creating worldwide calamities. He will continue to batter the planet with disastrous storms until world leaders surrender control to COBRA. At G.I. JOE headquarters, Sparks attempts to triangulate the signal to find the Cobra Temple.

Day 1: 2012 Hours

Rainfall activates mutant creeper vines with which Destro seeded the Pit of Chaos, creating a choking tangle meant to trap any G.I. JOE survivors. Flint and Roadblock try to hack their way through, and are saved by Mutt, who has rigged his crashed Skystriker engines to blast the vines away.

Day 2: 0812 Hours

Snake-Eyes and Duke overhear that Cobra Commander's next target will be Washington, D.C. Subverting the electronics used in the COBRA Arena of Sport, Snake-Eyes manages to get a warning signal off to headquarters using G.I. JOE code Ultra.

As Washington, D.C. begins evacuation procedures, Doc devises a plan to use specialized energy-absorbing mirrors to redirect the Weather Dominator energy threatening the capital.

Day 2: 1020 Hours

Mutt, Flint, and Roadblock engineer a makeshift helicopter from Skystriker parts, but it is not strong enough to lift all three fugitive G.I. JOEs. The creeper vines refuse to let loose their grip on Roadblock, and he opts to stay behind so that Mutt and Flint can escape. As COBRA plots to use the Weather Dominator again, the rainstorms over the Pit of Chaos cease.

Day 2: 1034 Hours

Destro fires a blast on Washington, D.C., starting a torrential rainstorm. The G.I. JOEs arrive with energy mirrors, but many of the fragile devices are smashed by enormous hailstones.

Day 2: 1112 Hours

Mutt and Flint secure COBRA uniforms from a guard detail and make their way to a small, rough town at the edge of the desert. Surviving a sudden brawl in a wretched hive of a bar, they meet the surly sailor Shipwreck, who offers them transportation away from COBRA.

Day 2: 1131 Hours

Displeased with the weather display over D.C., Cobra Commander orders Destro to create a lightning storm despite Destro's protestations. The G.I. JOEs harness the energy unleashed by the lightning with their remaining mirrors and redirect the flow back to the Dominator. The backfire blasts the device into orbit, where it splits into three fragments; each falls to the earth in a separate location. Its scattering has also triggered freak weather occurrences around the world; it is imperative that the device be reassembled in order to right the planet's weather.

Day 2: 1812 Hours

The ion correlator component has fallen into a remote atoll called the Island of No Return, which is surrounded by razor-sharp coral reef. The Baroness leads a COBRA nautical expedition to recover the fragment, while Cutter leads the G.I. JOE force.

Day 2: 2021 Hours

Flint and Mutt return to G.I. JOE headquarters with Shipwreck in tow.

Day 2: 2210 Hours

Lady Jaye and Recondo lead a Skystriker mission to Central America to locate the hydromaster component, which has fallen near the Meso-American ruins known as the Palace of Doom. Flint and Shipwreck accompany them.

Day 3: 0341 Hours

Roadblock, on foot, is chased by mountain lions but escapes into a civilian truck convoy. In the back of the truck, he finds Honda-Lou West of Wild West Hauling. Her truck of provisions has been commandeered by COBRA forces.

Day 3: 0510 Hours

At the reef battle, a freak whirlpool nearly swallows both G.I. JOE and COBRA forces. Spirit heads alone to the island to recover the ion correlator. He is confronted by Storm Shadow.

Day 3: 0610 Hours

Major Bludd leads COBRA to the Palace of Doom, while the G.I. JOE team—led by Recondo and Lady Jaye—sneaks past COBRA S.N.A.K.E. robots to recover the hydromaster. An earthquake suddenly strikes, providing enough distraction for Bludd to recover the component.

Day 3: 0619 Hours

The strange environmental conditions have caused a lava flow to open near the Island of No Return, beginning to swallow the whole atoll in geological conflagration.

Storm Shadow and Spirit must work together to escape a cavern filling with water. For saving his life, Storm Shadow concedes victory to Spirit and allows him to escape with the ion correlator. Zartan, operating secretly from a submarine, fires torpedoes to ensure COBRA agents cannot pursue the G.I. JOEs. Zartan's plot revolves around G.I. JOE and COBRA each having an element of the Weather Dominator.

Day 3: 0630 Hours

The COBRA convoy with Honda-Lou and Roadblock aboard arrives at the Cobra Temple.

Day 3: 1310 Hours

Destro leads the COBRA mission to the Himalayas, the so-called Roof of the World, where the final component of the Weather Dominator has been located. He and Major Bludd ride a tracked ice-borer as it digs its way to the plateau. The G.I. JOEs likewise send a cold-weather team through the glacial sluice tunnels cutting through the ice shelf. A third party, Zartan and the Dreadnoks, also close in on the coveted laser core.

Day 3: 1349 Hours

Cobra Commander is monitoring this progress from the Cobra Temple, and is confronted by Roadblock, who throws the Commander at a pursuing team of COBRA troopers as a distraction. Roadblock and Honda-Lou try to escape but are overwhelmed by COBRAs led by Scrap-Iron.

Day 3: 1415 Hours

The G.I. JOE and COBRA teams arrive at the ice plateau at the same time; a battle erupts for the laser core. The Dreadnoks capture it with the intent of selling it to the highest bidder. Zartan triggers an avalanche to cover his escape.

Day 4: 2112 Hours

Zartan returns to his headquarters, an abandoned Everglades amusement park called Bayou World. He issues his terms to G.I. JOE and COBRA. Both forces triangulate the transmission and dispatch forces to Florida.

Day 4: 2130 Hours

Roadblock and Honda-Lou are placed in the COBRA Arena of Sport along with Duke and Snake-Eyes. They overpower the various electronic menaces sicced upon them by Cobra Commander. They are now loose in COBRA headquarters.

Day 4: 2212 Hours

Ripcord and Breaker parachute into the bayou.

Day 4: 2218 Hours

Storm Shadow infiltrates G.I. JOE headquarters and steals back the ion correlator.

Day 4: 2231 Hours

COBRA Rattlers strafe Bayou World to little effect. COBRA infantry begin to investigate the grounds on foot and are repulsed by armed amusement park rides.

Ripcord and Breaker bomb a nearby generator station, cutting power to Zartan's defenses. The rest of the G.I. JOE strike team arrives.

Day 5: 0145 Hours

Zartan and the Dreadnoks flee into the swamps, but Destro apprehends the master of disguise. Zartan hands over the laser core.

Day 5: 0612 Hours

Duke is able to get a distress signal out of the Cobra Temple that G.I. JOE can home in on.

Day 5: 0704 Hours

Destro brings Zartan before Cobra Commander, but the COBRA leader doesn't punish the opportunistic mercenary. COBRA engineers begin reassembling the Weather Dominator.

During his escape from the Cobra Temple, Roadblock finds samples of COBRA's creeper vine sprigs and begins to develop a plan.

Day 5: 0745 Hours

G.I. JOEs attack the Cobra Temple in force, but the Weather Dominator is active. Destro unleashes a barrage of inclement weather on the G.I. JOEs, radically shifting from one extreme to the other.

Day 5: 0801 Hours

Roadblock unleashes the creeper vines at the base of the Weather Dominator and adds water. The vines grow out of control, choking the Weather Dominator. No longer plagued by the weather effect, the G.I. JOEs push their advantage.

Day 5: 0827 Hours

G.I. JOE forces conquer the temple. Cobra Commander is immobilized by the creeper vine. Destro and Zartan flee. Breaker uses the Weather Dominator to correct the weather patterns around the world...although he can't seem to stop it from snowing at G.I. JOE headquarters.

THE PYRAMID OF DARKNESS

Background: Cobra Commander plots to unleash his most powerful weapon yet—the Pyramid of Darkness. Funded by Extensive Enterprises, the device consists of an array of four Control Cubes powered by a satellite-based laser to create a linked energy field that encapsulates the planet within a square-based pyramid. Within this field, no electrically powered device can function. As the Control Cubes undergo construction, Cobra Commander targets an orbital space station that he needs to complete his plan.

Day 1: 0625 Hours

G.I. JOE serves as security escort for a space shuttle launch when it is suddenly attacked by COBRA forces. The assault, led by Tomax, Xamot, and Cobra Commander, is but an elaborate ruse meant to conceal the fact that COBRA agents have snuck a cargo canister aboard the shuttle.

Day 1: 0720 Hours

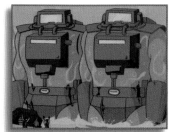

To cover their escape to their underwater lair, Cobra Commander and the Crimson Twins unleash enormous water robots—huge mechanical humanoids with transparent seawater circulation chambers—to fend off pursuing G.I. JOE S.H.A.R.C. crafts. Two S.H.A.R.C.s piloted by Snake-Eyes and Shipwreck dive past the robots and infiltrate the COBRA base.

Day 1: 0752 Hours

The space shuttle docks with G.I. JOE Space Station Delta. Odd inconsistencies with the shuttle's docking performance suggest that it has taken on unexpected weight.

G.I. JOE Orbital Personnel

Shuttle Crew: Mutt & Junkyard, Dusty, Breaker, and Steeler.
Space Station Crew: Duke, Scarlett, Clutch, and Rock 'N Roll.

Inspecting the cargo pods, the G.I. JOE crew finds strangely adorable bioengineered creatures dubbed "fatal fluffies." A member of the shuttle crew reveals himself as COBRA agent Zartan, who sounds a whistle that activates the fluffies' adrenal metamorphosis, transforming them from apparently harmless cuddly creatures to rampaging fire-breathing titans.

Zartan also releases from a second cargo capsule his Dreadnok shock assault team. Backed by the Dreadnoks and the fluffies, Zartan orders the G.I. JOEs to surrender.

Day 1: 0802 Hours

Shipwreck and Snake-Eyes abandon their S.H.A.R.C.s and proceed on foot within the COBRA base. They appropriate COBRA uniforms and try to blend in with the ranks as they investigate the COBRA operation.

Day 1: 0915 Hours

Zartan makes a transmission from Space Station Delta to G.I. JOE headquarters. By establishing a connection, Zartan is able to lock firing coordinates; he proceeds to devastate the headquarters through an orbital laser strike.

Day 1: 1411 Hours

In the underwater lair, Control Cube One is completed and readied for delivery. Shipwreck affixes a tracking beacon onto the cube.

Day 1: 2105 Hours

The second Control Cube is completed.

Day 2: 0701 Hours

The third Control Cube is completed.

Day 2: 0921 Hours

The G.I. JOEs, led by Flint, establish temporary headquarters aboard the USS *Flagg*. They track Shipwreck's beacon signal as it surfaces over the Pacific Ocean. A COBRA helicopter convoy is carrying the first Control Cube to a volcanic island known as the Devil's Playground. The G.I. JOEs scramble to intercept.

Day 2: 0941 Hours

Dusty, a prisoner aboard Space Station Delta, suddenly activates the artificial gravity system, taking his COBRA captors by surprise. In the ensuing confusion, he races to the station control room to uncover details about the COBRA plot, but doesn't get far before being recaptured.

Day 2: 1047 Hours

Destro and his forces arrive at the Devil's Playground. They must carefully align the cube in order for the pyramid to form. The G.I. JOEs, led by Flint and Lady Jaye, arrive in their Skystrikers. A battle erupts.

Day 2: 1101 Hours

In the underwater lair, Shipwreck and Snake-Eyes break into the chief engineer's office and capture a data disk with the full program specs for the automated cube assembly lines. Evading COBRA security, the two G.I. JOEs take a handcar through the rail tunnel network to escape the compound.

Day 2: 1114 Hours

Dusty and Mutt surreptitiously splice a circuit jumper across the space station's communications cables, allowing them to intercept and retransmit Zartan's contact with COBRA headquarters to other G.I. JOEs.

Day 2: 1401 Hours

The second cube, transported by the Crimson Twins, arrives at the City of the Dead—an area of Shanxi province, China. The third cube, meanwhile, approaches the Mountain of Glass, a glacier on the northwest coast of North America.

The G.I. JOE team receives Cobra Commander's status updates via Dusty's rigged communications line, and begins prepping missions to intercept these next two cubes.

Day 2: 2124 Hours
Snake-Eyes and Shipwreck evade COBRA pursuit and emerge from the underwater lair to arrive in the subway system in a sketchy part of Enterprise City. They are tailed by Colonel Slash, a COBRA agent, who follows them to the Snake Club, a nightclub. With the help of torch singer Satin, the two fugitive G.I. JOEs escape pursuit.

Day 2: 2315 Hours
At the Devil's Playground, Flint attempts to mine the Control Cube, but its built-in defenses repulse the G.I. JOE team.

Day 2: 2320 Hours
A G.I. JOE team led by Roadblock and including Footloose and Airtight arrives at the City of the Dead. The terra-cotta warriors found within an ancient temple suddenly spring to life and attack the G.I. JOEs, as the COBRAs—Tomax and Xamot—position the cube for activation.

Day 2: 2340 Hours
The G.I. JOE arctic forces, led by Alpine and Bazooka, arrive at the Mountain of Glass to stop Major Bludd from positioning his Control Cube.

Day 3: 0012 Hours
The City of the Dead Control Cube is activated, lancing a beam of energy to Space Station Delta. Though COBRA has successfully activated this cube, their forces are overrun by G.I. JOE. Roadblock captures Tomax.
Another cube, at the Devil's Playground, also activates.

Day 3: 0021 Hours
At the Mountain of Glass, Major Bludd activates the third cube. Alpine and Bazooka, meanwhile, are split from the rest of their unit and end up stranded on an ice floe until rescued by MacArthur Ito, an out-of-work stuntman left stuck out in the arctic wilderness by a swindling television commercial director. The two G.I. JOEs and Ito team up and stow away aboard the COBRA vehicles as they drive away from the ice shelf.

Day 3: 0421 Hours
Roadblock returns to the USS *Flagg* with Tomax as his prisoner. Due to his psychic link with his twin brother, Xamot is able to pinpoint the location of the *Flagg* and mounts a rescue effort. The *Flagg* is near the location for the fourth and final cube, the fabled Sea of Lost Souls, an area of shipwrecks in the Pacific.

Day 3: 0701 Hours
Satin's truck is stopped at a checkpoint leaving Enterprise City. Her stowaways—Snake-Eyes and Shipwreck—help her fight her way past COBRA guards.

Day 3: 0721 Hours
The *Flagg* enters the Sea of Lost Souls. Xamot infiltrates the aircraft carrier and frees Tomax from the brig.
Meanwhile, Baroness and Destro submerge the last cube, activating it and thus completing the Pyramid of Darkness. Electrical activity within the pyramid ceases. The G.I. JOEs are literally powerless to stop the escaping COBRAs.

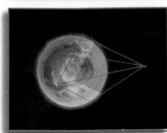

Day 3: 0945 Hours
Xamot and Tomax signal the Dreadnoks via a flare spotted by sensors within Space Station Delta. The Dreadnoks betray Zartan and take control of the fatal fluffies. The Dreadnoks are secretly on Extensive Enterprises' payroll; the Crimson Twins are taking over the pyramid operation.

Day 3: 1812 Hours
With enormous sails affixed to the USS *Flagg,* scavenged from the shipwrecks in the Sea of Lost Souls, the carrier begins to move forward.

Day 3: 1825 Hours

Satin drops off Snake-Eyes and Shipwreck on the outskirts of Enterprise City. The two G.I. JOEs are now left to return to their headquarters on their own.

Day 3: 1915 Hours

Tomax and Xamot confront Cobra Commander, revealing their treachery and command of Space Station Delta.

Day 4: 0821 Hours

Major Bludd's COBRA forces arrive at the Cobra Temple, hidden behind a waterfall in the Pacific Northwest. Ito, Alpine, and Bazooka commandeer a COBRA transport plane and take off. The COBRA crew rebels, dropping the plane, but the G.I. JOEs escape in Trouble Bubbles.

Day 4: 1700 Hours

Cobra Commander, held in thrall by the Crimson Twins, diminishes the pyramid effect to allow a transmission—an ultimatum to the world—giving seven hours to surrender control to COBRA.

Day 4: 1721 Hours

Snake-Eyes and Shipwreck return to G.I. JOE headquarters with the Control Cube data disk, but the G.I. JOEs are unable to read it without any electricity.

Day 4: 1825 Hours

Aboard Space Station Delta, Mutt grabs the control whistle from an inattentive Dreadnok and reverts the fatal fluffies back to their diminutive state. The G.I. JOEs rush the Dreadnoks, retaking control of the station.

Day 4: 1830 Hours

The orbital laser powering the Pyramid of Darkness dissipates, and the pyramid collapses. Cobra Commander resumes command from the Crimson Twins, and orders Destro to resurrect a low-altitude version of the pyramid.

The G.I. JOEs now have power and examine the data disk, uncovering the existence of a self-destruct mechanism at the Cobra Temple that can obliterate the cubes. Unfortunately, the disk provides no information on the location of the temple.

Day 5: 0911 Hours

Destro uses a laser projector to erect a low-altitude Pyramid of Darkness. Though the pyramid is smaller, it is still effective.

Alpine, Bazooka, and Ito arrive at G.I. JOE headquarters. They know the location of Cobra Temple, allowing the G.I. JOE team to act.

Day 5: 1421 Hours

The G.I. JOEs arrive at the Cobra Temple. COBRA counterattacks, using a dragon heat projector device.

Day 5: 1518 Hours

Tomax and Xamot retreat with Cobra Commander. Shipwreck locates the self-destruct device and detonates the Control Cubes.

Day 5: 1721 Hours

Tomax, Xamot, and Cobra Commander retreat to the twin-towered executive office building of Extensive Enterprises. An orbital rocket is concealed within the edifice. They attempt to launch, but have been pursued by G.I. JOE agents. With Satin's help, Shipwreck and Snake-Eyes infiltrate the towers and nearly sabotage the launch attempt.

Day 5: 1740 Hours

Zartan and the Dreadnoks break out of custody and escape Space Station Delta in launch capsules. Duke, aboard the station, configures a proton beam that destroys the Extensive Enterprises rocket. COBRA and the Crimson Twins, however, have fled in an escape pod.

ATTACK ON SPRINGFIELD

Background: At Cobra Commander's order, Dr. Mindbender and Destro have been collecting genetic samples from some of history's greatest military leaders to create a clone amalgam in the form of Serpentor. Meanwhile, G.I. JOE agent Ripcord infiltrated Cobra Island on a highly unauthorized personal mission to uncover the truth about his girlfriend, the daughter of a COBRA Crimson Guardsman. That Guardsman, concerned for his daughter's safety, let Ripcord escape custody disguised as Zartan aboard a pre-programmed Firebat that transported him to COBRA's secret mainland headquarters beneath the town of Springfield.

Day 1: 2122 Hours

Ripcord has duped the Dreadnoks into believing he is Zartan. While they dine at the Tiki Lounge, a Polynesian-themed eatery in Springfield, Ripcord surreptitiously makes a phone call to G.I. JOE headquarters, revealing Springfield's location. COBRA Tele-Vipers intercept the call and attempt to apprehend Ripcord, but he escapes on foot.

Day 1: 2148 Hours

Hawk gathers G.I. JOE personnel and mobilizes every active and able-bodied G.I. JOE to attack Springfield. The G.I. JOE team lifts off aboard two C-130 Hercules transports from McGuire Air Force Base.

Strike Team

Personnel: Hawk, Lady Jaye, Barbecue, Heavy Metal, Flint, Deep Six, Airtight, Footloose, Bazooka, Alpine, Crankcase, Blowtorch, and Shipwreck.

Vehicles: Mauler M.B.T. Tank; AWE Striker; Silver Mirage motorcycle.

Objective: Take and secure Springfield airport and then locate and neutralize COBRA headquarters.

Security Team

Personnel: Duke, Steeler, Grunt, Rock 'N Roll, Flash, Gung-Ho, Tripwire, Short-Fuze, Breaker, Mutt & Junkyard, Snow Job, Zap, Doc, Cover Girl, and Roadblock.

Vehicles: MOBAT; RAM; VAMP Mark II.

Objective: Coordinate with Strike Team to take out the airport, then branch out and block all the main roads leading out of Springfield.

Assault Team

Personnel: Stalker, Snake-Eyes, Scarlett, Quick Kick, Recondo, Spirit, Torpedo, Beachhead, and Leatherneck.

Objective: First insertion team, tasked with cutting off power, communications, and water.

Air Transport and Support Team

Aboard C-130 #1: (carrying the Strike Team) Ace.

Aboard C-130 #2: (carrying the Security Team) Slip-Stream.

Aboard Tomahawk: (carrying the Assault Team) Lift-Ticket.

Aboard Dragonfly XH-1: Wild Bill and Airborne.

Day 1: 2205 Hours

Ripcord is re-apprehended by the Dreadnoks, Scrap-Iron, and Firefly when his location is exposed by a young civilian girl who proves to be a COBRA collaborator.

Day 1: 2228 Hours

Ripcord is dragged to the Springfield Museum of Antiquities, site of Dr. Mindbender's laboratory. The G.I. JOE is placed into the brainwave scanner—currently set up to construct Serpentor's mind—in order to discover how much information Ripcord has divulged to the G.I. JOE team. The security breach is confirmed, and Cobra Commander is informed on Cobra Island.

Day 1: 2230 Hours

The Tomahawk deposits the Assault Team at the Springfield Power and Light Company. A COBRA security detail spots their approach but is quickly—and silently—neutralized by Quick Kick. The team detonates explosives at the central power station, plunging Springfield into darkness.

Day 1: 2235 Hours

Serpentor emerges from his nutrient tank. He quickly—and correctly—surmises the G.I. JOE attack strategy.

Day 1: 2248 Hours

The Assault Team neutralizes the central telephone exchange offices, cutting Springfield's outbound and inbound communications.

Day 1: 2305 Hours

The Assault Team takes Springfield Police Headquarters intact, securing access to their files, maps, and computers.

The C-130s transporting the Strike and Security teams approach Springfield Airport and begin taking anti-aircraft fire from A.S.P. emplacements. The Dragonfly blasts a clear path for the incoming planes.

Serpentor takes over defense command from Destro and the Baroness, tasking them with supervising evacuation efforts. Destro, wary of Serpentor, nonetheless grants him a company of COBRA infantry, four H.I.S.S. tanks, and two Stinger jeeps.

Day 1: 2310 Hours

A recon element of the Assault Team reports unusual activity at the Museum of Antiquities, citing it as a possible regimental headquarters. Stalker requests backup from Hawk.

Hawk's and Duke's teams quickly unload from the C-130s, which return to the skies. Duke's Security Team begins mounting roadblocks on major roads out of Springfield.

Serpentor rallies his troops to carry out a holding action while Springfield evacuates.

Day 2: 0010 Hours

The Assault Team engages Serpentor's forces on Main Street. Recondo and Scarlett are injured in the crossfire. Serpentor leads his troops in pushing toward the airport.

Hawk's strike team calls back the Security Team to the airport so that he can roll out to attack the museum. Because they cannot maintain manned roadblocks, the Security Team stops up the main roads with burning vehicles.

Day 2: 0012 Hours

Aboard a H.I.S.S. tank, Destro begins calling for the evacuation of the Springfield suburbs. All personnel and dependents are to report to their cell leaders at Springfield High School. Each evacuee is allowed one suitcase. All COBRA documents, equipment, and paraphernalia must be destroyed or brought with the evacuee.

Underneath the airport, COBRA's evacuation helicopters begin moving through an underground tunnel network.

Day 2: 0024 Hours

Serpentor presses the offensive against the Assault Team.

The Security Team returns to the airport. Hawk has them set up a defensive perimeter while the Strike Team rolls out into town. Recon units from the Security Team investigate the hangars and outbuildings for any COBRA presence.

Day 2: 0048 Hours

COBRA cells are assembled in the Springfield High School gymnasium and begin filing out to the football field in alphabetical order, with group Anaconda first.

Day 2: 0050 Hours

Retreating from Serpentor's advance, the Assault Team takes over an abandoned Springfield Department of Sanitation truck as transportation.

The Strike Team arrives at the museum. The few COBRAs left at the facility abandon it. The G.I. JOEs recover Ripcord from the brainwave scanner. Fearing that Serpentor's push to the airport is not a diversion but an actual tactic, Hawk regroups his Strike Team to reinforce the Security Team.

Flash, while scouting an empty hangar for the Security Team, finds a vast elevator system below the airfield rigged to explode.

Day 2: 0058 Hours

The underground explosives detonate, destroying the entire tunnel system that connects the airport to the high school.

Day 2: 0110 Hours

The assembled evacuation helicopters are ready at the football field and begin airlifting evacuees out of Springfield.

Day 2: 0112 Hours

The Assault Team's garbage truck arrives at the airport. They report a motorized COBRA column in close pursuit. The Assault Team joins the Security Team in defending the airport.

Day 2: 0115 Hours

The COBRA vehicles approach with headlamps lit and mufflers disengaged, producing a loud screen of engine noise that covers the escaping helicopters. The vehicles suddenly cut their headlamps and disappear in the darkness.

Strike Team members return to the airport and, together with the rest of the G.I. JOE team, wipe out the charging COBRA vehicles, only to discover they are unmanned. The rest of the COBRA vehicles are left stopped but with engines running on the airfield.

The G.I. JOEs launch a flare and discover a small group of COBRA transport helicopters lifting the drivers of the COBRA vehicles to safety.

Day 2: 0210 Hours

The G.I. JOE team completes a first reconnaissance of Springfield, finding it completely evacuated and all tangible evidence of COBRA occupation destroyed. The G.I. JOEs will receive harsh reprimands for their failure, including a momentary suspension of operations.

COBRA ISLAND CIVIL WAR

Background: A surgically enhanced COBRA agent, the Star Viper, infiltrated the G.I. JOE shuttle launch base in Utah and stole a vital piece of electronics: a top-secret L-VE "black box" that can read every signal from every US spy satellite. Returning to Cobra Island with the technological prize, the Star Viper discovers that the leadership rivalries between Cobra Commander and Serpentor have escalated to open conflict.

G.I. JOE dispatched a recon team, launched aboard a captured COBRA Mamba helicopter from the USS *Flagg,* to Cobra Island to gather intelligence.

Civil war erupts on Cobra Island, with Cobra Commander operating out of headquarters building and Serpentor based out of the landlocked freighter. Serpentor dispatches Dr. Mindbender to Washington, D.C., to broker a deal with the United States for military aid in overthrowing Cobra Commander in exchange for the return of the black box.

Meanwhile, in the Caribbean, an ocean liner carrying Destro's Iron Grenadier forces also approaches Cobra Island.

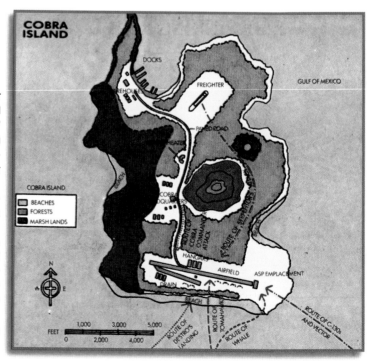

Alliances and Forces

Serpentor's Forces: Dr. Mindbender (operations); Croc-Master (security); Crimson Twins and Crimson Guardsmen (shock troops); Scrap-Iron; B.A.T.s (infantry); Rattlers (air arm); H.I.S.S. tanks (armor).

Cobra Commander's Forces: The Baroness (operations); Zartan and Family (security); the Dreadnoks (shock troops); Viper Corps (infantry); Mambas (air arm); Maggots, BUGGs (armor).

G.I. JOE Forces

Sea Transport and Support: Admiral Keel-Haul, Cutter, and Shipwreck.

Operations (aboard USS *Flagg*): Flint, Lady Jaye, and Mainframe.

Air Transport and Support: Wild Bill, Lift-Ticket, Slip-Stream, and Ace.

Mechanized Assault and Combined Aviation: Battle Force 2000 (Maverick, Knockdown, Avalanche, Blocker, Blaster, and Dodger).

Weapons Team and Field HQ: Hawk, Roadblock, Leatherneck, Fast Draw, Sci-Fi, Low-Light, Breaker, and Doc.

Security Team: Duke, Crazylegs, Beachhead, Wet-Suit, Airborne, Ripcord, and Lifeline.

Motorized Recon: Crankcase and Clutch.

Intelligence Recon Team: Falcon, Dial-Tone, Tunnel Rat, Spirit, Sneak Peek, and Gung-Ho.

Engineering Team (EOD and Demolitions): Stalker, Tripwire, Short-Fuze, and Mutt & Junkyard.

Amphibious Assault Team: Recondo, Psyche-Out, Torpedo, Thunder, Cross-Country, Armadillo, Tollbooth, Outback, Grand Slam, Heavy Metal, Charbroil, Law & Order, Alpine, Blowtorch, and Hardtop.

Day 1: 2118 Hours

The Intelligence Recon Team witnesses the lengthy siege of the COBRA landlocked freighter, as the Baroness's ground and air forces get whittled away despite a five-to-one numerical superiority over Serpentor's entrenched forces. Despite their growing losses, Cobra Commander orders the Baroness to continue the assault, for he cannot have Serpentor break through the lines and attack his headquarters.

Day 1: 2142 Hours

The Intelligence Recon Team is ordered south to the COBRA airfield to report on defenses and airfield conditions. The G.I. JOEs trudge through the edges of the marshes, shadowed by Captain Minh, a boat captain betrayed by Cobra Commander who has been living on the island for weeks.

Day 2: 0614 Hours

The G.I. JOE forces amass at the USS *Flagg* 30 miles east of Cobra Island. General Hollingsworth briefs them on their new mission—to support Serpentor in his bid to retake control of Cobra Island.

Day 2: 0652 Hours

Falcon's Recon Team reconnoiters the airfield. They spot ground defenses consisting of two A.S.P.s around the tower, a fortified A.S.P. battery at the end of the runway, three Maggots for mobile ground support, and at least three Mambas for air support. Falcon is given a new assignment: to attack and take control of the tower, no matter the cost.

Minh provides them with a secret underground route to infiltrate the tower without being seen: using the storm drain to reach a service access.

Day 2: 0810 Hours

The G.I. JOE forces approach the airfield. Tomahawk helicopters carrying the Weapons and Security teams approach from the south. Two C-130 transports carrying the Mechanized Assault and Motorized Recon teams approach from the southeast. The Killer W.H.A.L.E., with the Engineering Team, approaches from the southeast as well.

Day 2: 0816 Hours

The Intelligence Recon Team reaches the tower. Tunnel Rat decimates the tower crew. COBRA is unable to mount a coordinated defense against the G.I. JOE landing forces.

Day 2: 0819 Hours

The Air Transport and Support team Tomahawks touch down on the airstrip, depositing the Security and Weapons teams. A COBRA Mamba strafes Lift-Ticket's Tomahawk chopper as the Security Team exits his vehicle. Lift-Ticket and Crazylegs are incapacitated. Wild Bill provides air support, striking back at the Mambas in his Tomahawk.

Day 2: 0821 Hours

With attention riveted by the hangars, the fortified A.S.P. emplacement at the eastern end of the airstrip is unprepared for the sudden arrival of the Killer W.H.A.L.E. The G.I. JOE hovercraft wipes out half the A.S.P.s before it is knocked out of commission by the remaining gunpods. The Engineering Team proceeds on foot and uses satchel charges to wipe out the rest of the A.S.P. gunpods, clearing the path for the C-130s.

Day 2: 0824 Hours

Serpentor's H.I.S.S. column rushes out of the landlocked freighter, pushing through the Baroness's offensive lines to make its way to the airfield.

Cobra Commander orders Zartan to lead a column of Maggots from the headquarters building to the airfield, though Serpentor has a head start.

Day 2: 0829 Hours

The Security and Weapons teams take cover at the airfield hangars. The COBRA Maggots begin to close in, but are taken out by Weapons Team specialists Sci-Fi and Fast Draw.

Day 2: 0831 Hours

The C-130s land at the airfield, with cover fire provided by Wild Bill's Tomahawk and Maverick's Vector jet.

Just then, Cobra Commander and the Dreadnoks arrive at the airfield aboard the Thunder Machine. With the vehicle's forward cannons, they cripple the forward C-130, effectively blocking the runway.

Day 2: 0840 Hours

The Thunder Machine drives past the airstrip battle, and Dreadnok Buzzer grabs Hawk and takes him aboard the vehicle. This leads to a running fistfight aboard the Thunder Machine as it moves into the forests beyond the airstrip, only to come into contact with Serpentor's H.I.S.S. column. Serpentor has trussed up the captive Baroness on the hood of his H.I.S.S. tank to act as a human shield.

Day 2: 0842 Hours

Serpentor's forces arrive at the airfield.

Day 2: 0851 Hours

Destro's Iron Grenadier army arrives on the southern beach in force. Thrasher, having difficulty controlling the Thunder Machine with Hawk aboard, crashes into the lead Iron Grenadier D.E.M.O.N. tank holding Destro.

The D.E.M.O.N. tank blasts the Thunder Machine out of the way, flipping the Dreadnok vehicle and sending its occupants scattering.

Day 2: 0901 Hours

Destro's forces fully arrive and take control of the southern beach: two squadrons of armor, a battalion of elite infantry, as well as undefined air support. Duke orders Clutch, Crankcase and Roadblock aboard the AWE Striker to pick up Hawk. G.I. JOE air support begins to engage Destro's A.G.P. pods, pushing them back.

Zartan's Maggot column approaches from the northwest. Rather than engaging, Zartan orders his troops to take hold of the west end of the airfield and see what Destro is up to.

Day 2: 0912 Hours

The Dreadnoks flip the Thunder Machine back onto its wheels, driving Cobra Commander away from the battlefield.

Serpentor distributes his armored column into defensive positions at the east end of the runway, alongside the G.I. JOE Engineering Team. Rather than allow Serpentor an open field of fire down the runway, Zartan's Maggots open fire at the H.I.S.S. squadrons. Serpentor's forces return fire, catching G.I. JOE in the middle of this artillery duel. The AWE Striker is taken out, and Crankcase is injured.

The Security Team covers the withdrawal of G.I. JOE forces from the airstrip. Breaker orders the air support to suppress Zartan's artillery. Cutter and the Engineering Team use the captured A.S.P.s to return fire against Zartan's forces.

Day 2: 0930 Hours
Destro begins calling his troops to fall back for morning tea.
Cobra Commander rejoins Zartan and his armored forces and calls in an airstrike.

Day 2: 0931 Hours
Serpentor and Hawk discuss chain of command; Hawk will offer aid and support to Serpentor, but at his discretion. He will not hand over command of G.I. JOE to the COBRA Emperor.
Serpentor's B.A.T. infantry arrive on foot at the airfield.

Day 2: 0939 Hours
Cobra Commander's air support arrives in the form of a squadron of Mamba helicopters. The Vector jet engages them, but the Mambas shoot down the remaining Tomahawk. Wild Bill lands the helicopter at Serpentor's end of the airstrip.
Serpentor's air reinforcements arrive: Rattlers and F.A.N.G. helicopters.

Day 2: 1001 Hours
Serpentor leads his H.I.S.S. tank column in a full-frontal assault against the Maggots. Cobra Commander counterattacks. The G.I. JOE Weapons, Security, and Engineering teams charge with the H.I.S.S. tanks as cover.
The two forces engage at point-blank range. The competing COBRA air forces withdraw with weapons spent.

Day 2: 1015 Hours
Destro's forces, fully rested and replenished, advance, pushing all players off the airfield. Serpentor and the G.I. JOEs withdraw. Cobra Commander and his forces pull back to the northwest, placing the volcano directly between their retreating forces.

Day 2: 1021 Hours
A rain squall moves in, turning the weather.

Day 2: 1030 Hours
Destro takes control of the airfield, making the tower his operational headquarters. He orders the position reinforced with razor ribbon, claymores, and anti-tank trenches.
The G.I. JOE Intelligence Recon Team retreats to the drainage tunnels, which begin to fill with water due to the weather. Iron Grenadier patrols also begin to search the tunnels. With Captain Minh's guidance, the Recon Team is able to work its way through the sluice tunnels undetected.

Day 2: 1115 Hours
Cobra Commander returns to his headquarters building and attempts to pull up the broadcast signal from a specially modified B.A.T. trooper he has secreted within Serpentor's ranks. But Serpentor has spotted the modification and terminated that trooper.
Hawk radios the USS *Flagg,* requesting reinforcement and resupply, but he notes that the airfield is now in unfriendly hands.

Day 2: 1131 Hours
The weather conditions are too rough for an aerial insertion, so the Operations Team dispatches a fully loaded LCT (landing craft tank) for sea insertion. At the same time, Ghostrider lifts off in the Phantom X-19 stealth fighter to knock out the COBRA radar systems.

Day 2: 1139 Hours
The stealth fighter destroys two COBRA BUGG tracked submarines, then wipes out the radar before being detected. COBRA headquarters is now blind.

Day 2: 1204 Hours

Serpentor's forces, having navigated around the volcano, attack COBRA headquarters from the north.

Day 2: 1208 Hours

The Amphibious Assault Team arrives on the west beach and deploys the Slugger, Rolling Thunder, Mauler M.B.T., H.A.V.O.C., and Bridge Layer through a trail already blazed by Croc-Master.

Day 2: 1214 Hours

The Recon Team emerges back at the airfield between hangars to find the strip completely deserted. Tank trails lead north.

Day 2: 1221 Hours

The Amphibious Assault Team emerges from the western marshes and boxes in Cobra Commander's forces. The Dreadnoks surrender.

Day 2: 1229 Hours

Destro's forces march up from the south; Cobra Commander is now completely surrounded.

Day 2: 1231 Hours

Zartan strings up his compound bow and fires an arrow, killing Serpentor. Dr. Mindbender quickly runs over to Cobra Commander to establish a truce, combining Serpentor's forces with Cobra Commander in order to push Destro off the island.

Day 2: 1237 Hours

Destro arrives and offers to leave immediately if he can take custody of the Baroness. Cobra Commander and Mindbender agree. The G.I. JOEs, having no arrangement with the new COBRA command structure, are left with no option but to leave.

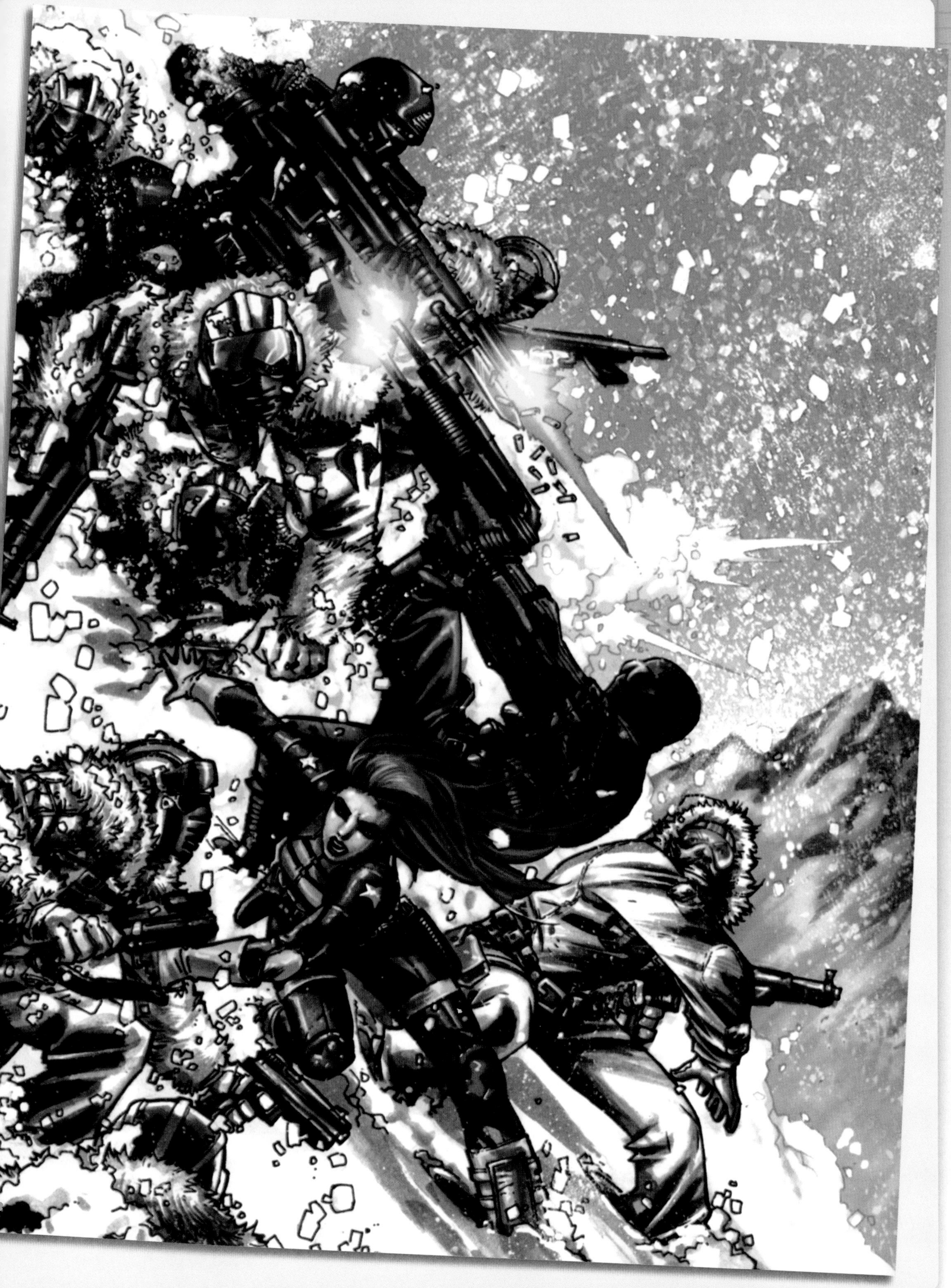

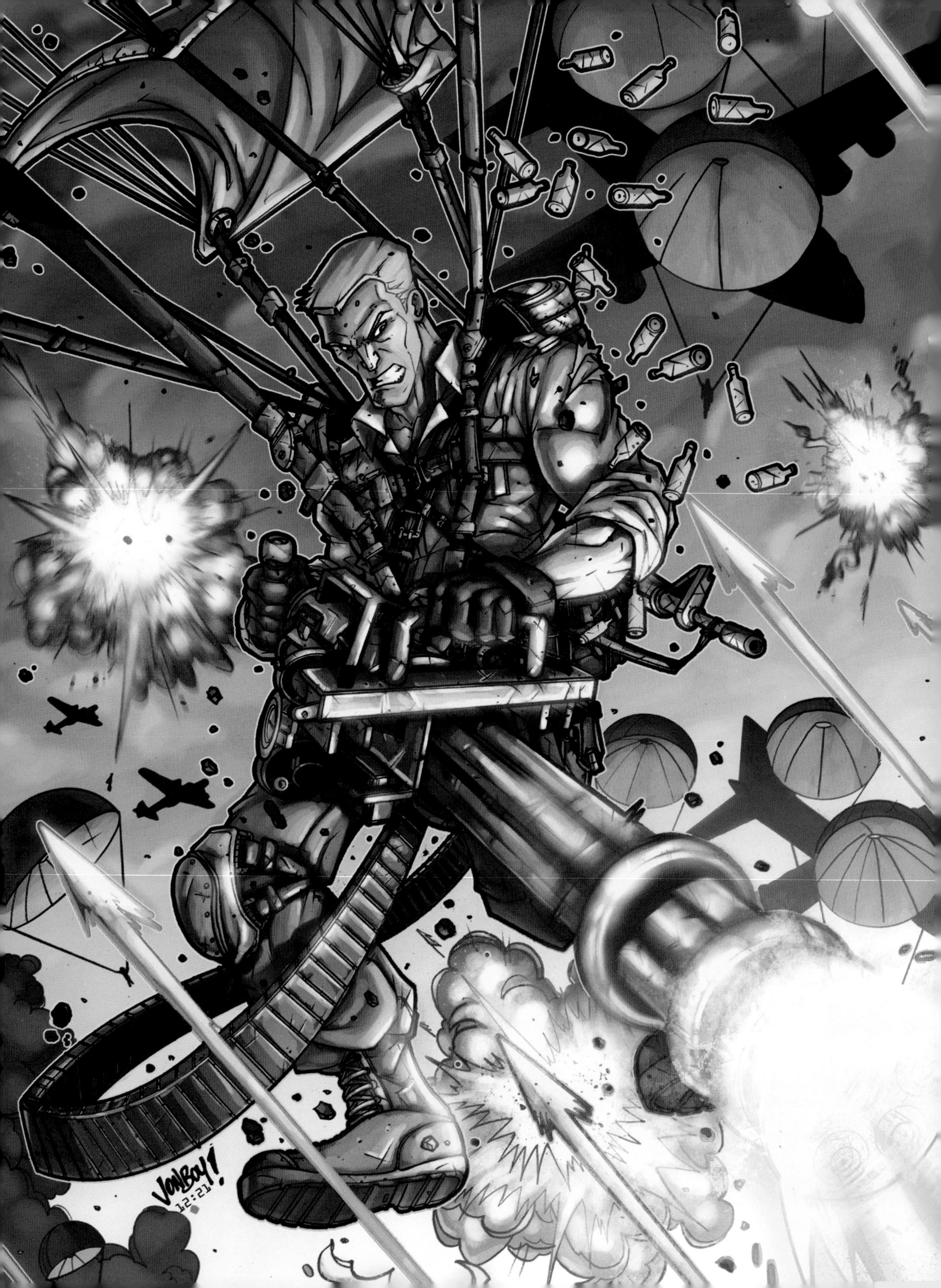

CHAPTER 5

THE MISSION CONTINUES...

"IN OR OUT?" Written by Larry Hama   Art and Color by Tom Feister

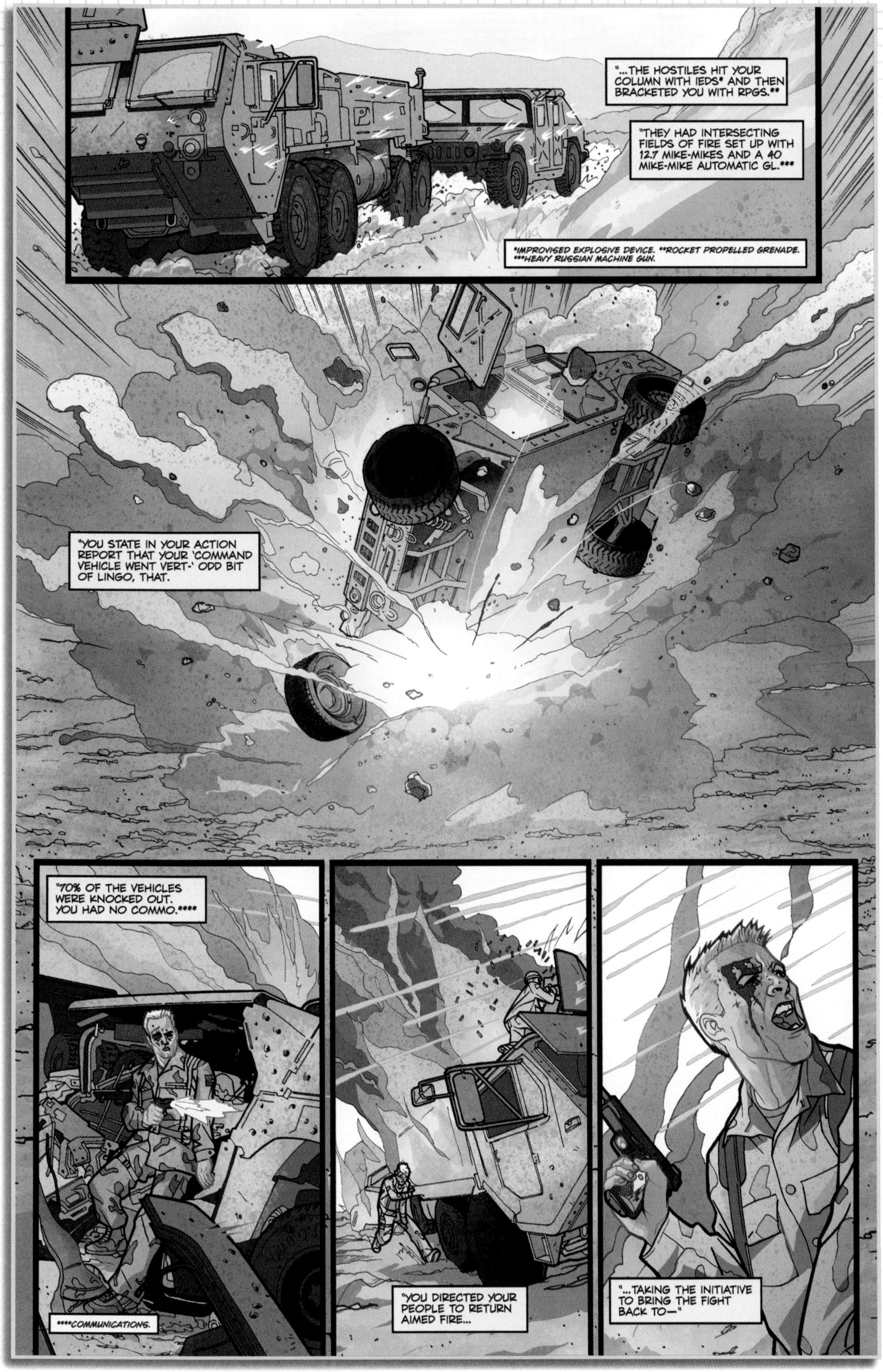
"...THE HOSTILES HIT YOUR COLUMN WITH IEDS* AND THEN BRACKETED YOU WITH RPGS.**
"THEY HAD INTERSECTING FIELDS OF FIRE SET UP WITH 12.7 MIKE-MIKES AND A 40 MIKE-MIKE AUTOMATIC GL.***
*IMPROVISED EXPLOSIVE DEVICE. **ROCKET PROPELLED GRENADE. ***HEAVY RUSSIAN MACHINE GUN.
"YOU STATE IN YOUR ACTION REPORT THAT YOUR 'COMMAND VEHICLE WENT VERT-' ODD BIT OF LINGO, THAT.
"70% OF THE VEHICLES WERE KNOCKED OUT. YOU HAD NO COMMO.****
****COMMUNICATIONS.
"YOU DIRECTED YOUR PEOPLE TO RETURN AIMED FIRE...
"...TAKING THE INITIATIVE TO BRING THE FIGHT BACK TO—"

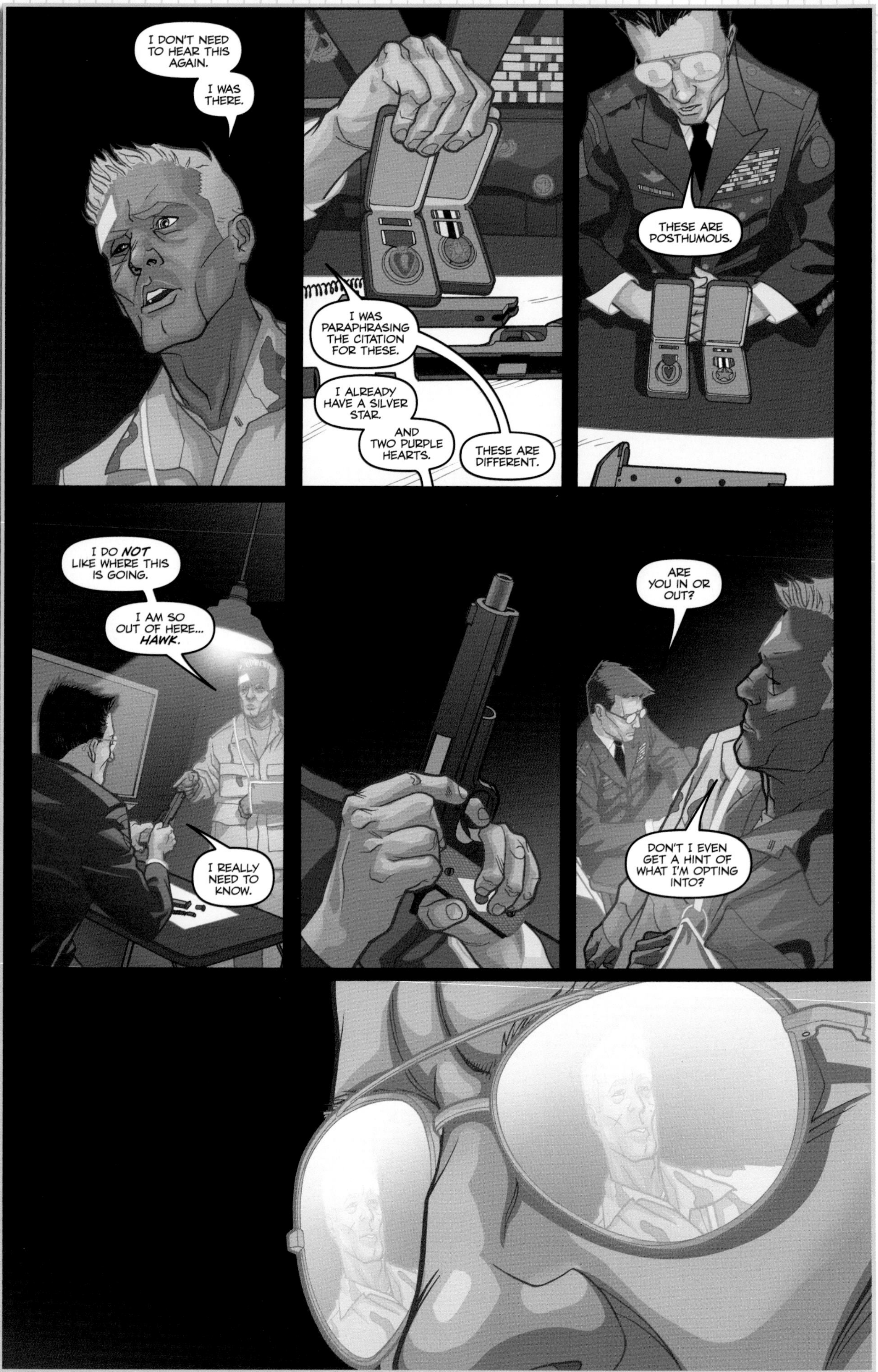
I DON'T NEED TO HEAR THIS AGAIN.
I WAS THERE.
I WAS PARAPHRASING THE CITATION FOR THESE.
I ALREADY HAVE A SILVER STAR.
AND TWO PURPLE HEARTS.
THESE ARE DIFFERENT.
THESE ARE POSTHUMOUS.
I DO ***NOT*** LIKE WHERE THIS IS GOING.
I AM SO OUT OF HERE... ***HAWK.***
I REALLY NEED TO KNOW.
ARE YOU IN OR OUT?
DON'T I EVEN GET A HINT OF WHAT I'M OPTING INTO?

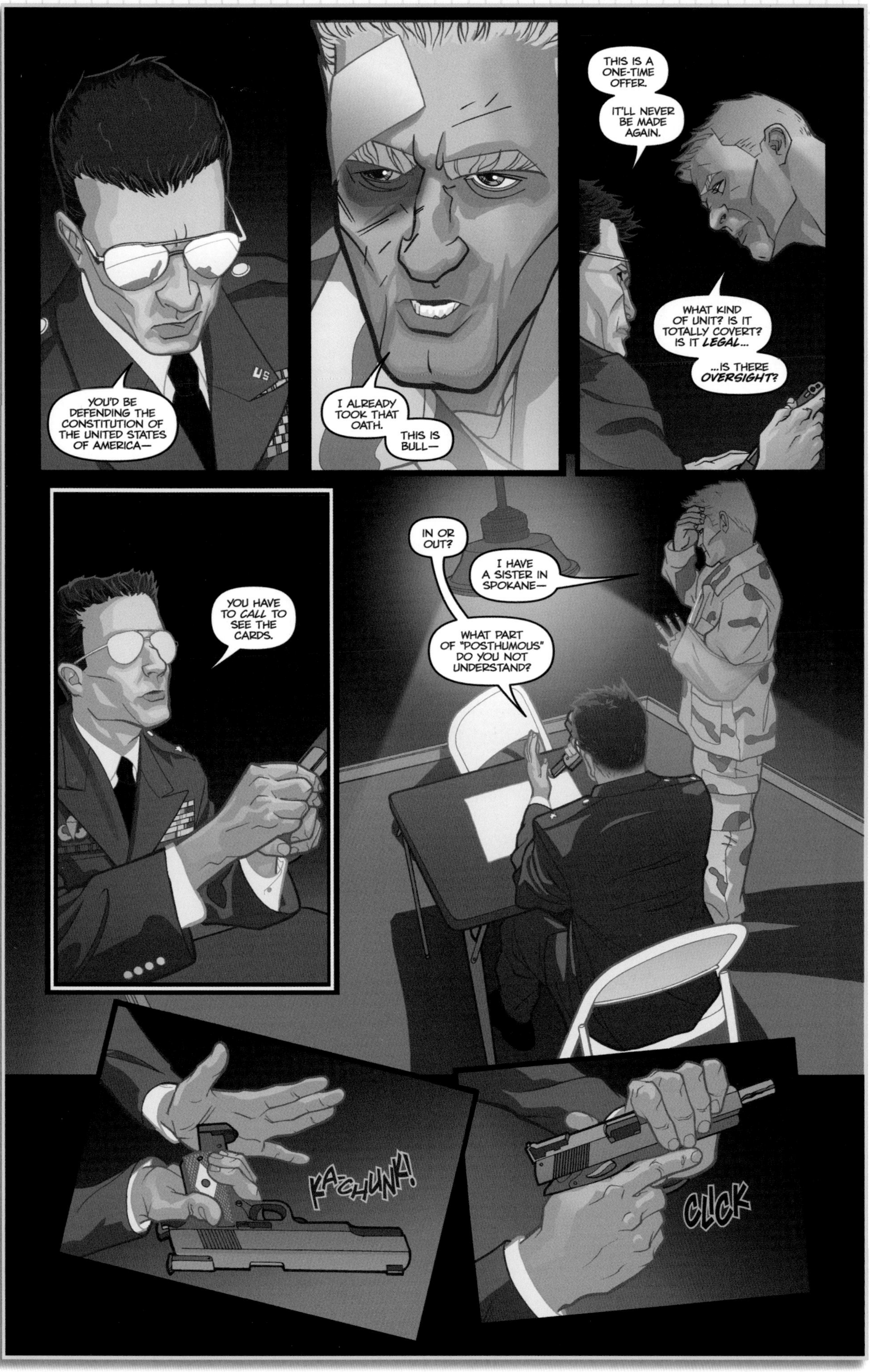

YOU'D BE DEFENDING THE CONSTITUTION OF THE UNITED STATES OF AMERICA—
I ALREADY TOOK THAT OATH.
THIS IS BULL—
THIS IS A ONE-TIME OFFER.
IT'LL NEVER BE MADE AGAIN.
WHAT KIND OF UNIT? IS IT TOTALLY COVERT? IS IT LEGAL...
...IS THERE OVERSIGHT?
YOU HAVE TO CALL TO SEE THE CARDS.
IN OR OUT?
I HAVE A SISTER IN SPOKANE—
WHAT PART OF "POSTHUMOUS" DO YOU NOT UNDERSTAND?
KA-CHUNK!
CLICK

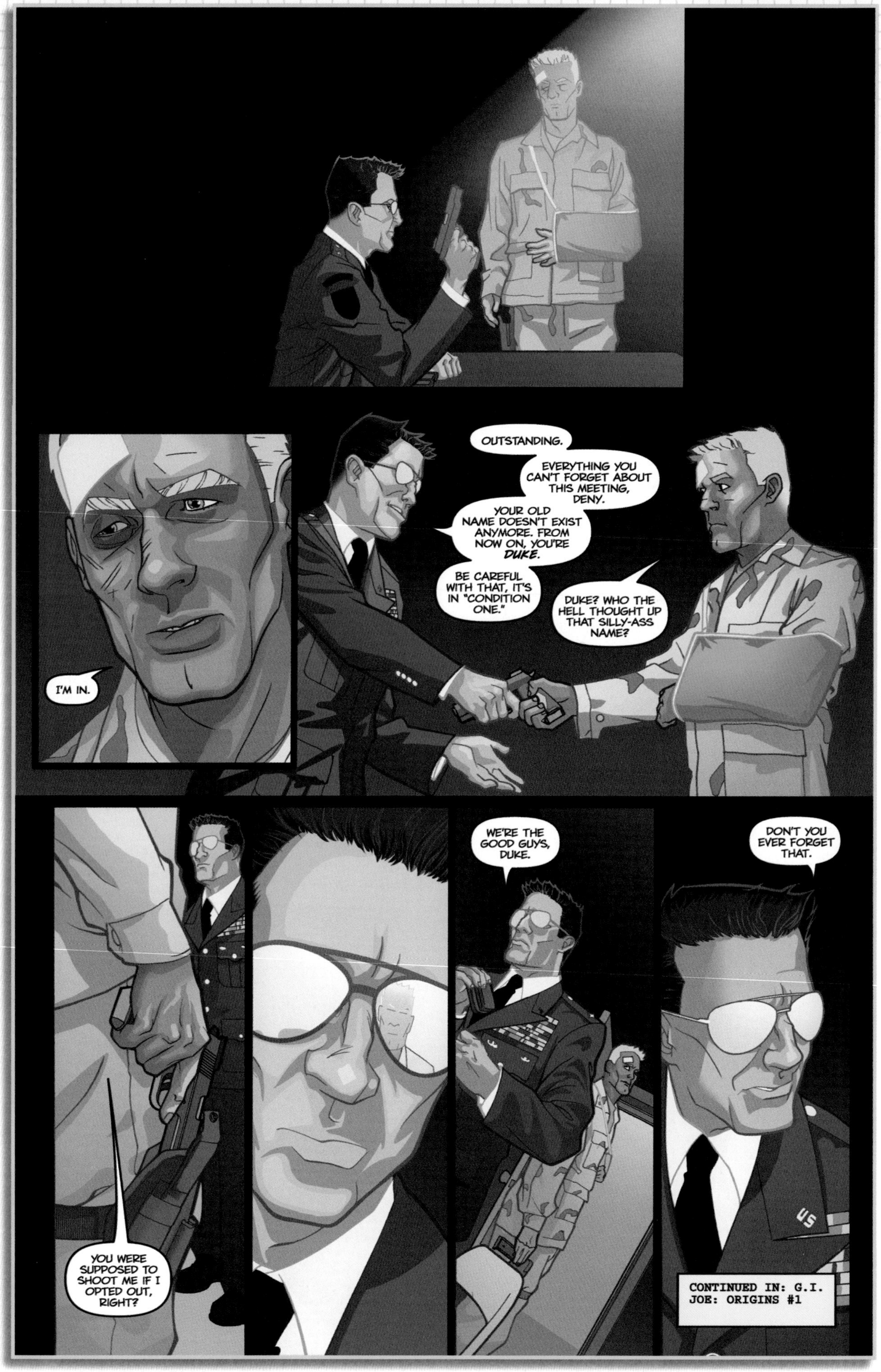
OUTSTANDING.
EVERYTHING YOU CAN'T FORGET ABOUT THIS MEETING, DENY.
YOUR OLD NAME DOESN'T EXIST ANYMORE. FROM NOW ON, YOU'RE DUKE.
BE CAREFUL WITH THAT, IT'S IN "CONDITION ONE."
DUKE? WHO THE HELL THOUGHT UP THAT SILLY-ASS NAME?
I'M IN.
YOU WERE SUPPOSED TO SHOOT ME IF I OPTED OUT, RIGHT?
WE'RE THE GOOD GUYS, DUKE.
DON'T YOU EVER FORGET THAT.
CONTINUED IN: G.I. JOE: ORIGINS #1

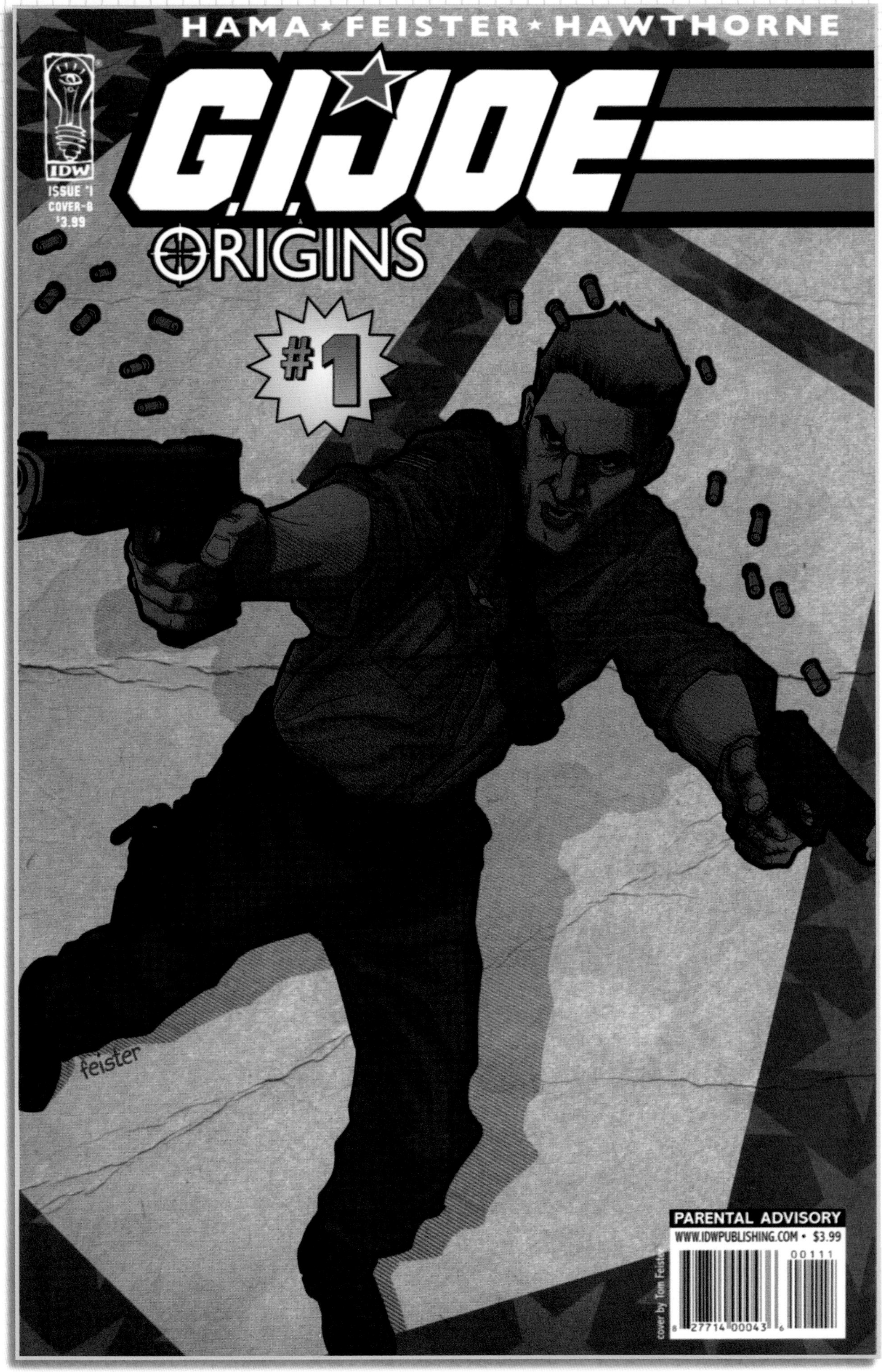
HAMA ★ FEISTER ★ HAWTHORNE
IDW
ISSUE #1
COVER-B
$3.99
G.I. JOE
ORIGINS
#1
feister
PARENTAL ADVISORY
WWW.IDWPUBLISHING.COM • $3.99
cover by Tom Feister

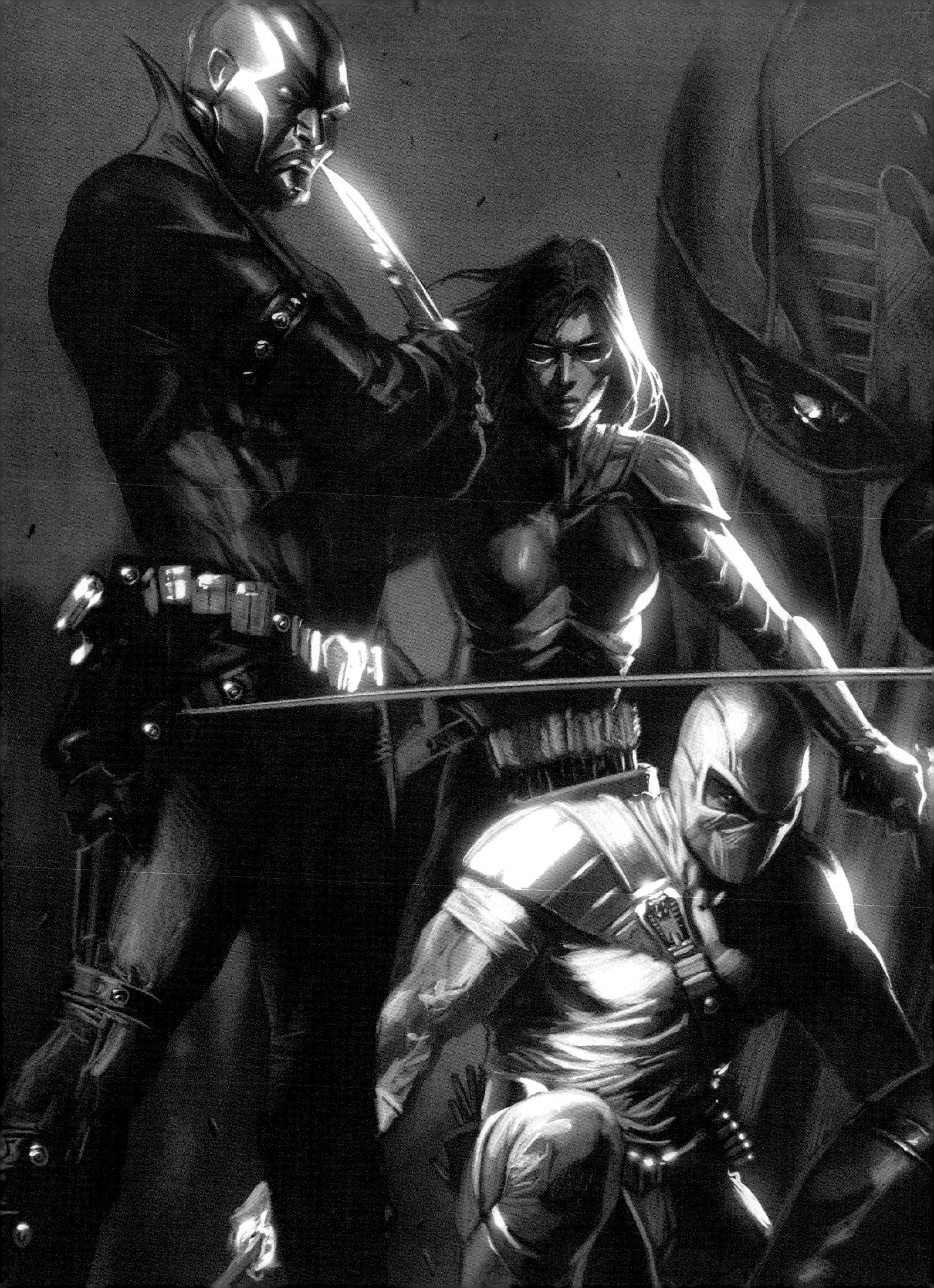

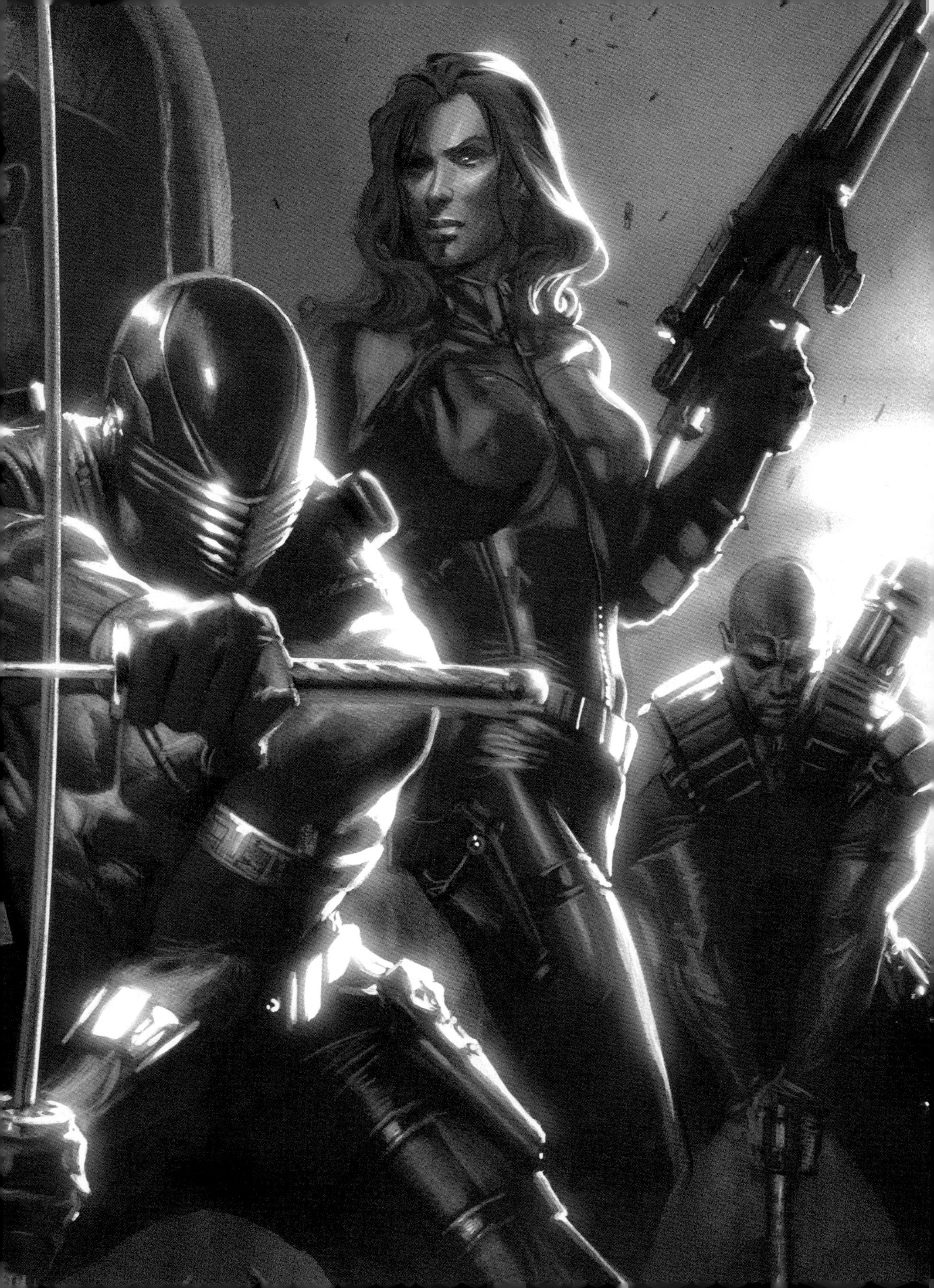

"DEEP COVER" Written by Mike Costa and Christos N. Gage   Art by Antonio Fuso   Color by Chris Chuckry

EIGHTEEN MONTHS AGO I WAS JASON WRIGHT, RUNNING GUNS THROUGH LAOTIAN MINEFIELDS.

LAST JANUARY I WAS DERRICK ATTELL, EXPLOSIVES EXPERT CONTRACTED BY THE TALIBAN.

AND AFTER THAT I WAS MARCUS QUINN, WORKING SECURITY FOR A COLOMBIAN DRUG LORD.

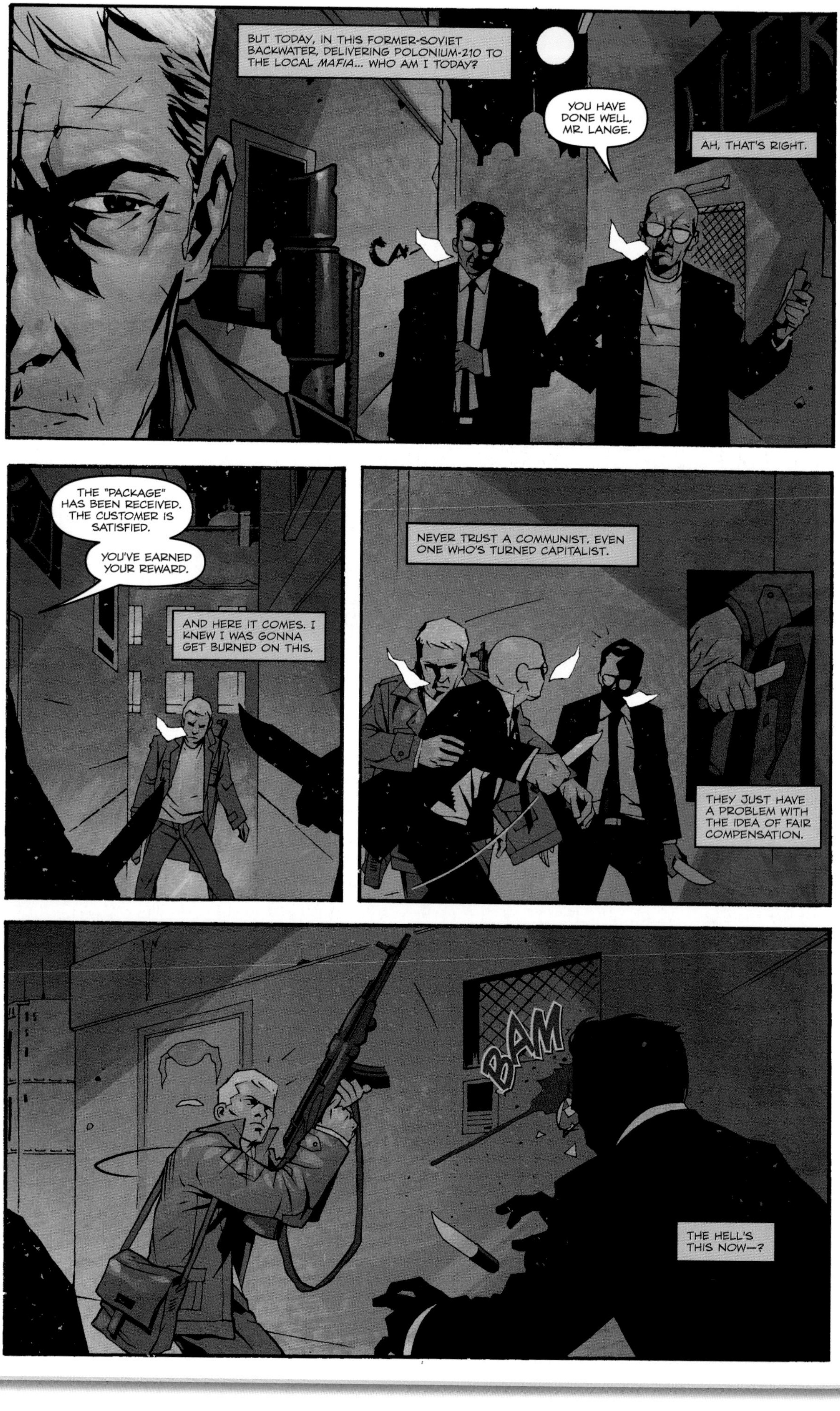
BUT TODAY, IN THIS FORMER-SOVIET BACKWATER, DELIVERING POLONIUM-210 TO THE LOCAL *MAFIA*... WHO AM I TODAY?
YOU HAVE DONE WELL, MR. LANGE.
AH, THAT'S RIGHT.
THE "PACKAGE" HAS BEEN RECEIVED. THE CUSTOMER IS SATISFIED.
YOU'VE EARNED YOUR REWARD.
AND HERE IT COMES. I KNEW I WAS GONNA GET BURNED ON THIS.
NEVER TRUST A COMMUNIST. EVEN ONE WHO'S TURNED CAPITALIST.
THEY JUST HAVE A PROBLEM WITH THE IDEA OF FAIR COMPENSATION.
BAM
THE HELL'S THIS NOW—?

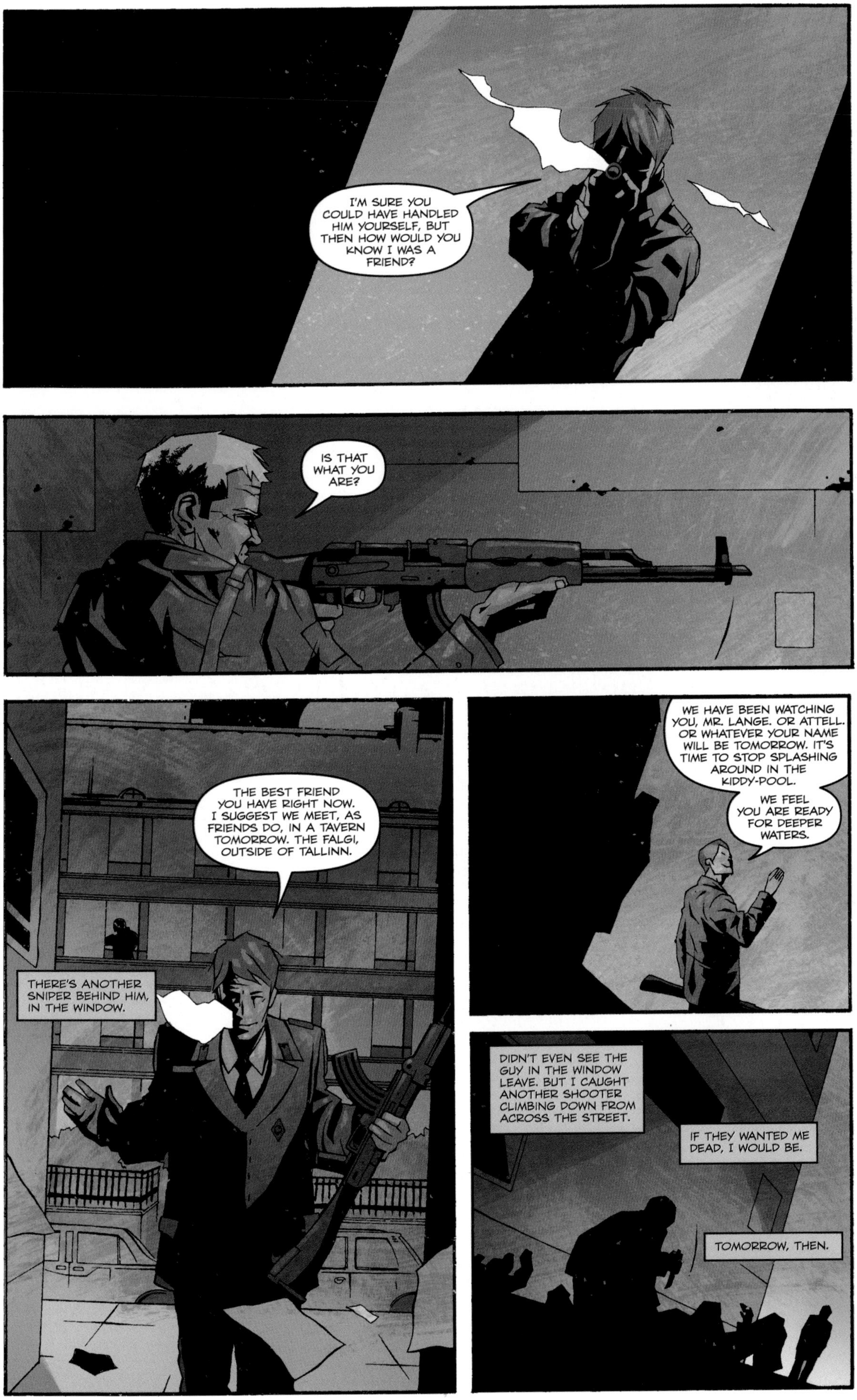
I'M SURE YOU COULD HAVE HANDLED HIM YOURSELF, BUT THEN HOW WOULD YOU KNOW I WAS A FRIEND?
IS THAT WHAT YOU ARE?
THE BEST FRIEND YOU HAVE RIGHT NOW. I SUGGEST WE MEET, AS FRIENDS DO, IN A TAVERN TOMORROW. THE FALGI, OUTSIDE OF TALLINN.
THERE'S ANOTHER SNIPER BEHIND HIM, IN THE WINDOW.
WE HAVE BEEN WATCHING YOU, MR. LANGE. OR ATTELL. OR WHATEVER YOUR NAME WILL BE TOMORROW. IT'S TIME TO STOP SPLASHING AROUND IN THE KIDDY-POOL.
WE FEEL YOU ARE READY FOR DEEPER WATERS.
DIDN'T EVEN SEE THE GUY IN THE WINDOW LEAVE. BUT I CAUGHT ANOTHER SHOOTER CLIMBING DOWN FROM ACROSS THE STREET.
IF THEY WANTED ME DEAD, I WOULD BE.
TOMORROW, THEN.

CONTINUED IN: G.I. JOE: COBRA #1

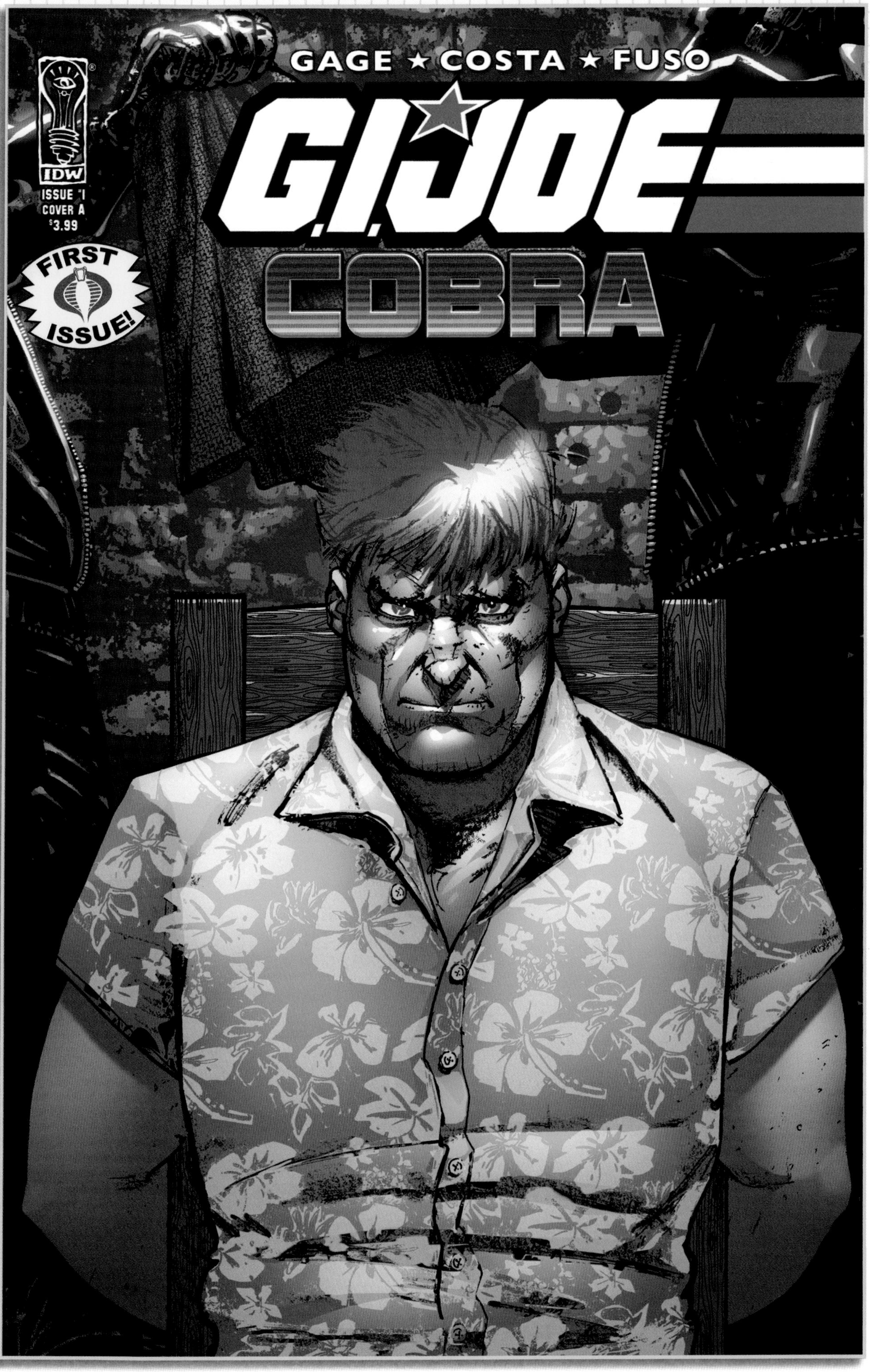

GAGE ★ COSTA ★ FUSO
G.I. JOE
COBRA
IDW
ISSUE #1
COVER A
$3.99
FIRST ISSUE!

COVER GALLERY

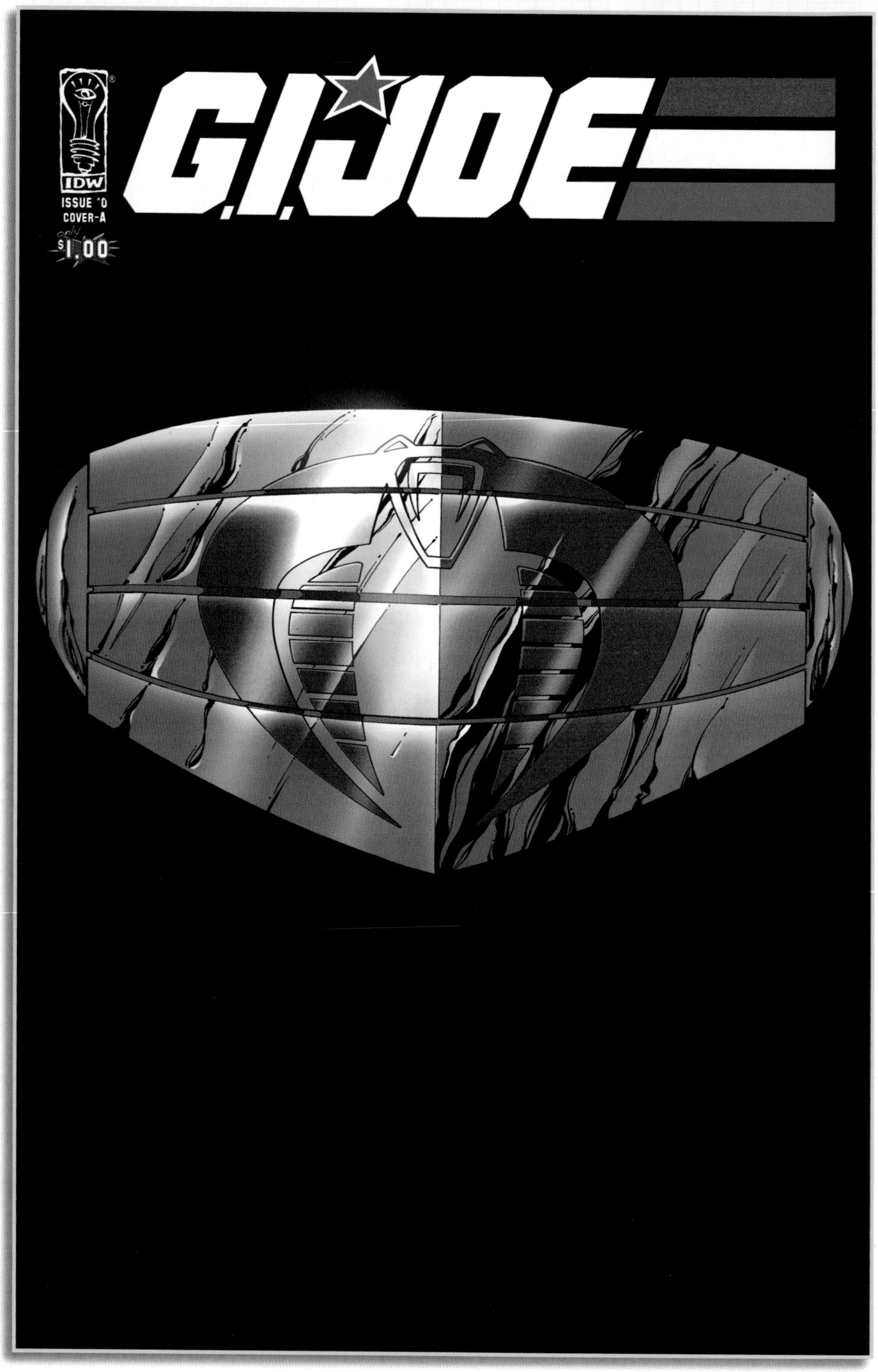
IDW
ISSUE #0
COVER-A
only $1.00
G.I. JOE

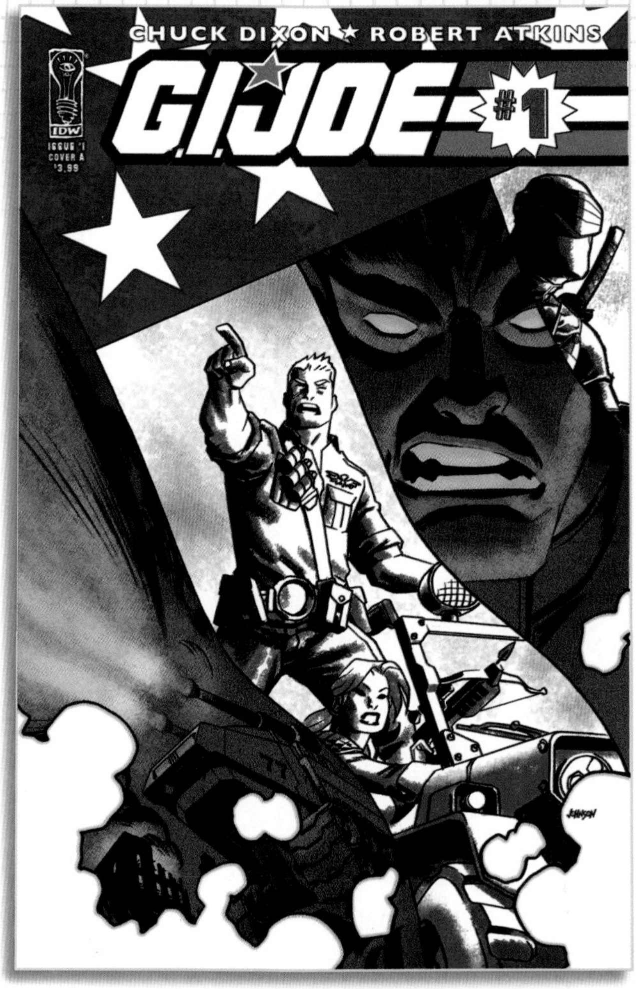
CHUCK DIXON ★ ROBERT ATKINS
G.I. JOE
#1
IDW
ISSUE 1
COVER A
$3.99

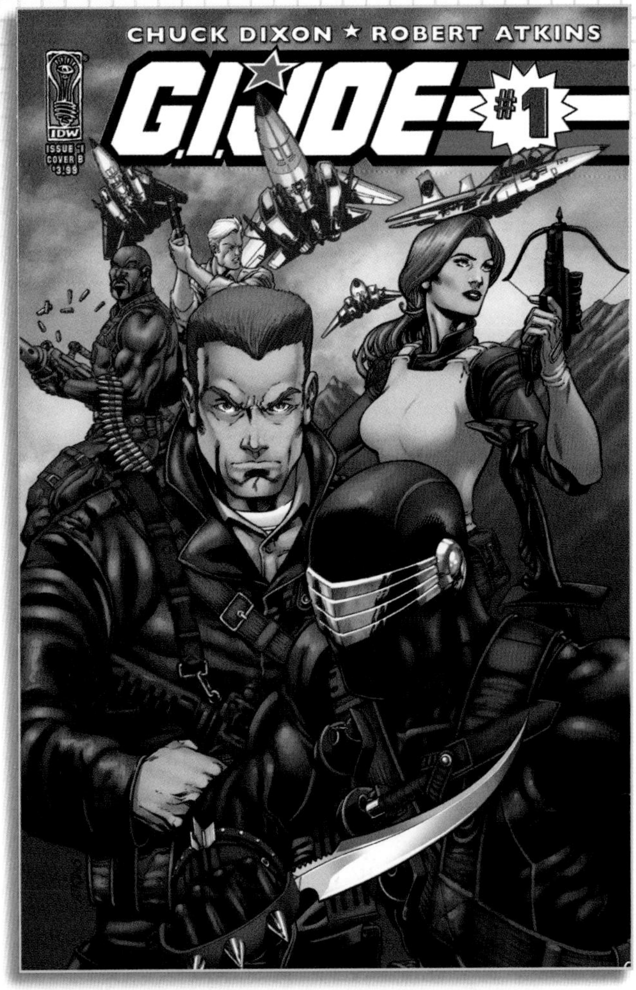
CHUCK DIXON ★ ROBERT ATKINS
G.I. JOE
#1
IDW
ISSUE 1
COVER B
$3.99

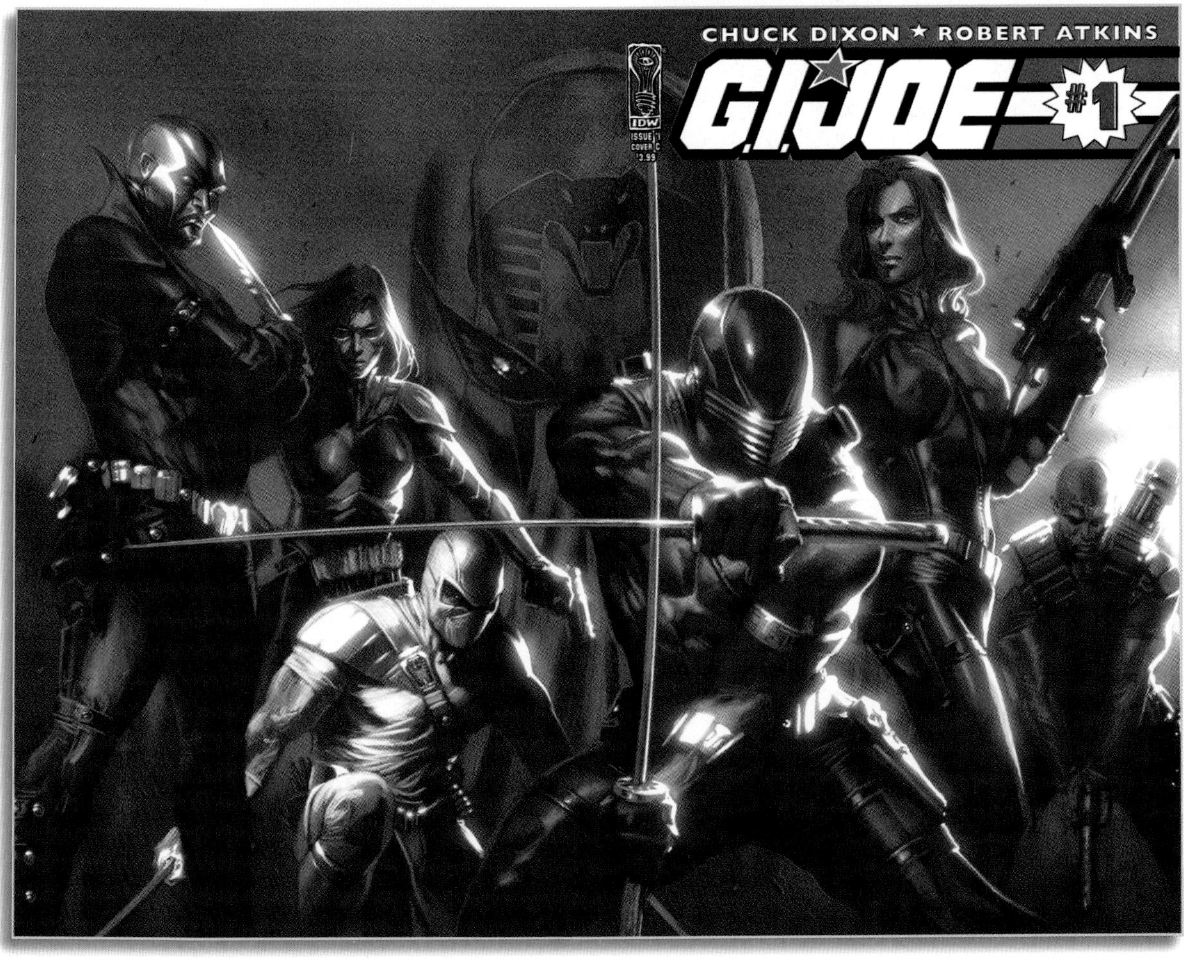
CHUCK DIXON ★ ROBERT ATKINS
G.I. JOE
#1
IDW
ISSUE 1
$3.99

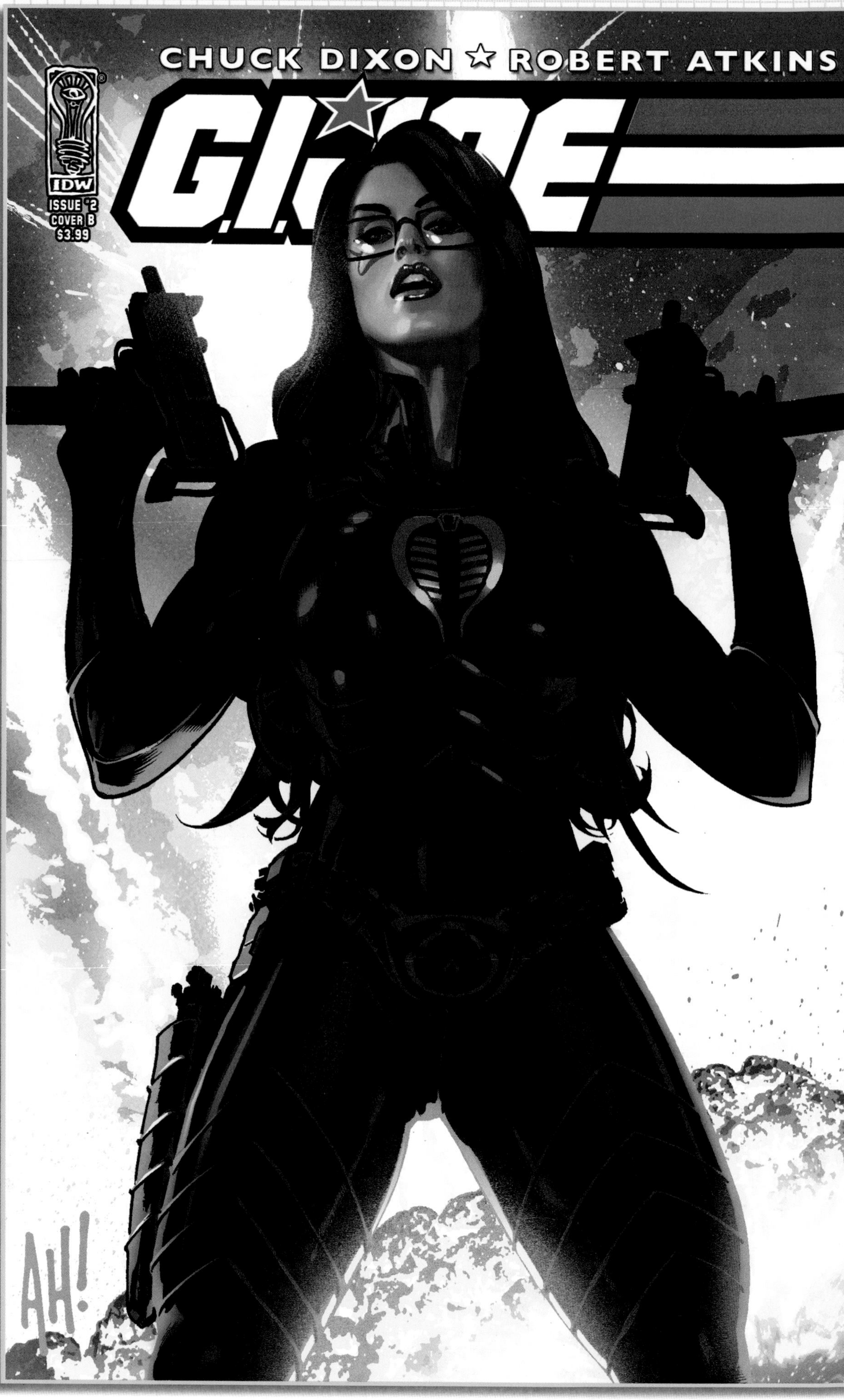
CHUCK DIXON ☆ ROBERT ATKINS
IDW
ISSUE #2
COVER B
$3.99
AH!

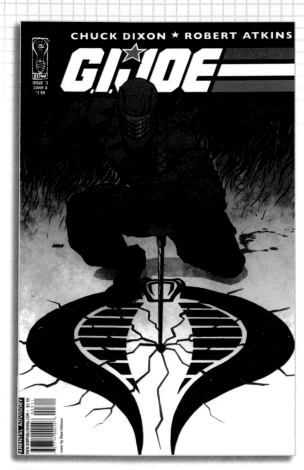

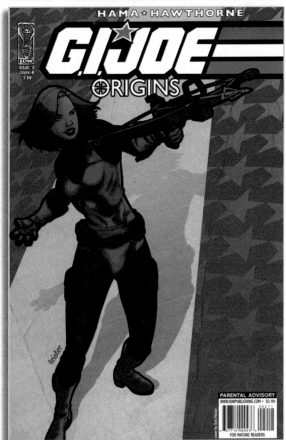

Follow the continuing story of G.I. JOE vs. COBRA in comic books from IDW Publishing.

NOW YOU KNOW!

An expert on a variety of genre obsessions, from classic animation to shape-shifting robots, PABLO HIDALGO started writing about fantastic subject matters professionally in 1995 as a freelance author for role-playing games.

In 2000, he changed careers from a visual-effects concept artist and digital compositor in Canada to a full-time *Star Wars* authority at Lucasfilm Ltd., working in their online department. Since then, he has overseen the development of websites, co-authored several books, and developed a number of online comic books and strips.

He is currently managing editor for StarWars.com, overseeing daily publication of content as well as developing special online spin-off projects for *Star Wars: The Clone Wars.* He lives in San Francisco.